Plato's Symposium

Greek Text with Facing Vocabulary and Commentary

Geoffrey Steadman

Plato's Symposium
Greek Text with Facing Vocabulary and Commentary

First Edition

© 2009 by Geoffrey D. Steadman

Revised July 2010, March 2011, July 2011, September 2012

The Greek text is the edition by John Burnet, first published by Oxford University Press in 1905.

ISBN-13: 978-0-9843065-1-0
ISBN-10: 0-9843065-1-X

Published by Geoffrey Steadman
Cover Design: David Steadman

Fonts: Times New Roman, SPIonic, GFS Porson

geoffreysteadman@gmail.com

Table of Contents

Symposium

Preface to the Series

The aim of this commentary is to make Plato's *Symposium* as accessible as possible to intermediate-level Greek readers so that they may experience the joy, insight, and lasting influence that comes from reading some of the greatest works in classical antiquity in the original Greek.

Facing each of the 72 pages of the Greek text (Burnet's Oxford Classical Text) is a single page of commentary, which is divided into halves. The top half includes all of the corresponding vocabulary words that occur six or fewer times in the dialogue, arranged alphabetically in two columns. The bottom half of each page is devoted to grammatical notes, which are organized according to the Stephanus page numbers and likewise arranged in two columns. The advantage of this format is that it allows me to include as much information as possible on a single page and yet insure that the numerous commentary entries are distinct and readily accessible to readers.

To complement the vocabulary within the commentary, I have added a Core Vocabulary List that includes all words occurring seven or more times (roughly 80% of all words in the dialogue) and strongly recommend that readers memorize this list as soon as they begin reading. A second list of core vocabulary occurring three to six times is available online. Together, this book has been designed in such a way that, once readers have mastered the Core List, they will be able to rely solely on the Greek text and facing commentary and not need to turn a page or consult outside dictionaries as they read.

The grammatical notes are designed to help beginning readers read the text, and so I have passed over detailed literary, historical, and philosophical explanations in favor of short, concise, and frequent entries that focus exclusively on grammar and morphology. The notes are intended to complement, not replace, an advanced level commentary. Assuming that readers finish elementary Greek with varying levels of ability, I draw attention to subjunctive and optative constructions, identify unusual aorist and perfect forms, and in general explain aspects of the Greek that they should have encountered in first year study but perhaps forgotten. As a rule, I prefer to offer too much assistance rather than too little.

Better Vocabulary-Building Strategies

One of the virtues of this commentary is that it eliminates time-consuming dictionary work. While there are certainly occasions where a dictionary is absolutely necessary for developing a nuanced reading of the Greek, in most instances any advantage that may come from looking up a word and exploring alternative meanings is outweighed by the time and effort spent in the process. Many continue to defend this practice, but I am convinced that such work has little pedagogical value for intermediate-level students and that the time saved by avoiding such drudgery can be better spent reading more Greek, reviewing morphology, learning core vocabulary, or reading secondary literature.

As an alternative to dictionary work, this commentary offers a two approaches to building knowledge of vocabulary. First, I isolate the most common words (7 or more times) for immediate drilling and memorization. Since these words are not found elsewhere in the commentary, readers are forced to consult the list until they have learned the words thoroughly. Second, I have marked every word in the *Symposium* that occurs between three and six times with an asterisk and compiled these words into a second list available online. I encourage readers who have mastered the core list to single out and memorize words with asterisks as they encounter them and devote comparatively little attention to words that occur once or twice. Altogether, I am confident that readers who follow this regimen will learn Plato's vocabulary more efficiently and develop fluency more quickly than with traditional methods.

Print on Demand Books

This volume is a self-published, print-on-demand (POD) book, and as such it gives its author distinct freedoms and limitations that are not found in traditional publications. After writing this commentary, I simply purchased an ISBN number (the owner is *de facto* the publisher) and submitted a digital copy for printing. The most significant limitation of a POD book is that it has not undergone extensive peer-review or general editing. This is a serious shortcoming that should make readers wary. Because there are so many vocabulary and commentary entries, there are sure to be typographical and factual errors that an extra pair of eyes would have spotted immediately. Until all of the mistakes have been identified and corrected, I hope the reader will excuse the occasional error.

The benefits of POD, however, outweigh the costs. This commentary and others in the series simply would not exist without POD. Since there is no traditional publisher acting as a middle man, there is no one to deny publication of this work because it may not be profitable *for the publisher*. In addition, since the production costs are so low and there is no publishing company which needs to recover its own investment, I am able to offer this text at a low price of my own choosing. If I wish to make revisions or publish a second, third, or fourth edition, I alone make the decision. Finally, since this book is no more than a .pdf file waiting to be printed, I am able to make corrections and place a revised edition of a POD book for sale in as short as 24 hours. In this regard, we should liken PODs to software instead of typeset books. Although the first edition of a POD may not be as polished as a traditional book, I am able to respond very quickly to readers' recommendations and criticisms and create an emended POD that is far superior to previous editions. Consider, therefore, what you hold in your hand as an inexpensive beta version of the commentary. If you would like to recommend changes or download a free .pdf copy of any of the books in this series, please see one of the addresses below. All criticisms are welcome, and I would be grateful for your help.

Lastly, I would like to thank Megan O'Donald for reading through an earlier version of this commentary and recommending changes. Her acute observations and generous spirit has save readers from numerous typographical errors in the latest revision.

Geoffrey Steadman Ph.D.
geoffreysteadman@gmail.com
www.geoffreysteadman.com

Introduction to Plato's *Symposium*

The *Symposium* tells the story of a drinking party in which the guests agree to put aside their desire for wine, women and music and deliver speeches in honor of erōs, a word often translated as "love" but more aptly described as "sexual desire" or "passionate love." The gathering takes place at the house of the tragedian Agathon just two days after he received first prize for one of his plays at the Lenaean festival in 416 BC, but the dialogue itself begins many years later, as Apollodorus, a follower of Socrates, agrees to recount the details of that party to an unnamed friend. Since Apollodorus mentions Agathon's departure from Athens in 408 (173b) but says nothing about Socrates' execution in 399, most scholars assume that Apollodorus is speaking some ten years after the drinking party, perhaps between 405 and 399 BC. Adding even more distance between the reader and the events that take place during the symposium, Plato has Apollodorus preface his account of the party with the revelation that he was not himself present at the banquet but learned everything that he is about to relate from Aristodemus, another follower of Socrates and first-hand witness to the symposium.

According to Apollodorus, soon after Aristodemus and Socrates arrive at Agathon's house, the guests agree to refrain from the sort of drinking that had consumed many of them on the previous night and deliver speeches in praise of Erōs, the god synonymous with erōs itself. As each speaker takes his turn, we become increasingly aware of how the view of love espoused in each speech is a reflection of the speaker's own character.[1] First, Phaedrus, a lover of literature, offers an account of erōs that draws heavily from the time-honored myths of the poets. Then Pausanias, the proud lover of Agathon, follows with a speech that highlights the educational value of a homoerotic relationship between a lover and his younger companion. The physician Eryximachus not surprisingly emphasizes the cosmic role of erōs and the ability of the physician to harness its power, while the comic playwright Aristophanes

---

[1] See Arieti, J. (1991). "The Symposium." In *Interpreting Plato: The Dialogues as Drama*. Lanham: Rowman and Littlefield Publishers, Inc. Both the interpretation noted throughout the introduction and the Xenophanes quote below comes from this accessible and insightful article.

offers a thoroughly amusing portrayal of humans as torn souls who seek through erōs to unite with their missing halves and become whole again. Agathon, a tragic poet known for being graceful and good-looking, describes erōs as a poet both graceful and good-looking. And finally Socrates, after chastising the other members of the party for indiscriminately praising erōs, claims to have learned all that he knows about such matters from Diotima, a prophetess who engages in the same sort of questioning and answering that Socrates does and who imagines erōs as an unshod, unkempt philosopher not unlike Socrates himself!

Though there is risk in oversimplifying what are in fact rich and subtly drawn portraits of love, this relationship between speech and speaker reminds us that we cannot easily separate the subject from its setting. Whether the guests are simply creating gods in their own image and imbuing erōs with the very qualities that they see in themselves or, quite the opposite, modeling their lives after their conceptions of erōs, the relationship between love and life, word and action, is continually brought to the reader's attention. This lesson becomes even more poignant when the charismatic general Alcibiades bursts into the party with his fellow revelers and, before reducing the gathering to a free for all, delivers a moving speech in honor not of erōs but of Socrates himself. For it is in Alcibiades' deeply personal portrait of Socrates that readers are able to revisit Socrates' speech on love and compare the philosopher's words with the life that he has lived and people that he has touched.

The Setting

When we read the *Symposium* in translation, it is easy to overlook that most of the dialogue is being retold by Apollodorus, who in turn learned of it from Aristodemus; but the same is not true for the Greek reader. With the exception of the speeches on erōs, most of the events in the dialogue are described in the common accusative and infinitive idiom of indirect discourse. And so, while English readers enjoy vivid descriptions such as "he found the door open" and "Aristophanes hiccupped" Greek readers repeatedly encounter the equivalent to "that he found the door open" and "that Aristophanes hiccupped," where they must assume the main clause "Aristodemus said" in order to make sense of the narrative. This feature of ancient Greek leaves English and Greek readers with very different impressions of the dialogue. While a refined English translation makes readers feel that they are experiencing the events first-hand and can trust what they read as if they were witnessing it themselves, the awkwardness of indirect discourse in the Greek serves as a constant reminder that readers are several people removed from the events that Apollodorus recalls and that the dialogue is a recollection of a drinking party rather than a drinking party itself.

The role of memory and oral history in the telling of the Symposium becomes even more meaningful when we realize that all the party's guests were real Athenians whom Plato's contemporary readers could place at a significant moment in the recent past. Imagine that instead of the *Symposium* we were reading about a nightlong seminar on the nature of love attended by the statesman Robert Kennedy, singer Mick Jagger, theologian Paul Tillich, actor Rock Hudson, minister and activist Martin Luther King, philosopher Michel Foucault and General William Westmoreland on the eve of the Gulf of Tonkin resolution in 1964.[1] Imagine once more that the narrative was not a word-for-word transcript of the seminar but a personal account recalled by a follower of Foucault, who in turn learned it from another follower of Foucault. Needless to say, there would be much more on our minds than the discussion of love. Our attention would turn not only to the topic of love but also to the past and often tragic, future lives of the speakers, their occupations, and the relationship between these figures and the view of love that each espouses. We would be sensitive to the distance that lies between the seminar and us, suspicious of our knowledge of the gathering, and at the same time conscious of the central role given to Foucault by his followers.

The same may be said about Plato's *Symposium*. Even if Plato's fellow Athenians did not know that the party which celebrated Agathon's victory occurred in 416 BC, they would be able to infer from the names of the guests that the gathering took place a short time before the disastrous Sicilian Expedition in 415-414. Early in 415 one of the dialogue's main characters, Alcibiades, persuaded the Athenian Assembly to

---

[1] This vivid scenario has been adapted from Halperin, D. (2005). "Love's Irony: Six Remarks on Platonic Eros" In *Erotikon: Essays on Eros, Ancient and Modern*. Chicago.

launch a second front in the intermittent war against Sparta (431-404) and attack the large, democratic Greek city of Syracuse. The decision proved to be catastrophic, and the Athenians and their allies lost some 40,000 men in addition to hundreds of warships and supply ships. The loss not only demoralized the Athenians but more importantly emboldened the Spartans, who would some ten years later in 404 BC defeat the Athenians, take control of their city and temporarily suspend their democracy.

In the days leading up to the failed expedition, there were two sacrilegious crimes that led to the eventual exile or death of almost half of the guests in the *Symposium*. First, in an event known as the "mutilation of the herms," groups of young Athenian men ran through the city in the cover of night and defaced many of the sacred herms, statues with the head and genitalia of Hermes, that populated public and private spaces throughout the city. Since Hermes was the god who granted or denied safe passage to travelers, the crime heightened the city's anxiety on the eve of the expedition to Sicily and made the Athenians more vigilant about the need for proper religious observance. Shortly afterward, however, another scandal arose when it was revealed that a number of Athenians were performing the rituals of the Eleusinian mysteries in private gatherings such as symposia. The Athenians considered the performance of such rites outside of their proper setting to be sacrilegious and vigorously pursued the matter as an offense punishable by death. In the investigation that followed, fellow symposiasts Eryximachus, Phaedrus and Alcibiades were among the many implicated in the crime. While it is unclear whether Eryximachus was simply exiled or in fact executed for his participation, Phaedrus fled the city, and the Athenians subsequently sold off all of his possessions. Alcibiades, who had just set out on the Sicilian expedition as one of its commanders, was recalled to Athens but chose to flee in exile rather than return and face trial. Soon afterwards, he became an advisor to the Spartans, and though it is not known for certain whether he provided accurate information to the enemy, many Athenians believed that his counsel gave the Spartans the support they needed to secure victories in the battles that followed.

The fact that both of these religious crimes likely arose from drinking parties such as the one in the *Symposium* must have made the setting of the dialogue troubling for Plato's readers, especially when we recall that a few years later in 399 BC Socrates himself would be convicted and executed on the charge of impiety. If Plato's sole concern in the dialogue were the topic of erōs, he could easily have avoided any confusion by choosing less controversial characters in a less controversial setting. Why then did he choose these particular Greeks to have a conversation of the nature of the god Erōs? What are we to think when Socrates uses terminology associated with the Eleusinian mysteries in his discussion of love (209e5ff.)? Is it significant that Alcibiades, Apollodorus and Aristodemus are all examples of the sort of youth that Socrates was accused of corrupting?

As with many of Plato's dialogues, the *Symposium* seems to elicit more questions than it answers. Though we may be tempted to brush aside these concerns and turn our attention solely to the loftier theme of *erōs*, Plato seems determined to ground his discussion of love in the turbulent and very real world of 5th century Athens.

Characters

Below are brief descriptions of various participants in the *Symposium*, adapted from Debra Nails' highly recommended study, *The People of Plato*. For a fuller examination of these and other characters throughout the Platonic corpus, please consult her book.

Agathon (~31 years old; 447-401): Though Agathon continued to build a reputation as a tragic poet, he left Athens in 408 BC to join the court of King Archelaus of Macedon, where he later died in 401. Though none of Agathon' tragedies have survived, Aristophanes alludes to him in several of his comedies and in the *Frogs* (405 BC) calls him a "fine poet who is missed by his friends."

Alcibiades (~35 yrs. old; 451-404): A member of the politically connected Alcmaeonid family, Alcibiades became the ward of the statesman Pericles after the death of his mother. According to Plato, Socrates saved Alcibiades' life during the siege of Potidaea in 432. In the retreat at the Battle of Delium (424 BC), Alcibiades watched on horseback as Socrates retreated on foot, saving both the general Laches and himself. After Alcibiades' involvement in the events surrounding the Sicilian expedition, Alcibiades was recalled from exile in 411 to command the Athenian fleet in the Hellespont and again in 407 for several months, during which time he was elected general in Athens. Alcibiades left Athens once more and died in 404, when he was likely assassinated by a member of the Persian court. The details of his death, however, are vague.

Apollodorus (~ 24 yrs. old, b. 429): A successful businessman born into a wealthy family, Apollodorus says in the *Symposium* that he became a follower of Socrates "a few years earlier" than the setting of the dialogue, perhaps between 408 and 405 BC. In the *Phaedo*, Plato's account of the death of Socrates, Apollodorus is described as the most distraught of the fourteen friends who are present when Socrates drinks the hemlock.

Aristodemus: We know nothing more about Aristodemus than what Plato says in the *Symposium*. A follower of Socrates, Aristodemus' decision to walk barefoot suggests that he was so enamored by Socrates that he imitated the philosopher's outward appearance and habits.

Aristophanes (~34 yrs. old; 450-386): Aristophanes was a playwright who wrote comedies for one of the several festivals on Athens' religious calendar. Among the eleven plays that have survived is the *Clouds* (ca. 423-418) a work that parodies both Socrates and the influence of sophistic education. In the *Apology*, Plato has Socrates point to Aristophanes (and presumably the *Clouds*) as one of the sources of the negative attitudes toward Socrates. Of all the guests at the party, this playwright alone survived to enjoy success and fame well into the 390's and 380's.

Eryximachus (~30 yrs. old; 448-415?): Eryximachus was a physician, like his father Acumenus (*Symposium* 214b). In both the *Protagoras* and the *Phaedrus*, we are told that Eryximachus was a friend of Phaedrus. In 400 BC, Andocides identified Eryximachus and his father as two Athenians who were either executed or exiled in 415 for performing the Eleusinian mysteries outside of their proper setting.

Glaucon: Nothing more is known about this character than his name. At the beginning of the dialogue, Apollodorus addresses an unnamed interlocutor in response to a question about the symposium and claims that he had just told the details of the party to Glaucon the day before. Since Plato had a brother named Glaucon and made him a main character in the *Republic*, we might conclude— in the absence of other evidence—that this Glaucon is Plato's brother.

Pausanias (fl. late 5th c.): Little more is known about Pausanias than his relationship with Agathon. In Plato's *Protagoras* Pausanias makes a brief appearance beside Agathon at Callias' house, which suggests that Pausanias was engaged in the traditional courtship with the young Agathon in 433-32 and that their relationship continued into Agathon's adulthood, well beyond the customary period for a typical pederastic relationship in Athens.

Phaedrus (~28 yrs. old, 444-393): Phaedrus appears in several of Plato's dialogues: the *Symposium*, *Protagoras*, and his namesake, the *Phaedrus*. In the *Protagoras*, set ca. 433-432 BC, Socrates spies Phaedrus sitting in a small group along with Eryximachus. In the *Phaedrus*, a dialogue preoccupied with the role of rhetoric, Phaedrus is depicted as a lover of all types of literature.

Socrates (~54 yrs. old; 470-399): A stonemason by trade, Socrates acquired a reputation of discussing philosophy in public places. He did not write down his philosophical beliefs, so whatever we know about him comes from the works of a number of his contemporaries including Plato, Xenophon, and Aristophanes.

Additional Readings

Arieti, J. (1991). "The *Symposium*." In *Interpreting Plato: The Dialogues as Drama*. Lanham: Rowman & Littlefield Publishers, Inc.

Blanckenhagen, P. H. von. (1992). "Stage and Actors in Plato's *Symposium*." *GRBS*, 33: 51-68.

Burnyeat, M. F. (1977). "Socratic Midwifery, Platonic Inspiration." *Bulletin of the Institute of Classical Studies*, 24: 7-17. Reprinted in H. H. Benson ed. (1992). *Essays on the Philosophy of Socrates*. New York. pp. 53-65.

Clay, D. (1975). "The Tragic and Comic Poet of the *Symposium*" *Arion*, 2:238-61

Corrigan, K. and Glazov-Corrigan E. (2004). *Plato's Dialectic at Play: Argument, Structure, and Myth in the Symposium.* University Park, Pennsylvania.

Dover, K. J. (1980). *Plato: Symposium.* Cambridge Greek and Latin Classics.

---. (1978). *Greek Homosexuality.* New York: Vintage Books.

---. (1970). "Excursus: The Herms and the Mysteries." In. A. W. Gomme *et al.*, eds. *A Historical Commentary on Thucydides.* 4: 264-88.

---. (1966). "Aristophanes' Speech in Plato's *Symposium*." *JHS,* 86: 41-50.

---. (1965). "The Date of Plato's *Symposium*", *Phronesis*, 10: 2-20.

Edelstein, L. (1945). "The Role of Eryximachus in Plato's *Symposium*." *TAPA*, 76.

Emlyn-Jones, C. (2004). "The Dramatic Poet and his audience: Agathon and Socrates in Plato's *Symposium*." *Hermes*, 132: 289-405.

Gagarin, M. (1977). "Socrates' Hybris and Alcibiades' Failure." *Phoenix*, 31:22-37.

Halperin, D. M. (1990). "Why Is Diotima a Woman?" In *One Hundred Years of Homosexuality.* New York. pp. 112-151.

Hobbs, A. (2000). "Alcibiades' Revenge: Thumos in the *Symposium*." In A. Hobbs, *Plato and the Hero.* Cambridge. pp. 250-261.

Hubbard, T. K. (1998). "Popular Perceptions of Elite Homosexuality in Classical Athens" *Arion*, 6:48-78.

Konstan, D. and Young-Bruehl, E. (1982. "Eryximachus' Speech in the *Symposium*." *Apeiron*, 16: 40-46.

Lesher, J. H. (2004). "The Afterlife of Plato's *Symposium*." *Ordia Prima.* 3:89-105.

Lesher, J. H., Nails, D. and Sheffield F. eds. (2006). *Plato's Symposium: Issues in Interpretation and Reception.* Cambridge: Harvard University Press.

Murray, O. ed. (1990). *Sympotica: A Symposium on the Symposion.* Oxford: Oxford University Press.

Nails, D. (2002). *The People of Plato: A Prosopography of Plato and Other Socratics.* Indianapolis: Hackett Publishing.

Nichols, M. (2009). *Socrates on Friendship and Community: Reflections on Plato's Symposium, Phaedrus, and Lysis.* Cambridge.

Nehamas, A. (2005). "Only in the Contemplation of Beauty is Human Life Worth Living." http://depts.washington.edu/schkatz/podcasts/nehamas_podcast.mp3 Solomon Katz Distinguished Lectures. MP3. (accessed September 8, 2012).

Nightingale, A. (1993). "The Folly of Praise: Plato's Critique of Encomiastic Discourse in the *Lysis* and *Symposium.*" *Classical Quarterly*, 43: 112-130.

Nussbaum, M. C. (1986). "The Speech of Alcibiades: a Reading of the *Symposium.*" In *The Fragility of Goodness.* Cambridge. pp. 165-199.

O'Brien, M. J., (1984). "Becoming Immortal in Plato's *Symposium.*" In D. Gerber ed., *Greek Poetry and Philosophy.* Chicago.

Osborne, C. (1994). "Eros, the Socratic Spirit: Inside and Outside the *Symposium*," in *Eros Unveiled: Plato and the God of Love.* Oxford. pp. 86-116

Osborne, R. (1985). "The Erection and Mutilation of the Hermai." *Proceedings of the Cambridge Philological Society*, 31: 47-73.

Price, A. W. (1981). "Loving Persons Platonically." *Phonesis*, 26: 25-34.

---. (1991). "Martha Nussbaum's *Symposium.*" *Ancient Philosophy*, 11: 285-99.

Reeve, C.D.C. (1992). "Telling the Truth About Love: Plato's *Symposium.*" *Proceedings of the Boston Area Colloquium in Ancient Philosophy*, 8: 89-114.

Rowe, C. J. (1998). "Socrates and Diotima: Eros, Creativity and Immortality." *Proceedings of the Boston Area Colloquium in Ancient Philosophy*, 14: 239-259.

Salman, C. (1993). "Phaedrus' Cosmology in the *Symposium.*" *Interpretation*, 20: 99

Scott, G. and Welton, W. (2008). *Erotic Wisdom: Philosophy and Immediacy in Plato's Symposium.* Albany: State University of New York Press.

Sheffield, F. (2006). *Plato's Symposium: The Ethics of Desire.* Oxford: Oxford University Press.

--- (2012). "The *Symposium* and Platonic Ethics: Plato, Vlastos and a Misguided Debate." *Phronesis*, 57: 117-141.

Usher, M. D. (2002). "Satyr play in Plato's *Symposium*" *AJP*, 123: 205-28.

Vlastos, Gregory. (1981). "The Individual as Object of Love in Plato." In Vlastos, *Platonic Studies*: 2nd ed. Princeton. pp. 3-42.

Wardy, R. (2002). "The Unity of Opposites in Plato's *Symposium.*" *Oxford Studies in Ancient Philosophy.* 23:1-61.

Vries, G. J. des. (1973). "Mystery Terminology in Aristophanes and Plato." *Mnemosyne*, 26:1-8.

How to Use this Commentary

Research shows that, as we learn how to read in a second language, a combination of reading and direct vocabulary instruction is statistically superior to reading alone. One of the purposes of this book is to encourage active acquisition of vocabulary.

1. Master the core vocabulary list as soon as possible.

A. Develop a daily regimen for memorizing vocabulary lists and forms before you begin reading. Start with an intensive review of the Core Vocabulary (pp. 150-158) and then turn to less frequent vocabulary words as you encounter them.

B. If you have to consult the core list as you read the dialogue, either photocopy the list or print it from online and keep it by your book to avoid page-flipping. More importantly, place a dot or similar mark by all core words that you consult. As review progresses, focus extra effort on the words that accumulate marks.

C. Download and use the core list flashcards available online (ppt or jpg format). Research has shown that you must review new words at least seven to nine times before you are able to commit them to long term memory, and flashcards are particularly efficient at promoting repetition. Develop the habit of deleting flashcards that you have mastered and focus your efforts on the remaining words.

2. Read actively and make lots of educated guesses

One of the benefits of traditional dictionary work is that it gives readers an interval between the time they encounter a questionable word or form and the time they find the dictionary entry. That span of time often compels readers to make educated guesses and actively seek out understanding of the Greek.

Despite the benefits of facing vocabulary lists (see the preface), there is a risk that without that interval of time you will become complacent in your reading habits and treat the Greek as a puzzle to be decoded rather than a language to be learned. *Your challenge, therefore, is to develop the habit of making an educated guess under your breath each time before you consult the facing vocabulary and grammar*. If you guess correctly, the commentary will reaffirm your understanding of the Greek. If you answer incorrectly, you will become more aware of your weaknesses and therefore more capable of correcting them.

3. Reread a passage immediately after you have completed it.

Repeated readings not only help you commit Greek to memory but also increase your ability to read the Greek as Greek. Always read the words out loud (or at least whisper it to yourself). While you may be inclined to translate the text into English as you reread, develop the habit of reading Greek and acquiring meaning without turning the text into English.

4. Reread the most recent passage immediately before you begin a new one.

This additional repetition will strengthen your ability to recognize vocabulary, forms, and syntax quickly, bolster your confidence, and most importantly provide you with much-needed context as you begin the next selection in the text.

Abbreviations

abs.	absolute	imp.	imperative	pf.	perfect
acc.	accusative	impf.	imperfect	pl.	plural
act.	active	imper.	impersonal	plpf.	pluperfect
adj.	adjective	indic.	indicative	pred.	predicate
adv.	adverb	i.o.	indirect object	prep.	preposition
aor.	aorist	inf.	infinitive	pres.	present
app.	appositive	inter.	interrogative	pron.	pronoun
comp.	comparative	m.	masculine	reflex.	reflexive
dat.	dative	n.	neuter	rel.	relative
dep.	deponent	nom.	nominative	seq.	sequence
d.o.	direct object	obj.	object	sg.	singular
f.	feminine	opt.	optative	subj.	subject
fut.	future	pple.	participle	superl.	superlative
gen.	genitive	pass	passive	voc.	vocative

Stephanus Page Numbers

The universal method for referring to pages in any of Plato's dialogues is through Stephanus page numbers. This paging system was developed by Henri Estienne (Lat., *Stephanus*), who published a multi-volume edition of Plato's dialogues in 1578. Stephanus divided each page in his edition into roughly equal sections, which he labeled with the letters a, b, c, d, and e. This system allowed his readers to locate a particular passage not only by the page number but by the section letter as well (e.g. 172a, 172b, 172c, 172d, 172e, 173a…). Many modern editions, including the Greek text in this volume, have adopted this system and gone one step further by dividing the sections into individual lines (e.g. 172a1, 172a2, 172a3…). This paging system offers the same advantages as chapters and verses in the Bible. Since most editions of Plato include the Stephanus page numbers in the margins of the text, a reader can pick up any volume of Plato—in Greek or in translation—and easily locate a particular passage in the dialogue.

Because Stephanus placed the *Symposium* on pages 172-223 in his first volume of Plato, the *Symposium* begins on Stephanus page 172a1 and ends on page 223d12. In this commentary all of the grammatical notes are arranged and labeled according to this paging system. Since most of the entries on a given page of commentary have the same Stephanus page number, I have identified the page number only once and labeled all subsequent grammatical note entries by the section letter and line number (e.g. 172a1, a2, a3…b1, b2, b3, b4…).

If oxen and horses and lions had hands
and were able to draw with their hands and do the same things as men,
horses would draw the figures of the gods like horses and oxen like oxen,
and each would make the gods' bodies have the same shape as they themselves had.

-Xenophanes

To make the ancients speak, we must feed them with our own blood.

-von Wilamowitz-Moellendorff

ΣΥΜΠΟΣΙΟΝ

ΑΠΟΛΛΟΔΩΡΟΣ ΕΤΑΙΡΟΣ

a   ΑΠΟΛ. Δοκῶ μοι περὶ ὧν πυνθάνεσθε οὐκ ἀμελέτητος
εἶναι. καὶ γὰρ ἐτύγχανον πρῴην εἰς ἄστυ οἴκοθεν ἀνιὼν Φαλη-
ρόθεν· τῶν οὖν γνωρίμων τις ὄπισθεν κατιδών με πόρρωθεν
ἐκάλεσε, καὶ παίζων ἅμα τῇ κλήσει, "ὦ Φαληρεύς," ἔφη,
5 "οὗτος Ἀπολλόδωρος, οὐ περιμένεις;" Κἀγὼ ἐπιστὰς περι-
έμεινα. Καὶ ὅς, "Ἀπολλόδωρε," ἔφη, "καὶ μὴν καὶ ἔναγχός
σε ἐζήτουν βουλόμενος διαπυθέσθαι τὴν Ἀγάθωνος συνουσίαν
b   καὶ Σωκράτους καὶ Ἀλκιβιάδου καὶ τῶν ἄλλων τῶν τότε ἐν
τῷ συνδείπνῳ παραγενομένων, περὶ τῶν ἐρωτικῶν λόγων
τίνες ἦσαν· ἄλλος γάρ τίς μοι διηγεῖτο ἀκηκοὼς Φοίνικος
τοῦ Φιλίππου, ἔφη δὲ καὶ σὲ εἰδέναι. ἀλλὰ γὰρ οὐδὲν εἶχε
5 σαφὲς λέγειν. σὺ οὖν μοι διήγησαι· δικαιότατος γὰρ εἶ
τοὺς τοῦ ἑταίρου λόγους ἀπαγγέλλειν. πρότερον δέ μοι,"
ἦ δ' ὅς, "εἰπέ, σὺ αὐτὸς παρεγένου τῇ συνουσίᾳ ταύτῃ ἢ οὔ;"
Κἀγὼ εἶπον ὅτι "Παντάπασιν ἔοικέ σοι οὐδὲν διηγεῖσθαι
c   σαφὲς ὁ διηγούμενος, εἰ νεωστὶ ἡγῇ τὴν συνουσίαν γεγονέναι
ταύτην ἣν ἐρωτᾷς, ὥστε καὶ ἐμὲ παραγενέσθαι." " Ἐγώ γε

2

ἀ-μελέτητος, -ον: unpracticed, unprepared
ἀν-έρχομαι: to go up, approach
ἀπ-αγγέλλω: to report, announce, relate*
Ἀπολλόδωρος, ὁ: Apollodorus*
ἄστυ, -εως, τό: city, town
γνώριμος, -ον: familiar; *sub.* an acquaintance
δια-πυνθάνομαι: to learn thoroughly by
    inquiry, by hearsay; inquire in detail
ἔναγχος: just now, lately
κλῆσις, -εως, ἡ: a calling, invitation; name
νεωστί: lately, just now, recently
οἴκο-θεν: from home
ὄπισ-θεν: behind, from behind (+ gen.)
παίζω: to play, joke, jest

παντά-πασι: all in all, altogether, absolutely*
παρα-γίγνομαι: to be present; to arrive*
περι-μένω: to wait for, await*
πόρρω-θεν: from afar, at a distance
πρῴην: day before yesterday, the other day
πυνθάνομαι: to learn by inquiry, learn by
    hearsay; inquire, ask about*
σαφής, -ές: clear, distinct, definite*
σύν-δειπνον, τό: dinner, banquet
Φαληρεύς: Phalerian, man from Phalerum
Φαληρό-θεν: from Phalerum
Φίλιππος, ὁ: Phillip
Φοῖνιξ, Φοινίκος, ὁ: Phoinix

172a1 Δοκῶ μοι: *I think*; "I seem to myself"
περὶ ὧν: *concerning the things which*;
    the acc. relative pronoun has assumed
    the gen. of the missing antecedent: περὶ
    ἐκείνων οὕς, *concerning those which*
a2 καὶ γάρ: *for in fact*; καὶ is adverbial
ἐτύγχανον: *happened to...*; impf., this
    verb takes a complementary pple. ἀνιὼν
ἀνιὼν: pres. pple. ἀνέρχομαι (-ι)
a3 κατιδὼν: *seeing*; aor. pple. καθ-οράω
a4 ἔφη: *he said*; 3rd sg. impf., see below
a5 οὗτος: *you there*
    Ἀπολλόδωρος: vocative nom. in form.
περιμένεις: *are you not...*; more suitable
    for a statement that a question
κἀγὼ: crasis καὶ ἐγὼ
ἐπιστὰς: *stopping*; aor. pple, ἐφ-ίστημι
a6 ὅς: *he*; pronoun used as a demonstrative
καὶ μὴν καὶ: *why, in fact...*; lit. "and
    indeed in fact"

b1 Σωκράτους: gen. sg., see page 7 below
b3 ἦσαν: 3rd pl. impf. εἰμί
ἀκηκοὼς: nom. perf. pple. ἀκούω + gen.
b4 τοῦ Φιλίππου: *(son of) Phillip*
εἰδέναι: inf., οἶδα
ἀλλὰ γάρ: *but, and yet*
εἶχε: *he was able, could*; ἔχω + inf.
    often means "to have ability to or able to"
b5 διήγησαι: *relate (it)*; aor. mid. imp.
διηγέομαι
εἶ: *you are*; 2nd sg. pres. εἰμί
b7 ἦ: *he said*; 3rd sg. impf. ἠμί, see below
εἰπέ: aor. imp. λέγω
παρεγένου: *were you present*; 2nd sg.
    aor. παρεγένε(σ)ο,
c1 ἡγῇ: *you believe*; ἡγέ(σ)αι, 2nd sg. mid.
γεγονέναι: pf. inf, γίγνομαι
c2 ἐρωτᾷς 2nd sg. pres. α-contract
ὥστε...ἐμὲ: *so that I also*; result clause
Ἐγώ γε δή: *Yes indeed I (believe)*

φημί, φήσω, ἔφησα: to say, claim and ἠμί: to say

Since Apollodorus is recalling the conversation that he heard from Aristodemus, he uses the
following two verbs frequently. Note that the verb ἠμί occurs only in the 1st and 3rd singular.

	Present		Imperfect		Present		Imperfect	
1st	φημί	φαμέν	ἔφην	ἔφαμεν	ἠμί	––	ἦν	––
2nd	φῆς	φατέ	ἔφης	ἔφατε	–––	–––	–––	–––
3rd	φησί(ν)	φασί(ν)	ἔφη	ἔφασαν	ἠσί	––	ἦ	––
Inf.	φάναι							

δή," ἔφη. "Πόθεν, ἦν δ' ἐγώ, ὦ Γλαύκων; οὐκ οἶσθ' ὅτι
5 πολλῶν ἐτῶν Ἀγάθων ἐνθάδε οὐκ ἐπιδεδήμηκεν, ἀφ' οὗ δ'
ἐγὼ Σωκράτει συνδιατρίβω καὶ ἐπιμελὲς πεποίημαι ἑκάστης
ἡμέρας εἰδέναι ὅτι ἂν λέγῃ ἢ πράττῃ, οὐδέπω τρία ἔτη ἐστίν;
173 πρὸ τοῦ δὲ περιτρέχων ὅπῃ τύχοιμι καὶ οἰόμενος τὶ ποιεῖν
ἀθλιώτερος ἢ ὁτουοῦν, οὐχ ἧττον ἢ σὺ νυνί, οἰόμενος δεῖν
πάντα μᾶλλον πράττειν ἢ φιλοσοφεῖν." Καὶ ὅς, "Μὴ
σκῶπτ'," ἔφη, "ἀλλ' εἰπέ μοι πότε ἐγένετο ἡ συνουσία
5 αὕτη." Κἀγὼ εἶπον ὅτι "παίδων ὄντων ἡμῶν ἔτι, ὅτε τῇ πρώτῃ
τραγῳδίᾳ ἐνίκησεν Ἀγάθων, τῇ ὑστεραίᾳ ἢ ᾗ τὰ ἐπινίκια
ἔθυεν αὐτός τε καὶ οἱ χορευταί." "πάνυ," ἔφη, "ἄρα πάλαι,
ὡς ἔοικεν. ἀλλὰ τίς σοι διηγεῖτο; ἢ αὐτὸς Σωκράτης;"
b "Οὐ μὰ τὸν Δία," ἦν δ' ἐγώ, "ἀλλ' ὥσπερ Φοίνικι. Ἀριστόδημος ἦν τις, Κυδαθηναιεύς, σμικρός, ἀνυπόδητος ἀεί· παρεγεγόνει δ' ἐν τῇ συνουσίᾳ, Σωκράτους ἐραστὴς ὢν ἐν τοῖς
μάλιστα τῶν τότε, ὡς ἐμοὶ δοκεῖ. οὐ μέντοι ἀλλὰ καὶ
5 Σωκράτη γε ἔνια ἤδη ἀνηρόμην ὧν ἐκείνου ἤκουσα, καί μοι
ὡμολόγει καθάπερ ἐκεῖνος διηγεῖτο." "Τί οὖν," ἔφη, "οὐ
διηγήσω μοι; πάντως δὲ ἡ ὁδὸς ἡ εἰς ἄστυ ἐπιτηδεία
πορευομένοις καὶ λέγειν καὶ ἀκούειν."

Οὕτω δὴ ἰόντες ἅμα τοὺς λόγους περὶ αὐτῶν ἐποιούμεθα,
c ὥστε, ὅπερ ἀρχόμενος εἶπον, οὐκ ἀμελετήτως ἔχω. εἰ οὖν
δεῖ καὶ ὑμῖν διηγήσασθαι, ταῦτα χρὴ ποιεῖν. καὶ γὰρ ἔγωγε
καὶ ἄλλως, ὅταν μέν τινας περὶ φιλοσοφίας λόγους ἢ αὐτὸς
ποιῶμαι ἢ ἄλλων ἀκούω, χωρὶς τοῦ οἴεσθαι ὠφελεῖσθαι
5 ὑπερφυῶς ὡς χαίρω· ὅταν δὲ ἄλλους τινάς, ἄλλως τε καὶ
τοὺς ὑμετέρους τοὺς τῶν πλουσίων καὶ χρηματιστικῶν, αὐτός
τε ἄχθομαι ὑμᾶς τε τοὺς ἑταίρους ἐλεῶ, ὅτι οἴεσθε τὶ ποιεῖν
d οὐδὲν ποιοῦντες. καὶ ἴσως αὖ ὑμεῖς ἐμὲ ἡγεῖσθε κακοδαίμονα

ἄθλιος, -α, -ον: miserable, wretched
ἀ-μελέτητος, -ον: unpracticed, unprepared
ἀν-έρομαι: to ask, question, inquire about
ἀν-υπόδητος, -η, -ον: unshod, barefoot*
ἄστυ, -εως, τό: a city, town
ἄχθομαι: to be annoyed, vexed
Γλαύκων, ὁ: Glaucon
ἐλεέω: to have pity, show mercy*
ἔνιοι, -αι, -α: some*
ἐπι-δημέω: to live at home, be in town
ἐπι-μελής, -ές: careful about, attentive
ἐπινίκιος, -ον: of victory
ἐπιτήδειος, -α, -ον: suitable, useful, friendly*
ἔτος, -εως, τό: a year*
θύω: to sacrifice, make a sacrifice*
κακο-δαίμων, -ον: unlucky, ill-fated
Κυδαθηναιεύς, ὁ: from Kydathenaion
μά: by (+ acc.); in exclamation*
νικάω: to conquer, defeat, win*
νυνί: now; as it is*
ὁδός, ἡ: road, way, path, journey*
οὐδέ-πω: not yet, not as yet

ὅπη: (to) where, by which way, in what way*
ὅτε: when, at some time*
πάλαι: long ago, formerly, of old*
πάντως: altogether, by all means, in any case
παρα-γίγνομαι: to be present; to arrive*
περι-τρέχω: to run round, run about
πλούσιος, -α, -ον: rich, wealthy, opulent*
πόθεν: whence? from where?*
πότε: when? at what time?*
σκώπτω: to joke, make fun of, mock
συν-διατρίβω: to spend together with
τραγῳδία, ἡ: a tragedy
τρεῖς, τρία: three*
ὑμέτερος, -α, -ον: your, yours*
ὑπερφυῶς: extraordinarily, marvelously
ὑστεραῖος, -α, -ον: next, later; the next (day)
φιλο-σοφέω: to pursue wisdom, investigate*
χορευτής, -οῦ, ὁ: a choral dancer
χρηματιστικός, -ή, -όν: of money-making,
      gain, profit
χωρίς: separately; apart from (+ gen.)*
ὠφελέω: to help, to be of use, benefit*

172c3 Πόθεν: (From) where in the world?
c4 οἶσθ᾽: οἶσθα, 2nd sg., οἶδα
  πολλῶν ἐτῶν: for...; gen. time within
  ἐπιδεδήμηκεν: pf. ἐπιδημέω
  ἀφ᾽ οὗ: since; "from which (time)"
c5 συνδιατρίβω: I have been spending;
  pres. but pf. progressive in translation
  ἐπιμελὲς πεποίημαι: I have made it my
  business; "have made it my care," pf.
  ἑκάστης ἡμέρας: each day; time within
c6 εἰδέναι: inf., οἶδα
  ὅτι ἄν: ὅ τι ἄν, whatever...; general rel.
  clause: ἄν + 3rd sg. pres. subjunctives
173a1 πρὸ τοῦ: before which (time)
  ὅπη τύχοιμι: wherever I happened (to
  run); indefinite clause in secondary seq.
  governs an opt., aor. τυγχάνω
a1 τὶ ποιεῖν: to do something (important)
a2 ἦ: I was; 1st sg. impf., variation of ἦν
  ὁτουοῦν: than anyone; gen., ὁστισ-οῦν
  ἧττον ἤ: less than; adv., ἥττων, -ον
  δεῖν: inf. δεῖ
a3 μὴ σκῶπτ᾽: μὴ σκῶπτε; sg. imperative
a4 εἰπέ: aor. imp. λέγω
a6 τῇ ὑστεραίᾳ ἢ ᾗ: on the day later than
  on which (day); two datives, time when

  τὰ ἐπινίκια: the victory-sacrifices
b1 ὅσπερ Φοίνικι: the very one who
  (related it) to Phoenix
b2 παρεγεγόνει: had been present; plpf.
b3 Σωκράτους: gen. sg., see page 7 below
  ἐν τοῖς μάλιστα τῶν τότε: among
  those in particular at that time
b4 οὐ μέντοι ἀλλὰ καί: (I had) not (been
  present), however, but
b5 Σωκράτη: Σωκράτεα, acc. sg., see pg. 7
  ὧν: (about) the things which; acc. rel.
  attracted by the missing gen. antecedent
b6 καθάπερ: just as; 'in the very way which'
b7 τί...διηγήσω: why have you; διηγήσασο
b9 ἰόντες: going; pres. pple. ἔρχομαι (-ι)
c1 ἀμελετήτως ἔχω: I am not unpracticed;
  ἔχω + adv. correspond to "I am" + adj.
c3 ὅταν...ποιῶμαι...ἀκούω: whenever...;
  general temporal clause, pres. subj.
c4 τοῦ οἴεσθαι: from thinking; articular inf.
c5 ὑπερφυῶς ὡς: It is extraordinary how;
  ὑπερφυές ἐστιν ὡς, attracted by adv.
  ἄλλους τινάς: supply λόγους
  ἄλλως τε καί: especially, in particular
d1 οὐδέν: nothing (important); see 173a1

εἶναι, καὶ οἴομαι ὑμᾶς ἀληθῆ οἴεσθαι· ἐγὼ μέντοι ὑμᾶς οὐκ
οἴομαι ἀλλ' εὖ οἶδα.

ΕΤΑΙ. Ἀεὶ ὅμοιος εἶ, ὦ Ἀπολλόδωρε· ἀεὶ γὰρ σαυτόν
5 τε κακηγορεῖς καὶ τοὺς ἄλλους, καὶ δοκεῖς μοι ἀτεχνῶς
πάντας ἀθλίους ἡγεῖσθαι πλὴν Σωκράτους, ἀπὸ σαυτοῦ
ἀρξάμενος. καὶ ὁπόθεν ποτὲ ταύτην τὴν ἐπωνυμίαν ἔλαβες
τὸ μαλακὸς καλεῖσθαι, οὐκ οἶδα ἔγωγε· ἐν μὲν γὰρ τοῖς
λόγοις ἀεὶ τοιοῦτος εἶ, σαυτῷ τε καὶ τοῖς ἄλλοις ἀγριαίνεις
10 πλὴν Σωκράτους.

e ΑΠΟΛ. Ὦ φίλτατε, καὶ δῆλόν γε δὴ ὅτι οὕτω δια-
νοούμενος καὶ περὶ ἐμαυτοῦ καὶ περὶ ὑμῶν μαίνομαι καὶ
παραπαίω;

ΕΤΑΙ. Οὐκ ἄξιον περὶ τούτων, Ἀπολλόδωρε, νῦν ἐρίζειν·
5 ἀλλ' ὅπερ ἐδεόμεθά σου, μὴ ἄλλως ποιήσῃς, ἀλλὰ διήγησαι
τίνες ἦσαν οἱ λόγοι.

ΑΠΟΛ. Ἦσαν τοίνυν ἐκεῖνοι τοιοίδε τινές—μᾶλλον δ'
174 ἐξ ἀρχῆς ὑμῖν ὡς ἐκεῖνος διηγεῖτο καὶ ἐγὼ πειράσομαι
διηγήσασθαι.

Ἔφη γάρ οἱ Σωκράτη ἐντυχεῖν λελουμένον τε καὶ τὰς
βλαύτας ὑποδεδεμένον, ἃ ἐκεῖνος ὀλιγάκις ἐποίει· καὶ ἐρέσθαι
5 αὐτὸν ὅποι ἴοι οὕτω καλὸς γεγενημένος.

Καὶ τὸν εἰπεῖν ὅτι ἐπὶ δεῖπνον εἰς Ἀγάθωνος. χθὲς γὰρ
αὐτὸν διέφυγον τοῖς ἐπινικίοις, φοβηθεὶς τὸν ὄχλον· ὡμολόγησα δ' εἰς τήμερον παρέσεσθαι. ταῦτα δὴ ἐκαλλωπι-
σάμην, ἵνα καλὸς παρὰ καλὸν ἴω. ἀλλὰ σύ, ἦ δ' ὅς, πῶς
b ἔχεις πρὸς τὸ ἐθέλειν ἂν ἰέναι ἄκλητος ἐπὶ δεῖπνον;

Κἀγώ, ἔφη, εἶπον ὅτι οὕτως ὅπως ἂν σὺ κελεύῃς.

Ἕπου τοίνυν, ἔφη, ἵνα καὶ τὴν παροιμίαν διαφθείρωμεν
μεταβαλόντες, ὡς ἄρα καὶ "Ἀγάθων' ἐπὶ δαῖτας ἴασιν

ἀγριαίνω: to be angered, provoked, chafed
ἄθλιος, -α, -ον: miserable, wretched
ἄ-κλητος, -ον: uncalled, unbidden*
ἀ-τεχνῶς: simply, really, entirely*
βλαύτη, ἡ: a slipper
δαίς, δαιτός, ἡ: meal, feast, banquet
δεῖπνον, τό: the principal meal, dinner*
δια-νοέομαι: to think, suppose, intend*
δια-φεύγω: to flee, escape, avoid*
δια-φθείρω: to destroy, corrupt, pervert*
ἐπινίκιος, -ον: of victory
ἐπωνυμία, ἡ: a nickname, surname
ἐρίζω: to quarrel, wrangle, strive
κακ-ηγορέω: to speak ill of, abuse, slander
καλλ-ωπίζω: to adorn, make look beautiful
λούω: to wash, bathe

μαίνομαι: to be mad, rage, be furious
μαλακός, -ή, -όν: soft, gentle, mild; weak
μετα-βάλλω: to change, alter; turn about*
ὀλιγάκις: a few times, seldom
ὅποι: to where, whither, to what place
ὁπόθεν: from where, whence, from what place
ὄχλος, ὁ: a crowd, throng, mob
παρα-παίω: to strike aside; strike a false
    note, lose one's wits, be dumbstruck
παρ-οιμία, ἡ: common saying, proverb*
πλήν: except, but (+ gen.)*
τήμερον: today
τοιόσδε, -άδε, -όνδε: such, the following*
ὑπο-δέω: to bind from under, put on shoes*
φοβέομαι: to fear, be seized with fear, flee*
χθές: yesterday*

173d2 ἀληθῆ: *the truth*; neut. pl., see below
    μέντοι ὑμᾶς: *that you...*; acc. subj., add
    κακοδαίμονας εἶναι from earlier
d3 εἶ: *you are*; 2nd sg. pres., εἰμί
d7 ὁπόθεν ποτέ: *where in the world?*;
    "from wherever," expression of surprise
    ἔλαβες: 2nd sg. aor. λαμβάνω
d8 τὸ μαλακὸς καλεῖσθαι: *to be called soft*;
    articular inf. with pred. adj. in apposition
    to τὴν ἐπωνυμίαν
e1 φίλτατε: *O most dear man*; superlative
    καὶ δῆλόν γε...ὅτι: *is it really clear that*;
    supply ἐστίν; καὶ γε stresses middle term
e4 οὐκ ἄξιον: *it is not worthwhile*; add ἐστίν
e5 μὴ...ποιήσῃς: neg. command, aor. subj
    διήγησαι: *relate...*;aor. mid. imperative
e6 ἦσαν: 3rd pl. impf. εἰμί
e7 τοιοίδε τινές: *somewhat as follows*
    μᾶλλον δ: *or rather*; "but rather"
174a1 πειράσομαι: 1st sg. fut. πειράζω
a3 οἱ: *(to) him*; dat. of ἕ, obj. of ἐντυχεῖν
    ἐντυχεῖν: aor. inf. ἐντυγχάνω + dat. obj.
    λελουμένον...ὑποδεδεμένον: pf. mid.
    pple. λούω, ὑποδέω

a4 ἐρέσθαι: *he asked*; governed by ἔφη,
    the subj. is Aristodemus, not Socrates.
a5 ὅποι ἴοι: *(to) where he was going*; ind.
    question, opt. ἔρχομαι in secondary seq.
    γεγενημένος: pf. mid. pple. γίγνομαι
a6 τὸν: *he*; "this one," acc. subj. (cf. 172a6)
    εἰς Ἀγάθωνος: *at Agathon's (house)*
a7 διέφυγον: 1st sg. aor. δια-φεύγω
    φοβηθείς: nom. sg., aor. dep. pple φοβέω
a8 παρέσεσθαι: *to be present*, fut. πάρ-ειμι
    ταῦτα δή: *that's why...*; "with respect
    to these very things," acc. of respect
a9 ἴω: *I may go*; purpose, subj. ἔρχομαι
    πῶς ἔχεις πρός: *how are you disposed
    towards*; "feel towards," ἔχω + adv.
b1 τὸ ἐθέλειν: *being willing*; articular inf.
    ἰέναι: inf. ἔρχομαι
b2 κἀγώ: crasis καὶ ἐγώ
    ὅπως ἂν σὺ κελεύῃς: *however you bid*;
    indefinite clause with pres. subjunctive
b3 Ἕπου: *follow!*; ἕπεσο, pres. mid. imp.
    διαφθείρωμεν: purpose with pres. subj.
b4 ὡς...ἀγαθοί: *that it turns out that the
    good willingly go to Agathon for feasts*

Common Third-Declension ε(σ)-stem Nouns and Adjectives

		m/f		n.	
Nom.	Σωκράτης	ἀληθής	ἀληθεῖς (ε-ες)	ἀληθές	ἀληθῆ (ε-α)
Gen.	Σωκράτους (ε-ος)	ἀληθοῦς	ἀληθῶν	ἀληθοῦς	ἀληθῶν
Dat.	Σωκράτει (ε-ι)	ἀληθεῖ	ἀληθέσιν	ἀληθεῖ	ἀληθέσιν
Acc.	Σωκράτη (ε-α)	ἀληθῆ	ἀληθεῖς (ε-ες)	ἀληθές	ἀληθῆ (ε-α)

5 αὐτόματοι ἀγαθοί". Ὅμηρος μὲν γὰρ κινδυνεύει οὐ μόνον
διαφθεῖραι ἀλλὰ καὶ ὑβρίσαι εἰς ταύτην τὴν παροιμίαν·
ποιήσας γὰρ τὸν Ἀγαμέμνονα διαφερόντως ἀγαθὸν ἄνδρα
c τὰ πολεμικά, τὸν δὲ Μενέλεων ""μαλθακὸν αἰχμητήν"
θυσίαν ποιουμένου καὶ ἑστιῶντος τοῦ Ἀγαμέμνονος ἄκλητον
ἐποίησεν ἐλθόντα τὸν Μενέλεων ἐπὶ τὴν θοίνην, χείρω ὄντα
ἐπὶ τὴν τοῦ ἀμείνονος.

5 Ταῦτ' ἀκούσας εἰπεῖν ἔφη ἴσως μέντοι κινδυνεύσω καὶ
ἐγὼ οὐχ ὡς σὺ λέγεις, ὦ Σώκρατες, ἀλλὰ καθ' Ὅμηρον
φαῦλος ὢν ἐπὶ σοφοῦ ἀνδρὸς ἰέναι θοίνην ἄκλητος. ὅρα οὖν
ἄγων με τί ἀπολογήσῃ, ὡς ἐγὼ μὲν οὐχ ὁμολογήσω ἄκλητος
d ἥκειν, ἀλλ' ὑπὸ σοῦ κεκλημένος.

"Σύν τε δύ'," ἔφη, "ἐρχομένω πρὸ ὁδοῦ" βουλευσόμεθα
ὅτι ἐροῦμεν. ἀλλ' ἴωμεν.

Τοιαῦτ' ἄττα σφᾶς ἔφη διαλεχθέντας ἰέναι. τὸν οὖν
5 Σωκράτη ἑαυτῷ πως προσέχοντα τὸν νοῦν κατὰ τὴν ὁδὸν
πορεύεσθαι ὑπολειπόμενον, καὶ περιμένοντος οὗ κελεύειν
προϊέναι εἰς τὸ πρόσθεν. ἐπειδὴ δὲ γενέσθαι ἐπὶ τῇ οἰκίᾳ
e τῇ Ἀγάθωνος, ἀνεῳγμένην καταλαμβάνειν τὴν θύραν, καί τι
ἔφη αὐτόθι γελοῖον παθεῖν. οἱ μὲν γὰρ εὐθὺς παῖδά τινα
τῶν ἔνδοθεν ἀπαντήσαντα ἄγειν οὗ κατέκειντο οἱ ἄλλοι, καὶ
καταλαμβάνειν ἤδη μέλλοντας δειπνεῖν· εὐθὺς δ' οὖν ὡς
5 ἰδεῖν τὸν Ἀγάθωνα, ὦ, φάναι, Ἀριστόδημε, εἰς καλὸν ἥκεις
ὅπως συνδειπνήσῃς· εἰ δ' ἄλλου τινὸς ἕνεκα ἦλθες, εἰς αὖθις
ἀναβαλοῦ, ὡς καὶ χθὲς ζητῶν σε ἵνα καλέσαιμι, οὐχ οἷός τ'
ἦ ἰδεῖν. ἀλλὰ Σωκράτη ἡμῖν πῶς οὐκ ἄγεις;

Καὶ ἐγώ, ἔφη, μεταστρεφόμενος οὐδαμοῦ ὁρῶ Σωκράτη

Ἀγαμέμνων, -ονος ὁ: Agamemnon
αἰχμητής, οῦ, ὁ: spearman
ἄ-κλητος, -ον: uncalled, unbidden*
ἀνα-βάλλω: to throw up or back; put off
ἀν-οίγνυμι: to open*
ἀπ-αντάω: to meet, to encounter
ἀπο-λογέομαι: to speak in defense, defend
αὖθις: back again, later*
αὐτό-θι: on the very spot or moment*
αὐτόματος, -η, -ον: of one's own will
βουλεύω: to deliberate, plan, take counsel*
δεῖπνον, τό: the principal meal, dinner*
δια-φερόντως: differently from; especially*
δια-φθείρω: to destroy, corrupt, pervert*
ἔνδο-θεν: from within*
ἑστιάω: to entertain, give a feast
εὐθύς: right away, straight, directly, at once*
θοίνη, ἡ: a feast, meal, banquet

κατα-λαμβάνω: to find; seize; comprehend*
μαλακός, -ή, -όν: soft, gentle, mild; weak
Μενέλαος, ὁ: Menelaos
μετα-στρέφω: to turn about, turn round*
ὁδός, ἡ: road, way, path, journey*
οἰκία, ἡ: a house, home, dwelling
οὐδαμοῦ: nowhere
παρ-οιμία, ἡ: common saying, proverb*
περι-μένω: to wait for, await*
πολεμικός, -ή, -όν: of or for war, warlike
προ-έρχομαι: to go forth, advance*
πρόσθεν: before*
σύν: along with, with, together (+ gen.)*
συν-δειπνέω: to dine together with
ὑβρίζω: to commit outrage, assault, insult*
ὑπο-λείπω: to leave behind; fail
χείρων, ον: worse, more severe, inferior*
χθές: yesterday*

174b6 διαφθεῖραι...ὑβρίσαι: aor. infinitives
c1 τὰ πολεμικά: in warfare; acc. respect
μαλθακὸν: soft; μαλακὸν
c2 θυσίαν...Ἀγαμέμνονος: gen. abs.
c3 ἐλθόντα: coming aor. pple. ἔρχομαι
χείρω: the worse; χείρονα, acc. sg.
c4 ἐπὶ τὴν: to the (feast); supply θοίνην
c6 καθ᾽ Ὅμηρον: according to Homer
c7 ὢν: being; nom. sg. pres. pple εἰμί
ἰέναι: inf ἔρχομαι
ἐπὶ...θοίνην: to the banquet
ὅρα: consider; "see," sg. imperative
c8 ἀπολογήσῃ: ἀπολογήσε(σ)αι; fut. 2nd s.
d1 κεκλημένος: pf. pass. pple. καλέω
d2 Σύν...ὁδοῦ: as we two go together
down the road; pple is a dual form
d3 ὅτι ἐροῦμεν: what we will say; ὅ τι
ἴωμεν: let us...; hortatory subj., ἔρχομαι
d4 ἄττα: τίνα
σφᾶς: that they; acc. subj. see below
διαλεχθέντας: discussing; acc. dep. pple
d5 προσέχοντα τὸν νοῦν: directing his
mind, paying attention, pondering

κατὰ τὴν ὁδόν: along the way
d6 περιμένοντος οὗ: while he...; gen. abs.
κελεύειν: (Socrates) bid (Aristodemus)
d7 προϊέναι: inf. προ-έρχομαι
εἰς τὸ πρόσθεν: in front, ahead
e1 ἀνεῳγμένην: opened; pf.. ἀν-οίγνυμι
e2 παθεῖν that (he) experienced; πάσχω
οἱ: him; see below, obj. ἀπαντήσαντα
παῖδά τινα: a boy; likely a slave-boy
e3 οὗ: where; relative adverb (cf. 174d6)
e5 ὡς ἰδεῖν: when Agathon saw; aor. ὁράω
φάναι: inf. φημί
εἰς καλὸν: at the right moment
e6 ὅπως...συνδειπνήσῃς: so that...; purpose,
aor. subjunctive
ἦλθες: 2nd sg. aor. ἔρχομαι
εἰς αὖθις: til later
e7 ἀναβαλοῦ: ἀναβαλέσο; aor. sg. imp.
ὡς: since...; ὡς + pple, causal
ἵνα καλέσαιμι: purpose, aor. opt.
οἷός τ᾽ ἦ: I was able; οἷος τε + εἰμί
often means "I am the sort (capable of)"

3rd Person Singular and Plural Pronoun -- ἕ

Nom.	--		σφεῖς	they (own)
Gen.	οὗ	his (own), her (own), its (own)	σφῶν	their (own)
Dat.	οἷ	to him(self), her(self), it(self)	σφίσι	to them(selves)
Acc.	ἕ	him(self), her(self), it(self)	σφᾶς	them(selves)

10 ἑπόμενον· εἶπον οὖν ὅτι καὶ αὐτὸς μετὰ Σωκράτους ἥκοιμι,
κληθεὶς ὑπ’ ἐκείνου δεῦρ’ ἐπὶ δεῖπνον.

Καλῶς γ’, ἔφη, ποιῶν σύ· ἀλλὰ ποῦ ἔστιν οὗτος;

175 Ὄπισθεν ἐμοῦ ἄρτι εἰσῄει· ἀλλὰ θαυμάζω καὶ αὐτὸς ποῦ
ἂν εἴη.

Οὐ σκέψῃ, ἔφη, παῖ, φάναι τὸν Ἀγάθωνα, καὶ εἰσάξεις
Σωκράτη; σὺ δ’, ᾗ δ’ ὅς, Ἀριστόδημε, παρ’ Ἐρυξίμαχον
5 κατακλίνου.

Καὶ ἓ μὲν ἔφη ἀπονίζειν τὸν παῖδα ἵνα κατακέοιτο· ἄλλον
δέ τινα τῶν παίδων ἥκειν ἀγγέλλοντα ὅτι “Σωκράτης οὗτος
ἀναχωρήσας ἐν τῷ τῶν γειτόνων προθύρῳ ἔστηκεν, κἀμοῦ
καλοῦντος οὐκ ἐθέλει εἰσιέναι.”

10 Ἄτοπόν γ’, ἔφη, λέγεις· οὔκουν καλεῖς αὐτὸν καὶ μὴ
ἀφήσεις;

b Καὶ ὃς ἔφη εἰπεῖν μηδαμῶς, ἀλλ’ ἐᾶτε αὐτόν. ἔθος γάρ
τι τοῦτ’ ἔχει· ἐνίοτε ἀποστὰς ὅποι ἂν τύχῃ ἔστηκεν. ἥξει
δ’ αὐτίκα, ὡς ἐγὼ οἶμαι. μὴ οὖν κινεῖτε, ἀλλ’ ἐᾶτε.

Ἀλλ’ οὕτω χρὴ ποιεῖν, εἰ σοὶ δοκεῖ, ἔφη φάναι τὸν
5 Ἀγάθωνα. ἀλλ’ ἡμᾶς, ὦ παῖδες, τοὺς ἄλλους ἑστιᾶτε.
πάντως παρατίθετε ὅτι ἂν βούλησθε, ἐπειδάν τις ὑμῖν μὴ
ἐφεστήκῃ—ὃ ἐγὼ οὐδεπώποτε ἐποίησα—νῦν οὖν, νομίζοντες
καὶ ἐμὲ ὑφ’ ὑμῶν κεκλῆσθαι ἐπὶ δεῖπνον καὶ τούσδε τοὺς
c ἄλλους, θεραπεύετε, ἵν’ ὑμᾶς ἐπαινῶμεν.

Μετὰ ταῦτα ἔφη σφᾶς μὲν δειπνεῖν, τὸν δὲ Σωκράτη
οὐκ εἰσιέναι. τὸν οὖν Ἀγάθωνα πολλάκις κελεύειν μετα-
πέμψασθαι τὸν Σωκράτη, ἓ δὲ οὐκ ἐᾶν. ἥκειν οὖν αὐτὸν οὐ

ἀγγέλλω: to announce, proclaim, report
ᾄδω: to sing*
ἀνα-χωρέω: to go back, withdraw, retreat*
ἀπο-νίζω: to wash, wash clean
ἄρτι: just, exactly*
ἄ-τοπος, -ον: strange, odd, extraordinary*
αὐτίκα: straightway, at once; presently*
ἀφ-ίστημι: to stand away from, remove*
γείτων, -ονος, ὁ, ἡ: a neighbor
δεῦρο: here, to this point, hither*
δεῖπνον, τό: the principal meal, dinner*
ἔθος, -εος, τό: custom, habit*
εἰσ-άγω: to lead in, to introduce, bring in*
ἐνί-οτε: sometimes, from time to time
ἑστιάω: to entertain, give a feast

θεραπεύω: to attend to, care for, serve
κατά-κλισις, -εως, ἡ: lying down at the table
κινέω: to set in motion, move; arouse, irritate*
μετα-πέμπω: to send after, send for, summon
μηδαμῶς: in no way, not at all
ὄπισθεν: (from) behind; in the future (+ gen.)
ὅποι: to where, whither, to what place
οὐδε-πώποτε: not yet ever, never in the world
οὔκ-ουν: certainly not, and so not
πάντως: altogether, by all means, certainly*
παρα-τίθημι: to place beside; offer, provide*
πρό-θυρον, τό: the front-door; porch, doorway
σκέπτομαι: to look at, examine, consider*
ὑβριστής, οῦ, ὁ: an outrageous person*

174e10 ἑπόμενον: *following*; pple. ἕπομαι
  ἥκοιμι: opt. of ἥκω, indirect discourse
  in secondary sequence
e11 κληθείς: aor. pass. pple, καλέω
175a1 εἰσῄει: 3rd sg. impf. εἰσέρχομαι
a2 ἂν εἴη: *would be*; potential opt. εἰμί
a3 οὐ σκέψῃ: *will you not look*; fut. 2nd sg.
  mid.; οὐ anticipates a *yes* response in
  this mild command
a5 κατακλίνου: κατακλίνε(σ)ο, mid. imp.
a6 κατακέοιτο: opt. κατάκειμαι in a
  purpose clause, secondary sequence
a7 οὗτος: *here*; the slave is pointing
a8 ἕστηκεν: 3rd sg. pf. ἵστημι
  κἀμοῦ: crasis καὶ ἐμοῦ
a10 οὔκουν καλεῖς: *will you not call*; fut. in a
  mild command (cf. 175a3)
  μὴ ἀφήσεις: *do not let him go*; lit. "you
  will not let him go, will you?", μὴ

anticipates a *no* response; fut. ἀφ-ίημι
b1 ὅς...εἰπεῖν: *he said that he;* the subj. is
  Aristodemus
b2 ἀποστάς: aor. pple. ἀφίστημι
  τύχῃ: *he happens (to stand)*; aor. subj.
  of τυγχάνω in an indefinite clause
  ἥξει: fut. ἥκω
b4 φάναι: inf. φημί
b6 ὅτι ἄν: *whatever...*; ὅ τι ἄν
  τις...μὴ ἐφεστήκῃ: *no one has stopped*
  you; 3rd sg. pf. subj. ἐφίστημι
b8 κεκλῆσθαι: pf. pass. inf. καλέω
c1 ἵν...ἐπαινῶμεν: *so that...*; purpose, subj.
c2 σφᾶς: *they*; acc. subject
c3 εἰσιέναι: inf. εἰσέρχομαι
  κελεύειν: assume τὸν παῖδα as object
c4 ἕ: *that he*; i.e. Aristodemus, acc. subj.
  ἐᾶν: inf. ἐάω
  αὐτὸν: *that he*; i.e. Socrates, acc. subj.

Common Constructions with ἄν

Indefinite (or General) Clauses

relative	ὅστις, ἥτις, ὅ τι + ἄν + subj.	ὅ τι ἄν ποιῇ	*whatever she does...*
temporal	ἐπειδάν, ὅταν, ἕως ἄν + subj.	ἐπειδάν ποιῇ	*whenever she does...*
conditional	ἐάν + subj.	ἐάν ποιῇ	*if ever she does...*

Potential Optative

	ἄν + optative	ἄν ποιοῖ	*she would/might do...*

Past Potential

	ἄν + past indicative	ἄν ἐποίησε	*she would have done...*

5 πολὺν χρόνον ὡς εἰώθει διατρίψαντα, ἀλλὰ μάλιστα σφᾶς
μεσοῦν δειπνοῦντας. τὸν οὖν Ἀγάθωνα—τυγχάνειν γὰρ
ἔσχατον κατακείμενον μόνον—δεῦρ᾽, ἔφη φάναι, Σώκρατες,
παρ᾽ ἐμὲ κατάκεισο, ἵνα καὶ τοῦ σοφοῦ ἁπτόμενός σου
d ἀπολαύσω, ὅ σοι προσέστη ἐν τοῖς προθύροις. δῆλον γὰρ
ὅτι ηὗρες αὐτὸ καὶ ἔχεις· οὐ γὰρ ἂν προαπέστης.

Καὶ τὸν Σωκράτη καθίζεσθαι καὶ εἰπεῖν ὅτι εὖ ἂν ἔχοι,
φάναι, ὦ Ἀγάθων, εἰ τοιοῦτον εἴη ἡ σοφία ὥστ᾽ ἐκ τοῦ πληρε-
5 στέρου εἰς τὸ κενώτερον ῥεῖν ἡμῶν, ἐὰν ἁπτώμεθα ἀλλήλων,
ὥσπερ τὸ ἐν ταῖς κύλιξιν ὕδωρ τὸ διὰ τοῦ ἐρίου ῥέον ἐκ τῆς
πληρεστέρας εἰς τὴν κενωτέραν. εἰ γὰρ οὕτως ἔχει καὶ ἡ
e σοφία, πολλοῦ τιμῶμαι τὴν παρὰ σοὶ κατάκλισιν· οἶμαι γάρ
με παρὰ σοῦ πολλῆς καὶ καλῆς σοφίας πληρωθήσεσθαι. ἡ μὲν
γὰρ ἐμὴ φαύλη τις ἂν εἴη, ἢ καὶ ἀμφισβητήσιμος ὥσπερ ὄναρ
οὖσα, ἡ δὲ σὴ λαμπρά τε καὶ πολλὴν ἐπίδοσιν ἔχουσα, ἥ γε
5 παρὰ σοῦ νέου ὄντος οὕτω σφόδρα ἐξέλαμψεν καὶ ἐκφανὴς
ἐγένετο πρῴην ἐν μάρτυσι τῶν Ἑλλήνων πλέον ἢ τρισμυρίοις.
Ὑβριστὴς εἶ, ἔφη, ὦ Σώκρατες, ὁ Ἀγάθων. καὶ ταῦτα
μὲν καὶ ὀλίγον ὕστερον διαδικασόμεθα ἐγώ τε καὶ σὺ περὶ
τῆς σοφίας, δικαστῇ χρώμενοι τῷ Διονύσῳ· νῦν δὲ πρὸς τὸ
10 δεῖπνον πρῶτα τρέπου.
176 Μετὰ ταῦτα, ἔφη, κατακλινέντος τοῦ Σωκράτους καὶ
δειπνήσαντος καὶ τῶν ἄλλων, σπονδάς τε σφᾶς ποιήσασθαι,
καὶ ᾄσαντας τὸν θεὸν καὶ τἆλλα τὰ νομιζόμενα, τρέπεσθαι
πρὸς τὸν πότον· τὸν οὖν Παυσανίαν ἔφη λόγου τοιούτου
5 τινὸς κατάρχειν. εἶεν, ἄνδρες, φάναι, τίνα τρόπον ῥᾷστα
πιόμεθα; ἐγὼ μὲν οὖν λέγω ὑμῖν ὅτι τῷ ὄντι πάνυ χαλεπῶς
ἔχω ὑπὸ τοῦ χθὲς πότου καὶ δέομαι ἀναψυχῆς τινος—οἶμαι
δὲ καὶ ὑμῶν τοὺς πολλούς· παρῆστε γὰρ χθές—σκοπεῖσθε
b οὖν τίνι τρόπῳ ἂν ὡς ῥᾷστα πίνοιμεν.

ᾄδω: to sing*
ἀμφισβητήσιμος, -ον: disputable, debatable
ἀνα-ψυχή, ἡ: relief, recovery, respite
ἀπο-λαύω: to enjoy, have enjoyment (gen.)*
δεῖπνον, τό: the principal meal, dinner*
δεῦρο: here, to this point, hither*
δια-δικάζω: to give judgment in a case, decide
δια-τρίβω: to pass time, consume, spend*
δικαστής, οῦ, ὁ: a juror, dicast*
Διόνυσος, ὁ: Dionysus
εἶεν: well! well now! *
ἐκ-λάμπω: to shine or beam forth
ἐκ-φανής, -ές: manifest, conspicuous, visible
Ἕλλην, Ἕλληνος, ὁ: a Greek
ἐπί-δοσις, -εως, ἡ: benefit, growth, progress
ἔριον, τό: wool
ἔσχατος, -η, -ον: extreme, last, furthest*
εὑρίσκω: to find, discover, devise, invent*
καθ-ίζω: to make sit down, seat
κατ-άρχω: to begin, commence (+ gen.)
κατά-κλισις, -εως, ἡ: lying down at the table
κενός, -ή, -όν: empty; void, destitute, bereft*

κύλιξ, -ικος, ἡ: a cup, drinking-cup
λαμπρός, -ά, -όν: bright, brilliant, radiant
μάρτυς, -υρος, ὁ, ἡ: a witness*
μεσόω: to be in the middle of
ὄναρ, τό: a dream, vision in sleep
πλήρης, -ες: full, filled*
πληρόω: to fill, make full of (+ gen.)*
πότος, ὁ: drinking, drink*
τρισ-μύριοι: thrice ten thousand
προ-αφίσταμαι: to depart, leave off, desist
    beforehand; to revolt beforehand
πρό-θυρον, τό: the front-door; porch, doorway
προσ-ίστημι: to set near, stand near
πρώην: day before yesterday, other day
ῥέω: to flow, run, stream*
σκοπέω: to look at, examine, consider*
σπονδή, ἡ: drink-offering, libation; treaty
ὑβριστής, -οῦ, ὁ: an outrageous person*
ὕδωρ, ὕδατος, τό: water
ὕστερον: later*
χθές: yesterday*

175c5 πολὺν χρόνον: *for...*; duration of time
   εἰώθει: *was accustomed*; plpf., εἴωθα
c6 μεσοῦν: *were in the middle of*; pres. inf.
   τυγχάνειν: *(he) happened to*; as often
   with a complementary pple
c8 κατάκεισο: *lie down*; pres. mid. imp.
   ἁπτόμενος σου: *(by) touching you*; pple
   governs a partitive gen., see d5 below
d1 ἀπολαύσω: *I may enjoy*; + gen. aor. subj.
   ὅ σοι προσέστη: *which set upon you*,
   3rd sg. aor. προσ-ίστημι
   δῆλον...ὅτι: *it is clear that*; (cf. 173e1)
d2 ηὗρες: 2nd sg. aor. εὑρίσκω
   οὐ...ἂν προαπέστης: *you would not*
   have departed beforehand; aor. ind. mid.
   προ-αφίστημι + ἂν = past potential
d3 εὖ ἂν ἔχοι: *it would be well*; lit. "would
   be well disposed," opt. ἔχω and εἰμί
   in a fut. less vivid (*if should, would*)
d4 τοιοῦτον...ὥστ': *such...that*
   ῥεῖν: inf. ῥέω
d6 τὸ...ῥέον: *flowing*; pple. modifies ὕδωρ
e1 πολλοῦ τιμῶμαι: *I value greatly*; "I
   consider of great (value)" gen. of value
e2 πληρωθήσεσθαι: *will be filled*; fut. pass.

e3 ἡ μὲν γὰρ ἐμὴ φαύλη τις ἂν εἴη: *my*
   (wisdom) is probably quite worthless
   ὥσπερ ὄναρ: *as if in a dream*
e4 οὖσα: *being*; pple. εἰμί
   ἥ γε: *since it...*; rel. pron. + γέ is causal
e5 ὄντος: *being*; gen. sg. with pred. νέου
e7 εἶ: *you are*; 2nd sg. pres. εἰμί
e8 ὀλίγον: *little*; acc. of extent
e10 πρῶτα: *first*; adverbial accusative
   πρέπου: *turn*; πρέπε(σ)ο; 2nd sg. mid.
176a1 κατακλινέντος: gen. abs., aor. dep.
a3 ᾄσαντες: *singing*; aor. pple ᾄδω
   τἆλλα: *other*; crasis τὰ ἄλλα
   τὰ νομιζόμενα: *customary things*
a5 τίνα τρόπον: *in what way*; acc. respect
   ῥᾷστα: *most easily*; superlative adv.
   from ῥᾴδιος
a6 πιόμεθα: 1st pl. fut dep. πίνω
   τῷ ὄντι: *really, in reality, actually*;
   dat. of respect from the pple of εἰμί
a8 παρῆστε: impf. πάρ-ειμι
b1 τίνι τρόπῳ: *in what way*; dat. manner
   ὡς ῥᾷστα: *as easily as possible*; superl.
   ἂν...πίνοιμεν: *we might*; potential opt.

Τὸν οὖν Ἀριστοφάνη εἰπεῖν, τοῦτο μέντοι εὖ λέγεις, ὦ
Παυσανία, τὸ παντὶ τρόπῳ παρασκευάσασθαι ῥᾳστώνην τινὰ
τῆς πόσεως· καὶ γὰρ αὐτός εἰμι τῶν χθὲς βεβαπτισμένων.

5   Ἀκούσαντα οὖν αὐτῶν ἔφη Ἐρυξίμαχον τὸν Ἀκουμενοῦ
Ἦ καλῶς, φάναι, λέγετε. καὶ ἔτι ἑνὸς δέομαι ὑμῶν ἀκοῦσαι
πῶς ἔχει πρὸς τὸ ἐρρῶσθαι πίνειν, Ἀγάθων⟨ος⟩.

   Οὐδαμῶς, φάναι, οὐδ᾽ αὐτὸς ἔρρωμαι.

c   Ἕρμαιον ἂν εἴη ἡμῖν, ἦ δ᾽ ὅς, ὡς ἔοικεν, ἐμοί τε καὶ
Ἀριστοδήμῳ καὶ Φαίδρῳ καὶ τοῖσδε, εἰ ὑμεῖς οἱ δυνατώτατοι
πίνειν νῦν ἀπειρήκατε· ἡμεῖς μὲν γὰρ ἀεὶ ἀδύνατοι. Σωκράτη δ᾽ ἐξαιρῶ λόγου· ἱκανὸς γὰρ καὶ ἀμφότερα, ὥστ᾽
5 ἐξαρκέσει αὐτῷ ὁπότερ᾽ ἂν ποιῶμεν. ἐπειδὴ οὖν μοι δοκεῖ
οὐδεὶς τῶν παρόντων προθύμως ἔχειν πρὸς τὸ πολὺν πίνειν
οἶνον, ἴσως ἂν ἐγὼ περὶ τοῦ μεθύσκεσθαι οἷόν ἐστι τἀληθῆ
λέγων ἧττον ἂν εἴην ἀηδής. ἐμοὶ γὰρ δὴ τοῦτό γε οἶμαι
d κατάδηλον γεγονέναι ἐκ τῆς ἰατρικῆς, ὅτι χαλεπὸν τοῖς
ἀνθρώποις ἡ μέθη ἐστίν· καὶ οὔτε αὐτὸς ἑκὼν εἶναι πόρρω
ἐθελήσαιμι ἂν πιεῖν οὔτε ἄλλῳ συμβουλεύσαιμι, ἄλλως τε
καὶ κραιπαλῶντα ἔτι ἐκ τῆς προτεραίας.

5   Ἀλλὰ μήν, ἔφη φάναι ὑπολαβόντα Φαῖδρον τὸν Μυρρινού-
σιον, ἔγωγέ σοι εἴωθα πείθεσθαι ἄλλως τε καὶ ἅττ᾽ ἂν περὶ
ἰατρικῆς λέγῃς· νῦν δ᾽, ἂν εὖ βουλεύωνται, καὶ οἱ λοιποί.
e ταῦτα δὴ ἀκούσαντας συγχωρεῖν πάντας μὴ διὰ μέθης
ποιήσασθαι τὴν ἐν τῷ παρόντι συνουσίαν, ἀλλ᾽ οὕτω πίνοντας
πρὸς ἡδονήν.

   Ἐπειδὴ τοίνυν, φάναι τὸν Ἐρυξίμαχον, τοῦτο μὲν δέδοκται, πίνειν ὅσον ἂν ἕκαστος βούληται, ἐπάναγκες δὲ μηδὲν

ἀ-ηδής, -ές: unpleasant, disagreeable
Ἀκουσίλεως, ὁ: Akousileus
ἀπ-ερέω: to renounce, speak against, gainsay
βαπτίζω: to soak, dip in or under water
βουλεύω: to deliberate, plan, take counsel*
δυνατός, -ή, -όν: capable, strong, possible*
ἐξ-αιρέω: to take out, remove, leave out*
ἐξ-αρκέω: to be enough, suffice, be sufficient*
ἐπ-ανάγκης, -ες: necessary, compulsory
ἕρμαιον, τό: god-send, stroke of luck
κατά-δηλος, -η, -ον: quite clear, evident*
κραιπαλάω: to have a headache, hangover
λοιπός, ὁ: remaining, the rest*
μέθη, ἡ: drunkenness
μεθύσκω: to make drunk, intoxicate, inebriate*
Μυρρινούσιος: of the deme Myrrhinus

οἶνος, ὁ: wine*
ὁπότερος, -α, -ον: which of two
οὐδαμῶς: in no way, not at all
παρασκευάζω: to prepare, get ready; procure*
πόρρω: far; advanced
πόσις, -εως, ὁ: drinking*
προ-θύμως: eagerly, zealously, readily
προτεραῖος, -α, -ον: on the day before
ῥᾳστώνη, ἡ: ease, comfort; relief, recovery
ῥώννυμι: to strengthen, make strong; be fit*
συγ-χωρέω: to come together; yield, concede*
συμ-βουλεύω: to deliberative together, advise*
ὑπο-λαμβάνω: to take up, reply; suppose*
χθές: yesterday*

176b2 μέντοι: *certainly*; here assertative
  b3 τὸ...παρασκευάσασθαι: an articular inf. in apposition to τοῦτο above
  παντὶ τρόπῳ: *in every way*; dat. respect
  b4 πόσεως: *from drinking*; gen. separation
  βεβαπτισμένων (one) of those...; pf. pass. pple., partitive gen.
  b5 τὸν Ἀκουμενοῦ: *son of Akoumenus*
  b6 ἑνός: *from one*...; gen. obj. of ἀκούω
  b7 πῶς ἔχει: *how he feels*; "is disposed"
  πρὸς τὸ ἐρρῶσθαι: *with regard to being fit to*...; perf. mid. inf. ῥώννυμι
  b8 ἔρρωμαι: *am fit*; perf. mid. ῥώννυμι
  c1 ἂν εἴη: *would be*; potential opt. εἰμί
  c2 δυνατώτατοι: superlative
  c3 ἀπειρήκατε: 2nd pl. pf. ἀπ-ερέω
  Σωκράτη...ἐξαιρῶ λόγου: *I make an exception for Socrates*; "I leave Socrates out from the account," gen. separation
  c4 ἱκανὸς...ἀμφότερα: *for in fact (he is) adequate in both ways*; acc. respect
  c5 ὁπότερ' ἂν: *whichever*...; general clause
  c6 προθύμως ἔχειν: *is eager*; see below
  πρὸς τὸ...πίνειν: *with regard to drinking*
  c7 οἷόν ἐστι: *what sort of thing it is*; related

to the with the preceding articular inf.
  c8 ἄν...ἂν εἴην: *I would be*; potential opt.
  εἰμί; the second ἂν is redundant
  ἧττον: *less*; adv. modifying ἀηδής
  d1 γεγονέναι: pf. inf. γίγνομαι
  ἰατρικῆς: *art of medicine*; add τέχνης
  d2 ἑκὼν εἶναι: *willingly*; Dover says εἶναι has the force of γέ: "willingly, anyway"
  d3 ἐθελήσαιμι ἄν: *I would*...; potential opt.
  πόρρω..πιεῖν: *drink heavily*; aor. πίνω
  ἄλλως τε καὶ: *in particular*; "both otherwise and…"
  d5 ἀλλὰ μήν: *very well*
  d6 εἴωθα: *I am accustomed*; pf., pres. sense
  ἅττ᾽: *whatever*; alternative to ἅτινα
  d7 ἄν: *if*; ἐάν, in a future-more-vivid
  d8 οἱ λοιποί: *the rest (will obey)*; supply πείσονταί σοι from above
  e2 ἐν τῷ παρόντι: *in the present moment*; pple. πάρ-ειμι
  οὕτω...πρὸς ἡδονήν: *just...for pleasure*
  e4 δέδοκται: *has seemed best (to us)*; pf.
  e5 ὅσον ἂν: *as much as*; general rel. + subj.
  ἐπάναγκες...μηδέν: *no compulsion*

Common Translations of ἔχω			
ἔχω + infinitive	→	*to be able + inf.*	εἶχε...λέγειν	*he was able to say...*
ἔχω + adverb	→	*to be + adjective*	ἀμελετήτως ἔχω	*I am unpracticed...*
ἔχω + obj.	→	*to know*	εἶχον ὅπως...	*I knew how...*

a εἶναι, τὸ μετὰ τοῦτο εἰσηγοῦμαι τὴν μὲν ἄρτι εἰσελθοῦσαν
αὐλητρίδα χαίρειν ἐᾶν, αὐλοῦσαν ἑαυτῇ ἢ ἂν βούληται ταῖς
γυναιξὶ ταῖς ἔνδον, ἡμᾶς δὲ διὰ λόγων ἀλλήλοις συνεῖναι
τὸ τήμερον· καὶ δι᾿ οἵων λόγων, εἰ βούλεσθε, ἐθέλω ὑμῖν
10 εἰσηγήσασθαι.

177 Φάναι δὴ πάντας καὶ βούλεσθαι καὶ κελεύειν αὐτὸν
εἰσηγεῖσθαι. εἰπεῖν οὖν τὸν Ἐρυξίμαχον ὅτι ἡ μέν μοι
ἀρχὴ τοῦ λόγου ἐστὶ κατὰ τὴν Εὐριπίδου Μελανίππην· οὐ
γὰρ ἐμὸς ὁ μῦθος, ἀλλὰ Φαίδρου τοῦδε, ὃν μέλλω λέγειν.
5 Φαῖδρος γὰρ ἑκάστοτε πρός με ἀγανακτῶν λέγει οὐ δεινόν,
φησίν, ὦ Ἐρυξίμαχε, ἄλλοις μέν τισι θεῶν ὕμνους καὶ
παίωνας εἶναι ὑπὸ τῶν ποιητῶν πεποιημένους, τῷ δὲ Ἔρωτι,
τηλικούτῳ ὄντι καὶ τοσούτῳ θεῷ, μηδὲ ἕνα πώποτε τοσούτων
b γεγονότων ποιητῶν πεποιηκέναι μηδὲν ἐγκώμιον; εἰ δὲ βούλει
αὖ σκέψασθαι τοὺς χρηστοὺς σοφιστάς, Ἡρακλέους μὲν καὶ
ἄλλων ἐπαίνους καταλογάδην συγγράφειν, ὥσπερ ὁ βέλτιστος
Πρόδικος—καὶ τοῦτο μὲν ἧττον καὶ θαυμαστόν, ἀλλ᾿ ἔγωγε
5 ἤδη τινὶ ἐνέτυχον βιβλίῳ ἀνδρὸς σοφοῦ, ἐν ᾧ ἐνῆσαν ἅλες
ἔπαινον θαυμάσιον ἔχοντες πρὸς ὠφελίαν, καὶ ἄλλα τοιαῦτα
c συχνὰ ἴδοις ἂν ἐγκεκωμιασμένα—τὸ οὖν τοιούτων μὲν πέρι
πολλὴν σπουδὴν ποιήσασθαι, ἔρωτα δὲ μηδένα πω ἀνθρώπων
τετολμηκέναι εἰς ταυτηνὶ τὴν ἡμέραν ἀξίως ὑμνῆσαι· ἀλλ᾿
οὕτως ἠμέληται τοσοῦτος θεός. ταῦτα δή μοι δοκεῖ εὖ
5 λέγειν Φαῖδρος. ἐγὼ οὖν ἐπιθυμῶ ἅμα μὲν τούτῳ ἔρανον
εἰσενεγκεῖν καὶ χαρίσασθαι, ἅμα δ᾿ ἐν τῷ παρόντι πρέπον
μοι δοκεῖ εἶναι ἡμῖν τοῖς παροῦσι κοσμῆσαι τὸν θεόν. εἰ οὖν
d συνδοκεῖ καὶ ὑμῖν, γένοιτ᾿ ἂν ἡμῖν ἐν λόγοις ἱκανὴ διατριβή·
δοκεῖ γάρ μοι χρῆναι ἕκαστον ἡμῶν λόγον εἰπεῖν ἔπαινον
Ἔρωτος ἐπὶ δεξιὰ ὡς ἂν δύνηται κάλλιστον, ἄρχειν δὲ

ἀγανακτέω: to be irritated, annoyed, angry
ἅλς, -ος, ὁ: salt
ἀμελέω: to have no care for, neglect (+ gen.)*
ἄρτι: just, exactly*
αὐλητρίς, -ίδος, ἡ: a flute-girl*
αὐλέω: to play on the flute*
βέλτιστος, -η, -ον: best*
βιβλίον, τό: scroll, book
δεξιός, -ά, -όν: right, right side*
δια-τριβή, ἡ: pastime; pursuit
ἐγ-κώμιον, τό: eulogy, speech of praise*
εἰσ-ηγέομαι: to propose, introduce; explain*
εἰσ-φέρω: to bring in, introduce; to contribute
ἑκάστοτε: each time, on each occasion
ἔνδον: within, at home*
ἐν-ειμί: to be in*
ἔρανος, ὁ: contribution, kindness, favor
Εὐριπίδης, ὁ: Euripides
Ἡρακλέης, -εεος, ὁ: Heracles
καταλογάδην: in prose, through conversation

κοσμέω: to order, arrange, adorn
Μελανίππη, ἡ: Melanippe (lost tragedy)
μῦθος, ὁ: story, word, speech*
παιων, -ωνος ὁ: paean, hymn, chant
πρέπω: to fit, suit; impers. it is fitting*
Πρόδικος, ὁ: Prodicus
πω: yet, up to this time*
πώ-ποτε: ever yet, ever
σκέπτομαι: to look at, examine, consider*
σοφιστής, ὁ: sophist, wise man*
σπουδή, ἡ: zeal, earnestness, seriousness
συγ-γράφω: to compose, write in prose
συν-δοκέω: to seem good also
συχνός, -ή, -όν: many, much, great, long
τηλικοῦτος, -αύτη, -οῦτο: at such an age
τήμερον: today
ὑμνέω: to sing, laud, praise in song; recite*
ὕμνος, ὁ: a hymn, festive song
χρηστός, -ή, -όν: good, worthy*
ὠφέλεια, ἡ: help, aid, use, advantage, benefit

176e6 τὸ μετὰ τοῦτο: *as the next thing;* "the thing after this"
εἰσελθοῦσαν: acc. aor. pple. εἰσέρχομαι
e7 χαίρειν ἐᾶν: *to dismiss;* lit. "allow (acc.) to say farewell"
ἢ ἂν βούληται: *or if she wishes;* ἂν contracted from ἐάν
e8 συνεῖναι: *to associatei;* inf. σύμ-ειμι
177a3 κατὰ τὴν...Μελανίππην: *according to Euripides' Melanippe*
a5 οὐ δεινόν: *isn't it terrible, isn't it strange;* add ἐστιν for impersonal verb
a7 εἶναι...πεποιημένους: *have been composed;* pf. pass. pple. + εἰμί = periphrastic perfect passive
a8 μηδὲ...μηδὲν: *not even...any;* double negative, translate 2nd term positively
τοσούτων γεγονότων: *(though) having been so many;* pf. pple., concessive
b1 βούλει: *you wish;* βούλε(σ)αι, 2nd sg.
b2 Ἡρακλέους: Ἡρακλέεος, gen. sg.
b3 συγγράφειν: add οὐ δεινόν ἐστιν above
b4 τοῦτο: supply ἐστιν
ἧττον καὶ θαυμαστόν: *less amazing in fact (than the following);* acc. of extent
b5 ἐνέτυχον: *encountered;* aor. ἐν-τυγχάνω
ἐνῆσαν: 3rd pl. impf., ἐν-ειμί

b6 πρὸς ὠφελίαν: *with regard to its benefit*
c1 ἴδοις ἄν: aor. potential opt. ὁράω
πέρι: accent on ε means the obj. of the preposition comes before περί
τὸ...ποιήσασθαι...τετολμηκέναι: *(to think) that...;* these infs. are exclamatory
c3 τετολμηκέναι: *to have dared;* pf. inf.
ταυτηνὶ: *this here;* deictic iota
ὑμνῆσαι: aor. inf.
c4 ἠμέληται: 3rd sg. pf. pass., ἀμελέω
c5 ἅμα μὲν...ἅμα δὲ: *both...and*
τούτῳ: i.e. Phaedrus
c6 εἰσενεγκεῖν: aor. inf., εἰσφέρω
ἐν τῷ παρόντι: *at the present time;* pres. pple. πάρ-ειμι
πρέπον...εἶναι: *to be fitting;* πρέπον is a neuter pres. pple, often used with εἰμί
c7 τοῖς παροῦσι: pple. πάρ-ειμι
d1 γένοιτ᾽ ἂν ἡμῖν: *we might have;* "there might be for us," potential opt., dat poss.
d2 χρῆναι ἕκαστον ἡμῶν: *each of us ought...;* inf. χρή, partitive gen.
d3 ἐπὶ δεξιὰ: *(from left) to right*
ὡς ἂν δύνηται κάλλιστον: *as beautiful as he is able;* or "as it is possible"

Φαῖδρον πρῶτον, ἐπειδὴ καὶ πρῶτος κατάκειται καὶ ἔστιν
5 ἅμα πατὴρ τοῦ λόγου.

Οὐδείς σοι, ὦ Ἐρυξίμαχε, φάναι τὸν Σωκράτη, ἐναντία
ψηφιεῖται. οὔτε γὰρ ἄν που ἐγὼ ἀποφήσαιμι, ὃς οὐδέν
φημι ἄλλο ἐπίστασθαι ἢ τὰ ἐρωτικά, οὔτε που Ἀγάθων καὶ
e Παυσανίας, οὐδὲ μὴν Ἀριστοφάνης, ᾧ περὶ Διόνυσον καὶ
Ἀφροδίτην πᾶσα ἡ διατριβή, οὐδὲ ἄλλος οὐδεὶς τουτωνὶ ὧν
ἐγὼ ὁρῶ. καίτοι οὐκ ἐξ ἴσου γίγνεται ἡμῖν τοῖς ὑστάτοις
κατακειμένοις· ἀλλ' ἐὰν οἱ πρόσθεν ἱκανῶς καὶ καλῶς
5 εἴπωσιν, ἐξαρκέσει ἡμῖν. ἀλλὰ τύχῃ ἀγαθῇ καταρχέτω
Φαῖδρος καὶ ἐγκωμιαζέτω τὸν ἔρωτα.

Ταῦτα δὴ καὶ οἱ ἄλλοι πάντες ἄρα συνέφασάν τε καὶ
178 ἐκέλευον ἅπερ ὁ Σωκράτης. πάντων μὲν οὖν ἃ ἕκαστος
εἶπεν, οὔτε πάνυ ὁ Ἀριστόδημος ἐμέμνητο οὔτ' αὖ ἐγὼ
ἃ ἐκεῖνος ἔλεγε πάντα· ἃ δὲ μάλιστα καὶ ὧν ἔδοξέ
μοι ἀξιομνημόνευτον, τούτων ὑμῖν ἐρῶ ἑκάστου τὸν
5 λόγον.

Πρῶτον μὲν γάρ, ὥσπερ λέγω, ἔφη Φαῖδρον ἀρξάμενον
ἐνθένδε ποθὲν λέγειν, ὅτι μέγας θεὸς εἴη ὁ Ἔρως καὶ
θαυμαστὸς ἐν ἀνθρώποις τε καὶ θεοῖς, πολλαχῇ μὲν καὶ ἄλλῃ,
οὐχ ἥκιστα δὲ κατὰ τὴν γένεσιν. τὸ γὰρ ἐν τοῖς πρεσβύ-
b τατον εἶναι τὸν θεὸν τίμιον, ἦ δ' ὅς, τεκμήριον δὲ τούτου·
γονῆς γὰρ Ἔρωτος οὔτ' εἰσὶν οὔτε λέγονται ὑπ' οὐδενὸς οὔτε
ἰδιώτου οὔτε ποιητοῦ, ἀλλ' Ἡσίοδος πρῶτον μὲν Χάος φησὶ
γενέσθαι—

5 αὐτὰρ ἔπειτα

Γαῖ' εὐρύστερνος, πάντων ἕδος ἀσφαλὲς αἰεί,
ἠδ' Ἔρος . . .

ἄλλη: in another place; in another way*
ἀξιο-μνημόνευτος, -ον: worth mentioning
ἀπό-φημι: to speak out; refuse, reject, deny
ἀ-σφαλής, -ές: safe, secure, not liable to fall
αὐτάρ: but, yet
γονεύς, -έως, ὁ: a begetter, parent*
δια-τριβή, ἡ: pastime; pursuit
ἕδος, -εος, τό: a seat, chair; dwelling-place
ἐνθένδε: from here, from this place
ἐξ-αρκέω: to be enough, suffice, be sufficient*
ἐπί-σταμαι: to know, know how, understand*
εὐρύ-στερνος, -ον: broad-breasted, -chested
ἠ-δέ: and
ἥκιστος, -η, -ον: least; not at all*
Ἡσίοδος, ὁ: Hesiod*

ἰδιώτης, -ου, ὁ: a private citizen, lay person
καίτοι: and yet, and indeed, and further
κατ-άρχω: to begin, commence
μιμνήσκω: to recall, remember*
ποθεν: from somewhere, from some place
πολλα-χῇ: many times, in many ways
που: anywhere, somewhere; I suppose
πρόσθεν: before*
σύμ-φημι: to assent, approve*
τεκμήριον, τό: sign, indication, proof*
τίμιος, -α, -ον: honored, valued, worthy*
τύχη, ἡ: chance, luck, fortune, success*
ὕστατος, -η, -ον: latter, last
Χάος, τό: Chaos
ψηφίζομαι: to vote

177d4 πρῶτος: *in the first position*; Phaedrus
is first in order on the dining couches
d7 ψηφιεῖται: ψηφιεεται, fut., stems ending
in -ιζ lose the ζ and add an ε in the future
που: *I suppose*; note the lack of accent
ἂν ἀποφήσαιμι: *would*; potential aor. opt.
d8 τὰ ἐρωτικά: *matters of desire*
e1 ᾧ: *who (has)*; dat. poss., add ἐστίν
περὶ Διόνυσον καὶ Ἀφροδίτην:
regarding Dionysus and Aphrodite
e2 τουτωνί: *of these here*; deictic iota
e3 ἐξ ἴσου: *on equal terms, fair*
e3 ἐάν...εἴπωσιν: aor. subj.
e4 οἱ πρόσθεν: *those (coming) before*
e5 ἐξαρκέσει: *it will suffice*; fut.
τύχῃ ἀγαθῇ: *with good luck*
καταρχέτω...ἐγκωμιαζέτω: *let...and
let...*; 3rd sg. imperatives
178a1 ἅπερ: *the very things which...*; supply
κελεύει from the main clause
πάντων: obj. ἐμέμνητο
a2 ἐμέμνητο: *(had) recalled*; plpf. μιμνήσκω
with simple past sense; object is gen.

ἐγώ: supply μιμνήσκω; the object
πάντα, has been attracted from the gen.
into the acc. by the preceding pronoun ἅ
a3 ἅ...ἀξιομνημόνευτον: *what in particular
and whom it seemed to me worth
mentioning...*
a7 ἐνθένδε ποθέν: *(from) here more or
less*; "from here (from) somewhere"
εἴη: opt. ind. discourse, secondary seq.
a9 πολλαχῇ...ἄλλη: *in many different
ways*; "in many another way"
ἥκιστα: *the least*; adverbial accusative
κατὰ: *in, in respect to*
τὸ...εἶναι: articular inf.; supply ἐστίν
as a main verb, τίμιον is a pred. adj.
ἐν τοῖς πρεσβύτατον: *among the
oldest*; (cf. 178c1-2)
b1 τεκμήριον δὲ τούτου: *and (the following
is) proof of this*; "and the proof of this:"
b2 γονῆς: *parents*; γονεῖς, nom. pl.
εἰσὶν: *are*; 3rd pl. εἰμί
Χάος: neuter acc. subject of γενέσθαι

	Present Tense of the α-contract verb ἐράω: to love, desire (+ gen.)		
1st	ἐρῶ	ἐρῶμεν	act. pple
2nd	ἐρᾷς	ἐρᾶτε	ἐρῶν (-ῶντος), -ῶσα, -ῶν: *loving, desiring*
3rd	ἐρᾷ	ἐρῶσι(ν)	ὁ ἐρῶν: *the lover*
		mid. pple	
Inf.	ἐρᾶν		ἐρώμενος, -η, -ον: *being loved, being desired*
			ὁ ἐρώμενος: *the beloved, the one loved*

Ἡσιόδῳ δὲ καὶ Ἀκουσίλεως σύμφησιν μετὰ τὸ Χάος δύο
τούτω γενέσθαι, Γῆν τε καὶ ἔρωτα. Παρμενίδης δὲ τὴν
10 γένεσιν λέγει—

πρώτιστον μὲν ἔρωτα θεῶν μητίσατο πάντων.

c οὕτω πολλαχόθεν ὁμολογεῖται ὁ Ἔρως ἐν τοῖς πρεσβύτατος εἶναι. πρεσβύτατος δὲ ὢν μεγίστων ἀγαθῶν ἡμῖν
αἴτιός ἐστιν. οὐ γὰρ ἔγωγ' ἔχω εἰπεῖν ὅτι μεῖζόν ἐστιν
ἀγαθὸν εὐθὺς νέῳ ὄντι ἢ ἐραστὴς χρηστὸς καὶ ἐραστῇ
5 παιδικά. ὃ γὰρ χρὴ ἀνθρώποις ἡγεῖσθαι παντὸς τοῦ βίου
τοῖς μέλλουσι καλῶς βιώσεσθαι, τοῦτο οὔτε συγγένεια οἵα
τε ἐμποιεῖν οὕτω καλῶς οὔτε τιμαὶ οὔτε πλοῦτος οὔτ' ἄλλο
d οὐδὲν ὡς ἔρως. λέγω δὲ δὴ τί τοῦτο; τὴν ἐπὶ μὲν τοῖς
αἰσχροῖς αἰσχύνην, ἐπὶ δὲ τοῖς καλοῖς φιλοτιμίαν· οὐ γὰρ
ἔστιν ἄνευ τούτων οὔτε πόλιν οὔτε ἰδιώτην μεγάλα καὶ
καλὰ ἔργα ἐξεργάζεσθαι. φημὶ τοίνυν ἐγὼ ἄνδρα ὅστις
5 ἐρᾷ, εἴ τι αἰσχρὸν ποιῶν κατάδηλος γίγνοιτο ἢ πάσχων
ὑπό του δι' ἀνανδρίαν μὴ ἀμυνόμενος, οὔτ' ἂν ὑπὸ πατρὸς
ὀφθέντα οὕτως ἀλγῆσαι οὔτε ὑπὸ ἑταίρων οὔτε ὑπ' ἄλλου
e οὐδενὸς ὡς ὑπὸ παιδικῶν. ταὐτὸν δὲ τοῦτο καὶ τὸν ἐρώμενον ὁρῶμεν, ὅτι διαφερόντως τοὺς ἐραστὰς αἰσχύνεται,
ὅταν ὀφθῇ ἐν αἰσχρῷ τινι ὤν. εἰ οὖν μηχανή τις γένοιτο
ὥστε πόλιν γενέσθαι ἢ στρατόπεδον ἐραστῶν τε καὶ παι-
5 δικῶν, οὐκ ἔστιν ὅπως ἂν ἄμεινον οἰκήσειαν τὴν ἑαυτῶν ἢ
ἀπεχόμενοι πάντων τῶν αἰσχρῶν καὶ φιλοτιμούμενοι πρὸς
179 ἀλλήλους, καὶ μαχόμενοί γ' ἂν μετ' ἀλλήλων οἱ τοιοῦτοι
νικῷεν ἂν ὀλίγοι ὄντες ὡς ἔπος εἰπεῖν πάντας ἀνθρώπους.
ἐρῶν γὰρ ἀνὴρ ὑπὸ παιδικῶν ὀφθῆναι ἢ λιπὼν τάξιν ἢ
ὅπλα ἀποβαλὼν ἧττον ἂν δήπου δέξαιτο ἢ ὑπὸ πάντων τῶν

αἰσχύνη, ἡ: shame, disgrace, dishonor*
Ἀκουσίλεως, ὁ: Akousileos
ἀλγέω: to feel pain, suffer
ἀμύνω: to keep off, ward off, defend*
ἀν-ανδρία, ἡ: unmanliness, cowardice
ἀπ-έχω: to be distant, keep away from*
ἀπο-βάλλω: to throw away, reject; lose
Γῆ, ἡ: Earth*
δέχομαι: to receive, accept, take*
δια-φερόντως: differently from; especially*
ἐξ-εργάζομαι: to work out, produce, perform
ἔπος, -εος, τό: a word*
εὐθύς: right away, straight, directly, at once*
Ἡσίοδος, ὁ: Hesiod
ἰδιώτης, -ου, ὁ: a private citizen, lay person
κατά-δηλος, -η, -ον: quite clear, visible*
μάχομαι: to fight, contend, quarrel, dispute*
μείζων, μείζον: larger, greater*

μητίομαι: to devise, contrive, plan
μηχανή, ἡ: means, device, contrivance*
νικάω: to conquer, defeat, win*
οἰκέω: to inhabit, dwell, live; manage, direct*
ὅπλον, τό: a tool, implement; arms*
Παρμενίδης, ὁ: Parmenides (a famous poet)
πλοῦτος, ὁ: wealth, riches*
πολλα-χόθεν: from many places
πρώτιστος, -η, -ον: the very first
στρατόπεδον, τό: camp, encampment; army*
συγ-γένεια, ἡ: kinship, relationship; family
connection
σύμ-φημι: to assent, approve, agree*
τάξις, -εως, ἡ: post, position, rank, array*
φιλο-τιμέομαι: to love honor, to be ambitious
φιλο-τιμία, ἡ: love of honor, ambition
Χάος, τό: Chaos
χρηστός, -ή, -όν: good, worthy*

178b8 δύο τούτω: *these two*; dual acc.

b9 τὴν γένεσιν λέγει: *says with respect to the birth*; acc. respect

b11 μητίσατο: *she devised*; (ἐ)μητίσατο, 3rd sg. aor.; the subject is unclear

c1 πολλα-χόθεν: *from many sources*
ἐν τοῖς πρεσβύτατος: *oldest among these*; superlative, pred. of εἶναι

c3 ἔχω εἰπεῖν: *I am able...*; ἔχω + inf.
ὅτι...ἀγαθόν: *what good...*; ὅ τι is a neuter adjective modifying ἀγαθόν

c4 εὐθὺς νέῳ ὄντι: *right from youth*; "right away for one being young," pple. εἰμί

c5 ὅ...τοῦτο: *this...which it is necessary*; τοῦτο is the antecedent of the pronoun ὅ, and ὅ is the acc. subject of ἡγεῖσθαι
ἡγεῖσθαι: *guide* (dat.) *through* (gen.)

c6 μέλλουσι: *for those intending*; dat. pl.
οἷα τε: *is able*; οἷα τε (ἐστίν), the verb agrees with the fem. subject συγ-γένεια but applies to all subjects in the series

c7 οὕτω...ὡς ἔρως: *so...as love*

d1 λέγω: *am I to tell (you)*; deliberative pres. subjunctive
τί τοῦτο: indirect question, add ἐστίν
ἐπὶ τοῖς αἰσχροῖς...ἐπὶ τοῖς καλοῖς: *in the case of shameful things...in the case of noble things*; substantive adjs.

d2 οὐ...ἔστιν: *it is not possible*

d4 ἄνδρα: acc. subj. of aor. inf. ἀλγῆσαι

d5 εἰ...γίγνοιτο...ἄν...ἀλγῆσαι: *if should be...would feel pain*; future less vivid in indirect discourse, secondary sequence an aor. inf. replaces an aor. optative

d6 ὑπό του: *by someone, because of someone*; ὑπό τινός

d7 ὀφθέντα: *being seen*; acc. aor. pass. pple. ὁράω (ὀπ-) modifying ἄνδρα
οὕτως...ὡς: *so...as*

e1 ταὐτόν...τοῦτο: *in this same way*; adverbial acc., crasis τὸ αὐτόν
ὀφθῇ: *he is seen*; 3rd sg aor. pass. ὁράω

e4 ὥστε...γενέσθαι: *so that...come to be*; result clause

e5 οὐκ ἔστιν ὅπως: *it is not possible that*; "there is no way how"
ἄμεινον...ἤ: *better than*; adverbial acc.
οἰκήσειαν: *they could manage*; aor. opt., potential optative

179a2 ἂν νικῷεν: *would defeat*; νικαοιεν, 3rd pl. pres. opt., potential opt.
ὡς ἔπος εἰπεῖν: *so to speak, as it were*

a3 ὀφθῆναι: *to be seen*; aor. pass. inf. ὁράω
λιπών: nom. sg. aor. pple. λείπω
ἤ...ἤ: *either...or*;

a4 ἂν δέξαιτο: *would accept*; opt. δέχομαι
ἧττον...ἤ: *less..than*; comparative adv.

5   ἄλλων, καὶ πρὸ τούτου τεθνάναι ἂν πολλάκις ἕλοιτο. καὶ
μὴν ἐγκαταλιπεῖν γε τὰ παιδικὰ ἢ μὴ βοηθῆσαι κινδυνεύοντι—
οὐδεὶς οὕτω κακὸς ὅντινα οὐκ ἂν αὐτὸς ὁ Ἔρως ἔνθεον
ποιήσειε πρὸς ἀρετήν, ὥστε ὅμοιον εἶναι τῷ ἀρίστῳ φύσει·
b   καὶ ἀτεχνῶς, ὃ ἔφη Ὅμηρος, "μένος ἐμπνεῦσαι" ἐνίοις
τῶν ἡρώων τὸν θεόν, τοῦτο ὁ Ἔρως τοῖς ἐρῶσι παρέχει
γιγνόμενον παρ' αὐτοῦ.

     Καὶ μὴν ὑπεραποθνῄσκειν γε μόνοι ἐθέλουσιν οἱ ἐρῶντες,
5   οὐ μόνον ὅτι ἄνδρες, ἀλλὰ καὶ αἱ γυναῖκες. τούτου δὲ καὶ
ἡ Πελίου θυγάτηρ Ἄλκηστις ἱκανὴν μαρτυρίαν παρέχεται
ὑπὲρ τοῦδε τοῦ λόγου εἰς τοὺς Ἕλληνας, ἐθελήσασα μόνη
ὑπὲρ τοῦ αὑτῆς ἀνδρὸς ἀποθανεῖν, ὄντων αὐτῷ πατρός τε
c   καὶ μητρός, οὓς ἐκείνη τοσοῦτον ὑπερεβάλετο τῇ φιλίᾳ διὰ
τὸν ἔρωτα, ὥστε ἀποδεῖξαι αὐτοὺς ἀλλοτρίους ὄντας τῷ υἱεῖ
καὶ ὀνόματι μόνον προσήκοντας, καὶ τοῦτ' ἐργασαμένη τὸ
ἔργον οὕτω καλὸν ἔδοξεν ἐργάσασθαι οὐ μόνον ἀνθρώποις
5   ἀλλὰ καὶ θεοῖς, ὥστε πολλῶν πολλὰ καὶ καλὰ ἐργασαμένων
εὐαριθμήτοις δή τισιν ἔδοσαν τοῦτο γέρας οἱ θεοί, ἐξ Ἅιδου
ἀνεῖναι πάλιν τὴν ψυχήν, ἀλλὰ τὴν ἐκείνης ἀνεῖσαν ἀγα-
d   σθέντες τῷ ἔργῳ· οὕτω καὶ θεοὶ τὴν περὶ τὸν ἔρωτα σπουδήν
τε καὶ ἀρετὴν μάλιστα τιμῶσιν. Ὀρφέα δὲ τὸν Οἰάγρου
ἀτελῆ ἀπέπεμψαν ἐξ Ἅιδου, φάσμα δείξαντες τῆς γυναικὸς
ἐφ' ἣν ἧκεν, αὐτὴν δὲ οὐ δόντες, ὅτι μαλθακίζεσθαι ἐδό-
5   κει, ἅτε ὢν κιθαρῳδός, καὶ οὐ τολμᾶν ἕνεκα τοῦ ἔρωτος
ἀποθνῄσκειν ὥσπερ Ἄλκηστις, ἀλλὰ διαμηχανᾶσθαι ζῶν
εἰσιέναι εἰς Ἅιδου. τοιγάρτοι διὰ ταῦτα δίκην αὐτῷ ἐπέθεσαν, καὶ ἐποίησαν τὸν θάνατον αὐτοῦ ὑπὸ γυναικῶν
e   γενέσθαι, οὐχ ὥσπερ Ἀχιλλέα τὸν τῆς Θέτιδος υἱὸν ἐτίμη-

ἄγαμαι: to wonder at, marvel at, admire*
αἱρέω: to size, take; *mid.* choose*
Ἄλκηστις, ἡ: Alcestis*
ἀλλότριος, -α, -ον: of another, alien, foreign*
ἀν-ίημι: to send up, let go, give up*
ἀπο-δείκνυμι: to show, demonstrate, prove*
ἀπο-πέμπω: to send away, to dismiss*
ἀ-τελής, -ές: unaccomplished, incomplete
ἀ-τεχνῶς: simply, really, entirely*
Ἀχιλλεύς, ὁ: Achilles*
βοηθέω: to come to aid, to assist, help, aid*
γέρας, -αος, τό: a gift of honor
δείκνυμι: to point out, display, show*
δια-μηχανάομαι: to bring about, contrive
δίκη, ἡ: custom, justice; lawsuit, trial; penalty
ἐγ-καταλείπω: to leave behind, leave out
Ἕλλην, Ἕλληνος, ὁ: Greek
ἐμ-πνέω: to breathe into
ἔνιοι, -αι, -α: some*

ἔν-θεος, -ον: inspired, possessed by god
εὐ-αρίθμητος, -ον: easy to count, few
ἥρως, ὁ: hero, warrior
θάνατος, ὁ: death*
Θέτις, -ιδος, ἡ: Thetis
θυγάτηρ, ἡ: a daughter*
κιθαρῳδός, ὁ: a lyre-player, singer with a lyre
μαλθακίζομαι: to be soft; to be softened, relax
μαρτυρία, ἡ: witness, testimony, evidence*
μένος, -εος, τό: might, strength, courage*
Ὀρφεύς, -εως, ὁ: Orpheus
Οἴαγρος, ὁ: Oeagrus
Πελίης, ὁ: Pelias
προσ-ήκων, προσήκοντος: relatives, kin*
τοι-γάρ-τοι: therefore, for that very reason
υἱός, -οῦ, ὁ: a son*
ὑπερ-αποθνήσκω: to die on behalf of, die for*
ὑπερ-βάλλω: to exceed, surpass; overthrow
φάσμα, -ατος, τό: an apparition, phantom

179a5 πρὸ τούτου: *in place of of this*
   τεθνάναι: perf. inf., ἀπο-θνήσκω
   ἂν...ἕλοιτο: *would choose*; potential opt.
   aor. mid. αἱρέω
   καὶ μὴν ἐγκαταλιπεῖν...κινδυνεύοντι:
   *and indeed (as for) leaving behind his
   darling or not helping him when he is in
   danger...*; with no main verb, translate
   the infinitives as articular infinitives, acc.
   of respect
a7 οὕτω κακός ὅντινα: *is so cowardly
   that*; lit. "so cowardly whom"; supply
   ἐστίν, ὅντινα begins a result clause
a8 ἂν ποιήσειε: *could make*; aor. opt.
   πρὸς ἀρετήν: *with regard to courage*
   φύσει: *by nature*; dat. of respect
b1 ἐμπνεῦσαι: aor. inf., τὸν θεόν is the
   acc. subj. and μένος is the direct obj.
b5 οὐ μόνον ὅτι: *not only*; conflation of οὐ
   μόνον, οὐχ ὅτι, i.e. "not to mention"
b7 εἰς...Ἕλληνας: *for the Greeks*
b8 τοῦ...ἀνδρός: *her husband*; ἑαυτῆς
   ἀποθανεῖν: aor. inf. ἀποθνήσκω
   ὄντων αὐτῷ...: *although he had*; dat.
   of possession in a concessive gen. abs.
c1 τοσοῦτον...ὥστε: *so much...(so) as...*;

adverbial acc. and a result clause
   τῇ φιλίᾳ: *in devotion*; dat. of respect
c2 ἀποδεῖξαι...ὄντας: *showed (acc.)
   to be*; "showed...being," aor. inf.
c3 ὀνόματι: *in name*; dat. of respect
c4 οὕτω καλόν: *so noble a (deed)*; obj. of
   ἐργάσασθαι, supply ἔργον
c5 πολλῶν...ἐργασαμένων: gen. abs.
c6 ἔδοσαν: 3rd pl. aor. δίδωμι
   γέρας: *as a gift of honor*; τοῦτο is the
   direct obj. and does not modify γέρας
c7 ἀνεῖναι: *to release, send up*; inf. ἀνίημι,
   in apposition to τοῦτο in c6
   ἀνεῖσαν: *they released*; 3rd pl. aor. ἀνίημι
d1 τῷ ἔργῳ: *because of her deed*; dat. cause
d3 ἀτελῆ: *without completing his goal*;
   ἀτελέα, acc. sg. modifies Ὀρφέα
d4 ἐφ' ἥν: *for whom*
d5 ἅτε: *inasmuch as he is*; "...as being"
   τολμᾶν: pres. inf. α-contract verb
d6 ζῶν: *though being alive*; concessive pple
   εἰσιέναι: pres. inf. εἰσ-έρχομαι
d7 δίκην ἐπέθεσαν: *imposed a punishment*;
   3rd pl. aor. ἐπιτίθημι
d8 ὑπὸ γυναικῶν: *at the hands of women*
e1 τὸν τῆς Θέτιδος: *son of Thetis*

σαν καὶ εἰς μακάρων νήσους ἀπέπεμψαν, ὅτι πεπυσμένος
παρὰ τῆς μητρὸς ὡς ἀποθανοῖτο ἀποκτείνας Ἕκτορα, μὴ
ποιήσας δὲ τοῦτο οἴκαδε ἐλθὼν γηραιὸς τελευτήσοι,
5 ἐτόλμησεν ἑλέσθαι βοηθήσας τῷ ἐραστῇ Πατρόκλῳ καὶ
180 τιμωρήσας οὐ μόνον ὑπεραποθανεῖν ἀλλὰ καὶ ἐπαποθανεῖν
τετελευτηκότι· ὅθεν δὴ καὶ ὑπεραγασθέντες οἱ θεοὶ διαφερόντως αὐτὸν ἐτίμησαν, ὅτι τὸν ἐραστὴν οὕτω περὶ πολλοῦ
ἐποιεῖτο. Αἰσχύλος δὲ φλυαρεῖ φάσκων Ἀχιλλέα Πα-
5 τρόκλου ἐρᾶν, ὃς ἦν καλλίων οὐ μόνον Πατρόκλου ἀλλ'
ἅμα καὶ τῶν ἡρώων ἁπάντων, καὶ ἔτι ἀγένειος, ἔπειτα
νεώτερος πολύ, ὡς φησιν Ὅμηρος. ἀλλὰ γὰρ τῷ ὄντι
μάλιστα μὲν ταύτην τὴν ἀρετὴν οἱ θεοὶ τιμῶσιν τὴν περὶ
b τὸν ἔρωτα, μᾶλλον μέντοι θαυμάζουσιν καὶ ἄγανται καὶ
εὖ ποιοῦσιν ὅταν ὁ ἐρώμενος τὸν ἐραστὴν ἀγαπᾷ, ἢ ὅταν
ὁ ἐραστὴς τὰ παιδικά. θειότερον γὰρ ἐραστὴς παιδικῶν·
ἔνθεος γάρ ἐστι. διὰ ταῦτα καὶ τὸν Ἀχιλλέα τῆς Ἀλκή-
5 τιδος μᾶλλον ἐτίμησαν, εἰς μακάρων νήσους ἀποπέμψαντες.

Οὕτω δὴ ἔγωγέ φημι ἔρωτα θεῶν καὶ πρεσβύτατον καὶ
τιμιώτατον καὶ κυριώτατον εἶναι εἰς ἀρετῆς καὶ εὐδαιμονίας
κτῆσιν ἀνθρώποις καὶ ζῶσι καὶ τελευτήσασιν.

c Φαῖδρον μὲν τοιοῦτόν τινα λόγον ἔφη εἰπεῖν, μετὰ δὲ
Φαῖδρον ἄλλους τινὰς εἶναι ὧν οὐ πάνυ διεμνημόνευε· οὓς
παρεὶς τὸν Παυσανίου λόγον διηγεῖτο. εἰπεῖν δ' αὐτὸν
ὅτι οὐ καλῶς μοι δοκεῖ, ὦ Φαῖδρε, προβεβλῆσθαι ἡμῖν
5 ὁ λόγος, τὸ ἁπλῶς οὕτως παρηγγέλθαι ἐγκωμιάζειν Ἔρωτα.
εἰ μὲν γὰρ εἷς ἦν ὁ Ἔρως, καλῶς ἂν εἶχε, νῦν δὲ οὐ γάρ
ἐστιν εἷς· μὴ ὄντος δὲ ἑνὸς ὀρθότερόν ἐστι πρότερον προρ-
d ρηθῆναι ὁποῖον δεῖ ἐπαινεῖν. ἐγὼ οὖν πειράσομαι τοῦτο

ἄγαμαι: to wonder at, marvel at, admire*
ἀγαπάω: to love, show affection, be fond of*
ἀ-γένειος, -ον: beardless
αἱρέω: to seize, take; mid. choose*
Αἰσχύλος, ὁ: Aeschylus
Ἄλκηστις, ἡ: Alcestis*
ἅπας, ἅπασα, ἅπαν: every, quite all*
ἁπλῶς: singly, plainly, absolutely*
ἀπο-κτείνω: to kill, slay*
ἀπο-πέμπω: to send away, to dismiss*
Ἀχιλλεύς, ὁ: Achilles*
βοηθέω: to come to aid, to assist, aid*
γηραιός, -ά, -όν: aged, in old age
δια-μνημονεύω: to recall, remember (+ gen.)
δια-φερόντως: differently from; especially*
Ἕκτωρ, ὁ: Hector
ἔν-θεος, -ον: inspired, possessed by god
ἐπ-αποθνήσκω: to die after
εὐ-δαιμονία, ἡ: happiness, good fortune*
ἥρως, ὁ: hero, warrior
κτῆσις, -εως, ἡ: possession, acquisition

κύριος, -α, -ον: authoritative, supreme*
μάκαρ, -αρος, ὁ: the blessed, happy
νεώτερος, -α, -ον: younger; rather recent*
νῆσος, -ου, ἡ: an island*
ὅ-θεν: from where, from which*
οἴκα-δε: homeward, home
ὁποῖος, -α, -ον: what sort or kind*
παρ-αγγέλλω: to tell, give orders, pass word
παρ-ίημι: to pass over, yield, allow, permit*
Πάτροκλος, ὁ: Patroclus*
προ-βάλλω: to put forward, advance
προ-ερέω: to say first, say beforehand*
πυνθάνομαι: to learn by inquiry, learn by
    hearsay; inquire, ask about*
τίμιος, -α, -ον: honored, worthy*
τιμωρέω: to avenge, exact vengeance*
ὑπερ-άγαμαι: to be exceedingly pleased
ὑπερ-αποθνήσκω: to die on behalf of, die for*
φάσκω: to say, affirm, claim*
φλυαρέω: to talk nonsense, play the fool

179e2 πεπυσμένος: *having learned*; perf. mid. pple. πυνθάνομαι with gen. of source
e3 ἀποθανοῖτο...τελευτήσοι: *would die ...would die;* both are unusual fut. opt. replacing fut. ind. in secondary sequence
ἀποκτείνας: nom. sg. aor. pple.
e5 ἑλέσθαι: *to choose*; aor. mid. inf. αἱρέω
180a2 τετελευτηκότι: *the one having died*; pf. pple, dat. obj. of ἐπ-αποθνήσκω
ὅθεν δή: *for this very reason*; "from which very thing"
ὑπεραγασθέντες: aor. dep. pple
a3 ὅτι: *because*
περὶ πολλοῦ ἐποιεῖτο: *considered of great importance*; common idiom
a5 ἐρᾶν: *was the lover of*; inf., Phaedrus is distinguishing a lover from his beloved
ἦν: 3rd sg. impf. εἰμί
καλλίων: comparative degree, καλός governing a gen. of comparison (than...)
a7 ἀλλὰ γάρ: *but in any case, but really*
τῷ ὄντι: *actually, really*; dat. respect
a8 τὴν περὶ: *(excellence) with regard to...*
b3 θειότερον: *more god-like*; neuter adj.

modifying a masc. ἐραστής, add ἐστίν
b4 τῆς Ἀλκήστιδος: *than...*; comparison
b6 πρεσβύτατον, κυριώτατον: superlatives
b7 εἰς...κτῆσιν: *for the possession of...*
b8 ζῶσι...τελευτήσασιν: dat. pl., pples.
c2 ἄλλους τινάς: *any other (words)*
διεμνημόνευε: subject is Aristodemus
οὓς παρεὶς: *passing over which*; nom. sg. aor. pple, παρ-ίημι
c3 αὐτὸν: Pausanias, subj. acc. of εἰπεῖν
c4 προβεβλῆσθαι: pf. pass. προ-βάλλω governing a dat. of agent
c5 τὸ...παρηγγέλθαι: *to have been told*; articular inf. in apposition to ὁ λόγος, pf. pass. inf. παρ-αγγέλλω
c6 εἰ...ἦν...ἂν εἶχε: *If...were...I would have*; contrary-to-fact condition
εἷς: *one*; notice the breathing accent
c7 μὴ ὄντος: *if (Eros) is not...*; gen. abs. is conditional
ὀρθότερόν ἐστι: *it is more correct...*
προρρηθῆναι: pf. inf. προ-ερέω
d1 πειράσομαι: fut. πειράζω

ἐπανορθώσασθαι, πρῶτον μὲν ἔρωτα φράσαι ὃν δεῖ ἐπαινεῖν, ἔπειτα ἐπαινέσαι ἀξίως τοῦ θεοῦ. πάντες γὰρ ἴσμεν
ὅτι οὐκ ἔστιν ἄνευ Ἔρωτος Ἀφροδίτη. μιᾶς μὲν οὖν
5 οὔσης εἷς ἂν ἦν Ἔρως· ἐπεὶ δὲ δὴ δύο ἐστόν, δύο ἀνάγκη
καὶ Ἔρωτε εἶναι. πῶς δ' οὐ δύο τὼ θεά; ἡ μέν γέ που
πρεσβυτέρα καὶ ἀμήτωρ Οὐρανοῦ θυγάτηρ, ἣν δὴ καὶ
Οὐρανίαν ἐπονομάζομεν· ἡ δὲ νεωτέρα Διὸς καὶ Διώνης,
e ἣν δὴ Πάνδημον καλοῦμεν. ἀναγκαῖον δὴ καὶ ἔρωτα τὸν
μὲν τῇ ἑτέρᾳ συνεργὸν Πάνδημον ὀρθῶς καλεῖσθαι, τὸν δὲ
Οὐράνιον. ἐπαινεῖν μὲν οὖν δεῖ πάντας θεούς, ἃ δ' οὖν
ἑκάτερος εἴληχε πειρατέον εἰπεῖν. πᾶσα γὰρ πρᾶξις ὧδ'
5 ἔχει· αὐτὴ ἐφ' ἑαυτῆς πραττομένη οὔτε καλὴ οὔτε αἰσχρά.
181 οἷον ὃ νῦν ἡμεῖς ποιοῦμεν, ἢ πίνειν ἢ ᾄδειν ἢ διαλέγεσθαι,
οὐκ ἔστι τούτων αὐτὸ καλὸν οὐδέν, ἀλλ' ἐν τῇ πράξει, ὡς
ἂν πραχθῇ, τοιοῦτον ἀπέβη· καλῶς μὲν γὰρ πραττόμενον
καὶ ὀρθῶς καλὸν γίγνεται, μὴ ὀρθῶς δὲ αἰσχρόν. οὕτω δὴ
5 καὶ τὸ ἐρᾶν καὶ ὁ Ἔρως οὐ πᾶς ἐστι καλὸς οὐδὲ ἄξιος
ἐγκωμιάζεσθαι, ἀλλὰ ὁ καλῶς προτρέπων ἐρᾶν.

  Ὁ μὲν οὖν τῆς Πανδήμου Ἀφροδίτης ὡς ἀληθῶς πάν-
b δημός ἐστι καὶ ἐξεργάζεται ὅτι ἂν τύχῃ· καὶ οὗτός ἐστιν
ὃν οἱ φαῦλοι τῶν ἀνθρώπων ἐρῶσιν. ἐρῶσι δὲ οἱ τοιοῦτοι
πρῶτον μὲν οὐχ ἧττον γυναικῶν ἢ παίδων, ἔπειτα ὧν καὶ
ἐρῶσι τῶν σωμάτων μᾶλλον ἢ τῶν ψυχῶν, ἔπειτα ὡς ἂν
5 δύνωνται ἀνοητοτάτων, πρὸς τὸ διαπράξασθαι μόνον βλέ-
ποντες, ἀμελοῦντες δὲ τοῦ καλῶς ἢ μή· ὅθεν δὴ συμβαίνει
αὐτοῖς ὅτι ἂν τύχωσι τοῦτο πράττειν, ὁμοίως μὲν ἀγαθόν,
ὁμοίως δὲ τοὐναντίον. ἔστι γὰρ καὶ ἀπὸ τῆς θεοῦ νεωτέρας
c τε οὔσης πολὺ ἢ τῆς ἑτέρας, καὶ μετεχούσης ἐν τῇ γενέσει

ᾄδω: to sing*
ἀμελέω: to have no care for, neglect (+ gen.)*
ἀ-μήτωρ, -ορος, ἡ, ὁ: motherless
ἀ-νόητος, -ον: foolish, unintelligent*
ἀπο-βαίνω: to turn out, result; disembark*
δια-πράττω: to accomplish, achieve*
Διώνη, ἡ: Dione
ἑκάτερος, -α, -ον: each of two, either*
ἐξ-εργάζομαι: to accomplish, perform
ἐπαν-ορθόω: to set upright, restore, correct
ἐπ-ονομάζω: to give a surname, an epithet
θυγάτηρ, ἡ: a daughter*
λαγχάνω: to obtain by lot*

νεώτερος, -α, -ον: younger; rather recent*
ὅ-θεν: from where, from which*
Οὐρανία, ἡ: Urania, the heavenly one*
Οὐρανός, ὁ: heaven
πρᾶξις, -εως, ἡ: action, deed, activity,
  business*
προ-τρέπω: to turn forward, urge on, impel
που: anywhere, somewhere; I suppose
συμ-βαίνω: to happen, occur*
συν-εργός, -όν: fellow-worker, accomplice
φράζω: to point out, tell, indicate*
ὧδε: in this way, so, thus*

180d2 ἐπανορθώσασθαι: *to correct*; aor. mid.
  Ἔρωτα...ὅν: *which Eros*; "the Eros
  whom..."
  φράσαι: *first...to say*; in apposition to
  ἐπανοθρώσασθαι, aor. inf. φράζω
d3 ἴσμεν: 1st pl. οἶδα
d4 μιᾶς...οὔσης: *if she were one*; gen.
  abs. is conditional, contrary-to-fact
d5 ἂν ἦν: *would be*; ἄν + impf. of εἰμί in a
  contrary-to-fact condition
  ἐστόν..Ἔρωτε...τὼ θεά: *are...
  Eroses...the two goddesses*; dual forms
d6 ἡ μὲν..ἡ δὲ: *one (goddess) is...the
  other is*; add ἐστίν to each subject
d8 Διὸς καὶ Διώνης: *daughter of Zeus
  and Dione*; supply θυγάτηρ
e1 ἀναγκαῖον: *it is necessary*; add ἐστίν
  τὸν μὲν...τὸν δὲ: *the one (Eros)...the
  other (Eros)*
e4 εἴληχε: *presides over*; "has obtained as
  his portion", 3rd sg. pf. λαγχάνω
  πειρατέον: *I must try*; "it is to be tried
  (by me)," verbal adjective, supply ἐστίν
e5 αὐτὴ ἐφ' ἑαυτῆς πραττομένη: *(every
  action) itself in itself being carried out*;
  supply ἐστίν as the main verb
181a1 οἷον: *for example*
a2 οὐκ...τούτων...οὐδὲν: *not any of these
  things...*; double negative
  ὡς ἂν πραχθῇ: *however it was done*;
  ἄν + aor. pass. subj., πράττω (πρακ-)
a3 ἀπέβη: *turns out*; gnomic aor. of
  ἀποβαίνω to express general truth

a5 τὸ ἐρᾶν: *to desire, desiring*; art. inf.
a6 ὁ...προτρέπων: *the one urging...*;
  καλῶς modifies ἐρᾶν, supply ἐστι
  καλὸς from the previous line
a7 ὁ μὲν τῆς Πανδήμου Ἀφροδίτης: *the
  Eros of Pandemus Aphrodite*; answered
  by ὁ δὲ in 181c2
  ὡς ἀληθῶς: *truly*
b1 ὅτι ἂν τύχῃ: *whatever he happens (to
  do)*; ὅτι is ὅ τι, aor. subj. τυγχάνω
b2 ὅν: *which (love)*; inner accusative
b3 ἧττον: *less than*; adv. from ἥττων, -ον
  ὧν καὶ ἐρῶσι: *and (among those) whom
  they in fact love (they love)...*; add ἐρῶσι
b4 ὡς ἂν δύνωνται ἀνοητοτάτων: *they
  love the most foolish as they are able*;
  supply ἐρῶσι (cf. 177d3)
b5 πρὸς τὸ διαπράξασθαι: *with regard
  to accomplishing (their goal)*; art. inf.
b6 τοῦ καλῶς: *for accomplishing it well*;
  supply διαπράξασθαι for this art. inf.
  ὅθεν δὴ: *for this very reason*; "from
  which very thing"
b7 ὅτι ἂν τύχωσι: *whatever they happen to
  do*; see b1 above, antecedent is τοῦτο
b8 τοὐναντίον: *the opposite*; τὸ ἐναντίον
  ἐστι: *this Eros is*; add οὗτος ὁ Ἔρως
  νεωτέρας...ἤ: *younger than*; gen. sg.
  pred. of οὔσης
c1 τῆς ἑτέρας: *the other (goddess)*; objects
  of comparison in same case as subj. θεοῦ

καὶ θήλεος καὶ ἄρρενος. ὁ δὲ τῆς Οὐρανίας πρῶτον μὲν οὐ
μετεχούσης θήλεος ἀλλ᾽ ἄρρενος μόνον—καὶ ἔστιν οὗτος ὁ
τῶν παίδων ἔρως—ἔπειτα πρεσβυτέρας, ὕβρεως ἀμοίρου· ὅθεν
5 δὴ ἐπὶ τὸ ἄρρεν τρέπονται οἱ ἐκ τούτου τοῦ ἔρωτος ἔπιπνοι,
τὸ φύσει ἐρρωμενέστερον καὶ νοῦν μᾶλλον ἔχον ἀγαπῶντες.
καί τις ἂν γνοίη καὶ ἐν αὐτῇ τῇ παιδεραστίᾳ τοὺς εἰλικρινῶς
d ὑπὸ τούτου τοῦ ἔρωτος ὡρμημένους· οὐ γὰρ ἐρῶσι παίδων,
ἀλλ᾽ ἐπειδὰν ἤδη ἄρχωνται νοῦν ἴσχειν, τοῦτο δὲ πλησιάζει
τῷ γενειάσκειν. παρεσκευασμένοι γὰρ οἶμαί εἰσιν οἱ ἐντεῦθεν ἀρχόμενοι ἐρᾶν ὡς τὸν βίον ἅπαντα συνεσόμενοι
5 καὶ κοινῇ συμβιωσόμενοι, ἀλλ᾽ οὐκ ἐξαπατήσαντες, ἐν
ἀφροσύνῃ λαβόντες ὡς νέον, καταγελάσαντες οἰχήσεσθαι
ἐπ᾽ ἄλλον ἀποτρέχοντες. χρῆν δὲ καὶ νόμον εἶναι μὴ ἐρᾶν
e παίδων, ἵνα μὴ εἰς ἄδηλον πολλὴ σπουδὴ ἀνηλίσκετο· τὸ
γὰρ τῶν παίδων τέλος ἄδηλον οἷ τελευτᾷ κακίας καὶ ἀρετῆς
ψυχῆς τε πέρι καὶ σώματος. οἱ μὲν οὖν ἀγαθοὶ τὸν νόμον
τοῦτον αὐτοὶ αὑτοῖς ἑκόντες τίθενται, χρῆν δὲ καὶ τούτους
5 τοὺς πανδήμους ἐραστὰς προσαναγκάζειν τὸ τοιοῦτον, ὥσπερ
καὶ τῶν ἐλευθέρων γυναικῶν προσαναγκάζομεν αὐτοὺς καθ᾽
182 ὅσον δυνάμεθα μὴ ἐρᾶν. οὗτοι γάρ εἰσιν οἱ καὶ τὸ ὄνειδος
πεποιηκότες, ὥστε τινὰς τολμᾶν λέγειν ὡς αἰσχρὸν χαρίζεσθαι ἐρασταῖς· λέγουσι δὲ εἰς τούτους ἀποβλέποντες,
ὁρῶντες αὐτῶν τὴν ἀκαιρίαν καὶ ἀδικίαν, ἐπεὶ οὐ δήπου
5 κοσμίως γε καὶ νομίμως ὁτιοῦν <πρᾶγμα> πραττόμενον ψόγον
ἂν δικαίως φέροι.

Καὶ δὴ καὶ ὁ περὶ τὸν ἔρωτα νόμος ἐν μὲν ταῖς ἄλλαις
πόλεσι νοῆσαι ῥᾴδιος, ἁπλῶς γὰρ ὥρισται· ὁ δ᾽ ἐνθάδε
b καὶ ἐν Λακεδαίμονι ποικίλος. ἐν Ἤλιδι μὲν γὰρ καὶ ἐν
Βοιωτοῖς, καὶ οὗ μὴ σοφοὶ λέγειν, ἁπλῶς νενομοθέτηται

ἀγαπάω: to love, show affection, be fond of*
ἄ-δηλος, -ον: unclear, unknown, obscure
ἀ-δικία, ἡ: wrong-doing, injustice*
ἀ-καιρία, ἡ: ill-timedness, unseasonableness
ἄ-μοιρος: without a share in (+ gen.)*
ἀν-αλίσκω: to use up, to spend, squander
ἅπας, ἅπασα, ἅπαν: every, quite all*
ἁπλῶς: simply, plainly, singly, absolutely*
ἀπο-βλέπω: to look off to, look at, gaze*
ἀπο-τρέχω: to run off or away
ἀ-φροσύνη, ἡ: folly, thoughtlessness
Βοιωτός, ὁ: Boeotian
γενειάσκω: to grow a beard
εἰλικρινῶς: purely, simply, absolutely
ἐλεύθερος, -α, -ον: free*
ἐντεῦθεν: from here, from there*
ἐπί-πνοος, -ον: inspired, breathed on
ἐρρωμένος, -η, -ον: stout, vigorous, strong
Ἦλις, ὁ: Elis
θῆλυς, -εια, -υ: female, feminine*
ἴσχω: to have; hold back, check, restrain*

κακία, ἡ: wickedness, vice, cowardice*
κατα-γελάω: to laugh at, mock*
κοινῇ: in common, together, in concert*
Λακεδαίμων, -ονος, ἡ: Lacedaemon, Sparta*
νοέω: to think, mean, indicate, suppose
νόμιμος, -η, -ον: customary, lawful, rightful
νομο-θετέω: to make laws, to ordain by law
ὅ-θεν: from where, from which*
οἷ: to where, to which
ὄνειδος, τό: reproach, censure, rebuke*
ὁρίζω: to define, mark out, limit*
ὁρμάω: to set in motion; set out, begin*
παιδεραστία, ἡ: love of boys, pederasty
παρα-σκευάζω: to prepare, get ready*
πλησιάζω: to approach; associate with (+dat.)
ποικίλος, -η, -ον: various, diverse, complex*
προσ-αναγκάζω: to press, compel, force*
συμ-βιόω: to live with, live together
τέλος, -εος, τό: end, goal, result; sacred rites*
ὕβρις, -εως, ἡ: outrage, assault, violence*
ψόγος, ὁ: blame, censure

181c2 θήλεος...ἄρρενος: gen. obj. of μετέχω
c2 ὁ δὲ τῆς Οὐρανίας: the Eros of Heavenly (Aphrodite); cf. 181a7 above
c4 ὕβρεως ἀμοίρου: having no share of outrage; modifies τῆς Οὐρανίας
  ὅθεν δή: for this very reason
c6 τὸ φύσει ἐρρωμενέστερον...ἔχον: (what is) stronger by nature and having more sense; dat. of respect
c7 τις ἄν γνοίη: one might recognize; aor. potential opt., γιγνώσκω
d1 ὡρμημένους pf. pass. pple. ὁρμάω
d2 τοῦτο...πλησιάζει: and this (i.e. having sense) is associated with
d3 τῷ γενειάσκειν: articular inf.
  παρεσκευασμένοι... εἰσιν: are prepared; "have been prepared" pf. pass. pple + εἰμί is pf. pass. periphrastic; ἐρᾶν is a complementary inf.
d4 ὡς: so that...; ὡς + fut. pple expresses purpose or alleged cause
  συνεσόμενοι: be together; fut. συν-ειμί
d5 ἐν ἀφροσύνῃ...νέον: catching him in his folly, since (he is) young; ὡς + pple is causal, assume the pple ὄντα
d6 οἰχήσεσθαι: (they are prepared) to go

d7 χρῆν: there ought...; inf. χρή, usually χρῆναι but here identical to impf.
e1 ἵνα μὴ... ἀνηλίσκετο: so that...not be spent...; μὴ +impf. as unfulfilled purpose
  εἰς ἄδηλον: for an unclear (purpose)
e2 τό...τέλος: subject of 3rd sg. τελευτᾷ
  ἄδηλον: it is unclear; supply ἐστίν
  οἷ...κακίας καὶ ἀρετῆς: to what point of badness or goodness; partitive gen.
e4 αὐτοῖς: for themselves; ἑαυτοῖς
  τίθενται: set down, made; pres. mid.
  χρῆν..προσαναγκάζειν τὸ τοιοῦτον: they ought to force this sort (of law) on
e6 καθ᾽ ὅσον: insofar as
182a1 εἰσιν: are; 3rd pl. pres. εἰμί
  οἱ πεποιηκότες: those having caused; pf.
a2 ὡς αἰσχρὸν: that (it is) shameful...
a5 ὁτιοῦν: whatever (deed); nom. subj.
a6 ἄν...φέροι: would...; potential opt.
a8 νοῆσαι: to perceive; explanatory inf.
  ὥρισται: has been defined; pf. ὁρίζω
b2 οὗ: where; relative adv.
  σοφοὶ λέγειν: clever at speaking
  νενομοθέτηται: it has been established; pf. pass.

καλὸν τὸ χαρίζεσθαι ἐρασταῖς, καὶ οὐκ ἄν τις εἴποι οὔτε
νέος οὔτε παλαιὸς ὡς αἰσχρόν, ἵνα οἶμαι μὴ πράγματ᾽
5 ἔχωσιν λόγῳ πειρώμενοι πείθειν τοὺς νέους, ἅτε ἀδύνατοι λέγειν· τῆς δὲ Ἰωνίας καὶ ἄλλοθι πολλαχοῦ αἰσχρὸν
νενόμισται, ὅσοι ὑπὸ βαρβάροις οἰκοῦσιν. τοῖς γὰρ βαρβάροις διὰ τὰς τυραννίδας αἰσχρὸν τοῦτό γε καὶ ἥ γε
c φιλοσοφία καὶ ἡ φιλογυμναστία· οὐ γὰρ οἶμαι συμφέρει
τοῖς ἄρχουσι φρονήματα μεγάλα ἐγγίγνεσθαι τῶν ἀρχομένων, οὐδὲ φιλίας ἰσχυρὰς καὶ κοινωνίας, ὃ δὴ μάλιστα
φιλεῖ τά τε ἄλλα πάντα καὶ ὁ ἔρως ἐμποιεῖν. ἔργῳ δὲ
5 τοῦτο ἔμαθον καὶ οἱ ἐνθάδε τύραννοι· ὁ γὰρ Ἀριστογεί-
τονος ἔρως καὶ ἡ Ἁρμοδίου φιλία βέβαιος γενομένη κατ-
έλυσεν αὐτῶν τὴν ἀρχήν. οὕτως οὗ μὲν αἰσχρὸν ἐτέθη
d χαρίζεσθαι ἐρασταῖς, κακίᾳ τῶν θεμένων κεῖται, τῶν μὲν
ἀρχόντων πλεονεξίᾳ, τῶν δὲ ἀρχομένων ἀνανδρίᾳ· οὗ δὲ
καλὸν ἁπλῶς ἐνομίσθη, διὰ τὴν τῶν θεμένων τῆς ψυχῆς
ἀργίαν. ἐνθάδε δὲ πολὺ τούτων κάλλιον νενομοθέτηται, καὶ
5 ὅπερ εἶπον, οὐ ῥᾴδιον κατανοῆσαι. ἐνθυμηθέντι γὰρ ὅτι
λέγεται κάλλιον τὸ φανερῶς ἐρᾶν τοῦ λάθρᾳ, καὶ μάλιστα
τῶν γενναιοτάτων καὶ ἀρίστων, κἂν αἰσχίους ἄλλων ὦσι, καὶ
ὅτι αὖ ἡ παρακέλευσις τῷ ἐρῶντι παρὰ πάντων θαυμαστή,
οὐχ ὥς τι αἰσχρὸν ποιοῦντι, καὶ ἑλόντι τε καλὸν δοκεῖ εἶναι
e καὶ μὴ ἑλόντι αἰσχρόν, καὶ πρὸς τὸ ἐπιχειρεῖν ἑλεῖν ἐξουσίαν ὁ νόμος δέδωκε τῷ ἐραστῇ θαυμαστὰ ἔργα ἐργαζομένῳ
ἐπαινεῖσθαι, ἃ εἴ τις τολμῴη ποιεῖν ἀλλ᾽ ὁτιοῦν διώκων καὶ
183 βουλόμενος διαπράξασθαι πλὴν τοῦτο, †φιλοσοφίας τὰ μέγιστα καρποῖτ᾽ ἂν ὀνείδη—εἰ γὰρ ἢ χρήματα βουλόμενος
παρά του λαβεῖν ἢ ἀρχὴν ἄρξαι ἤ τινα ἄλλην δύναμιν
ἐθέλοι ποιεῖν οἷάπερ οἱ ἐρασταὶ πρὸς τὰ παιδικά, ἱκετείας

αἱρέω: to seize, take; mid. choose*
ἄλλο-θι: in another place, elsewhere*
ἀν-ανδρία, ἡ: unmanliness, cowardice
ἁπλῶς: singly, simply, plainly, absolutely*
ἀ-ργία, ἡ: idleness, laziness; inactivity
Ἀριστογείτων, ὁ: Aristogeiton
Ἁρμόδιος, ὁ: Harmodius
βάρβαρος, ὁ: foreigner, a non-Greek*
βέβαιος, -ον: firm, steadfast, sure, certain*
γενναῖος, -α, -ον: noble, well-bred*
δια-πράττω: to accomplish, achieve, affect*
ἐγ-γίγνομαι: to come about; be possible*
ἐν-θυμέομαι: to consider, reflect, ponder*
ἐξουσία, ἡ: opportunity power, authority*
ἱκετεία, ἡ: supplication
Ἰωνία, ἡ: Ionia
κακία, ἡ: wickedness, vice, cowardice*
καρπόω: to bear fruit; mid. enjoy, profit*
κατα-λύω: to dissolve, break up, abolish*
κατα-νοέω: to observe, understand, consider

κεῖμαι: to lie down*
κοινωνία, ἡ: association, partnership*
λάθρᾳ: secretly, covertly, by stealth
μανθάνω: to learn, understand*
νομο-θετέω: to make laws, to ordain by law
οἰκέω: to inhabit, dwell, live*
ὄνειδος, τό: reproach, censure, rebuke*
οἷοσπερ, -απερ, -ονπερ: very sort who, which
παρα-κέλευσις, -εως, ἡ: encouragement
πλεον-εξία, ἡ: greediness, grasping, arrogance
πλήν: except, but (+ gen.)*
πολλα-χοῦ: in many places
συμ-φέρω: to gather; be useful, be expedient*
τυραννίς, -ίδος, ἡ: absolute power, tyranny
τύραννος, ὁ: absolute sovereign, tyrant*
φανερῶς: clearly, visibly, openly*
φιλέω: to love, befriend; strive to, tend to*
φιλο-γυμναστία, ἡ: fondness for exercise
φρόνημα, -ατος, τό: mind, thought, purpose

182b3 καλόν: *that (it is) noble*; supply εἶναι
οὐκ...τις..οὔτε...οὔτε: *not anyone either...or*; double negative
b4 ὡς αἰσχρόν: *that it is shameful*
ἵνα...μὴ πράγματ᾽ ἔχωσιν: *so that they may not make trouble*; neg. purpose
b5 ἅτε: *since (they are)*; supply ὄντες
b6 τῆς...Ἰωνίας: *within Ionia*; paritive
b7 νενόμισται: pf. pass., νομίζω
ὑπὸ βαρβάροις: *under the Barbarians*
b8 αἰσχρόν: *is shameful*; supply ἐστίν
c1 συμφέρει: *it is useful*; impersonal + dat.
c2 φρονήματα μεγάλα: *big thoughts, haughty thoughts, prideful thoughts*
c4 φιλεῖ...ἐμποιεῖν: *tends/strives to create*
ἔργῳ: *through experience*; "in deed"
c5 ἔμαθον: 3rd pl. aor. μανθάνω
οἱ ἐνθάδε τύραννοι: *the tyrants here*
c6 βέβαιος: fem. adj. following γενομένη
c7 οὗ...ἐτέθη: *where it is set forth that it is shameful...*; aor. pass. τίθημι
d1 κεῖται: *it is set forth*
κακίᾳ τῶν θεμένων: *because of the wickedness of those having proposed (it)*; dat. cause, aor. mid. pple. τίθημι
d3 ἐνομίσθη: *it was believed*; aor. pass.
d4 τούτων: *than these*; gen. of comparison

νενομοθέτηται: *it has been ordained*
d5 οὐ ῥάδιον: *it is not easy*; supply ἐστίν
κατανοῆσαι: explanatory inf., aor. inf.
ἐνθυμηθέντι: *for one considering*; dat.
aor. dep. pple in an incomplete sentence
d6 τοῦ λάθρα: *than (to love) in secret*; gen. of comparison, supply ἐρᾶν
d7 τῶν γενναιοτάτων...: obj. of ἐρᾶν
κἄν...ὦσι: *even if they are*; καὶ ἐάν; καὶ is adverbial, 3rd pl. pres. subj. εἰμί
αἰσχίους: *more ugly*; αἰσχίονες, nom. pl
d8 ἡ παρακέλευσις...παρὰ πάντων: *the encouragement for the lover from all is...*
d9 οὐχ ὡς...ποιοῦντι: *not because he is doing...*; causal, dat. sg. modifies ἐρῶντι
ἑλόντι...μὴ ἑλόντι: *for one catching a beloved...for one not catching a beloved*; aor. pple. αἱρέω
e1 πρὸς...ἑλεῖν: *in regard to...*; inf. αἱρέω
ἐξουσίαν ἐπαινεῖσθαι: *opportunity to be praised*; obj. of δέδωκε, pf. δίδωμι
τολμῷη: *should..*; τολμαοιη, pres. opt.
e3 ἀλλ᾽ ὁτιοῦν: *something other*; ἄλλο
183a1 φιλοσοφίας: the meaning is unclear
a3 παρά του: *from someone*; παρά τινός
ἀρχὴν ἄρξαι: *to hold office*; aor. inf.
δύναμιν: *position of power*; add λαβεῖν

5 τε καὶ ἀντιβολήσεις ἐν ταῖς δεήσεσιν ποιούμενοι, καὶ ὅρκους
ὀμνύντες, καὶ κοιμήσεις ἐπὶ θύραις, καὶ ἐθέλοντες δουλείας
δουλεύειν οἵας οὐδ' ἂν δοῦλος οὐδείς, ἐμποδίζοιτο ἂν μὴ
πράττειν οὕτω τὴν πρᾶξιν καὶ ὑπὸ φίλων καὶ ὑπὸ ἐχθρῶν,
b τῶν μὲν ὀνειδιζόντων κολακείας καὶ ἀνελευθερίας, τῶν δὲ
νουθετούντων καὶ αἰσχυνομένων ὑπὲρ αὐτῶν—τῷ δ' ἐρῶντι
πάντα ταῦτα ποιοῦντι χάρις ἔπεστι, καὶ δέδοται ὑπὸ τοῦ
νόμου ἄνευ ὀνείδους πράττειν, ὡς πάγκαλόν τι πρᾶγμα
5 διαπραττομένου· ὃ δὲ δεινότατον, ὥς γε λέγουσιν οἱ πολλοί, ὅτι καὶ ὀμνύντι μόνῳ συγγνώμη παρὰ θεῶν ἐκβάντι
τῶν ὅρκων—ἀφροδίσιον γὰρ ὅρκον οὔ φασιν εἶναι· οὕτω
c καὶ οἱ θεοὶ καὶ οἱ ἄνθρωποι πᾶσαν ἐξουσίαν πεποιήκασι τῷ
ἐρῶντι, ὡς ὁ νόμος φησὶν ὁ ἐνθάδε—ταύτῃ μὲν οὖν οἰηθείη
ἄν τις πάγκαλον νομίζεσθαι ἐν τῇδε τῇ πόλει καὶ τὸ ἐρᾶν καὶ
τὸ φίλους γίγνεσθαι τοῖς ἐρασταῖς. ἐπειδὰν δὲ παι-
5 δαγωγοὺς ἐπιστήσαντες οἱ πατέρες τοῖς ἐρωμένοις μὴ ἐῶσι
διαλέγεσθαι τοῖς ἐρασταῖς, καὶ τῷ παιδαγωγῷ ταῦτα προστεταγμένα ᾖ, ἡλικιῶται δὲ καὶ ἑταῖροι ὀνειδίζωσιν ἐάν τι
ὁρῶσιν τοιοῦτον γιγνόμενον, καὶ τοὺς ὀνειδίζοντας αὖ οἱ
d πρεσβύτεροι μὴ διακωλύωσι μηδὲ λοιδορῶσιν ὡς οὐκ ὀρθῶς
λέγοντας, εἰς δὲ ταῦτά τις αὖ βλέψας ἡγήσαιτ' ἂν πάλιν
αἴσχιστον τὸ τοιοῦτον ἐνθάδε νομίζεσθαι. τὸ δὲ οἶμαι ὧδ'
ἔχει· οὐχ ἁπλοῦν ἐστιν, ὅπερ ἐξ ἀρχῆς ἐλέχθη οὔτε καλὸν
5 εἶναι αὐτὸ καθ' αὑτὸ οὔτε αἰσχρόν, ἀλλὰ καλῶς μὲν πραττ-
τόμενον καλόν, αἰσχρῶς δὲ αἰσχρόν. αἰσχρῶς μὲν οὖν
ἐστι πονηρῷ τε καὶ πονηρῶς χαρίζεσθαι, καλῶς δὲ χρηστῷ
τε καὶ καλῶς. πονηρὸς δ' ἐστὶν ἐκεῖνος ὁ ἐραστὴς ὁ πάν-

32

ἀν-ελευθερία, ἡ: servility, conduct unbefitting
   a free person
ἀντι-βόλησις, -εως, ἡ: entreaty, prayer
ἁπλόος, -η, -ον: single, simple, absolute*
ἀφροδίσιος, -α, -ον: belonging to Aphrodite
δέησις, -εως, ἡ: request, entreaty
δια-κωλύω: to hinder, prevent
δια-πράττω: to accomplish, effect*
δουλεία, ἡ: servitude, slavery, bondage*
δουλεύω: to be a slave, serve, be subject to*
δοῦλος, ὁ: a slave*
ἐκ-βαίνω: disembark; come to pass, turn out
ἐμ-ποδίζω: to hinder, impede, prevent
ἐξουσία, ἡ: power, authority, opportunity*
ἔπ-ειμι: to be upon, be set upon
ἐφ-ίστημι: to set, stop, stand near or over
ἐχθρός, -οῦ, ὁ: enemy
ἡλικιώτης, -ου, ὁ: an equal in age, peer

κοίμησις, -εως, ἡ: lying down to sleep
κολακεία, ἡ: flattery, fawning*
λοιδορέω: to abuse, rail against, revile
νου-θετέω: to admonish, warn, advise
ὄμνυμι: to swear, take an oath*
ὀνειδίζω: to object, reproach, rebuke
ὄνειδος, τό: reproach, censure, rebuke*
ὅρκος, ὁ: an oath*
πάγκαλος, -η, -ον: all-beautiful, good, noble*
παιδαγωγός, ὁ: a boy-ward, tutor
πονηρός, -ά, -όν: wicked, base; defective*
πονηρῶς: badly, wickedly*
πρᾶξις, -εως, ἡ: action, deed, business*
προσ-τάττω: to order, assign, appoint*
συγ-γνώμη, ἡ: confession, forgiveness, pardon
χάρις, χάριτος, ἡ: grace, favor, gratitude*
χρηστός, -ή, -όν: good, noble, worthy*
ὧδε: in this way, so, thus*

183a6 ὀμνύντες: pres. pple, ὄμνυμι
  κοιμήσεις ἐπὶ θύραις: *lying down to sleep near their doorways*
a7 οἵας οὐδ᾽ ἂν δοῦλος οὐδείς: *which (sort of slavery) not even a slave would...*; supply ἔθελοι δουλεύειν
  ἐμποδίζοιτο ἄν: *he would be hindered*; pres. pass. opt. with genitive of agents
  μὴ πράττειν: *from doing*; untranslated μὴ + inf. follow verbs of hindering
b1 τῶν μὲν...τῶν δὲ: *some (i.e. enemies)... others (i.e. friends)*; gen. absolutes
  κολακείας καὶ ἀνελευθερίας: *on the charge of..*; gen. of charge or accusation
b2 ὑπὲρ αὐτῶν: *on their behalf*
  τῷ δ᾽ ἐρῶντι...χάρις ἔπεστι: *but for the lover there is (a certain) charm...*
b3 δέδοται: *he is granted*; pf. pass. δίδωμι
b4 ὡς: *on the grounds that he...*; gen. abs.
b5 ὃ δὲ δεινότατον...ὅτι: *and what is most strange...is that*; supply ἐστιν
b6 ὀμνύντι μόνῳ: *for (this) swearer alone*; "swearing" pres. pple ὄμνυμι
  συγγνώμη: supply ἐστίν
  παρὰ θεῶν: *from the gods*
  ἐκβάντι: *having transgressed*; aor. pple ἐκβαίνω governing a gen. separation
b7 οὔ φασιν εἶναι: *deny that...is (genuine)*

c1 πεποιήκασι: *have provided*; pf. ποιέω
c2 ταύτῃ: *in this way, thus*
  οἰηθείη ἄν τις: *one might think*; aor. dep. opt. οἴομαι
c3 νομίζεσθαι: articular infs. are the subject
c5 ἐπιστήσαντες: *(by) putting...in charge*; "setting over" aor. pple, ἐφ-ίστημι; ἐῶσι: *allow*; 3rd pl. pres., ἐάω
c6 προστεταγμένα ᾖ: *have been imposed on* (+ dat.); pf. pass. pple προσ-τάττω, 3rd sg pres. subj. εἰμί is pf. periphrastic
d1 ὡς: *on the grounds that they are not speak correctly*; suggesting alleged cause
d2 ἡγήσαιτ᾽ ἄν: *one might think*; aor. opt.
d3 αἴσχιστον...νομίζεσθαι: *that such action is believed most shameful here*
  τὸ δὲ ὧδ᾽ ἔχει: *but this is as follows*; ἔχω + adv. = "is disposed" or "to be" + adj.
d4 ὅπερ...ἐλέχθη: *just as it was said from the beginning*; aor. pass. λέγω
d5 αὐτὸ καθ᾽ αὑτό: *itself in itself*
d6 αἰσχρῶς δὲ: supply πραττόμενον
  αἰσχρῶς μὲν: *to act shamefully*; add πράττειν as subject
d7 καλῶς δὲ: *to act nobly*; add πράττειν
d8 χρηστῷ τε καὶ καλῶς: add χαρίζεσθαι to complete parallelism with d5

e δημος, ὁ τοῦ σώματος μᾶλλον ἢ τῆς ψυχῆς ἐρῶν· καὶ γὰρ
οὐδὲ μόνιμός ἐστιν, ἅτε οὐδὲ μονίμου ἐρῶν πράγματος.
ἅμα γὰρ τῷ τοῦ σώματος ἄνθει λήγοντι, οὗπερ ἤρα, "οἴχεται ἀποπτάμενος," πολλοὺς λόγους καὶ ὑποσχέσεις καται-
5 σχύνας· ὁ δὲ τοῦ ἤθους χρηστοῦ ὄντος ἐραστὴς διὰ βίου
μένει, ἅτε μονίμῳ συντακείς. τούτους δὴ βούλεται ὁ
184 ἡμέτερος νόμος εὖ καὶ καλῶς βασανίζειν, καὶ τοῖς μὲν
χαρίσασθαι, τοὺς δὲ διαφεύγειν. διὰ ταῦτα οὖν τοῖς μὲν
διώκειν παρακελεύεται, τοῖς δὲ φεύγειν, ἀγωνοθετῶν καὶ
βασανίζων ποτέρων ποτέ ἐστιν ὁ ἐρῶν καὶ ποτέρων ὁ
5 ἐρώμενος. οὕτω δὴ ὑπὸ ταύτης τῆς αἰτίας πρῶτον μὲν τὸ
ἁλίσκεσθαι ταχὺ αἰσχρὸν νενόμισται, ἵνα χρόνος ἐγγένηται,
ὃς δὴ δοκεῖ τὰ πολλὰ καλῶς βασανίζειν, ἔπειτα τὸ ὑπὸ
χρημάτων καὶ ὑπὸ πολιτικῶν δυνάμεων ἁλῶναι αἰσχρόν,
b ἐάν τε κακῶς πάσχων πτήξῃ καὶ μὴ καρτερήσῃ, ἄν τ'
εὐεργετούμενος εἰς χρήματα ἢ εἰς διαπράξεις πολιτικὰς μὴ
καταφρονήσῃ· οὐδὲν γὰρ δοκεῖ τούτων οὔτε βέβαιον οὔτε
μόνιμον εἶναι, χωρὶς τοῦ μηδὲ πεφυκέναι ἀπ' αὐτῶν γεν-
5 ναίαν φιλίαν. μία δὴ λείπεται τῷ ἡμετέρῳ νόμῳ ὁδός, εἰ
μέλλει καλῶς χαριεῖσθαι ἐραστῇ παιδικά. ἔστι γὰρ ἡμῖν
νόμος, ὥσπερ ἐπὶ τοῖς ἐρασταῖς ἦν δουλεύειν ἐθέλοντα
c ἡντινοῦν δουλείαν παιδικοῖς μὴ κολακείαν εἶναι μηδὲ ἐπο-
νείδιστον, οὕτω δὴ καὶ ἄλλη μία μόνη δουλεία ἑκούσιος
λείπεται οὐκ ἐπονείδιστος· αὕτη δ' ἐστὶν ἡ περὶ τὴν ἀρετήν.
νενόμισται γὰρ δὴ ἡμῖν, ἐάν τις ἐθέλῃ τινὰ θεραπεύειν
5 ἡγούμενος δι' ἐκεῖνον ἀμείνων ἔσεσθαι ἢ κατὰ σοφίαν τινὰ

ἀγωνο-θετέω: to judge or set up a contest
αἰτία, ἡ: cause, reason; charge, blame*
ἁλίσκομαι: to be caught, be taken*
ἄνθος, -εος, τό: a blossom, flower, bloom*
ἀπο-πέτομαι: to fly off or away
βασανίζω: to put to the test; examine closely
βέβαιος, -ον: firm, steadfast, sure, certain*
γενναῖος, -α, -ον: noble, well-bred*
διά-πραξις, -εως, ἡ: (dispatch of) business
δια-φεύγω: to flee, get away from, escape*
δουλεία, ἡ: servitude, slavery, bondage*
δουλεύω: to be a slave, serve, be subject to*
ἐγ-γίγνομαι: to be in, intervene; be possible*
ἑκούσιος, -ον: voluntary, willing
ἐπ-ονείδιστος, -ον: shameful, reproachable
εὐ-εργετέω: to do well, treat well, treat kindly
ἦθος, -εος, τό: custom; disposition, character*
θεραπεύω: to attend to, care for, serve

καρτερέω: to endure, be steadfast, staunch*
κατ-αισχύνω: to dishonor, disgrace, degrade
κατα-φρονέω: to think down upon, despise*
κολακεία, ἡ: flattery, fawning*
λήγω: to stop, cease, leave off, fade*
μένω: to stay, remain*
μόνιμος, -α, -ον: stable, steadfast, lasting*
ὁδός, ἡ: road, way, path, journey*
παρα-κελεύομαι: to order, urge, encourage*
πολιτικός, -ή, -όν: of the city, political, civic*
πότερος, -α, -ον: which (of two)?, whether?*
πτήσσω: to frighten, scare; cower, crouch
συν-τήκω: to melt together; fuse, join with*
ὑπόσχεσις, -εως, ἡ: a promise, undertaking
φεύγω: to flee, escape; defend in court*
χρηστός, -ή, -όν: good, worthy, noble*
χωρίς: separately; apart from (+ gen.)*

183e1 καὶ γάρ: *for also, for even*
e2 ἅτε...ἐρῶν: *since he loves*; ἅτε + pple
e3 ἅμα...ἄνθει λήγοντι: *as soon as the flower...fades*; "fading flower"
ἤρα: *he used to love*; 3rd sg. impf. ἐράω
οἴχεται ἀποπτάμενος: *goes flittering away*; aor. pple, ἀπο-πέτομαι
e4 καταισχύνας: nom. sg., aor. pple
e6 ἅτε...συντακείς: *since he was fused with...*; aor. pass. pple, συν-τήκω
τούτους: τοὺς ἐραστάς
184a1 τοῖς μὲν...τοὺς δέ: *some...others*; i.e. erastai; both are objects of infinitives
a2 χαρίσασθαι...διαφεύγειν: supply "beloved," τοὺς ἐρωμένους as subj. acc.
τοῖς μὲν...τοῖς δέ: *these (erastai) ...those (eromenoi)*; objects of main verb
a4 ποτέρων: *in which group*; partitive gen.
a5 τὸ ἁλίσκεσθαι ταχύ: *to be caught quickly*; the beloved should not submit to the lover quickly; subj. of νενόμισται
a6 νενόμισται: pf. pass., νομίζω; add εἶναι
ἵνα χρόνος ἐγγένηται: *so that time may intervene*; "come about," purpose
a8 τὸ ἁλῶναι *to be caught*; aor. pass. inf. supply νενόμισται εἶναι as main verb
ὑπὸ χρημάτων: *because of money*
b1 ἐάν τε...ἄν τ᾿: *whether...or*

κακῶς πάσχων: *(when) suffering badly*
πτήξῃ καὶ μὴ καρτερήσῃ: *cowers and is not steadfast* 3rd sg. aor. subj. πτήσσω
b2 εἰς χρήματα ἤ..καταφρονήσῃ: *despise upon money or...*; prepositional phrases governed by καταφρονήσῃ, aor. subj.
b4 χωρὶς τοῦ μηδὲ πεφυκέναι...φιλίαν: *apart from genuine friendship not being brought forth from these*; articular inf.
b5 μία λείπεται...ὁδός: *one way is left over*
b6 μέλλει: subject is (τὰ) παιδικά
ἔστι...ἡμῖν: *we have*; dat. of possession
b7 ἐπὶ τοῖς ἐρασταῖς ἦν: *in the case of lovers there was a law that*; add νόμος
δουλεύειν...παιδικοῖς: *to engage willingly in whatsoever form of slavery for his darling*; this is subject of the inf.
εἶναι, ἐθέλοντα is lit. "being willing"
c3 ἡ περὶ τὴν ἀρετήν: *(slavery) pertaining to excellence*; ἡ (δουλεία)
c4 νενόμισται: *is believed*; pf. pass., the subject is ἡ ἐθελοδουλεία below
ἡμῖν: *by us*; dat. of agent with pf. pass.
ἐάν...ἐθέλῃ: *if one wishes*: pres. subj.
c5 ἔσεσθαι: *to be better*; fut. inf. εἰμί governed by ἡγούμενος
κατὰ σοφίαν τινά: *in some skill*

ἢ κατὰ ἄλλο ὁτιοῦν μέρος ἀρετῆς, αὕτη αὖ ἡ ἐθελοδουλεία
οὐκ αἰσχρὰ εἶναι οὐδὲ κολακεία. δεῖ δὴ τὼ νόμω τούτω
συμβαλεῖν εἰς ταὐτόν, τόν τε περὶ τὴν παιδεραστίαν καὶ
d τὸν περὶ τὴν φιλοσοφίαν τε καὶ τὴν ἄλλην ἀρετήν, εἰ
μέλλει συμβῆναι καλὸν γενέσθαι τὸ ἐραστῇ παιδικὰ χαρίσασθαι. ὅταν γὰρ εἰς τὸ αὐτὸ ἔλθωσιν ἐραστής τε καὶ
παιδικά, νόμον ἔχων ἑκάτερος, ὁ μὲν χαρισαμένοις παιδικοῖς
5 ὑπηρετῶν ὁτιοῦν δικαίως ἂν ὑπηρετεῖν, ὁ δὲ τῷ ποιοῦντι
αὐτὸν σοφόν τε καὶ ἀγαθὸν δικαίως αὖ ὁτιοῦν ἂν ὑπουρ-
γῶν ⟨ὑπουργεῖν⟩, καὶ ὁ μὲν δυνάμενος εἰς φρόνησιν καὶ τὴν
e ἄλλην ἀρετὴν συμβάλλεσθαι, ὁ δὲ δεόμενος εἰς παίδευσιν
καὶ τὴν ἄλλην σοφίαν κτᾶσθαι, τότε δὴ τούτων συνιόντων
εἰς ταὐτὸν τῶν νόμων μοναχοῦ ἐνταῦθα συμπίπτει τὸ καλὸν
εἶναι παιδικὰ ἐραστῇ χαρίσασθαι, ἄλλοθι δὲ οὐδαμοῦ. ἐπὶ
5 τούτῳ καὶ ἐξαπατηθῆναι οὐδὲν αἰσχρόν· ἐπὶ δὲ τοῖς ἄλλοις
πᾶσι καὶ ἐξαπατωμένῳ αἰσχύνην φέρει καὶ μή. εἰ γάρ τις
185 ἐραστῇ ὡς πλουσίῳ πλούτου ἕνεκα χαρισάμενος ἐξαπατηθείη
καὶ μὴ λάβοι χρήματα, ἀναφανέντος τοῦ ἐραστοῦ πένητος,
οὐδὲν ἧττον αἰσχρόν· δοκεῖ γὰρ ὁ τοιοῦτος τό γε αὑτοῦ
ἐπιδεῖξαι, ὅτι ἕνεκα χρημάτων ὁτιοῦν ἂν ὁτῳοῦν ὑπηρετοῖ,
5 τοῦτο δὲ οὐ καλόν. κατὰ τὸν αὐτὸν δὴ λόγον κἂν εἴ τις
ὡς ἀγαθῷ χαρισάμενος καὶ αὐτὸς ὡς ἀμείνων ἐσόμενος διὰ
τὴν φιλίαν ἐραστοῦ ἐξαπατηθείη, ἀναφανέντος ἐκείνου κακοῦ
b καὶ οὐ κεκτημένου ἀρετήν, ὅμως καλὴ ἡ ἀπάτη· δοκεῖ γὰρ
αὖ καὶ οὗτος τὸ καθ᾽ αὑτὸν δεδηλωκέναι, ὅτι ἀρετῆς γ᾽
ἕνεκα καὶ τοῦ βελτίων γενέσθαι πᾶν ἂν παντὶ προθυμηθείη,
τοῦτο δὲ αὖ πάντων κάλλιστον· οὕτω πᾶν πάντως γε καλὸν

ἄλλο-θι: in another place, elsewhere*
ἀνα-φαίνω: to bring to light, show, display*
ἀπάτη, -ης, ἡ: a trick, fraud, deceit
βελτίων, -ον: better
δηλόω: to make clear, show, reveal, exhibit*
ἐθελο-δουλεία, ἡ: willing slavery
ἑκάτερος, -α, -ον: each of two, either*
ἐπι-δείκνυμι: to show forth, display, point out*
κολακεία, ἡ: flattery, fawning*
μέρος, -έος, τό: a part, share, portion*
μοναχοῦ: alone, only
οὐδαμοῦ: nowhere
παιδ-εραστία, ἡ: love of young men
παίδευσις, -εως, ἡ: education, learning

πάντως: altogether, by all means, certainly*
πένης, -ητος, ὁ: a poor man, a day-laborer*
πλούσιος, -α, -ον: rich, wealthy, opulent*
πλοῦτος, ὁ: wealth, riches*
προ-θυμέομαι: to be eager, zealous, ready
συμ-βαίνω: to occur, happen, turn out*
συμ-βάλλω: to join, combine, contribute*
συμ-πίπτω: to fall together, clash; happen
συν-έρχομαι: to come or go together, go with*
ὑπ-ηρετέω: to serve, minister (+ dat.)*
ὑπ-ουργέω: to render service, serve, assist
φρόνησις, -εως, ἡ: wisdom, intelligence,
    prudence*

184c6 κατὰ...μέρος: *in whatever other part*
c7 τὼ νόμω τούτω: *these 2 rules*; dual acc.
c8 συμβαλεῖν: *to come together, combine*
εἰς ταὐτόν: *to the same thing*; τὸ αὐτό
τὸν...τὸν: *the one (nomos)...the other*; in
apposition to τὼ νόμω τούτω
d2 συμβῆναι: *to turn out*; aor. συμβαίνω
τὸ...χαρίσασθαι: *that the beloved gratify
his lover*; subject of μέλλει
d3 ὅταν εἰς τὸ αὐτὸ ἔλθωσιν: *whenever
they come together*; "to the same thing"
d4 ὁ μὲν...ὁ δὲ...ἂν ὑπουργεῖν: *the one
(possessing the law) that, in offering
whatever service for a darling gratifying
him, he would offer the service justly,
the other (possessing the law) that, for
the one making him both wise and good,
he would offer in turn whatever service
justly*; ἂν + inf. replaces a potential opt.
in direct speech
d7 ὁ μὲν δυνάμενος...συμβάλλεσθαι: *the
one being able to contribute (towards)*;
i.e. the lover
e1 ὁ δὲ: *the other asking...*; i.e. the beloved
εἰς παίδευσιν: *with regard to education*;
awkward parallel with d7
e2 συνιόντων...τῶν νόμων: gen. abs.,
pres. pple. συν-έρχομαι (stem -ι)
e3 εἰς ταὐτόν: *to the same thing*; τὸ αὐτό
μοναχοῦ ἐνταῦθα: *only at this point*
συμπίπτει: *it happens that*; impersonal
τὸ...εἶναι: art. inf., καλόν is the pred.
e4 ἐπὶ τούτῳ: *in this case*
e5 ἐξαπατηθῆναι: *to be deceived*; aor. pass.

supply ἐστίν
ἐπὶ...ἄλλοις πᾶσι: *in all other cases*
e6 φέρει: *carries*; supply τὸ χαρίζεσθαι
ἐρασταῖς "to gratify lovers" as the subj.
καὶ...καὶ μὴ: *both the one deceived and
not (deceived)*; supply ἐξαπατωμένῳ
185a1 ὡς πλουσίῳ: *on the grounds that he is
rich*; ὡς + pple is causal, supply ὄντος
ἐξαπατηθείη...λάβοι: *should...should*;
aor. pass. and aor. act. opt. λαμβάνω
protasis of a future-less-vivid condition
a2 ἀναφανέντος: *being shown (to be)*;
aor. pass. pple, ἀνα-φαίνω, in gen. abs.
a3 οὐδὲν ἧττον: *not at all less*; adverbial
αἰσχρόν: *would be shameful*; add ἂν εἴη,
opt. εἰμί to complete the future-less-vivid
τὸ γε αὑτοῦ: *his own character*; "that of
his own", ἑαυτοῦ
a4 ἐπιδεῖξαι: aor. inf.
ὁτιοῦν...ὑπηρετοῖ: *he would offer
whatever (service) for anyone*
a5 κατὰ...λόγον: *in the same argument*
κἂν εἰ...ἐξαπατηθείη: *even if...should be
deceived*; aor. pass. opt.
a6 ὡς ἀγαθῷ: *since he is good*; + ὄντι
ὡς...ἐσόμενος: *so that he will be*; fut.
b1 κεκτημένου: pf. mid. pple, κτάομαι
ἡ ἀπάτη: *deceit would be*; supply ἂν εἴη
b2 τὸ καθ᾽ αὑτὸν: see τὸ γε αὑτοῦ in a3
δεδηλωκέναι: pf. δηλόω follows δοκεῖ
τοῦ...γένεσθαι: *of becoming*; with ἕνεκα
b3 πᾶν ἂν παντὶ προθυμηθείη: *would desire
(to do) anything for anyone*

5 ἀρετῆς γ' ἕνεκα χαρίζεσθαι. οὗτός ἐστιν ὁ τῆς οὐρανίας θεοῦ
ἔρως καὶ οὐράνιος καὶ πολλοῦ ἄξιος καὶ πόλει καὶ ἰδιώταις,
πολλὴν ἐπιμέλειαν ἀναγκάζων ποιεῖσθαι πρὸς ἀρετὴν τόν
c τε ἐρῶντα αὐτὸν αὑτοῦ καὶ τὸν ἐρώμενον· οἱ δ' ἕτεροι
πάντες τῆς ἑτέρας, τῆς πανδήμου. ταῦτά σοι, ἔφη, ὡς ἐκ
τοῦ παραχρῆμα, ὦ Φαῖδρε, περὶ Ἔρωτος συμβάλλομαι.

Παυσανίου δὲ παυσαμένου—διδάσκουσι γάρ με ἴσα λέγειν
5 οὑτωσὶ οἱ σοφοί—ἔφη ὁ Ἀριστόδημος δεῖν μὲν Ἀριστοφάνη
λέγειν, τυχεῖν δὲ αὐτῷ τινα ἢ ὑπὸ πλησμονῆς ἢ ὑπό τινος
ἄλλου λύγγα ἐπιπεπτωκυῖαν καὶ οὐχ οἷόν τε εἶναι λέγειν,
d ἀλλ' εἰπεῖν αὐτόν—ἐν τῇ κάτω γὰρ αὐτοῦ τὸν ἰατρὸν Ἐρυξίμαχον κατακεῖσθαι—"ὦ Ἐρυξίμαχε, δίκαιος εἶ ἢ παῦσαί
με τῆς λυγγὸς ἢ λέγειν ὑπὲρ ἐμοῦ, ἕως ἂν ἐγὼ παύσωμαι."
καὶ τὸν Ἐρυξίμαχον εἰπεῖν "ἀλλὰ ποιήσω ἀμφότερα ταῦτα·
5 ἐγὼ μὲν γὰρ ἐρῶ ἐν τῷ σῷ μέρει, σὺ δ' ἐπειδὰν παύσῃ, ἐν
τῷ ἐμῷ. ἐν ᾧ δ' ἂν ἐγὼ λέγω, ἐὰν μέν σοι ἐθέλῃ ἀπνευστὶ
ἔχοντι πολὺν χρόνον παύεσθαι ἡ λύγξ· εἰ δὲ μή, ὕδατι
e ἀνακογχυλίασον. εἰ δ' ἄρα πάνυ ἰσχυρά ἐστιν, ἀναλαβών
τι τοιοῦτον οἵῳ κινήσαις ἂν τὴν ῥῖνα, πτάρε· καὶ ἐὰν τοῦτο
ποιήσῃς ἅπαξ ἢ δίς, καὶ εἰ πάνυ ἰσχυρά ἐστι, παύσεται."
"Οὐκ ἂν φθάνοις λέγων," φάναι τὸν Ἀριστοφάνη· "ἐγὼ
5 δὲ ταῦτα ποιήσω."

Εἰπεῖν δὴ τὸν Ἐρυξίμαχον, δοκεῖ τοίνυν μοι ἀναγκαῖον
εἶναι, ἐπειδὴ Παυσανίας ὁρμήσας ἐπὶ τὸν λόγον καλῶς οὐχ
186 ἱκανῶς ἀπετέλεσε, δεῖν ἐμὲ πειρᾶσθαι τέλος ἐπιθεῖναι τῷ
λόγῳ. τὸ μὲν γὰρ διπλοῦν εἶναι τὸν ἔρωτα δοκεῖ μοι
καλῶς διελέσθαι· ὅτι δὲ οὐ μόνον ἐστὶν ἐπὶ ταῖς ψυχαῖς

ἀνακογχυλιάζω: to gargle
ἀνα-λαμβάνω: to take up, assume, regain, restore*
ἅπαξ: once, once only, once for all*
ἀ-πνευστί: breathless (adv.)
ἀπο-τελέω: to complete, accomplish, fulfill, realize
δι-αιρέω: to divide, distinguish*
διδάσκω: to teach, instruct*
δι-πλόος, -η, -ον: twofold, double*
δίς: twice, doubly
ἐπι-μέλεια, ἡ: care, care for, attention; pursuit
ἐπι-πίπτω: to fall upon, attack, assail
ἰατρός, ὁ: physician, doctor*
ἰδιώτης, -ου, ὁ: a private citizen, lay person

κάτω: down, below (+ gen.)
κινέω: to set in motion, move; arouse, irritate*
λύγξ, λυγγός, ἡ: hiccup, hiccough*
μέρος, -εος, τό: a part, share, portion*
οἶος, -η, -ον: alone, lone, lonely*
ὁρμάω: to set in motion; set out, begin*
παραχρῆμα: on the spot, off hand, straightway
πλησμονή, ἡ: fullness, satiety, satisfaction*
πταίρω: to sneeze
ῥίς, ῥινός, ἡ: the nose
συμ-βάλλω: to join, combine, contribute*
τέλος, -εος, τό: end, goal, result; sacred rites*
ὕδωρ, ὕδατος, τό: water
φθάνω: to anticipate, do beforehand (+ pple)*

185b6 πολλοῦ ἄξιος: *worth much to both the city and citizens;* "worthy of much"

b7 πολλὴν ἐπιμέλειαν...ποιεῖσθαι: *have much care;* τὸν ἐρῶντα...τὸν ἐρώμενον are acc. subj. and obj. of ἀναγκάζων
πρὸς ἀρετὴν: *with regard to excellence*

c1 αὑτοῦ: *his own, of himself;* ἑαυτοῦ, object of ἐπιμέλειαν
οἱ...ἕτεροι: *all other (forms of love)*

c2 τῆς ἑτέρας: *(are the eros) of the other (goddess);* parallel with b5 above
ὡς...παραχρῆμα: *as (best I can) on the spot;* ἂν δύνωμαι or its equivalent is implicit after ὡς

c4 ἴσα: *balanced phrases;* lit. "equal things", the preceding gen. abs. has two words with assonance, an equal number of syllables, and similar scansion
οἱ σοφοί: *those skilled (in speaking)*

c5 δεῖν: *was supposed to;* inf.

c6 τινα...λύγγα: *a sort of hiccup, some hiccups;* acc. subject of τυχεῖν
τυχεῖν...ἐπιπεπτωκυῖαν: *happened to have fall upon;* complementary pf. pple

c7 οἶόν τε εἶναι: *(he was able;* common translation for οἶός τε εἰμί

d1 ἐν τῇ κάτω: *on the (couch) below;* supply κλίνῃ, κάτω governs a genitive

d2 δίκαιος εἶ: *you are right to...;* + inf.

d3 τῆς λυγγὸς: *from hiccups;* gen. of separation with aor. inf. παῦσαι

d5 ἐρῶ: *I will speak;* ἐρέω.
ἐν τῷ σῷ μέρει: *during your turn*
παύσῃ: *it stops;* 3rd sg. aor. subj.
ἐν τῷ ἐμῷ: *(you will speak) during my (turn);* add ἐρεῖς and μέρει to complete the parallel construction

d6 ἐν ᾧ: *while;* "in which (time)"
ἐὰν ἐθέλῃ: the main clause is missing
ἀπνευστὶ ἔχοντι: *while holding your breath;* "keeping breathless" or "being breathless"

d7 πολὺν χρόνον: *for...;* duration of time with σοι...ἀπνευστὶ ἔχοντι
ὕδατι: *with water;* dat. of means

e1 ἀνακογχυλίασον: aor. imperative

e2 τι τοιοῦτον οἴῳ: *some sort of thing by which...*
πτάρε: aor. imperative

e3 παύσεται: fut. dep. παύω

e4 οὐκ ἂν φθάνοις λέγων: *you could not speak sooner;* "anticipate by speaking"

e7 ὁρμήσας ἐπὶ τὸν λόγον: *having set out upon his speech;* aor. pple ὁρμάω

186a1 ἐπιθεῖναι: *impose (acc.) upon (dat.);* aor. inf. ἐπι-τίθημι

a2 τὸ...εἶναι: art. inf., subject of δοκεῖ

a3 διελέσθαι: *to be chosen;* aor. pass. inf., δι-αιρέω (stem -ελ)
ἐπὶ ταῖς ψυχαῖς: *in the case of souls*

τῶν ἀνθρώπων πρὸς τοὺς καλοὺς ἀλλὰ καὶ πρὸς ἄλλα πολλὰ
5 καὶ ἐν τοῖς ἄλλοις, τοῖς τε σώμασι τῶν πάντων ζῴων καὶ
τοῖς ἐν τῇ γῇ φυομένοις καὶ ὡς ἔπος εἰπεῖν ἐν πᾶσι τοῖς
οὖσι, καθεωρακέναι μοι δοκῶ ἐκ τῆς ἰατρικῆς, τῆς ἡμετέρας
b τέχνης, ὡς μέγας καὶ θαυμαστὸς καὶ ἐπὶ πᾶν ὁ θεὸς τείνει
καὶ κατ᾽ ἀνθρώπινα καὶ κατὰ θεῖα πράγματα. ἄρξομαι δὲ
ἀπὸ τῆς ἰατρικῆς λέγων, ἵνα καὶ πρεσβεύωμεν τὴν τέχνην.
ἡ γὰρ φύσις τῶν σωμάτων τὸν διπλοῦν ἔρωτα τοῦτον ἔχει·
5 τὸ γὰρ ὑγιὲς τοῦ σώματος καὶ τὸ νοσοῦν ὁμολογουμένως
ἕτερόν τε καὶ ἀνόμοιόν ἐστι, τὸ δὲ ἀνόμοιον ἀνομοίων ἐπιθυμεῖ καὶ ἐρᾷ. ἄλλος μὲν οὖν ὁ ἐπὶ τῷ ὑγιεινῷ ἔρως, ἄλλος
δὲ ὁ ἐπὶ τῷ νοσώδει. ἔστιν δή, ὥσπερ ἄρτι Παυσανίας
ἔλεγεν τοῖς μὲν ἀγαθοῖς καλὸν χαρίζεσθαι τῶν ἀνθρώπων,
c τοῖς δ᾽ ἀκολάστοις αἰσχρόν, οὕτω καὶ ἐν αὐτοῖς τοῖς σώμασιν
τοῖς μὲν ἀγαθοῖς ἑκάστου τοῦ σώματος καὶ ὑγιεινοῖς καλὸν
χαρίζεσθαι καὶ δεῖ, καὶ τοῦτό ἐστιν ᾧ ὄνομα τὸ ἰατρικόν,
τοῖς δὲ κακοῖς καὶ νοσώδεσιν αἰσχρόν τε καὶ δεῖ ἀχαριστεῖν,
5 εἰ μέλλει τις τεχνικὸς εἶναι. ἔστι γὰρ ἰατρική, ὡς ἐν
κεφαλαίῳ εἰπεῖν, ἐπιστήμη τῶν τοῦ σώματος ἐρωτικῶν πρὸς
πλησμονὴν καὶ κένωσιν, καὶ ὁ διαγιγνώσκων ἐν τούτοις τὸν
d καλόν τε καὶ αἰσχρὸν ἔρωτα, οὗτός ἐστιν ὁ ἰατρικώτατος,
καὶ ὁ μεταβάλλειν ποιῶν, ὥστε ἀντὶ τοῦ ἑτέρου ἔρωτος τὸν
ἕτερον κτᾶσθαι, καὶ οἷς μὴ ἔνεστιν ἔρως, δεῖ δ᾽ ἐγγενέσθαι,
ἐπιστάμενος ἐμποιῆσαι καὶ ἐνόντα ἐξελεῖν, ἀγαθὸς ἂν εἴη
5 δημιουργός. δεῖ γὰρ δὴ τὰ ἔχθιστα ὄντα ἐν τῷ σώματι
φίλα οἷόν τ᾽ εἶναι ποιεῖν καὶ ἐρᾶν ἀλλήλων. ἔστι δὲ ἔχθιστα
τὰ ἐναντιώτατα, ψυχρὸν θερμῷ, πικρὸν γλυκεῖ, ξηρὸν ὑγρῷ,
e πάντα τὰ τοιαῦτα· τούτοις ἐπιστηθεὶς ἔρωτα ἐμποιῆσαι καὶ
ὁμόνοιαν ὁ ἡμέτερος πρόγονος Ἀσκληπιός, ὥς φασιν οἴδε οἱ

ἀ-κόλαστος, -ον: licentious, intemperate
ἀνθρώπινος, -η, -ον: human, of a human*
ἀν-όμοιος, -ον: unlike, dissimilar*
ἀντί: instead of, in place of (+ gen.) *
ἄρτι: just, exactly*
ἀ-χαριστέω: to show disfavor, discourage
γῆ, ἡ: earth*
γλυκύς, -εῖα, -ύ: sweet, pleasant, delightful*
δια-γιγνώσκω: to distinguish, discern, resolve
διπλόος, -η, -ον: twofold, double*
ἐγ-γίγνομαι: to come about; be possible*
ἐν-ειμί: to be in, exist in*
ἐξ-αιρέω: to take out, remove, leave out*
ἐπί-σταμαι: to know, know how, understand*
ἔπος, -εος, τό: a word*
ἔχθιστος, -η, -ον: most hated, most hostile
θερμός, -ή, -όν: hot, warm; *subst.* heat
κένωσις, -εως, ἡ: emptiness; an emptying

κεφάλαιον, τό: main or chief point, gist, sum*
μετα-βάλλω: to change, alter; turn about*
νοσέω: to be sick, ill*
νοσώδης, -ες: sickly, diseased, unwholesome
ξηρός, -ά, -όν: dry
ὁμο-λογουμένως: by general agreement
ὁμό-νοια, ἡ: oneness of mind, unity, concord
πικρός, -ά, -όν: sharp, keen, bitter*
πλησμονή, ἡ: fullness, satiety, satisfaction*
πρεσβεύω: to revere, venerate, honor
πρό-γονος, ὁ: a forefather, ancestor
τείνω: to tend, extend, direct; stretch, spread*
τεχνικός, -ή, -όν: skillful, skilled, artistic
ὑγιεινός, -ή, -όν: sound, healthy, wholesome
ὑγιής, -ές: sound, healthy, wholesome*`
ὑγρός, -ά, -όν: moist, wet, fluid*
ψυχρός, -ά, -όν: cold, chill, frigid*

186a3 ὅτι...τοῖς ἄλλοις: *that (the twofold eros) is not only in the souls of humans regarding beautiful (men) but also regarding other things and in other things*; governed by καθεωρακέναι in a7

a5 σώμασι,φυομένοις: apposition, ἄλλοις

a6 ὡς ἔπος εἰπεῖν: *so to speak*
τοῖς οὖσι: *things that exist*; dat. pple. εἰμί

a7 καθεωρακέναι: pf. inf. καθ-οράω
μοι δοκῶ: *I think*; "I seem to myself"

b1 ὡς μέγας: *how great...*; governed by καθεωρακέναι above
ἐπὶ πᾶν: *over everything*

b2 κατὰ: *in the area of...*

b3 ἰατρικῆς: *art of medicine*; add τέχνης

b5 τὸ ὑγιὲς...τὸ νοσοῦν: *the healthy (part)...the sick (part)*; "the being sick", neuter pres. pple. νοσέω

b7 ἄλλος...ἄλλος: *one...the other*
ἐπὶ: *in the case of*

b9 καλὸν: *that (it is) noble*; supply εἶναι

c1 αἰσχρόν: *that (it is) shameful to gratify*; parallel with b9 above

c2 καλὸν...δεῖ: *it is noble and necessary*

c3 ᾧ: *(that) which has*; "(that) to which there is" dat. of possession, add ἐστίν

c4 αἰσχρὸν...δεῖ: *it is shameful and necessary*; parallel with c2-3 above

c5 ὡς...εἰπεῖν: *so to speak in sum*

c6 πρὸς: *with regard to*

d2 ὁ μεταβάλλειν ποιῶν: *the one bringing about change*; subject of ἂν εἴη in d4
ἑτέρου...ἕτερον: *one love...the other*

d3 ὥστε...κτᾶσθαι: *so that (the body) possesses*; result, add τὸ σῶμα as subj.
οἷς...ἐγγενέσθαι: *(the bodies) in which eros does not exist but in is necessary to engender*; obj. of ἐμποιῆσαι

d4 ἐμποιῆσαι...ἐξελεῖν: *to create (an eros) in...and take (an eros) out*; aor. inf. ἐξ-αιρέω governed by ἐπιστάμενος

d5 ἔχιστα: *most hated*; superlative
δεῖ...οἷόν τ' εἶναι: *one ought to be able*

d7 θερμῷ...ὑγρῷ: *(most opposite) to...*; dat. are governed by missing ἐναντιώτατα

e1 ἐπιστηθείς: *having come to know how*; ingressive aor. aor. dep. pple. ἐπίσταμαι

ποιηταὶ καὶ ἐγὼ πείθομαι, συνέστησεν τὴν ἡμετέραν τέχνην.
ἥ τε οὖν ἰατρική, ὥσπερ λέγω, πᾶσα διὰ τοῦ θεοῦ τούτου
187 κυβερνᾶται, ὡσαύτως δὲ καὶ γυμναστικὴ καὶ γεωργία· μουσικὴ
δὲ καὶ παντὶ κατάδηλος τῷ καὶ σμικρὸν προσέχοντι τὸν νοῦν
ὅτι κατὰ ταὐτὰ ἔχει τούτοις, ὥσπερ ἴσως καὶ Ἡράκλειτος
βούλεται λέγειν, ἐπεὶ τοῖς γε ῥήμασιν οὐ καλῶς λέγει.   τὸ
5 ἓν γάρ φησι "διαφερόμενον αὐτὸ αὑτῷ συμφέρεσθαι,"
"ὥσπερ ἁρμονίαν τόξου τε καὶ λύρας." ἔστι δὲ πολλὴ
ἀλογία ἁρμονίαν φάναι διαφέρεσθαι ἢ ἐκ διαφερομένων ἔτι
εἶναι. ἀλλὰ ἴσως τόδε ἐβούλετο λέγειν, ὅτι ἐκ διαφερομένων
b πρότερον τοῦ ὀξέος καὶ βαρέος, ἔπειτα ὕστερον ὁμολογη-
σάντων γέγονεν ὑπὸ τῆς μουσικῆς τέχνης.   οὐ γὰρ δήπου
ἐκ διαφερομένων γε ἔτι τοῦ ὀξέος καὶ βαρέος ἁρμονία ἂν
εἴη· ἡ γὰρ ἁρμονία συμφωνία ἐστίν, συμφωνία δὲ ὁμολογία
5 τις—ὁμολογίαν δὲ ἐκ διαφερομένων, ἕως ἂν διαφέρωνται,
ἀδύνατον εἶναι· διαφερόμενον δὲ αὖ καὶ μὴ ὁμολογοῦν ἀδύνατον ἁρμόσαι—ὥσπερ γε καὶ ὁ ῥυθμὸς ἐκ τοῦ ταχέος καὶ
c βραδέος, ἐκ διενηνεγμένων πρότερον, ὕστερον δὲ ὁμολογη-
σάντων γέγονε.   τὴν δὲ ὁμολογίαν πᾶσι τούτοις, ὥσπερ
ἐκεῖ ἡ ἰατρική, ἐνταῦθα ἡ μουσικὴ ἐντίθησιν, ἔρωτα καὶ
ὁμόνοιαν ἀλλήλων ἐμποιήσασα· καὶ ἔστιν αὖ μουσικὴ περὶ
5 ἁρμονίαν καὶ ῥυθμὸν ἐρωτικῶν ἐπιστήμη. καὶ ἐν μέν γε
αὐτῇ τῇ συστάσει ἁρμονίας τε καὶ ῥυθμοῦ οὐδὲν χαλεπὸν τὰ
ἐρωτικὰ διαγιγνώσκειν, οὐδὲ ὁ διπλοῦς ἔρως ἐνταῦθά πω
ἔστιν· ἀλλ' ἐπειδὰν δέῃ πρὸς τοὺς ἀνθρώπους καταχρῆσθαι
d ῥυθμῷ τε καὶ ἁρμονίᾳ ἢ ποιοῦντα, ὃ δὴ μελοποιίαν καλοῦσιν,
ἢ χρώμενον ὀρθῶς τοῖς πεποιημένοις μέλεσί τε καὶ μέτροις,
ὃ δὴ παιδεία ἐκλήθη, ἐνταῦθα δὴ καὶ χαλεπὸν καὶ ἀγαθοῦ
δημιουργοῦ δεῖ. πάλιν γὰρ ἥκει ὁ αὐτὸς λόγος, ὅτι τοῖς μὲν
5 κοσμίοις τῶν ἀνθρώπων, καὶ ὡς ἂν κοσμιώτεροι γίγνοιντο
οἱ μήπω ὄντες,   δεῖ χαρίζεσθαι καὶ φυλάττειν τὸν τούτων

ἀ-λογία, ἡ: unreasonableness, absurdity
ἁρμόζω: to harmonize, fit together, attune
βαρύς, -εῖα, -ύ: low, heavy; grievous
βραδύς, -εῖα, -ύ: slow
γε-ωργία, ἡ: farming, agriculture
γυμναστικός, -ή, -όν: gymnastic
δια-γιγνώσκω: to distinguish, discern, resolve
δι-πλόος, -η, -ον: twofold, double*
ἐκεῖ: there, in that place*
ἐν-τίθημι: to put in or into, impose; inspire
Ἡράκλειτος, ὁ: Heraclitus
κατα-χράομαι: to apply, use; misuse (+ dat.)
κατά-δηλος, -η, -ον: quite clear, evident*
κυβερνάω: to take the helm; steer, govern
λύρα, ἡ: lyre
μελο-ποιία, ἡ: the making of music or strains
μέλος, -εος, τό: song, tune, strain

μέτρον, τό: meter, measure, verse; length*
μή-πω: not yet
ὁμο-λογία, ἡ: agreement*
ὁμό-νοια, ἡ: oneness of mind, unity, concord
ὀξύς, -εῖα, -ύ: sharp, keen*
παιδεία, ἡ: education, culture, learning
πω: yet, up to this time*
ῥῆμα, τό: word, wording, saying, phrase*
ῥυθμός, ὁ: rhythm, proportion, symmetry*
συμ-φέρω: to agree, gather; be useful*
συμ-φωνία, ἡ: harmony, unison, agreement
συν-ίστημι: to set together, organize, compose
σύς-τασις, -εως, ἡ: construction, composition
τόξον, τό: a bow
ὕστερον: later*
φυλάττω: keep watch, guard, keep in mind*
ὡσ-αύτως: in the same manner, just so*

186e3 συνέστησεν: 3rd sg. aor. συν-ίστημι
  e4 ἰατρική: *art of medicine*; supply τέχνη
      πᾶσα: *the entire*; modifies ἡ ἰατρική
187a1 γυμναστική, μουσική: supply τέχνη
  a2 παντί...τῷ...νοῦν: *to everyone paying even a little attention*; καὶ is adverbial,
  a3 ὅτι κατὰ ταὐτὰ ἔχει τούτοις: *that it is (disposed) in the same way as these*; crasis τὰ αὐτά, "holds in the same things to these," αὐτὰ governs a dat.
  a4 βούλεται λέγειν: *intends to say, means*
      ἐπεὶ...γε: *(I say "intends") because...*; this collocation is often used to explain the preceding statement
      τὸ ἕν... διαφερόμενον...συμφερέσθαι: *the One, itself being at variance, agrees with itself*; αὑτῷ is reflexive ἑαυτῷ reflexive
  a6 ἐστι...ἄλογια...φάναι: *there is much absurdity to say that...*"
  a8 τόδε...ὅτι: *this...(namely) that*
  b1 τοῦ ὀξέος καὶ βαρέος: *high and low*; in apposition to διαφερομένων
  b2 γέγονεν: *(harmony) has come to be*; pf.. γίγνομαι, subject is ἡ ἁρμονία; ὑπό...τέχνης *because of...*; causal
  b3 ἂν εἴη: *would be*; potential opt. εἰμί
  b5 ὁμολογίαν: acc. subj. of εἶναι in b6
  b6 ἀδύνατον: *it is impossible*; add ἐστίν
      ὁμολογοῦν: *agreeing*; neuter pres. pple.

  b7 ἁρμόσαι: aor. inf., ἁρμόζω
  c1 διενηνεγμένων: *things having differed*; pf. pple, δια-φέρω
  c2 ὥσπερ ἐκεῖ...ἐνταῦθα: *just as in that case... so here*; "just as there...here"
  c4 περὶ: *regarding, in regard to*
  c6 οὐδὲν χαλεπὸν: *it is not at all difficult*; supply ἐστίν
  c8 δέῃ...καταχρῆσθαι: *it is necessary that (one) use*; 3rd sg. subj. δεῖ
      πρὸς: *in relation to*
  d1 ἢ ποιοῦντα...ἢ χρώμενον: *either composing...or employing*; both modify the missing acc. subj. of καταχρῆσθαι
      πεποιημένοις: *composed*; pf. pass. pple
  d2 μέλεσι: dat. pl.
  d3 ἐκλήθη: *is called*; aor. pass., καλέω; general truths are often expressed in the aorist (gnomic aorist)
      χαλεπὸν: *it is difficult*; supply ἐστίν
  d4 δεῖ: *there is need of* (+ gen.)
      ὁ αὐτὸς λόγος, ὅτι: *the same argument ...(namely) that*
  d5 τοῖς...κοσμίοις: object of χαρίζεσθαι
      καὶ ὡς...ὄντες: *and in a way that those not yet being (well-ordered) may become more well-ordered*; rel. clause with a potential opt.

ἔρωτα, καὶ οὗτός ἐστιν ὁ καλός, ὁ οὐράνιος, ὁ τῆς Οὐρανίας

e μούσης Ἔρως· ὁ δὲ Πολυμνίας ὁ πάνδημος, ὃν δεῖ εὐλαβούμενον προσφέρειν οἷς ἂν προσφέρῃ, ὅπως ἂν τὴν μὲν ἡδονὴν
αὐτοῦ καρπώσηται, ἀκολασίαν δὲ μηδεμίαν ἐμποιήσῃ, ὥσπερ
ἐν τῇ ἡμετέρᾳ τέχνῃ μέγα ἔργον ταῖς περὶ τὴν ὀψοποιικὴν

5 τέχνην ἐπιθυμίαις καλῶς χρῆσθαι, ὥστ’ ἄνευ νόσου τὴν
ἡδονὴν καρπώσασθαι. καὶ ἐν μουσικῇ δὴ καὶ ἐν ἰατρικῇ
καὶ ἐν τοῖς ἄλλοις πᾶσι καὶ τοῖς ἀνθρωπείοις καὶ τοῖς θείοις,
καθ’ ὅσον παρείκει, φυλακτέον ἑκάτερον τὸν ἔρωτα· ἔνεστον

188 γάρ. ἐπεὶ καὶ ἡ τῶν ὡρῶν τοῦ ἐνιαυτοῦ σύστασις μεστή
ἐστιν ἀμφοτέρων τούτων, καὶ ἐπειδὰν μὲν πρὸς ἄλληλα τοῦ
κοσμίου τύχῃ ἔρωτος ἃ νυνδὴ ἐγὼ ἔλεγον, τά τε θερμὰ καὶ
τὰ ψυχρὰ καὶ ξηρὰ καὶ ὑγρά, καὶ ἁρμονίαν καὶ κρᾶσιν λάβῃ

5 σώφρονα, ἥκει φέροντα εὐετηρίαν τε καὶ ὑγίειαν ἀνθρώποις
καὶ τοῖς ἄλλοις ζῴοις τε καὶ φυτοῖς, καὶ οὐδὲν ἠδίκησεν·
ὅταν δὲ ὁ μετὰ τῆς ὕβρεως Ἔρως ἐγκρατέστερος περὶ τὰς
τοῦ ἐνιαυτοῦ ὥρας γένηται, διέφθειρέν τε πολλὰ καὶ ἠδίκησεν.

b οἵ τε γὰρ λοιμοὶ φιλοῦσι γίγνεσθαι ἐκ τῶν τοιούτων καὶ
ἄλλα ἀνόμοια πολλὰ νοσήματα καὶ τοῖς θηρίοις καὶ τοῖς
φυτοῖς· καὶ γὰρ πάχναι καὶ χάλαζαι καὶ ἐρυσῖβαι ἐκ
πλεονεξίας καὶ ἀκοσμίας περὶ ἄλληλα τῶν τοιούτων γίγνεται

5 ἐρωτικῶν, ὧν ἐπιστήμη περὶ ἄστρων τε φορὰς καὶ ἐνιαυτῶν
ὥρας ἀστρονομία καλεῖται. ἔτι τοίνυν καὶ αἱ θυσίαι πᾶσαι
καὶ οἷς μαντικὴ ἐπιστατεῖ—ταῦτα δ’ ἐστὶν ἡ περὶ θεούς τε

c καὶ ἀνθρώπους πρὸς ἀλλήλους κοινωνία—οὐ περὶ ἄλλο τί
ἐστιν ἢ περὶ Ἔρωτος φυλακήν τε καὶ ἴασιν. πᾶσα γὰρ
ἀσέβεια φιλεῖ γίγνεσθαι ἐὰν μή τις τῷ κοσμίῳ Ἔρωτι

ἀ-δικέω: to be unjust, do wrong, injure*
ἀ-κολασία, ἡ: licentiousness, intemperance
ἀ-κοσμία, ἡ: disorder
ἀνθρώπειος, -α, -ον: human, of a human*
ἀν-όμοιος, -ον: unlike, dissimilar*
ἀ-σέβεια, ἡ: impiety, ungodliness
ἄστρον, τό: a star
ἀστρο-νομία, ἡ: astronomy
δια-φθείρω: to destroy, corrupt, pervert*
ἐγ-κρατής, -ές: powerful, in control
ἑκάτερος, -α, -ον: each of two, either*
ἐν-ειμί: to be in*
ἐνιαυτός, ὁ: year, long period of time*
ἐπι-στατέω: to be set over, oversee
ἐρυσίβη, ἡ: red blight. blight
εὐ-ετηρία, ἡ: a good year, good season
εὐλαβέομαι: to be cautious, be careful, beware
θερμός, -ή, -όν: hot, warm; subst. heat
θηρίον, τό: a wild animal, beast*
ἴασις, -εως, ὁ: healing, cure, remedy
καρπόω: to bear fruit; mid. enjoy, profit*
κοινωνία, ἡ: association, partnership*
κρᾶσις, -εως, ἡ: a mixing, blending
λοιμός, ὁ: a plague, pestilence
μεστός, -ή, -όν: full, filled, filled full (+ gen.)*

μοῦσα, ἡ: muse*
νόσημα, -ατος, τό: a sickness, disease, plague
νόσος, ὁ: sickness, illness, disease*
νυν-δή: just now*
ξηρός, -ά, -όν: dry
Οὐρανία, ἡ: Urania, the heavenly one*
ὀψο-ποιικός, -ή, -όν: of cooking
παρ-είκω: to permit, allow; yield, give way
πάχνη, ἡ: frost
πλεον-εξία, ἡ: greediness, grasping, arrogance
Πολύμνια, ἡ: Polyhymnia
προσ-φέρω: to bring to, apply*
σύσ-τασις, -εως, ἡ: construction, composition
σώφρων, -ον: prudent, moderate, temperate*
ὕβρις, ἡ: outrage, assault, insult, violence*
ὑγίεια, ἡ: soundness, health, wholesomeness
ὑγρός, -ά, -όν: moist, wet, fluid*
φιλέω: to love, befriend; strive to, tend to*
φορά, ἡ: courses, movements, bringing forth
φυλακή, ἡ: a watch, guard, protection
φυλάττω: keep watch, guard, keep in mind*
φυτόν, τό: a plant, tree
χάλαζα, -ης, ἡ: hail, hail shower, hailstorm
ψυχρός, -ά, -όν: cold, chill, frigid*
ὥρα, ἡ: season, time, period of time; youth*

187e1 ὁ δὲ Πολυμνίας: the (Eros) of
Polyhymnia is; supply ἐστίν
e1 εὐλαβούμενον προσφέρειν: (the player)
being cautious apply...; supply a subject
e2 οἷς ἂν προσφέρῃ: to whatever (the
player) applies (it); 3ʳᵈ sg. subj.
e3 καρπώσηται: so that (the listener) enjoy;
aor. subj. in a purpose clause; ὅπως
unlike ἵνα retains an ἄν
e3 ἐμποιήσῃ: (the player) implant; 3ʳᵈ sg.
aor. subj. in the same ὅπως clause; the
subject is the same as for προσφέρῃ
e4 μέγα ἔργον: it is a great task; add ἐστί
e8 καθ᾽ ὅσον: insofar as
e8 φυλακτέον: one must keep watch over;
verbal adj. of φυλάττω, add ἐστίν
ἔνεστον: both are in (all things); 3ʳᵈ dual
188a1 ἐπεὶ καί: for even; causal, not temporal
a2 πρὸς ἄλληλα...κοσμίου: well-ordered
with regard to one another
a3 τύχῃ: (these things) get, hit upon (+ gen);

aor. subj.; subject is τὰ θερμὰ..ὑγρά
ἅ...ἔλεγον: that which...; modifies θερμά
a4 κρᾶσιν...σώφρονα: right mixture
λάβῃ: take on, receive; 3ʳᵈ sg. aor. subj.
λαμβάνω; subject still τὰ θερμὰ..ὑγρά
a5 ἥκει: subject still τὰ θερμὰ..ὑγρά
φέροντα: bringing ; modifies subject
a6 οὐδὲν ἠδίκησεν: they do no harm, do no
wrong; gnomic aorist, inner acc.
a7 ἐγκρατέστερος: more in control; i.e. this
love prevails over the other love; pred.
b1 φιλοῦσι γίγνεσθαι: tend to arise; cf. c3
b4 τοιούτων...ἐρωτικῶν: of such loves
γίγνεται: the subjects are plural in b3
ὧν ἐπιστήμη: knowledge of which...
b7 οἷς...ἐπιστατεῖ: that over which the art
of prophecy is set; supply τέχνη
ταῦτα δ᾽ ἐστίν: these things are; fem.
pl. subj. in b6 is here neuter; same in c2
c1 ἄλλο τί...ἤ: anything other...than
c3 φιλεῖ γίγνεσθαι: tends to arise; cf. b1

χαρίζηται μηδὲ τιμᾷ τε αὐτὸν καὶ πρεσβεύῃ ἐν παντὶ ἔργῳ,
5 ἀλλὰ τὸν ἕτερον, καὶ περὶ γονέας καὶ ζῶντας καὶ τετελευτηκότας καὶ περὶ θεούς· ἃ δὴ προστέτακται τῇ μαντικῇ
ἐπισκοπεῖν τοὺς ἐρῶντας καὶ ἰατρεύειν, καὶ ἔστιν αὖ ἡ
d μαντικὴ φιλίας θεῶν καὶ ἀνθρώπων δημιουργὸς τῷ ἐπίστασθαι τὰ κατὰ ἀνθρώπους ἐρωτικά, ὅσα τείνει πρὸς θέμιν
καὶ εὐσέβειαν.

Οὕτω πολλὴν καὶ μεγάλην, μᾶλλον δὲ πᾶσαν δύναμιν ἔχει
5 συλλήβδην μὲν ὁ πᾶς Ἔρως, ὁ δὲ περὶ τἀγαθὰ μετὰ σωφροσύνης καὶ δικαιοσύνης ἀποτελούμενος καὶ παρ' ἡμῖν καὶ
παρὰ θεοῖς, οὗτος τὴν μεγίστην δύναμιν ἔχει καὶ πᾶσαν ἡμῖν
εὐδαιμονίαν παρασκευάζει καὶ ἀλλήλοις δυναμένους ὁμιλεῖν
καὶ φίλους εἶναι καὶ τοῖς κρείττοσιν ἡμῶν θεοῖς. ἴσως μὲν
e οὖν καὶ ἐγὼ τὸν ἔρωτα ἐπαινῶν πολλὰ παραλείπω, οὐ μέντοι
ἑκών γε. ἀλλ' εἴ τι ἐξέλιπον, σὸν ἔργον, ὦ Ἀριστόφανες,
ἀναπληρῶσαι· ἢ εἴ πως ἄλλως ἐν νῷ ἔχεις ἐγκωμιάζειν τὸν
θεόν, ἐγκωμίαζε, ἐπειδὴ καὶ τῆς λυγγὸς πέπαυσαι.

189 Ἐκδεξάμενον οὖν ἔφη εἰπεῖν τὸν Ἀριστοφάνη ὅτι Καὶ
μάλ' ἐπαύσατο, οὐ μέντοι πρίν γε τὸν πταρμὸν προσενεχθῆναι
αὐτῇ, ὥστε με θαυμάζειν εἰ τὸ κόσμιον τοῦ σώματος ἐπιθυμεῖ τοιούτων ψόφων καὶ γαργαλισμῶν, οἷον καὶ ὁ πταρμός
5 ἐστιν· πάνυ γὰρ εὐθὺς ἐπαύσατο, ἐπειδὴ αὐτῷ τὸν πταρμὸν
προσήνεγκα.

Καὶ τὸν Ἐρυξίμαχον, ὠγαθέ, φάναι, Ἀριστόφανες, ὅρα
τί ποιεῖς. γελωτοποιεῖς μέλλων λέγειν, καὶ φύλακά με τοῦ
b λόγου ἀναγκάζεις γίγνεσθαι τοῦ σεαυτοῦ, ἐάν τι γελοῖον
εἴπῃς, ἐξόν σοι ἐν εἰρήνῃ λέγειν.

Καὶ τὸν Ἀριστοφάνη γελάσαντα εἰπεῖν Εὖ λέγεις, ὦ

ἀνα-πληρόω: to fill up, fill, supply
ἀπο-τελέω: to accomplish, fulfill, realize
γαργαλισμός, ὁ: a tickling
γελάω: to laugh*
γελωτο-ποιέω: to create laughter
γονεύς, -έως, ὁ: a begetter, parent*
δικαιοσύνη, ἡ: justice, righteousness*
εἰρήνη, ἡ: peace*
ἐκ-δέχομαι: to take or receive from; take up
ἐκ-λείπω: to leave out, omit, pass over
ἔξ-εστι: it is allowed, permitted, possible*
ἐπι-σκοπέω: to look at, examine, inspect
ἐπί-σταμαι: to know, know how, understand*
εὐ-δαιμονία, ἡ: happiness, good fortune*
εὐθύς: right away, straight, directly, at once*
εὐ-σέβεια, ἡ: piety, reverence*

θέμις, ἡ: custom, right
ἰατρεύω: to heal, treat medically
κρείττων, -ον: stronger, mightier, better*
λύγξ, λυγγός, ἡ: hiccup, hiccough*
μάλα: very, very much, exceedingly*
ὁμιλέω: to associate, consort, converse with
παρα-λείπω: to pass over, pass by
παρα-σκευάζω: to prepare, get ready*
πρεσβεύω: to revere, venerate, honor
προσ-τάττω: to order, assign, appoint*
προσ-φέρω: to bring to, apply to*
πταρμός, ὁ: a sneeze*
συλλήβδην: collectively, in sum, in general
τείνω: to tend, extend, direct; stretch, spread*
φύλαξ, -κος, ὁ: watcher, guard, sentinel
ψόφος, ὁ: noise, sound

188c4 τιμᾷ...πρεσβεύῃ: *both honor and revere it*; pres. subj., present general
τὸν ἕτερον: *(but they honor and revere) the other (Eros)*; parallel with c4

c5 περὶ...περὶ: *in regard to...in regard to*
καὶ ζῶντας καὶ τετελευτηκότας: *both... and...*; pres. and pf. pples. with γονέας

c6 ἃ δὴ: *that's why...*; "with respect to which very things," acc. of respect
προστέτακται: *it has been assigned to* (+ dat); perf. pass. προσ-τάττω
μαντικῇ: *the art of a seer*; add τέκνη

d1 φιλίας...δημιουργός: *craftsman of friendships between the gods and humans*; acc. respect, "in friendships"
τῷ ἐπίστασθαι: *by understanding*; art. inf. as a dative of means

d2 κατὰ ἀνθρώπους: *among humans*

d4 μᾶλλον δὲ: *or rather*

d5 ὁ πᾶς Ἔρως: *Eros in its entirety*
τἀγαθὰ: crasis τὰ ἀγαθά

d6 ὁ δὲ...ἀποτελούμενος: *but the one (i.e. eros) being realized*; pres. pass. pple.
παρὰ: *among*

d8 δυναμένους: *makes (us) capable*; add ἡμᾶς, as double acc. of παρασκευάζει

d9 τοῖς κρείττοσιν...θεοῖς: dat. governed by φίλους, "friends to"
ἡμῶν: *than us*; gen. of comparison

e1 οὐ μέντοι ἑκών γε: *not willing at any rate*

e2 ἐξέλιπον: 1st sg. aor., ἐκ-λείπω

σὸν ἔργον: *it is your task*; supply ἐστίν

e3 ἐν νῷ ἔχεις: *you have in mind, intend*

e4 τῆς λυγγὸς: *from...*; gen. of separation
πέπαυσαι: 2nd sg. perf. mid., παύω

189a1 ἐκδεξάμενον: *taking up, taking over (the conversation)* with Ἀριστοφάνη
καὶ μάλα: *very much indeed*; in reply to Eryximachus' request

a2 ἐπαύσατο: the subject is ἡ λύγξ
οὐ μέντοι πρίν γε: *but not until, at any rate,...* (+ inf.); usually translated "before" with an inf.
προσενεχθῆναι: *was applied*; aor. pass. inf. from προσ-φέρω, cf. 187e2

a3 ὥστε..θαυμάζειν: *so that...*; result
εἰ: *that...*; "if"
τὸ κόσμιον: *the well-ordered (part)*

a4 τοιούτων...οἷον: *the sort...that*; "the sort...which sort...," correlatives

a6 προσήνεγκα: 1st sg. aor. προσ-φέρω

a7 Ὠγαθέ: *my good man*; crasis ὦ Ἀγαθέ
ὅρα: *see, consider*; imperative ὁράω

a8 φύλακά με: acc. predicate and subject respectively for γίγνεσθαι
τοῦ λόγου...τοῦ σεαυτοῦ: *your own speech*; "the speech...yours!"

b1 ἐάν...εἴπῃς: *if you say*; aor. subj., in a present general condition

b2 ἐξόν: *although it is possible*; pres. pple from ἔξεστι in an accusative absolute

Ἐρυξίμαχε, καί μοι ἔστω ἄρρητα τὰ εἰρημένα. ἀλλὰ μή με
5 φύλαττε, ὡς ἐγὼ φοβοῦμαι περὶ τῶν μελλόντων ῥηθήσεσθαι,
οὔ τι μὴ γελοῖα εἴπω — τοῦτο μὲν γὰρ ἂν κέρδος εἴη καὶ τῆς
ἡμετέρας μούσης ἐπιχώριον — ἀλλὰ μὴ καταγέλαστα.

Βαλών γε, φάναι, ὦ Ἀριστόφανες, οἴει ἐκφεύξεσθαι·
ἀλλὰ πρόσεχε τὸν νοῦν καὶ οὕτως λέγε ὡς δώσων λόγον.
c ἴσως μέντοι, ἂν δόξῃ μοι, ἀφήσω σε.

Καὶ μήν, ὦ Ἐρυξίμαχε, εἰπεῖν τὸν Ἀριστοφάνη, ἄλλῃ
γέ πῃ ἐν νῷ ἔχω λέγειν ἢ ᾗ σύ τε καὶ Παυσανίας εἰπέτην.
ἐμοὶ γὰρ δοκοῦσιν ἄνθρωποι παντάπασι τὴν τοῦ ἔρωτος
5 δύναμιν οὐκ ᾐσθῆσθαι, ἐπεὶ αἰσθανόμενοί γε μέγιστ᾽ ἂν
αὐτοῦ ἱερὰ κατασκευάσαι καὶ βωμούς, καὶ θυσίας ἂν ποιεῖν
μεγίστας, οὐχ ὥσπερ νῦν τούτων οὐδὲν γίγνεται περὶ αὐτόν,
δέον πάντων μάλιστα γίγνεσθαι. ἔστι γὰρ θεῶν φιλαν-
d θρωπότατος, ἐπίκουρός τε ὢν τῶν ἀνθρώπων καὶ ἰατρὸς
τούτων ὧν ἰαθέντων μεγίστη εὐδαιμονία ἂν τῷ ἀνθρωπείῳ
γένει εἴη. ἐγὼ οὖν πειράσομαι ὑμῖν εἰσηγήσασθαι τὴν
δύναμιν αὐτοῦ, ὑμεῖς δὲ τῶν ἄλλων διδάσκαλοι ἔσεσθε.
5 δεῖ δὲ πρῶτον ὑμᾶς μαθεῖν τὴν ἀνθρωπίνην φύσιν καὶ τὰ
παθήματα αὐτῆς. ἡ γὰρ πάλαι ἡμῶν φύσις οὐχ αὑτὴ ἦν
ἥπερ νῦν, ἀλλ᾽ ἀλλοία. πρῶτον μὲν γὰρ τρία ἦν τὰ γένη
τὰ τῶν ἀνθρώπων, οὐχ ὥσπερ νῦν δύο, ἄρρεν καὶ θῆλυ,
e ἀλλὰ καὶ τρίτον προσῆν κοινὸν ὂν ἀμφοτέρων τούτων, οὗ
νῦν ὄνομα λοιπόν, αὐτὸ δὲ ἠφάνισται· ἀνδρόγυνον γὰρ ἓν
τότε μὲν ἦν καὶ εἶδος καὶ ὄνομα ἐξ ἀμφοτέρων κοινὸν τοῦ
τε ἄρρενος καὶ θήλεος, νῦν δὲ οὐκ ἔστιν ἀλλ᾽ ἢ ἐν ὀνείδει
5 ὄνομα κείμενον. ἔπειτα ὅλον ἦν ἑκάστου τοῦ ἀνθρώπου τὸ

αἰσθάνομαι: to perceive, feel, learn, realize*
ἄλλῃ: in another place; in another way*
ἀλλοῖος, -α, -ον: of another kind, different
ἀνδρό-γυνος, ὁ: man-woman, hermaphrodite
ἀνθρώπειος, -α, -ον: human, of a human*
ἀνθρώπινος, -η, -ον: human, of a human*
ἄρ-ρητος, -ον: unmentioned, not to be said
ἀ-φανίζω: make invisible, conceal, destroy*
βάλλω: to throw, pelt, hit, strike*
βωμός, ὁ: altar, platform
διδάσκαλος, ὁ: a teacher
εἰσ-ηγέομαι: to propose, introduce; explain*
ἐκ-φεύγω: to flee away, escape
ἐπί-κουρος, ὁ: assistant, helper, ally
ἐπι-χώριος, -α, -ον: native, customary of
εὐ-δαιμονία, ἡ: happiness, good fortune*
θῆλυς, -εια, -υ: female, feminine*
ἰάομαι: to heal, cure*
ἰατρός, ὁ: physician, doctor*

ἱερά, τά: offerings, sacrifices, victims
κατα-γέλαστος, -ον: ridiculous
κατα-σκευάζω: to prepare, construct, equip*
κεῖμαι: to lie down, be set, be assigned*
κέρδος, -εος, τό: profit, advantage, gain
λοιπός, ὁ: remaining, the rest*
μανθάνω: to learn, understand*
μοῦσα, ἡ: muse*
ὄνειδος, τό: reproach, censure, rebuke*
πάθημα, -ατος, τό: suffering, misfortune*
πάλαι: long ago, formerly, of old*
παντά-πασι: all in all, altogether, absolutely*
πῃ: in some way, in any way, somehow
πρόσ-ειμι: to be present, be in addition
τρεῖς, τρία: three*
τρίτος, -η, -ον: the third*
φιλ-άνθρωπος, -ον: humane, benevolent
φοβέομαι: to fear, be seized with fear, flee*
φυλάττω: keep watch, guard, keep in mind*

189b4 καί μοι: *and so for my sake*; ethical dat.
  ἔστω: *let...be*; 3rd sg. imperative, εἰμί
  τὰ εἰρημένα: *things said*; pf. pass. pple
    from ἐρέω in the neuter plural
  μή...φύλαττε: negative imperative
b5 ὡς φοβοῦμαι...οὔ τι μὴ...ἀλλὰ μὴ: *since
    I fear...not at all lest...but lest*; μὴ (+
    subj.) introduces a clause of fearing
  μελλόντων ῥηθήσεσθαι: μέλλω governs
    a fut. inf., in this case, fut. pass. inf. ἐρέω
b6 εἴπω: 1st sg. aor. subj., fearing clause
  τοῦτο: i.e. saying funny things; subject
b7 καταγέλαστα: add εἴπω from b6
b8 βαλών: *taking a shot (at me)*; aor. pple
  οἴει: *you think*; 2nd sg. pres. mid. οἴομαι
  ἐκφεύξεσθαι: fut. inf.
b9 πρόσεχε τὸν νοῦν: *pay attention!*; imp.
  ὡς δώσων: *so that I...*; ὡς + fut. pple
    (δίδωμι) expressing purpose
c1 ἂν δόξῃ: *if it seems good*; aor. subj. δοκεῖ
  ἀφήσω: *I shall release*; fut. ἀφ-ίημι
c2 ἄλλῃ...πῃ...ᾗ ἧ: *in any other way ...than
    in which (way)*; dat. of manner
c3 ἐν νῷ ἔχω: *I have in mind, intend*
  εἰπέτην: *spoke*; dual form of εἶπον
c5 ᾐσθῆσθαι: *to perceive*; aor. pass. dep. inf.,
    αἰσθάνομαι
  αἰσθανόμενοί γε... ἂν κατασκευάσαι

...ἂν ποιεῖν:: *(if they were) perceiving
it...they would...and they would;* the pple
is a protasis and the infinitives, governed
by ἐμοὶ δοκοῦσιν, are the apodosis in a
counterfactual condition
c6 αὑτοῦ ἱερὰ: *temples for him*
c7 περὶ αὐτόν *regarding him*
c8 δέον: *although it being necessary*; pres.
  pple δεῖ in an acc. abs. (cf. 189b2)
  πάντων μάλιστα: *most of all*; partitive
d1 ὤν: nom. sg. pres. pple. εἰμί
d2 ὧν ἰαθέντων: *which (when) having been
  healed*; gen. abs., aor. pass. pple ἰάομαι
  ἄν...εἴη: potential opt. εἰμί
d3 πειράσομαι: fut. πειράζω
d4 ἔσεσθε: *you will be*; 2nd pl. fut. dep. εἰμί
d5 μαθεῖν: aor. inf. μανθάνω
d6 αὐτὴ: *the same;* crasis ἡ αὐτὴ
d7 ἥπερ νῦν: *what (it is) now, just as now*
e1 προσῆν: 3rd sg. impf., πρόσ-ειμι
  κοινὸν ὄν: *partaking of (+ gen.)*; "being a
  share of", pres. pple. εἰμί
  οὗ: *whose*; gen. sg. relative pronoun
e2 ἠφάνισται: perf. pass. ἀ-φανίζω
e3 εἶδος...ὄνομα: *in...in...*;acc. of respect
e4 ἀλλ' ἤ: *except*; ἄλλο ἤ, "other than"
e5 ὄνομα κείμενον: *as a name assigned...*

εἶδος στρογγύλον, νῶτον καὶ πλευρὰς κύκλῳ ἔχον, χεῖρας
δὲ τέτταρας εἶχε, καὶ σκέλη τὰ ἴσα ταῖς χερσίν, καὶ πρόσωπα
190 δύ᾽ ἐπ᾽ αὐχένι κυκλοτερεῖ, ὅμοια πάντῃ· κεφαλὴν δ᾽ ἐπ᾽
ἀμφοτέροις τοῖς προσώποις ἐναντίοις κειμένοις μίαν, καὶ
ὦτα τέτταρα, καὶ αἰδοῖα δύο, καὶ τἆλλα πάντα ὡς ἀπὸ
τούτων ἄν τις εἰκάσειεν. ἐπορεύετο δὲ καὶ ὀρθὸν ὥσπερ
5 νῦν, ὁποτέρωσε βουληθείη· καὶ ὁπότε ταχὺ ὁρμήσειεν θεῖν,
ὥσπερ οἱ κυβιστῶντες καὶ εἰς ὀρθὸν τὰ σκέλη περιφερό-
μενοι κυβιστῶσι κύκλῳ, ὀκτὼ τότε οὖσι τοῖς μέλεσιν
ἀπερειδόμενοι ταχὺ ἐφέροντο κύκλῳ. ἦν δὲ διὰ ταῦτα τρία
b τὰ γένη καὶ τοιαῦτα, ὅτι τὸ μὲν ἄρρεν ἦν τοῦ ἡλίου τὴν
ἀρχὴν ἔκγονον, τὸ δὲ θῆλυ τῆς γῆς, τὸ δὲ ἀμφοτέρων μετέχον
τῆς σελήνης, ὅτι καὶ ἡ σελήνη ἀμφοτέρων μετέχει· περιφερῆ
δὲ δὴ ἦν καὶ αὐτὰ καὶ ἡ πορεία αὐτῶν διὰ τὸ τοῖς γονεῦσιν
5 ὅμοια εἶναι. ἦν οὖν τὴν ἰσχὺν δεινὰ καὶ τὴν ῥώμην, καὶ
τὰ φρονήματα μεγάλα εἶχον, ἐπεχείρησαν δὲ τοῖς θεοῖς,
καὶ ὃ λέγει Ὅμηρος περὶ Ἐφιάλτου τε καὶ Ὤτου, περὶ
ἐκείνων λέγεται, τὸ εἰς τὸν οὐρανὸν ἀνάβασιν ἐπιχειρεῖν
c ποιεῖν, ὡς ἐπιθησομένων τοῖς θεοῖς. ὁ οὖν Ζεὺς καὶ οἱ
ἄλλοι θεοὶ ἐβουλεύοντο ὅτι χρὴ αὐτοὺς ποιῆσαι, καὶ ἠπό-
ρουν· οὔτε γὰρ ὅπως ἀποκτείναιεν εἶχον καὶ ὥσπερ τοὺς
γίγαντας κεραυνώσαντες τὸ γένος ἀφανίσαιεν—αἱ τιμαὶ
5 γὰρ αὐτοῖς καὶ ἱερὰ τὰ παρὰ τῶν ἀνθρώπων ἠφανίζετο—
οὔτε ὅπως ἐῷεν ἀσελγαίνειν. μόγις δὴ ὁ Ζεὺς ἐννοήσας
λέγει ὅτι "Δοκῶ μοι," ἔφη, "ἔχειν μηχανήν, ὡς ἂν εἶέν
τε ἄνθρωποι καὶ παύσαιντο τῆς ἀκολασίας ἀσθενέστεροι
d γενόμενοι. νῦν μὲν γὰρ αὐτούς, ἔφη, διατεμῶ δίχα ἕκαστον,
καὶ ἅμα μὲν ἀσθενέστεροι ἔσονται, ἅμα δὲ χρησιμώτεροι
ἡμῖν διὰ τὸ πλείους τὸν ἀριθμὸν γεγονέναι· καὶ βαδιοῦνται

αἰδοῖον, τό: the genitals
ἀ-κολασία, ἡ: licentiousness, intemperance
ἀνά-βασις, -εως, ἡ: a going up, ascent
ἀπ-ερείδω: to rest upon, fix upon, settle upon
ἀπο-κτείνω: to kill, slay*
ἀριθμός, ὁ: number, amount, quantity*
ἀσελγαίνω: to behave outrageously
ἀ-σθενής, -ές: without strength, weak, feeble*
αὐχήν, -ενος, ὁ: the neck, throat
ἀ-φανίζω: make invisible, conceal, destroy*
βαδίζω: to walk, to go*
βουλεύω: to deliberate, plan, take counsel*
γίγας, -αντος, ὁ: giant; mighty
γονεύς, -έως, ὁ: a begetter, parent*
δια-τέμνω: to cut through, cut in two, dissever
δίχα: apart, asunder; apart from (+ gen.)*
εἰκάζω: to portray, imagine
ἔκ-γονος, -ον: offspring, a child
ἐν-νοέω: to have in mind, notice, consider*
Ἐφιάλτης, ὁ: Ephialtes
ἥλιος, ὁ: the sun*
θέω: to run, rush*
θῆλυς, -εια, -υ: female, feminine
ἱερά, τά: offerings, sacrifices, victims
ἰσχύς, ὁ: strength, power, force
κεῖμαι: to lie down*
κεραυνόω: to strike with thunderbolts
κυβιστάω: to tumble, to tumble head foremost

κύκλος, ὁ: a circle, round, ring*
κυκλοτερής, -ές: round, circular
μέλος, -εος, τό: limb
μηχανή, ἡ: means, device, contrivance*
μόγις: with difficulty, reluctantly, scarcely
νῶτον, τό: the back
ὀκτώ: eight
ὁποῖος, -α, -ον: what sort or kind*
ὁπότε: when, by what time*
ὁποτέρω-σε: in which (of two) way
ὁρμάω: to set in motion; set out, begin*
οὐρανός, ὁ: sky, heaven
οὖς, ωτός, τό: ear*
πάντη: in every way, by all means, entirely*
περι-φερής, -ές: circular, round, surrounding
περι-φέρω: to carry around, move about
πλευρά, ἡ: a rib, side*
πορεία, ἡ: a journey, way, passage
πρόσ-ωπον, τό: the face, countenance*
ῥώμη, ἡ: bodily strength, might*
σελήνη, ἡ: the moon
σκέλος, -εος, τό: the leg*
στρογγύλος, -η, -ον: round, spherical
τέτταρες, -α: four*
τρεῖς, τρία: three*
φρόνημα, -ατος, τό: mind, thought, purpose
χρήσιμος, -η, -ον: useful, serviceable, apt, fit*
Ὦτος, ὁ: Otus

189e6 τὸ εἶδος: *the shape*; subject of ἦν
  κύκλῳ: *in a circle*; same for 190a7, a8
  ἔχον: *having*; neuter pple.
  εἶχε: 3rd sg. impf. ἔχω
190a1 ἐπ᾽: *over, upon, on top of*; ἐπί
a1 ὅμοια πάντη: *alike in every way*
a2 ἐναντίοις κειμένοις: *facing in opposite
    directions*; "lying opposite," pred. dat.
a3 τἆλλα: *other things*; crasis τὰ ἄλλα
    ὡς...εἰκάσειεν: *as one might imagine*;
    aor. potential opt.
a5 ὁποτέρωσε βουληθείη: *in whichever way
    it wishes*; general clause, aor. dep. opt.
    replaces ἄν + subj. in secondary seq.
    ὁπότε...ὁρμήσειεν: *whenever*; see above
a6 εἰς ὀρθὸν: *upright*
b1 τὴν ἀρχὴν: *in the beginning*; adv. acc.
b2 μετέχον *having a share of* (gen.); pple
b3 ὅτι: *because*
b4 διὰ τὸ...εἶναι: *on account of being*

b5 τὴν ἰσχὺν..τὴν ῥώμην: *in...*; acc. respect
b6 φρονήματα μεγάλα: *haughty thoughts*
    ἐπεχείρησαν: *began to attack*
c1 ὡς ἐπιθησομένων: *in order to rush upon*;
    ὡς + fut. pple expressing purpose
c2 ὅτι: *what*; ὅ τι, "that which"
    ἠπόρουν: 3rd pl. impf. ἀ-πορέω
c3 εἶχον: *did know*; governs ὅπως below
    ὅπως ἀποκτείναιεν...ἀφανίσαιεν
    ...ἐῷεν: *how they were to...*; optatives
    replacing deliberative subjunctives;
    ἐῷεν (ἐάοιεν), 3rd pl. pres. opt., ἐάω
c5 ἠφανίζετο: *would...*; impf. past potential
c7 ὡς ἂν εἶεν: *how they might exist*; opt.
c8 τῆς ἀκολασίας: *from..*; gen. separation
d1 διατεμῶ: fut. διατέμνω
d2 ἔσονται: *they will be*; 3rd pl. fut., εἰμί
d3 τὸν ἀριθμὸν: *in number*; acc. respect
    βαδιοῦνται: 3rd pl. fut. dep., βαδίζω

ὀρθοὶ ἐπὶ δυοῖν σκελοῖν. ἐὰν δ' ἔτι δοκῶσιν ἀσελγαίνειν
5 καὶ μὴ 'θέλωσιν ἡσυχίαν ἄγειν, πάλιν αὖ, ἔφη, τεμῶ δίχα,
ὥστ' ἐφ' ἑνὸς πορεύσονται σκέλους ἀσκωλιάζοντες." ταῦτα
εἰπὼν ἔτεμνε τοὺς ἀνθρώπους δίχα, ὥσπερ οἱ τὰ ὄα τέμ-
e νοντες καὶ μέλλοντες ταριχεύειν, ἢ ὥσπερ οἱ τὰ ᾠὰ ταῖς
θριξίν· ὅντινα δὲ τέμοι, τὸν Ἀπόλλω ἐκέλευεν τό τε
πρόσωπον μεταστρέφειν καὶ τὸ τοῦ αὐχένος ἥμισυ πρὸς
τὴν τομήν, ἵνα θεώμενος τὴν αὑτοῦ τμῆσιν κοσμιώτερος
5 εἴη ὁ ἄνθρωπος, καὶ τἆλλα ἰᾶσθαι ἐκέλευεν. ὁ δὲ τό τε
πρόσωπον μετέστρεφε, καὶ συνέλκων πανταχόθεν τὸ δέρμα
ἐπὶ τὴν γαστέρα νῦν καλουμένην, ὥσπερ τὰ σύσπαστα
βαλλάντια, ἓν στόμα ποιῶν ἀπέδει κατὰ μέσην τὴν γαστέρα,
ὃ δὴ τὸν ὀμφαλὸν καλοῦσι. καὶ τὰς μὲν ἄλλας ῥυτίδας
191 τὰς πολλὰς ἐξελέαινε καὶ τὰ στήθη διήρθρου, ἔχων τι
τοιοῦτον ὄργανον οἷον οἱ σκυτοτόμοι περὶ τὸν καλάποδα
λεαίνοντες τὰς τῶν σκυτῶν ῥυτίδας· ὀλίγας δὲ κατέλιπε,
τὰς περὶ αὐτὴν τὴν γαστέρα καὶ τὸν ὀμφαλόν, μνημεῖον
5 εἶναι τοῦ παλαιοῦ πάθους. ἐπειδὴ οὖν ἡ φύσις δίχα
ἐτμήθη, ποθοῦν ἕκαστον τὸ ἥμισυ τὸ αὑτοῦ συνῄει, καὶ
περιβάλλοντες τὰς χεῖρας καὶ συμπλεκόμενοι ἀλλήλοις,
ἐπιθυμοῦντες συμφῦναι, ἀπέθνησκον ὑπὸ λιμοῦ καὶ τῆς
b ἄλλης ἀργίας διὰ τὸ μηδὲν ἐθέλειν χωρὶς ἀλλήλων ποιεῖν.
καὶ ὁπότε τι ἀποθάνοι τῶν ἡμίσεων, τὸ δὲ λειφθείη, τὸ
λειφθὲν ἄλλο ἐζήτει καὶ συνεπλέκετο, εἴτε γυναικὸς τῆς
ὅλης ἐντύχοι ἡμίσει—ὃ δὴ νῦν γυναῖκα καλοῦμεν—εἴτε
5 ἀνδρός· καὶ οὕτως ἀπώλλυντο. ἐλεήσας δὲ ὁ Ζεὺς ἄλλην
μηχανὴν πορίζεται, καὶ μετατίθησιν αὐτῶν τὰ αἰδοῖα εἰς

αἰδοῖον, τό: the genitals
Ἀπόλλων, ὁ: Apollo
ἀπο-δέω: to tie up, tie off, bind fast, fasten
ἀπ-όλλυμι: to destroy, kill, ruin*
ἀ-ργία, ἡ: idleness, laziness; inactivity
ἀσελγαίνω: to behave outrageously
ἀσκωλιάζω: to hop
αὐχήν, -ένος, ὁ: the neck, throat
βαλλάντιον, τό: a bag, pouch, purse
γαστήρ, -έρος, ὁ: belly, stomach*
δέρμα, -ατος, τό: the skin, hide
δι-αρθρόω: to articulate; divide by joints
δίχα: apart, asunder; apart from (+ gen.)*
εἴτε: whether...or, either...or*
ἐλεέω: to have pity, show mercy*
ἐκ-λεαίνω: to smooth out, polish, grind
ἡσυχία, ἡ: silence, quiet, stillness, rest
θρίξ, τριχός, ὁ: the hair of the head, hair
ἰάομαι: to heal, cure*
καλάπους, ὁ: a last, wooden form (of a shoe)
κατα-λείπω: to leave behind, abandon*
λεαίνω: to smooth, polish, grind
λιμός, ὁ, ἡ: hunger, famine
μέσος, -η, -ον: middle, in the middle of*6
μετα-στρέφω: to turn about, turn round*
μετα-τίθημι: to transpose, change, alter
μηχανή, ἡ: means, device, contrivance*
μνημεῖον, τό: monument, memorial, reminder

ὀμφαλός, ὁ: the navel
ὄον, τό: sorb-apple
ὁπότε: when, by what time*
ὄργανον, τό: instrument, tool, organ*
πάθος, τό: suffering, experience, misfortune
παντα-χόθεν: from all places, on every side
περι-βάλλω: to throw round, enclose; clothe*
ποθέω: to long for, yearn after
πορίζω: to provide, procure, furnish, supply*
πρόσ-ωπον, τό: the face, countenance*
ῥυτίς, -ιδος, ἡ: wrinkle, fold of skin
σκέλος, -εος, τό: the leg*
σκῦτος, τό: a skin, hide, leather
σκυτο-τόμος, ὁ: a leather-cutter, shoemaker
στῆθος, -εος, ὁ: chest, breast, heart
στόμα, -ατος, τό: the mouth*
συν-έλκω: to draw together, draw up
συν-έρχομαι: to come or go together, go with*
συμ-πλέκω: to twist together, entwine*
συμ-φύω: to grow together,
σύ-σπαστος, -ον: closed by drawing together
ταριχεύω: to preserve by drying, cure
τέμνω: to cut, hew, slice, ravage*
τμῆσις, -εως, ὁ: a cutting, a ravaging
τομή, ἡ: stump; end left by cutting
χωρίς: separately; apart from (+ gen.)*
ᾠόν, τό: egg

190d4 δυοῖν σκελοῖν: dual datives
  d5 ᾽θέλωσιν: ἐθέλωσιν, 3ʳᵈ pl. pres. subj.
    ἡσυχίαν ἄγειν: *keep quiet, keep still*
    τεμῶ: fut. τέμνω
  d6 σκέλους: σκέλεος, gen. with ἑνός, "one"
  e1 ταῖς θριξίν: *with hair*; dat. of means
  e2 ὅντινα δὲ τέμοι: *whomever he cut*; aor.
    opt. τέμνω, replacing ἄν + subj. in
    secondary sequence, general rel. clause
  e4 αὑτοῦ: *his own*; ἑαυτοῦ
  e5 εἴη: opt. εἰμί in purpose, secondary seq.
  e7 νῦν καλουμένην: *(what is)* now called
  e8 ἀπέδει: *tied off*; impf., ἀπο-δέω
    κατὰ: *over* (+ acc.)
191a1 διήρθρου: 3ʳᵈ sg. impf., δι-αρθρόω
  a2 τοιοῦτον...οἷον: *the sort...that*
  a3 κατέλιπε: 3ʳᵈ sg. aor. καταλείπω
  a6 ἐτμήθη: *was cut*; 3ʳᵈ sg. aor. pass., τέμνω

ποθοῦν: *longing*; neuter nom. pres. pple;
  τὸ αὑτοῦ is its object
  τὸ αὑτοῦ: *it's own (half)*; ἑαυτοῦ
  συνῄει: 3ʳᵈ sg. impf., συν-έρχομαι
a8 συμφῦναι: inf. συμφύω
  τῆς ἄλλης ἀργίας: *other (forms)*
  of laziness
b1 τὸ...ἐθέλειν: *being willing*; articular inf.
b2 ὁπότε τι ἀποθάνοι: *whenever...*; opt.
  replacing generalizing ἄν + subj.
  τὸ δὲ: *and the other half*; supply ἥμισυ
  λειφθείη: 3ʳᵈ sg. aor. pass. opt., λείπω
  τὸ λειφθέν: *the one left behind*; aor.
  pass. pple, λείπω
b4 ἐντύχοι: *encountered*; ἐντυγχάνω, aor.
  opt.; τὸ λειφθέν is the subject
b5 ἀπώλλυντο: impf. pass., ἀπ-όλλυμι
  ἐλεήσας: *struck by pity*; ingressive aor.

τὸ πρόσθεν—τέως γὰρ καὶ ταῦτα ἐκτὸς εἶχον, καὶ ἐγέννων
καὶ ἔτικτον οὐκ εἰς ἀλλήλους ἀλλ' εἰς γῆν, ὥσπερ οἱ τέτ-
c τιγες—μετέθηκέ τε οὖν οὕτω αὐτῶν εἰς τὸ πρόσθεν καὶ
διὰ τούτων τὴν γένεσιν ἐν ἀλλήλοις ἐποίησεν, διὰ τοῦ
ἄρρενος ἐν τῷ θήλει, τῶνδε ἕνεκα, ἵνα ἐν τῇ συμπλοκῇ
5 ἅμα μὲν εἰ ἀνὴρ γυναικὶ ἐντύχοι, γεννῷεν καὶ γίγνοιτο τὸ
γένος, ἅμα δ' εἰ καὶ ἄρρην ἄρρενι, πλησμονὴ γοῦν γίγνοιτο
τῆς συνουσίας καὶ διαπαύοιντο καὶ ἐπὶ τὰ ἔργα τρέποιντο
καὶ τοῦ ἄλλου βίου ἐπιμελοῖντο. ἔστι δὴ οὖν ἐκ τόσου
d ὁ ἔρως ἔμφυτος ἀλλήλων τοῖς ἀνθρώποις καὶ τῆς ἀρχαίας
φύσεως συναγωγεὺς καὶ ἐπιχειρῶν ποιῆσαι ἓν ἐκ δυοῖν καὶ
ἰάσασθαι τὴν φύσιν τὴν ἀνθρωπίνην. ἕκαστος οὖν ἡμῶν
ἐστιν ἀνθρώπου σύμβολον, ἅτε τετμημένος ὥσπερ αἱ ψῆτται,
5 ἐξ ἑνὸς δύο· ζητεῖ δὴ ἀεὶ τὸ αὑτοῦ ἕκαστος σύμβολον.
ὅσοι μὲν οὖν τῶν ἀνδρῶν τοῦ κοινοῦ τμῆμά εἰσιν, ὃ δὴ
τότε ἀνδρόγυνον ἐκαλεῖτο, φιλογύναικές τέ εἰσι καὶ οἱ
πολλοὶ τῶν μοιχῶν ἐκ τούτου τοῦ γένους γεγόνασιν, καὶ
e ὅσαι αὖ γυναῖκες φίλανδροί τε καὶ μοιχεύτριαι ἐκ τούτου
τοῦ γένους γίγνονται. ὅσαι δὲ τῶν γυναικῶν γυναικὸς
τμῆμά εἰσιν, οὐ πάνυ αὗται τοῖς ἀνδράσι τὸν νοῦν προσέχουσιν, ἀλλὰ μᾶλλον πρὸς τὰς γυναῖκας τετραμμέναι
5 εἰσί, καὶ αἱ ἑταιρίστριαι ἐκ τούτου τοῦ γένους γίγνονται.
ὅσοι δὲ ἄρρενος τμῆμά εἰσι, τὰ ἄρρενα διώκουσι, καὶ τέως
μὲν ἂν παῖδες ὦσιν, ἅτε τεμάχια ὄντα τοῦ ἄρρενος, φιλοῦσι
τοὺς ἄνδρας καὶ χαίρουσι συγκατακείμενοι καὶ συμπεπλε-
192 γμένοι τοῖς ἀνδράσι, καί εἰσιν οὗτοι βέλτιστοι τῶν παίδων
καὶ μειρακίων, ἅτε ἀνδρειότατοι ὄντες φύσει. φασὶ δὲ δή
τινες αὐτοὺς ἀναισχύντους εἶναι, ψευδόμενοι· οὐ γὰρ ὑπ'

ἀν-αίσχυντος, -ον: shameless, impudent
ἀνδρό-γυνος, ὁ: man-woman, hermaphrodite
ἀνθρώπινος, -η, -ον: human, of a human*
ἀρχαῖος, -α, -ον: ancient, old, original*
βέλτιστος, -η, -ον: best*
γῆ, ἡ: earth*
γοῦν: γε οὖν, at least, at any rate, any way*
δια-παύομαι: to rest, pause, stop for a time
ἐκτός: outside; out of, far from (+ gen.) *
ἔμ-φυτος, -ον: implanted, innate, natural
ἐπι-μελέομαι: to take care of (gen.) for (dat.)
ἑταιρίστρια, ἡ: lesbian
θῆλυς, -εια, -υ: female, feminine*
ἰάομαι: to heal, cure*
μειράκιον, τό: adolescent, boy, young man*
μετα-τίθημι: to transpose, change, alter
μοιχεύτρια, ἡ: an adulteress
μοιχός: an adulterer, debaucher

πλησμονή, ἡ: fullness, satiety, satisfaction*
πρόσθεν: before*
συγ-κατάκειμαι: to lie down together
σύμβολον, τό: token
συμ-πλέκω: to twist together, entwine*
συμ-πλοκή, ἡ: an intertwining, complication
συν-αγωγεύς, ὁ: a convener, bringer together
τεμάχιον, τό: slice (of fish or meat)
τέμνω: to cut, hew, slice, ravage*
τέττιξ, τέττιγος, ὁ: a cicada
τέως: till then, up to that time; as long as
τμῆμα, -ατος, τό: the part cut-off, a section*
τόσος, -η, -ον: so much, so many, so great
φιλέω: to love, befriend; strive to, tend to*
φίλ-ανδρος, -ον: fond of men
φιλο-γύνης, -ου, ὁ: one fond of women
ψεύδομαι: to lie, cheat, beguile*
ψῆττα, ἡ: a flat fish (e.g. plaice, sole, turbot)

191b7 εἰς τὸ πρόσθεν: *to the front*
   εἶχον: 3ʳᵈ pl. impf. ἔχω
   ἐγέννων: ἐγέννᾱον, 3ʳᵈ pl. impf.
   εἰς γῆν: i.e. semen falls onto the ground
c1 μετέθηκέ: 3ʳᵈ sg. aor., μετα-τίθημι
   αὐτῶν...πρόσθεν: *to their front*
c4 τῶνδε...ἵνα: *for the sake of the following,*
   (namely) so that
c5 γεννῷεν...γίγνοιτο: *they might beget*
   and the race be continued; γεννάοιεν,
   both are opt. in a purpose clause in
   secondary seq.; note change of subject
c6 εἰ καί: *even if*
   ἄρρην ἄρρενι: supply ἐντύχοι from c5
   πλησμονὴ γίγνοιτο: *satisfaction... might*
   come about; in same ἵνα clause
c8 τοῦ ἄλλου βίου: *the rest of (their) life*
   ἐκ τόσου: *from long ago*
d2 ἔμφυτος...συναγωγεύς...ἐπιχειρῶν:
   innate...a convener...one who tries...;
   predicate nominatives following ἐστίν
   δυοῖν: dual genitive

d4 ἅτε τετμημένος: *since (each) has been*
   cut; ἅτε + pple is causal; pf. pass. τέμνω
d6 ὅσοι...τῶν ἀνδρῶν: *as many men*
d8 γεγόνασιν: *have been born*; pf. act.
e2 ὅσαι...τῶν γυναικῶν: *as many women*
e3 οὐ πάνυ: *not at all*; lit. "not quite"
   τὸν νοῦν προσέχουσιν: *pay attention*
e4 τετραμμέναι εἰσί: *have turned*; pf.
   mid/pass. + εἰμί is a periphrastic form of
   the pf. mid/pass., τρέπω
e7 ὦσιν: *are*; 3ʳᵈ pl. pres. subjunctive, εἰμί
   ἅτε ὄντα: *since they are*; ἅτε + pple is
   causal; ὄντα, modifying παῖδες, is
   attracted into the acc. sg. by τεμάχια
e8 συμπεπλεγμένοι: *being entwined*
   together; pf. pass. pple. συμ-πλέκω
192a2 ἅτε...ὄντες: see e7 above
   φύσει: *by nature*; dat. of respect
a3 ψευδόμενοι: *but they speak falsely*;
   concessive pple. " though lying"

ἅτε + pple asserts a cause from the speaker's point of view, while ὡς + pple asserts the same from a character's point of view (alleged cause). ὡς + fut. pple expresses purpose.

ἅτε ἀνδρειότατοι ὄντες   *since/inasmuch as/seeing that they are very brave*
ὡς ἀνδρειότατοι ὄντες   *since/on the grounds that/as if they are very brave*
ὡς ἀνδρειότατοι ἐσόμενοι   *to/in order to /in order that they be very brave*

5 ἀναισχυντίας τοῦτο δρῶσιν ἀλλ᾽ ὑπὸ θάρρους καὶ ἀνδρείας
καὶ ἀρρενωπίας, τὸ ὅμοιον αὑτοῖς ἀσπαζόμενοι. μέγα δὲ
τεκμήριον· καὶ γὰρ τελεωθέντες μόνοι ἀποβαίνουσιν εἰς
τὰ πολιτικὰ ἄνδρες οἱ τοιοῦτοι. ἐπειδὰν δὲ ἀνδρωθῶσι,
b παιδεραστοῦσι καὶ πρὸς γάμους καὶ παιδοποιίας οὐ προσέχουσι τὸν νοῦν φύσει, ἀλλ᾽ ὑπὸ τοῦ νόμου ἀναγκάζονται·
ἀλλ᾽ ἐξαρκεῖ αὐτοῖς μετ᾽ ἀλλήλων καταζῆν ἀγάμοις. πάντως
μὲν οὖν ὁ τοιοῦτος παιδεραστής τε καὶ φιλεραστὴς γίγνεται,
5 ἀεὶ τὸ συγγενὲς ἀσπαζόμενος. ὅταν μὲν οὖν καὶ αὐτῷ
ἐκείνῳ ἐντύχῃ τῷ αὑτοῦ ἡμίσει καὶ ὁ παιδεραστὴς καὶ
ἄλλος πᾶς, τότε καὶ θαυμαστὰ ἐκπλήττονται φιλίᾳ τε καὶ
c οἰκειότητι καὶ ἔρωτι, οὐκ ἐθέλοντες ὡς ἔπος εἰπεῖν χωρί-
ζεσθαι ἀλλήλων οὐδὲ σμικρὸν χρόνον. καὶ οἱ διατελοῦντες
μετ᾽ ἀλλήλων διὰ βίου οὗτοί εἰσιν, οἳ οὐδ᾽ ἂν ἔχοιεν εἰπεῖν
ὅτι βούλονται σφίσι παρ᾽ ἀλλήλων γίγνεσθαι.   οὐδενὶ
5 γὰρ ἂν δόξειεν τοῦτ᾽ εἶναι ἡ τῶν ἀφροδισίων συνουσία, ὡς
ἄρα τούτου ἕνεκα ἕτερος ἑτέρῳ χαίρει συνὼν οὕτως ἐπὶ
μεγάλης σπουδῆς· ἀλλ᾽ ἄλλο τι βουλομένη ἑκατέρου ἡ ψυχὴ
d δήλη ἐστίν, ὃ οὐ δύναται εἰπεῖν, ἀλλὰ μαντεύεται ὃ βούλεται, καὶ αἰνίττεται. καὶ εἰ αὐτοῖς ἐν τῷ αὐτῷ κατακει-
μένοις ἐπιστὰς ὁ Ἥφαιστος, ἔχων τὰ ὄργανα, ἔροιτο· "Τί
ἔσθ᾽ ὃ βούλεσθε, ὦ ἄνθρωποι, ὑμῖν παρ᾽ ἀλλήλων γενέ-
5 σθαι;" καὶ εἰ ἀποροῦντας αὐτοὺς πάλιν ἔροιτο· "ἆρά γε
τοῦδε ἐπιθυμεῖτε, ἐν τῷ αὐτῷ γενέσθαι ὅτι μάλιστα ἀλλήλοις, ὥστε καὶ νύκτα καὶ ἡμέραν μὴ ἀπολείπεσθαι ἀλλήλων; εἰ γὰρ τούτου ἐπιθυμεῖτε, θέλω ὑμᾶς συντῆξαι καὶ
e συμφυσῆσαι εἰς τὸ αὐτό, ὥστε δύ᾽ ὄντας ἕνα γεγονέναι
καὶ ἕως τ᾽ ἂν ζῆτε, ὡς ἕνα ὄντα, κοινῇ ἀμφοτέρους ζῆν,
καὶ ἐπειδὰν ἀποθάνητε, ἐκεῖ αὖ ἐν Ἅιδου ἀντὶ δυοῖν ἕνα
εἶναι κοινῇ τεθνεῶτε· ἀλλ᾽ ὁρᾶτε εἰ τούτου ἐρᾶτε καὶ

ἄ-γαμος, -ον: unmarried, unwedded, single
Ἅδης, ὁ: Hades
αἰνίττομαι: to speak in riddles, disguise
ἀν-αισχυντία, ἡ: shamelessness
ἀνδρεία, ἡ: manliness, bravery, courage*
ἀνδρόω: to rear to manhood; *pass.* reach
   manhood
ἀπο-βαίνω: to turn out, result; disembark*
ἀπο-λείπω: to leave behind, abandon*
ἀρρεν-ωπία, ἡ: a manly look, manliness
ἀσπάζομαι: to welcome, embrace*
ἀφροδίσια, τά: sex, sexual pleasure
γάμος, ὁ: a wedding, wedding-feast*
δια-τελέω: to live, continue, persevere
δράω: to do*
ἑκάτερος, -α, -ον: each of two, either*
ἐκεῖ: there, in that place*
ἐκ-πλήγνυμι: to strike, amaze, astound*
ἐξ-αρκέω: to be enough, suffice, be sufficient*
ἔπος, -εος, τό: a word*

θάρρος, -εος, ὁ: confidence, boldness
κατα-ζάω: to live on, go through life
κοινῇ: in common, together, in concert*
μαντεύομαι: to prophesy, divine
νύξ, νυκτός, ἡ: a night*
οἰκειότης, ἡ: intimacy, affection, relationship
ὄργανον, τό: instrument, tool, organ*
παιδ-εραστέω: to be a lover of young men
παιδ-εραστής, οῦ, ὁ: a lover of young men
παιδο-ποιΐα, ἡ: procreation of children
πάντως: altogether, by all means, certainly*
πολιτικός, -ή, -όν: of the city, political, civic*
συγ-γενής, -ές: own kind, kin; natural, inborn
συμ-φυσάω: to blow together (w/ bellow),
   fuse
συν-τήκω: to melt together; fuse, join*
τεκμήριον, τό: sign, indication, proof*
τελεόω: to mature, complete, finish
φιλ-εραστής, -οῦ, ὁ: fond of having a lover
χωρίζω: to separate, sever, divide

192a6 μέγα...τεκμήριον: *there is substantial
   evidence*; supply ἐστίν
   καὶ γὰρ: *for in fact*
   τελεωθέντες: *having matured*; aor.
   pass. dep. pple, τελεόω
   ἀποβαίνουσιν...ἄνδρες: *turn out (to
   be real) men*; supply εἶναι
   εἰς τὰ πολιτικά: *with regard to...*
a7 ἀνδρωθῶσι: 3rd pl. aor. pass. subj.
b2 προσέχουσι...νοῦν: *direct their attention*
   φύσει *by nature*
b3 ἐξαρκεῖ: *it is enough*; impersonal
b6 πάντως μὲν οὖν: *and so in any case*
   ἐντύχῃ: 3rd sg. aor. subj., ἐν-τυγχάνω
   τῷ αὑτοῦ ἡμίσει: *his own half*; ἑαυτοῦ
b7 θαυμαστά: *amazingly*; adverbial acc.
   φιλίᾳ...ἔρωτι: *by...*; dat. of cause
c1 ὡς ἔπος εἰπεῖν: *so to speak, as it were*
c2 ἀλλήλων: *from...*; gen. of separation
   σμικρὸν χρόνον: *for...*; acc. of duration
c3 ἂν ἔχοιεν: *would be able*; ἔχω + inf.
c4 ὅτι: *what*; ὅ τι, relative pronoun
   σφίσι γίγνεσθαι: *to get, to possess, to
   gain*; dat. of possession, from σφεῖς
c5 ὡς ἄρα: *as if*
c6 ἕτερος ἑτέρῳ: *each one...the other*
   χαίρει συνὼν: *enjoys associating with*;
   pres. pple, σύν-ειμι (+ dat.)

οὕτως ἐπὶ μεγάλης σπουδῆς: *with
   such great enthusiasm*
c7 ἄλλο τι βουλομένη...δήλη ἐστίν: *clearly
   wants something else; "is clear wanting"*
   ἑκατέρου: *from each one*; gen. source
d1 μαντεύεται...αἰνίττεται: *divines and
   disguises what it wants*
d2 εἰ...ἔροιτο: *if he should ask*; future less
   vivid, the protasis is restated at d5, and
   the apodosis appears after ἴσμεν ὅτι, e5
   ἐν τῷ αὐτῷ: *in the same spot, together*
d3 ἐπιστάς: *standing over* (+ dat.); aor. pple
   Τί ἐσθ᾽: *what is it that?*; Τί ἔστι
d4 ὑμῖν...γενέσθαι: *to get, to possess, to
   gain*; dat. of possession
d6 τοῦδε... ἐν τῷ αὐτῷ γενέσθαι: *the
   following, namely to be in the same place*
   ὅτι μάλιστα: *as much as possible*
d7 νύκτα...ἡμέραν: *for...*; acc. of duration
d8 θέλω: *I am willing*; ἐθέλω (+ inf.)
   συντῆξαι, συμφυσῆσαι: aor. inf.
e1 εἰς τὸ αὐτό: *to the same (place)*
   ὥστε...γεγονέναι...ζῆν: pf. and pres. inf.
e2 ὡς ἕνα ὄντα: *since (you) are one*
e3 ἀποθάνητε: aor. subj. ἀποθνήσκω
   ἐν Ἅιδου: *In Hades' (realm)*; underworld
   ἀντὶ δυοῖν: *instead of two*; dual form
e4 τεθνεῶτε: *being dead*; dual pf. pple

5 ἐξαρκεῖ ὑμῖν ἂν τούτου τύχητε·" ταῦτ᾽ ἀκούσας ἴσμεν ὅτι
οὐδ᾽ ἂν εἷς ἐξαρνηθείη οὐδ᾽ ἄλλο τι ἂν φανείη βουλόμενος,
ἀλλ᾽ ἀτεχνῶς οἴοιτ᾽ ἂν ἀκηκοέναι τοῦτο ὃ πάλαι ἄρα ἐπε-
θύμει, συνελθὼν καὶ συντακεὶς τῷ ἐρωμένῳ ἐκ δυοῖν εἷς
γενέσθαι. τοῦτο γάρ ἐστι τὸ αἴτιον, ὅτι ἡ ἀρχαία φύσις
10 ἡμῶν ἦν αὕτη καὶ ἦμεν ὅλοι· τοῦ ὅλου οὖν τῇ ἐπιθυμίᾳ
193 καὶ διώξει ἔρως ὄνομα. καὶ πρὸ τοῦ, ὥσπερ λέγω, ἓν
ἦμεν, νυνὶ δὲ διὰ τὴν ἀδικίαν διῳκίσθημεν ὑπὸ τοῦ θεοῦ,
καθάπερ Ἀρκάδες ὑπὸ Λακεδαιμονίων· φόβος οὖν ἔστιν,
ἐὰν μὴ κόσμιοι ὦμεν πρὸς τοὺς θεούς, ὅπως μὴ καὶ αὖθις
5 διασχισθησόμεθα, καὶ περίιμεν ἔχοντες ὥσπερ οἱ ἐν ταῖς
στήλαις καταγραφὴν ἐκτετυπωμένοι, διαπεπρισμένοι κατὰ
τὰς ῥῖνας, γεγονότες ὥσπερ λίσπαι. ἀλλὰ τούτων ἕνεκα
πάντ᾽ ἄνδρα χρὴ ἅπαντα παρακελεύεσθαι εὐσεβεῖν περὶ
b θεούς, ἵνα τὰ μὲν ἐκφύγωμεν, τῶν δὲ τύχωμεν, ὡς ὁ Ἔρως
ἡμῖν ἡγεμὼν καὶ στρατηγός. ᾧ μηδεὶς ἐναντία πραττέτω—
πράττει δ᾽ ἐναντία ὅστις θεοῖς ἀπεχθάνεται—φίλοι γὰρ
γενόμενοι καὶ διαλλαγέντες τῷ θεῷ ἐξευρήσομέν τε καὶ
5 ἐντευξόμεθα τοῖς παιδικοῖς τοῖς ἡμετέροις αὐτῶν, ὃ τῶν νῦν
ὀλίγοι ποιοῦσι. καὶ μή μοι ὑπολάβῃ Ἐρυξίμαχος, κωμῳδῶν
τὸν λόγον, ὡς Παυσανίαν καὶ Ἀγάθωνα λέγω—ἴσως μὲν
c γὰρ καὶ οὗτοι τούτων τυγχάνουσιν ὄντες καί εἰσιν ἀμφότεροι
τὴν φύσιν ἄρρενες—λέγω δὲ οὖν ἔγωγε καθ᾽ ἁπάντων καὶ
ἀνδρῶν καὶ γυναικῶν, ὅτι οὕτως ἂν ἡμῶν τὸ γένος εὔδαιμον
γένοιτο, εἰ ἐκτελέσαιμεν τὸν ἔρωτα καὶ τῶν παιδικῶν τῶν
5 αὑτοῦ ἕκαστος τύχοι εἰς τὴν ἀρχαίαν ἀπελθὼν φύσιν. εἰ
δὲ τοῦτο ἄριστον, ἀναγκαῖον καὶ τῶν νῦν παρόντων τὸ
τούτου ἐγγυτάτω ἄριστον εἶναι· τοῦτο δ᾽ ἐστὶ παιδικῶν τυχεῖν

ἀ-δικία, ἡ: wrong-doing, injustice*
αἴτιον, τό: cause, reason
ἅπας, ἅπασα, ἅπαν: every, quite all*
ἀπ-εχθάνομαι: to be hated, incur hatred
ἀρχαῖος, -α, -ον: ancient, old, original*
Ἀρκάδες, οἱ: Arcadians
ἀ-τεχνῶς: simply, really, entirely*
αὖθις: back again, later*
δι-αλλάττω: to reconcile, give in an exchange
δια-πρίω: to saw through, saw asunder
δια-σχίζω: to cleave or rend asunder
δι-οικίζω: to make to live apart
δίωξις, -εως, ἡ: pursuit, chase; prosecution
ἐγγύς: near, close to (+ gen.); adv. nearby*
ἐκ-τελέω: to accomplish, fulfill
ἐκ-τυπόω: to model or work in relief
ἐκ-φεύγω: to flee away, escape
ἐξ-αρκέω: to be enough, suffice, be sufficient*
ἐξ-αρνέομαι: to deny utterly, deny

ἐξ-ευρίσκω: to find out, discover
εὐ-σεβέω: to live or act piously and religiously
ἡγεμών, -όνος, ὁ: leader, commander, guide*
κατα-γραφή, ἡ: low-relief
κωμῳδέω: to treat as funny, to satirize
Λακεδαιμόνιος, -α, -ον: Lacedaemonian
λίσπαι, αἱ: half-dice (split among two friends)
νυνί: now; as it is*
πάλαι: long ago, formerly, of old*
παρα-κελεύομαι: to order, urge, encourage*
περι-έρχομαι: to go around, come round
ῥίς, ῥινός, ἡ: the nose
στήλη, ἡ: a block of stone, slab, gravestone
στρατηγός, ὁ: a general, leader*
συν-έρχομαι: to come or go together, go with*
συν-τήκω: to melt together; fuse, join with*
ὑπο-λαμβάνω: to take up, reply; suppose*
φόβος, ὁ: fear, terror, panic*

192e5 ἄν...τύχητε: *if you get (gen.)*; ἐάν +
aor. subj., τυγχάνω ; see 193b1, c5
ταῦτ᾽ ἀκούσας: modifies εἷς below
ἴσμεν: 1st pl. οἶδα

e6 ἄν...ἐξαρνηθείη: aor. dep., potential opt.,
ἐξ-αρνέομαι
ἄν φανείη βουλόμενος: *would clearly
want*; aor. dep., potential opt. "would
show himself wanting"

e7 οἴοιτ᾽ ἄν: *one would think;* οἴοιτο, opt.
ἀκηκοέναι: pf. act. inf., ἀκούω

e8 συνελθών: aor. pple, συν-έρχομαι
συντακείς: aor. pass. pple, συν-τήκω
ἐκ δυοῖν: dual gen.

e9 τοῦτο...ὅτι: *this...(namely) that*

e10 ἦμεν: *we were*; impf. εἰμί
ἐπιθυμίᾳ καὶ διώξει: both dat. poss.
τοῦ ὅλου is objective gen.; add ἐστίν

193a1 πρὸ τοῦ: *before this (time)*

a2 διῳκίσθημεν: aor. pass., δι-οικίζω

a3 καθάπερ...: *just as the Arcadians*

a4 φόβος..ὅπως μὴ: *a fear...that we will*;
mixed effort (ὅπως + fut.) and fearing
(μή + subj.) clause following φόβος
ὦμεν: *we are*; 1st pl. subj. εἰμί

a5 διασχισθησόμεθα: fut. pass. διασχίζω
περίιμεν: 1st pl. fut. περι-έρχομαι (ι-)
ἔχοντες: *being (disposed)*; ἔχω + adv.

a6 καταγραφὴν: *in low-relief*; adverbial acc.
ἐκτετυπωμένοι: pf. pass. pple
κατὰ τὰς ῥῖνας: *down through the noses*

a7 γεγονότες: *having become*; pf. pple.

a8 πάντ᾽ ἄνδρα: subj. of παρακελεύσθαι,
supply "people" as the dative object
ἅπαντα: *(to do) all things pious*; perhaps
inner acc. object of εὐσεβεῖν

b1 τὰ μὲν...τῶν δὲ: *some things...others*
τύχωμεν: *get, attain*; see 192e5 above
ὡς: *since...(is)*; add pres. pple. ὤν

b2 ᾧ...ἐναντία: *opposing whom*; "things
opposite to whom"
πραττέτω: *let...*; 3rd sg. imperative

b4 διαλλαγέντες: aor. dep., δι-αλλάττω

b5 ἐξευρήσομέν: 1st pl. fut. ἐξ-ευρίσκω
ἐντευξόμεθα: fut. dep. ἐν-τυγχάνω
ἡμετέροις αὐτῶν: *our very own*

b6 μὴ...ὑπολάβῃ: *let...reply*; prohibitive
subj. 3rd sg. aor. ὑπολαμβάνω

b7 ὡς...λέγω: *as if I am talking about*

c1 τούτων: *among these*; partitive gen.
ὄντες *happen to be*; τυγχάνω + pple.

c2 τὴν φύσιν: *by nature*; acc. of respect

c3 ἄν...γένοιτο, εἰ ἐκτελέσαιμεν...τύχοι:
would, if...should; future less vivid

c6 παρόντων: *of the things now at hand*

c7 ἐγγυτάτω: *closest*; treat adv. as an adj

κατὰ νοῦν αὐτῷ πεφυκότων· οὗ δὴ τὸν αἴτιον θεὸν ὑμνοῦντες
d δικαίως ἂν ὑμνοῖμεν ἔρωτα, ὃς ἔν τε τῷ παρόντι ἡμᾶς
πλεῖστα ὀνίνησιν εἰς τὸ οἰκεῖον ἄγων, καὶ εἰς τὸ ἔπειτα
ἐλπίδας μεγίστας παρέχεται, ἡμῶν παρεχομένων πρὸς θεοὺς
εὐσέβειαν, καταστήσας ἡμᾶς εἰς τὴν ἀρχαίαν φύσιν καὶ
5 ἰασάμενος μακαρίους καὶ εὐδαίμονας ποιῆσαι.

Οὗτος, ἔφη, ὦ Ἐρυξίμαχε, ὁ ἐμὸς λόγος ἐστὶ περὶ
Ἔρωτος, ἀλλοῖος ἢ ὁ σός. ὥσπερ οὖν ἐδεήθην σου, μὴ
κωμῳδήσῃς αὐτόν, ἵνα καὶ τῶν λοιπῶν ἀκούσωμεν τί ἕκαστος
e ἐρεῖ, μᾶλλον δὲ τί ἑκάτερος· Ἀγάθων γὰρ καὶ Σωκράτης
λοιποί.

Ἀλλὰ πείσομαί σοι, ἔφη φάναι τὸν Ἐρυξίμαχον· καὶ
γάρ μοι ὁ λόγος ἡδέως ἐρρήθη. καὶ εἰ μὴ συνῄδη Σω-
5 κράτει τε καὶ Ἀγάθωνι δεινοῖς οὖσι περὶ τὰ ἐρωτικά, πάνυ
ἂν ἐφοβούμην μὴ ἀπορήσωσι λόγων διὰ τὸ πολλὰ καὶ
παντοδαπὰ εἰρῆσθαι· νῦν δὲ ὅμως θαρρῶ.

194 Τὸν οὖν Σωκράτη εἰπεῖν καλῶς γὰρ αὐτὸς ἠγώνισαι,
ὦ Ἐρυξίμαχε· εἰ δὲ γένοιο οὗ νῦν ἐγώ εἰμι, μᾶλλον δὲ
ἴσως οὗ ἔσομαι ἐπειδὰν καὶ Ἀγάθων εἴπῃ εὖ, καὶ μάλ᾽ ἂν
φοβοῖο καὶ ἐν παντὶ εἴης ὥσπερ ἐγὼ νῦν.

5 Φαρμάττειν βούλει με, ὦ Σώκρατες, εἰπεῖν τὸν Ἀγάθωνα,
ἵνα θορυβηθῶ διὰ τὸ οἴεσθαι τὸ θέατρον προσδοκίαν μεγάλην
ἔχειν ὡς εὖ ἐροῦντος ἐμοῦ.

Ἐπιλήσμων μεντἂν εἴην, ὦ Ἀγάθων, εἰπεῖν τὸν Σω-
b κράτη, εἰ ἰδὼν τὴν σὴν ἀνδρείαν καὶ μεγαλοφροσύνην
ἀναβαίνοντος ἐπὶ τὸν ὀκρίβαντα μετὰ τῶν ὑποκριτῶν, καὶ
βλέψαντος ἐναντία τοσούτῳ θεάτρῳ, μέλλοντος ἐπιδείξεσθαι
σαυτοῦ λόγους, καὶ οὐδ᾽ ὁπωστιοῦν ἐκπλαγέντος, νῦν
5 οἰηθείην σε θορυβήσεσθαι ἕνεκα ἡμῶν ὀλίγων ἀνθρώπων.

ἀγωνίζομαι: to contend, compete, fight*
ἀλλοῖος, -α, -ον: of another kind, different
ἀνα-βαίνω: to go up, climb, mount*
ἀνδρεία, ἡ: manliness, bravery, courage*
ἀρχαῖος, -α, -ον: ancient, old, original*
ἑκάτερος, -α, -ον: each of two, either*
ἐκ-πλήγνυμι: to strike with fear, amaze, astound, to drive out of one senses*
ἐλπίς, -ίδος, ἡ: hope, expectation*
ἐπι-δείκνυμι: to show forth, display, point out*
ἐπι-λήσμων, -ον: forgetful
εὐ-σέβεια, ἡ: piety, reverence*
ἡδέως: sweetly, pleasantly, gladly*
θαρρέω: to be confident, bold; take courage*
θέατρον, τό: theater; the spectators, audience*
θορυβέω: to throw into confusion, make an uproar; raise a shout; applaud*
ἰάομαι: to heal, cure*
καθ-ίστημι: to establish, put into a state, make become; fall into a state, become*

κωμῳδέω: to treat…as funny, to satirize
λοιπός, ὁ: remaining, the rest*
μακάριος, -α, -ον: blessed, happy*
μάλα: very, very much, exceedingly*
μεγαλο-φροσύνη, ἡ: magnanimity, greatness of mind, self-confidence; pride
οἰκεῖος, -α, -ον: one's own; belonging to one, private, subst. relatives*
ὀκρίβας, -αντος, ὁ: platform on the stage
ὀνίνημι: to benefit, profit, help, assist
ὁπωσ-τι-οῦν: in any way whatsoever
παντο-δαπός, -ή, -όν: of every sort, varied*
πλεῖστος, -η, -ον: most, very many, greatest*
προσ-δοκία, ἡ: expectation
σύν-οιδα: to be conscious, cognizant of, know*
ὑμνέω: to sing, laud, praise in song; recite*
ὑπο-κριτής, οῦ, ὁ: an actor, player; interpreter
φαρμάττω: to bewitch
φοβέομαι: to fear, be seized with fear, flee*

193c8 κατὰ νοῦν αὐτῷ: in accordance with one's own character

c8 πεφυκότων: being naturally; pf. pple
οὗ…θεόν: the god responsible for this "for which;" gen. modifies αἴτιον

d1 ἔν…τῷ παρόντι: at the present (time); pres. pple of πάρ-ειμι

d2 πλεῖστα: very greatly; adverbial acc.
εἰς τὸ οἰκεῖον ἄγων: leading (us) to our own; or "…to what belongs to us"
εἰς τὸ ἔπειτα: for the future; "thereafter"

d4 ἐλπίδας…ποιῆσαι: expectations…that (he) make (us); aor. inf. with double acc.
καταστήσας: setting…back; aor. pple

d7 ἐδεήθην: I asked; aor. pass. dep. δέομαι

d8 μὴ κωμῳδήσῃς: don't…; μὴ + aor. subj. is, as often, a prohibitive subjunctive
τῶν λοιπῶν: from the remaining (speakers); gen. of source with ἀκούω

e1 μᾶλλον δὲ: but rather

e2 λοιποί: pred. adj., add εἰσίν

e3 πείσομαι: fut. πείθομαι

e4 ἐρρήθη: was said; 3rd sg. aor. dep., ἐρέω
συνῄδη…ἂν ἐφοβούμην: if I did not know…I would; counterfactual; past, σύν-οιδα

e6 μὴ ἀπορήσωσι: lest…; aor. subj.

ἀπορέω (+ gen.), clause of fearing
τό…εἰρῆσθαι: pf. pass. articular inf. ἐρέω

194a1 ἠγώνισαι: 2nd sg. pf. mid., ἀγωνίζω

a2 γένοιο…φοβοῖο: you should…would; fut. less vivid; opt. γένοι(σ)ο, φοβοῖ(σ)ο;
οὗ: where; same in a3
ἔσομαι: 1st sg. fut. εἰμί
εἴπῃ: 3rd sg. aor. subj. λέγω

a4 ἐν παντὶ εἴης: you would be in complete despair; an idiom "in everything"

a5 βούλει: you wish; βούλε(σ)αι 2nd sg.

a6 θορυβηθῶ: I be thrown into confusion; aor. pass. subjunctive, purpose clause
τὸ θέατρον…ἔχειν: that spectators have

a7 ὡς…ἐμοῦ: on the grounds that I will speak; ὡς + pple expresses alleged cause

a8 μεντἄν: however; μέντοι ἄν

b1 ἰδών: nom. sg. pple. ὁράω
σὴν…ἀναβαίνοντος…ἐκπλαγέντος: of yours…;series of gen. sg. pples modify σην, a possessive which is implicitly gen.

b4 ἐκπλαγέντος: astounded; aor. pass.

b5 εἰ…οἰηθείην: if I should think; aor. dep. opt., οἴομαι, protasis in a fut. less vivid
θορυβήσεσθαι: will be thrown into confusion; fut. inf. in indirect discourse

Τί δέ, ὦ Σώκρατες; τὸν Ἀγάθωνα φάναι, οὐ δήπου με οὕτω θεάτρου μεστὸν ἡγῇ ὥστε καὶ ἀγνοεῖν ὅτι νοῦν ἔχοντι ὀλίγοι ἔμφρονες πολλῶν ἀφρόνων φοβερώτεροι;

c Οὐ μεντἂν καλῶς ποιοίην, φάναι, ὦ Ἀγάθων, περὶ σοῦ τι ἐγὼ ἄγροικον δοξάζων· ἀλλ᾽ εὖ οἶδα ὅτι εἴ τισιν ἐντύχοις οὓς ἡγοῖο σοφούς, μᾶλλον ἂν αὐτῶν φροντίζοις ἢ τῶν πολλῶν. ἀλλὰ μὴ οὐχ οὗτοι ἡμεῖς ὦμεν—ἡμεῖς μὲν γὰρ
5 καὶ ἐκεῖ παρῆμεν καὶ ἦμεν τῶν πολλῶν—εἰ δὲ ἄλλοις ἐντύχοις σοφοῖς, τάχ᾽ ἂν αἰσχύνοιο αὐτούς, εἴ τι ἴσως οἴοιο αἰσχρὸν ὂν ποιεῖν· ἢ πῶς λέγεις;

Ἀληθῆ λέγεις, φάναι.

Τοὺς δὲ πολλοὺς οὐκ ἂν αἰσχύνοιο εἴ τι οἴοιο αἰσχρὸν ποιεῖν;

d Καὶ τὸν Φαῖδρον ἔφη ὑπολαβόντα εἰπεῖν ὦ φίλε Ἀγάθων, ἐὰν ἀποκρίνῃ Σωκράτει, οὐδὲν ἔτι διοίσει αὐτῷ ὁπῃοῦν τῶν ἐνθάδε ὁτιοῦν γίγνεσθαι, ἐὰν μόνον ἔχῃ ὅτῳ διαλέγηται, ἄλλως τε καὶ καλῷ. ἐγὼ δὲ ἡδέως μὲν ἀκούω
5 Σωκράτους διαλεγομένου, ἀναγκαῖον δέ μοι ἐπιμεληθῆναι τοῦ ἐγκωμίου τῷ Ἔρωτι καὶ ἀποδέξασθαι παρ᾽ ἑνὸς ἑκάστου ὑμῶν τὸν λόγον· ἀποδοὺς οὖν ἑκάτερος τῷ θεῷ οὕτως ἤδη διαλεγέσθω.

e Ἀλλὰ καλῶς λέγεις, ὦ Φαῖδρε, φάναι τὸν Ἀγάθωνα, καὶ οὐδέν με κωλύει λέγειν· Σωκράτει γὰρ καὶ αὖθις ἔσται πολλάκις διαλέγεσθαι.

Ἐγὼ δὲ δὴ βούλομαι πρῶτον μὲν εἰπεῖν ὡς χρή με εἰπεῖν,
5 ἔπειτα εἰπεῖν. δοκοῦσι γάρ μοι πάντες οἱ πρόσθεν εἰρηκότες οὐ τὸν θεὸν ἐγκωμιάζειν ἀλλὰ τοὺς ἀνθρώπους εὐδαιμονίζειν τῶν ἀγαθῶν ὧν ὁ θεὸς αὐτοῖς αἴτιος· ὁποῖος δέ τις αὐτὸς ὢν
195 ταῦτα ἐδωρήσατο, οὐδεὶς εἴρηκεν. εἷς δὲ τρόπος ὀρθὸς παντὸς ἐπαίνου περὶ παντός, λόγῳ διελθεῖν οἷος οἵων αἴτιος ὢν

ἀ-γνοέω: to be ignorant of, not know*
ἄγρ-οικος, -ον: rustic, unsophisticated, crude
ἀπο-δέχομαι: to accept, receive
ἀπο-δίδωμι: to give back, give duly, render*
ἀπο-κρίνομαι: to answer, reply*
αὖθις: back again, later*
ἄ-φρων, -ον: senseless, foolish, silly
διέρχομαι: go through, pass; relate, explain*
δοξάζω: to opine, think, suppose, imagine*
δωρέω: to give, present, offer
ἐγ-κώμιον, τό: eulogy, speech of praise*
ἑκάτερος, -α, -ον: each of two, either*
ἐκεῖ: there, in that place*
ἔμ-φρων, -ον: sensible, shrewd, intelligent

ἐπι-μελέομαι: to take care of (gen.) for (dat.)
εὐ-δαιμονίζω: to call (acc.) happy for (gen.)
ἡδέως: sweetly, pleasantly, gladly*
θέατρον, τό: theater; the spectators, audience*
κωλύω: to hinder, prevent, check
μεστός, -ή, -όν: full, filled, filled full*
ὀπη-οῦν: by any way at all, in any way at all*
ὁποῖος, -α, -ον: what sort or kind*
πρόσθεν: before*
τάχα: perhaps, possibly; quickly
ὑπο-λαμβάνω: to take up, reply; suppose*
φοβερός, -ά, -όν: formidable, frightening
φροντίζω: to worry, give heed to (+ gen.)

194b6 τί δέ: *What?*

οὐ δήπου: *surely you don't*; "you do not, I suppose," anticipating a negative response

b7 ἡγῇ: *you believe*; ἡγέε(σ)αι, 2nd sg. pres.
οὕτω θεάτρου μεστόν: *so obsessed with the audience*; pred. adj., add εἶναι
νοῦν ἔχοντι: *to (anyone) having sense*; dat. of reference

b8 ἀφρόνων: *than...*; gen. of comparison
μεντἄν: μέντοι ἄν

c1 ποιοίην: *I would do*; 1st sg. potential opt.; an alternative form of ποιοῖμι

c2 τι...ἄγροικον: *something crude, something unsophisticated*

c3 εἰ...ἐντύχοις...ἄν φροντίζοις: *if should, would*; fut. less vivid ἐν-τυγχάνω
ἡγοῖο: *you believe (to be)*; ἡγοῖ(σ)ο, 2nd sg. pres. opt.

c4 μὴ οὐχ...ὦμεν: *perhaps we are not*; "(I suspect that) we are not"; μή + subj. in main verb suggest a doubtful assertion

c5 παρῆμεν...ἦμεν: impf. παρεῖμι, εἰμί

c6 ἄν αἰσχύνοιο, εἰ...οἴοιο: *if you should, you would*; fut. less vivid, 2nd sg. opt., αἰσχύνοι(σ)ο, οἴοι(σ)ο; same for c9-10

c7 αἰσχρὸν ὄν: *being shameful*; neuter pple εἰμί modifies the indefinite pronoun τι
πῶς λέγεις: *Is that what you mean?*

d2 ἀποκρίνῃ: 2nd sg. pres. mid. subj.
οὐδέν...διοίσει αὐτῷ: *it will make no difference any longer to him*; οὐδέν is an internal acc. with the fut., δια-φέρω

d3 ὁπηοῦν...γίγνεσθαι: *that any at all of the things here come about in any way at all*; ὁτιοῦν is the accusative subject
ἔχῃ: *he has*; 3rd sg. pres. subj.
ὅτῳ: *(someone) with whom*; ὅ-τινι, the acc. antecedent is missing; supply τινα

d4 ἄλλως τε καί: *especially, in particular*

d5 ἀναγκαῖον: *(it is) necessary*; add ἐστίν
ἐπιμεληθῆναι: *to take care*; aor. dep. inf.

d6 ἀποδέξασθαι: *to exact*; aor. inf.

d7 ἀποδούς: nom. aor. pple, ἀπο-δίδωμι
οὕτως ἤδη: *thus then*; i.e. only then

d8 διαλεγέσθω: *let...*; 3rd sg. mid. imp.

e2 λέγειν: *from speaking*; inf. following a verb of hindering
ἔσται: *there will be (a time)*; 3rd sg. fut.

e4 ὡς...εἰπεῖν: *how I ought to speak*

e5 οἱ...εἰρηκότες: *speakers*; "those having spoken," pf. pple, ἐρέω

e7 ὧν: *for which*; governed by αἴτιος
ὁποῖος...ἐδωρήσατο: *being of what sort he himself gave these things*; ὧν is nom. sg. εἰμί
εἴρηκεν: 3rd sg. pf. ἐρέω

e7 εἷς δὲ τρόπος: *there is one...*; add ἐστίν

195a2 διελθεῖν: aor. inf. δι-έρχομαι in apposition to εἷς τρόπος
οἷος...τυγχάνει: *(being) of what sort he happens to be responsible for what sort of things*; there are two interrogatives here, add a second pple. ὧν after οἷος

τυγχάνει περὶ οὗ ἂν ὁ λόγος ᾖ. οὕτω δὴ τὸν Ἔρωτα καὶ
ἡμᾶς δίκαιον ἐπαινέσαι πρῶτον αὐτὸν οἷός ἐστιν, ἔπειτα
5 τὰς δόσεις. φημὶ οὖν ἐγὼ πάντων θεῶν εὐδαιμόνων ὄντων
ἔρωτα, εἰ θέμις καὶ ἀνεμέσητον εἰπεῖν, εὐδαιμονέστατον
εἶναι αὐτῶν, κάλλιστον ὄντα καὶ ἄριστον. ἔστι δὲ κάλλιστος
ὢν τοιόσδε. πρῶτον μὲν νεώτατος θεῶν, ὦ Φαῖδρε. μέγα
b δὲ τεκμήριον τῷ λόγῳ αὐτὸς παρέχεται, φεύγων φυγῇ τὸ
γῆρας, ταχὺ ὂν δῆλον ὅτι· θᾶττον γοῦν τοῦ δέοντος ἡμῖν
προσέρχεται. ὃ δὴ πέφυκεν Ἔρως μισεῖν καὶ οὐδ᾽ ἐντὸς
πολλοῦ πλησιάζειν. μετὰ δὲ νέων ἀεὶ σύνεστί τε καὶ ἔστιν·
5 ὁ γὰρ παλαιὸς λόγος εὖ ἔχει, ὡς ὅμοιον ὁμοίῳ ἀεὶ πελάζει.
ἐγὼ δὲ Φαίδρῳ πολλὰ ἄλλα ὁμολογῶν τοῦτο οὐχ ὁμολογῶ,
ὡς Ἔρως Κρόνου καὶ Ἰαπετοῦ ἀρχαιότερός ἐστιν, ἀλλά
c φημι νεώτατον αὐτὸν εἶναι θεῶν καὶ ἀεὶ νέον, τὰ δὲ παλαιὰ
πράγματα περὶ θεούς, ἃ Ἡσίοδος καὶ Παρμενίδης λέγουσιν,
Ἀνάγκῃ καὶ οὐκ Ἔρωτι γεγονέναι, εἰ ἐκεῖνοι ἀληθῆ ἔλεγον·
οὐ γὰρ ἂν ἐκτομαὶ οὐδὲ δεσμοὶ ἀλλήλων ἐγίγνοντο καὶ ἄλλα
5 πολλὰ καὶ βίαια, εἰ Ἔρως ἐν αὐτοῖς ἦν, ἀλλὰ φιλία καὶ
εἰρήνη, ὥσπερ νῦν, ἐξ οὗ Ἔρως τῶν θεῶν βασιλεύει. νέος
μὲν οὖν ἐστι, πρὸς δὲ τῷ νέῳ ἁπαλός· ποιητοῦ δ᾽ ἔστιν
d ἐνδεὴς οἷος ἦν Ὅμηρος πρὸς τὸ ἐπιδεῖξαι θεοῦ ἁπαλότητα.
Ὅμηρος γὰρ Ἄτην θεόν τέ φησιν εἶναι καὶ ἁπαλήν—τοὺς
γοῦν πόδας αὐτῆς ἁπαλοὺς εἶναι—λέγων

τῆς μένθ᾽ ἁπαλοὶ πόδες· οὐ γὰρ ἐπ᾽ οὔδεος
5 πίλναται, ἀλλ᾽ ἄρα ἥ γε κατ᾽ ἀνδρῶν κράατα βαίνει.

καλῶ οὖν δοκεῖ μοι τεκμηρίῳ τὴν ἁπαλότητα ἀποφαίνειν,
ὅτι οὐκ ἐπὶ σκληροῦ βαίνει, ἀλλ᾽ ἐπὶ μαλθακοῦ. τῷ αὐτῷ

Ἀνάγκη, ἡ: Necessity, Force, Constraint
ἀ-νεμέσητος, -ον: without blame or offence
ἀπαλότης, -ητος, ὁ: softness, tenderness
ἀπο-φαίνω: to show, make clear; perform*
ἀρχαῖος, -α, -ον: ancient, old, original*
Ἄτη, ἡ: Ate, Bewilderment, Ruin
βαίνω: to walk, step, go*
βασιλεύω: to rule, be king, reign*
βίαιος, -α, -ον: forcible, violent
γῆρας, τό: old age
γοῦν: γε οὖν, at least, at any rate, any way*
δεσμός, ὁ: binding, bond, fetter
δόσις, -εως, ἡ: a gift
εἰρήνη, ἡ: peace*
ἐκ-τομή, ἡ: a piece cut out, segment; castration
ἐντός: within, inside*
ἐπι-δείκνυμι: to show forth, display, point out*
Ἡσίοδος, ὁ: Hesiod*

θάττων, -ον: quicker, swifter
θέμις, ἡ: custom, right; law, ordinance
Ἰαπετός, ὁ: Iapetos
κράς, κρατός, ἡ: the head*
Κρόνος, ὁ: Cronus
μαλθακός, -ή, -όν: soft, gentle, mild; weak
μισέω: to hate, despise*
οὖδας, -εος, τό: the ground, earth
Παρμενίδης, ὁ: Parmenides
πελάζω: to approach, come near
πιλνάω: to bring near, approach
πλησιάζω: to approach; associate with (+dat.)
πούς, ποδός, ὁ: a foot*
σκληρός, -ά, -όν: hard, harsh, severe*
τεκμήριον, τό: sign, indication, proof*
τοιόσδε, -άδε, -όνδε: such, the following*
φεύγω: to flee, escape; defend in court*
φυγή, ἡ: flight, escape, exile*

195a3 ἦ: *is*; 3ʳᵈ sg. pres. subj., εἰμί
   τὸν Ἔρωτα: *in respect to Eros*; acc. of
   respect, antecedent of αὐτὸν below
a4 δίκαιον: *(it is) just*; add ἐστίν
   ἐπαινέσαι: aor. inf. ἐπαινέω
   αὐτὸν οἷός ἐστιν: *what sort he is*; "him
   (i.e. Eros) what sort he is,"
a6 θέμις καὶ ἀνεμέσητον: *it is right and
   without offence*; add ἐστίν
b2 δῆλον ὅτι: *clearly*; lit. "(it is) clear that"
   θᾶττον: comparative adverb
   τοῦ δέοντος: *than it ought*; "gen. of
   comparison, pres pple, δεῖ
b3 ὃ δή: *which very thing*; i.e. old age
   πέφυκεν...μισεῖν: *by its nature hates*; "is
   disposed by nature to hate," pf. of φύω
   with a pres. sense
   ἐντός πολλοῦ: *within a mile*, "within
   much (distance)"
b4 ἔστιν: *is (young)*; supply νέος
b5 εὖ ἔχει: *holds up well*; ἔχω + adv.
   ὡς: *(namely) that*; same in b7
b7 Κρόνου, Ἰαπετοῦ: gen. of comparison
c2 περὶ θεούς: *regarding the gods*
c3 Ἀνάγκῃ καὶ οὐκ Ἔρωτι: *because of...*,

   at the hands of...; dat. of cause
c4 ἂν...ἐγίγνοντο, εἰ...ἦν: *would have
   occurred...if...were*; pres. contrafactual,
   εἰ + impf., ἂν + impf.
c5 φιλία καὶ εἰρήνη: add ἂν ἐγίγνοντο to
   preserve the parallelism from above
c6 ἐξ οὗ: *since*; "from which (time)"
   βασιλεύει: *has been ruling*; pres. with pf.
   progressive sense
c7 πρὸς τῷ νέῳ: *in addition to his youth*
d1 οἷος...Ὅμηρος: *such as Homer was*
   πρὸς τὸ ἐπιδεῖξαι: *with regard to
   presenting*; articular inf. ἐπι-δείκνυμι
d4 τῆς: *her*; genitive of the pronoun ἥ
   μένθ': *truly*; μέν τοι
   ἐπ': *upon* (+ gen.); ἐπί
d5 ἥ: *she*; personal pronoun, cf. d4
   κατ'...κράατα: *over the heads*; κατά,
   neuter pl. of κράς
d6 καλῷ τεκμηρίῳ: *with beautiful proof*;
   dat. of means
d7 ὅτι: *(namely) that*; following τεκμηρίῳ
   ἐπί: *upon* (+ gen.)
   τῷ αὐτῷ...τεκμηρίῳ: *the same proof*;
   obj. of fut. χρησόμεθα in e1

e δὴ καὶ ἡμεῖς χρησόμεθα τεκμηρίῳ περὶ ἔρωτα ὅτι ἁπαλός.
οὐ γὰρ ἐπὶ γῆς βαίνει οὐδ' ἐπὶ κρανίων, ἅ ἐστιν οὐ πάνυ
μαλακά, ἀλλ' ἐν τοῖς μαλακωτάτοις τῶν ὄντων καὶ βαίνει
καὶ οἰκεῖ. ἐν γὰρ ἤθεσι καὶ ψυχαῖς θεῶν καὶ ἀνθρώπων τὴν
5 οἴκησιν ἵδρυται, καὶ οὐκ αὖ ἐξῆς ἐν πάσαις ταῖς ψυχαῖς, ἀλλ'
ᾗτινι ἂν σκληρὸν ἦθος ἐχούσῃ ἐντύχῃ, ἀπέρχεται, ᾗ δ' ἂν
μαλακόν, οἰκίζεται. ἁπτόμενον οὖν ἀεὶ καὶ ποσὶν καὶ πάντῃ
ἐν μαλακωτάτοις τῶν μαλακωτάτων, ἁπαλώτατον ἀνάγκη
196 εἶναι.   νεώτατος μὲν δή ἐστι καὶ ἁπαλώτατος, πρὸς δὲ
τούτοις ὑγρὸς τὸ εἶδος. οὐ γὰρ ἂν οἷός τ' ἦν πάντῃ περι-
πτύσσεσθαι οὐδὲ διὰ πάσης ψυχῆς καὶ εἰσιὼν τὸ πρῶτον
λανθάνειν καὶ ἐξιών, εἰ σκληρὸς ἦν. συμμέτρου δὲ καὶ
5 ὑγρᾶς ἰδέας μέγα τεκμήριον ἡ εὐσχημοσύνη, ὃ δὴ δια-
φερόντως ἐκ πάντων ὁμολογουμένως Ἔρως ἔχει· ἀσχημοσύνη
γὰρ καὶ Ἔρωτι πρὸς ἀλλήλους ἀεὶ πόλεμος.   χρόας δὲ
κάλλος ἡ κατ' ἄνθη δίαιτα τοῦ θεοῦ σημαίνει· ἀνανθεῖ γὰρ
b καὶ ἀπηνθηκότι καὶ σώματι καὶ ψυχῇ καὶ ἄλλῳ ὁτῳοῦν οὐκ
ἐνίζει Ἔρως, οὗ δ' ἂν εὐανθής τε καὶ εὐώδης τόπος ᾖ,
ἐνταῦθα δὲ καὶ ἵζει καὶ μένει.

Περὶ μὲν οὖν κάλλους τοῦ θεοῦ καὶ ταῦτα ἱκανὰ καὶ ἔτι
5 πολλὰ λείπεται, περὶ δὲ ἀρετῆς Ἔρωτος μετὰ ταῦτα λεκτέον,
τὸ μὲν μέγιστον ὅτι Ἔρως οὔτ' ἀδικεῖ οὔτ' ἀδικεῖται οὔτε
ὑπὸ θεοῦ οὔτε θεόν, οὔτε ὑπ' ἀνθρώπου οὔτε ἄνθρωπον. οὔτε
γὰρ αὐτὸς βίᾳ πάσχει, εἴ τι πάσχει—βία γὰρ Ἔρωτος οὐχ
c ἅπτεται· οὔτε ποιῶν ποιεῖ—πᾶς γὰρ ἑκὼν Ἔρωτι πᾶν
ὑπηρετεῖ, ἃ δ' ἂν ἑκὼν ἑκόντι ὁμολογήσῃ, φασὶν ""οἱ πόλεως
βασιλῆς νόμοι"" δίκαια εἶναι. πρὸς δὲ τῇ δικαιοσύνῃ σωφροσύνης πλείστης μετέχει. εἶναι γὰρ ὁμολογεῖται σωφροσύνη
5 τὸ κρατεῖν ἡδονῶν καὶ ἐπιθυμιῶν, Ἔρωτος δὲ μηδεμίαν

ἀ-δικέω: to be unjust, do wrong, injure*
ἀν-ανθής, -ές: without bloom, past its bloom
ἄνθος, -εος, τό: a blossom, flower, bloom*
ἀπ-ανθέω: to lose one's bloom, fade, wither
ἀ-σχημοσύνη, ἡ: gracelessness, awkwardness
βαίνω: to walk, step, go*
βασιλεύς, ὁ: a king, chief*
βία, βιας, ἡ: violence; strength, force, might*
γῆ, ἡ: earth*
δίαιτα, ἡ: a way of living, living
δια-φερόντως: differently from; especially*
δικαιοσύνη, ἡ: justice, righteousness*
ἐν-ίζω: to sit in or on, settle in or on (+ dat.)
ἐξ-έρχομαι: to go out, come out*
ἑξῆς: one after another, in order, in succession
εὐ-ανθής, -ές: blooming; flowered, bright
εὐ-σχημοσύνη, ἡ: gracefulness, decorum
εὐ-ώδης, -ες: sweet-smelling, fragrant
ἦθος, -εος, τό: custom; disposition, character*
ἰδέα, ἡ: look, appearance, form, kind*
ἱδρύω: to make sit down; set up, establish
ἵζω: to sit, sit down, settle; make sit, place

κρανίον, τό: skull, head
κρατέω: to overcome (gen.); rule; be strong*
λανθάνω: to escape notice of, act unnoticed*
λεκτέος, -α, -ον: to be said, speakable
μαλακός, -α, -ον: soft, gentle; weak, feeble*
μένω: to stay, remain*
οἰκέω: to inhabit, dwell, live*
οἴκησις, ἡ: dwelling, house, household
οἰκίζω: to settle, colonize, make a home
πάντη: in every way, by all means, entirely*
περι-πτύσσω: to enfold, enwrap, fold around
πλεῖστος, -η, -ον: most, very many, greatest*
πόλεμος, ὁ: battle, fight, war*
πούς, ποδός, ὁ: a foot*
σημαίνω: to show, indicate, point out
σκληρός, -ά, -όν: hard, harsh, severe*
σύμ-μετρος, -ον: proportionate, balanced
τεκμήριον, τό: sign, indication, proof*
τόπος, ὁ: a place, region*
ὑγρός, -ά, -όν: moist, wet, fluid*
ὑπ-ηρετέω: to serve, minister (+ dat.)*
χροά, ἡ: color (of skin), complexion; skin

195e1 ὅτι ἁπαλός: supply ἐστίν

e3 τῶν ὄντων: *of the things that exist*; pres.
pple, εἰμί

e5 ἵδρυται: *has set up*; pf. mid., ἱδρύω

e6 ᾗτινι...ἐντύχῃ: *any (soul) he meets...*;
dat. object of ἐντύχῃ, 3rd sg. aor. subj.
ᾗ...μαλακόν: *whichever (soul) he meets*;
add ἦθος ἐχούσῃ ἐντύχῃ for parallelism

e7 ποσὶν: *with his feet*; dat. pl. πούς

e8 ἀνάγκη: *it is a necessity*; supply ἐστίν

196a1 πρὸς δὲ τούτοις: *in addition to these*

a2 τὸ εἶδος: *in form*; acc. of respect
ἂν οἷός τ᾽ ἦν...εἰ...ἦν: *would be able,
if...were*; contrafactual (impf. ἄν impf.)

a3 εἰσιών, ἐξιών: nom. sg., pres. pples
εἰσ-έρχομαι and ἐξ-έρχομαι (stem ι-)
ἐκ πάντων ὁμολογουμένως: *by the
consensus of all*; gen. of source or agent

a6 ἔχει: *possesses, has*; not ἔχω + adv.
ἀσχημοσύνη...Ἔρωτι: dat. of possession

a7 πρὸς ἀλλήλους: *against one another*
χρόας δὲ κάλλος: *beauty of the skin*

a8 ἡ κατ᾽ ἄνθη δίαιτα: *living among
flowers*; κατὰ ἄνθεα

b1 ἀπηνθηκότι: *fading*; pf. ἀπ-ανθέω

ἄλλῳ ὁτῳοῦν: *whatever else*

b2 οὗ δ᾽ ἂν...ᾖ: *but wherever...is*; 3rd sg.
pres. subj., εἰμί

b5 λείπεται: *remain*; "is left," pres. pass.
λεκτέον: *I must speak*; "(it is) to be said
(by me)"; verbal adj. expressing obligation

b6 τὸ μὲν μέγιστον ὅτι: *the greatest (is) that*

b7 ὑπὸ θεοῦ...ἀνθρώπου: add ἀδικεῖται
θεόν...ἄνθρωπον: ad ἀδικεῖ from above

b8 βία: *with violence*; dat. of means

c1 ποιῶν ποιεῖ: *and, if doing (something),
Eros does not do it (with violence)*; add
τι and βία for the parallelism with b7-
8, the pres. pple is conditional
Ἔρωτι...ὑπηρετεῖ: *everyone performs
every service for Eros willingly*; πᾶν is
an inner acc.

c2 ἃ δ᾽...ὁμολογήσῃ: *and what one willingly
agrees with one willingly*; the entire
clause is subject of εἶναι
οἱ...νόμοι: *the royal laws of the city*;
subject of φασὶν

c3 πρός: *in addition to* (+ dat.)

c5 τὸ κρατεῖν: *the thing overpowering* +gen.
Ἔρωτος: gen. of comparison

ἡδονὴν κρείττω εἶναι· εἰ δὲ ἥττους, κρατοῖντ᾽ ἂν ὑπὸ Ἔρωτος,
ὁ δὲ κρατοῖ, κρατῶν δὲ ἡδονῶν καὶ ἐπιθυμιῶν ὁ Ἔρως δια-
φερόντως ἂν σωφρονοῖ. καὶ μὴν εἴς γε ἀνδρείαν Ἔρωτι
d "οὐδ᾽ Ἄρης ἀνθίσταται." οὐ γὰρ ἔχει Ἔρωτα Ἄρης,
ἀλλ᾽ Ἔρως Ἄρη—Ἀφροδίτης, ὡς λόγος—κρείττων δὲ ὁ ἔχων
τοῦ ἐχομένου· τοῦ δ᾽ ἀνδρειοτάτου τῶν ἄλλων κρατῶν πάντων
ἂν ἀνδρειότατος εἴη. περὶ μὲν οὖν δικαιοσύνης καὶ σωφρο-
5 σύνης καὶ ἀνδρείας τοῦ θεοῦ εἴρηται, περὶ δὲ σοφίας λείπεται·
ὅσον οὖν δυνατόν, πειρατέον μὴ ἐλλείπειν. καὶ πρῶτον μέν,
ἵν᾽ αὖ καὶ ἐγὼ τὴν ἡμετέραν τέχνην τιμήσω ὥσπερ Ἐρυξί-
e μαχος τὴν αὑτοῦ, ποιητὴς ὁ θεὸς σοφὸς οὕτως ὥστε καὶ
ἄλλον ποιῆσαι· πᾶς γοῦν ποιητὴς γίγνεται," "κἂν ἄμουσος
ᾖ τὸ πρίν,'''' οὗ ἂν Ἔρως ἅψηται. ᾧ δὴ πρέπει ἡμᾶς
μαρτυρίῳ χρῆσθαι, ὅτι ποιητὴς ὁ Ἔρως ἀγαθὸς ἐν κεφαλαίῳ
5 πᾶσαν ποίησιν τὴν κατὰ μουσικήν· ἃ γάρ τις ἢ μὴ ἔχει ἢ
μὴ οἶδεν, οὔτ᾽ ἂν ἑτέρῳ δοίη οὔτ᾽ ἂν ἄλλον διδάξειεν. καὶ
197 μὲν δὴ τήν γε τῶν ζῴων ποίησιν πάντων τίς ἐναντιώσεται
μὴ οὐχὶ Ἔρωτος εἶναι σοφίαν, ᾗ γίγνεταί τε καὶ φύεται
πάντα τὰ ζῷα; ἀλλὰ τὴν τῶν τεχνῶν δημιουργίαν οὐκ
ἴσμεν, ὅτι οὗ μὲν ἂν ὁ θεὸς οὗτος διδάσκαλος γένηται,
5 ἐλλόγιμος καὶ φανὸς ἀπέβη, οὗ δ᾽ ἂν Ἔρως μὴ ἐφά-
ψηται, σκοτεινός; τοξικήν γε μὴν καὶ ἰατρικὴν καὶ μαντικὴν
Ἀπόλλων ἀνηῦρεν ἐπιθυμίας καὶ ἔρωτος ἡγεμονεύσαντος,
b ὥστε καὶ οὗτος Ἔρωτος ἂν εἴη μαθητής, καὶ Μοῦσαι
μουσικῆς καὶ Ἥφαιστος χαλκείας καὶ Ἀθηνᾶ ἱστουργίας
καὶ Ζεὺς κυβερνᾶν θεῶν τε καὶ ἀνθρώπων. ὅθεν δὴ
καὶ κατεσκευάσθη τῶν θεῶν τὰ πράγματα Ἔρωτος ἐγγε-
5 νομένου, δῆλον ὅτι κάλλους—αἴσχει γὰρ οὐκ ἔπι ἔρως—πρὸ
τοῦ δέ, ὥσπερ ἐν ἀρχῇ εἶπον, πολλὰ καὶ δεινὰ θεοῖς ἐγίγνετο,

Ἀθήνη, ἡ: Athena
αἶσχος, -εος, τό: shame, disgrace; ugliness*
ἄ-μουσος, -ον: unmusical, unrefined, rude
ἀνδρεία, ἡ: manliness, bravery, courage*
ἀν-ευρίσκω: to find out, discover
ἀνθ-ίστημι: to withstand, stand against (+ dat.)
ἀπο-βαίνω: to turn out, result; disembark*
Ἄρης, ὁ: Ares*
γοῦν: γε οὖν, at least, at any rate, any way*
δημιουργία, ἡ: practicing, workmanship
δια-φερόντως: differently from; especially*
διδάσκαλος, ὁ: a teacher*
διδάσκω: to teach, instruct*
δικαιοσύνη, ἡ: justice, righteousness*
δυνατός, -ή, -όν: capable, strong, possible*
ἐγ-γίγνομαι: to be born, come about*
ἐλ-λείπω: to leave out or undone, fall short
ἐλ-λόγιμος, -ον: famous, in high account
ἐναντιόομαι: to deny, oppose, contradict
ἐφ-άπτω: to grab hold of, grasp, bind onto*

ἡγεμονεύω: to guide, lead, rule, command
Ἥφαιστος, ὁ: Hephaestus
ἱστ-ουργία, ἡ: weaving
κατα-σκευάζω: to prepare, construct, equip*
κεφάλαιον, τό: main or chief point, gist, sum*
κρατέω: overcome (+ gen.); rule; be strong*
κρείττων, -ον: stronger, mightier, better*
κυβερνάω: to govern, guide; act as helmsman
μαθητής, οῦ, ὁ: a learner, student, pupil*
μαρτύριον, τό: witness, testimony, proof
μοῦσα, ἡ: muse*
ὅ-θεν: from where, from which*
πρέπω: to fit, suit; impers. it is fitting*
πρίν: until, before*
σκοτεινός, -ά, -όν: dark; obscure
σωφρονέω: be moderate, temperate, prudent
τοξικός, -ή, -όν: of the bow; subst. archery
φανός, -ή, -όν: conspicuous; light, bright
χαλκεία, ἡ: blacksmith's work, bronze work

196c6 κρείττω: mightier; κρείττο(ν)α, acc.
ἥττους: they (i.e. the pleasures should
be) weaker; ἥττο(ν)ες, nom. pl.; future
less vivid (should, would) condition
κρατοῖντ᾽: κρατοῖνται, pres. pass. opt.

c7 ὁ δὲ κρατοῖ: and Eros would be strong;
supply ἄν, potential opt.

c8 εἴς...ἀνδρείαν: with regard to courage

d2 Ἄρη: Ἄρεα, acc. sg.; supply ἔχει
Ἀρφροδίτης ὡς λόγος: (i.e.) Aphrodite,
as the story (goes); following Ἔρως

d3 τοῦ ἐχομένου: that the one being
possessed; gen. of comparison

d4 τοῦ ἀνδρειοτάτου: gen. obj. of κρατῶν

d5 εἴρηται: it has been said; i.e. I have
spoken already, pf. pass., ἐρέω
λείπεται: it remains; "is left," pass.

d6 ὅσον οὖν δυνατόν: and so as much as
it is possible; impersonal, supply ἐστίν
πειρατέον: I must try; lit. "it is to be
tried (by me)," verbal adj. of πειράω

d7 τιμήσω: aor. subj. of purpose, τιμάω

e1 τὴν αὑτοῦ: his own (skill); add τέχνην,
reflexive ἑαυτοῦ
ὥστε...ποιῆσαι: so as to make another
(a poet) as well; result, aor. inf., ποιέω

e2 κἄν: even if; καὶ ἐάν

e3 τὸ πρίν: before; adverbial

οὗ ἄν: whomever; gen. obj. of ἅψηται
ἅψηται: 3rd sg. aor. mid. subj., ἅπτω
ᾧ...μαρτυρίῳ...ὅτι: which it is proper to
use as a witness that; dat. obj. χράομαι

e4 ἐν κεφαλαίῳ: in sum

e5 πᾶσαν ποίησιν...μουσικήν: in every
creation regarding the arts; acc. respect

e6 ἄν..δοίη: would give; 3rd sg. aor. opt.
ἄν...διδάξειεν: would teach; aor. opt.
διδάσκω, governing two accusatives

197a1 τὴν...ποίησιν: in the creation; respect
μὴ οὐχὶ: untranslatable, introduces inf.
following the verb ἐναντιώσεται "deny"
ᾗ: by which; dat. of means

a4 οὐκ ἴσμεν: don't we know..?; 1st pl., οἶδα
οὗ: whose teacher; with διδάσκαλος

a5 ἀπέβη: turns out (to be); gnomic aorist
οὗ: (the one) whom: obj. ἐφ-άπτω

a7 ἀνηῦρεν: invented; aor. ἀνευρίσκω

b1 καὶ οὗτος: even this one; i.e. Apollo

b2 κυβερνᾶν: to
ὅθεν δὴ: for which very reason, whence

b4 κατεσκευάσθη: 3rd sg. aor. pass.

b5 δῆλον ὅτι κάλλους: clearly from beauty;
"it is clear that," gen. source καλε-ος
αἴσχει...ἔπι: for (there is) no desire in
ugliness; ἐπ-εστι
πρὸ τοῦ δὲ: and before that (time)

ὡς λέγεται, διὰ τὴν τῆς ἀνάγκης βασιλείαν· ἐπειδὴ δ' ὁ
θεὸς οὗτος ἔφυ, ἐκ τοῦ ἐρᾶν τῶν καλῶν πάντ' ἀγαθὰ γέγονεν
καὶ θεοῖς καὶ ἀνθρώποις.

c   Οὕτως ἐμοὶ δοκεῖ, ὦ Φαῖδρε, Ἔρως πρῶτος αὐτὸς ὢν
κάλλιστος καὶ ἄριστος μετὰ τοῦτο τοῖς ἄλλοις ἄλλων τοιούτων
αἴτιος εἶναι. ἐπέρχεται δέ μοί τι καὶ ἔμμετρον εἰπεῖν, ὅτι
οὗτός ἐστιν ὁ ποιῶν

5   εἰρήνην μὲν ἐν ἀνθρώποις, πελάγει δὲ γαλήνην
    νηνεμίαν, ἀνέμων κοίτην ὕπνον τ' ἐνὶ κήδει.

d οὗτος δὲ ἡμᾶς ἀλλοτριότητος μὲν κενοῖ, οἰκειότητος δὲ πληροῖ,
τὰς τοιάσδε συνόδους μετ' ἀλλήλων πάσας τιθεὶς συνιέναι,
ἐν ἑορταῖς, ἐν χοροῖς, ἐν θυσίαισι γιγνόμενος ἡγεμών·
πρᾳότητα μὲν πορίζων, ἀγριότητα δ' ἐξορίζων· φιλόδωρος
5 εὐμενείας, ἄδωρος δυσμενείας· ἵλεως ἀγαθός· θεατὸς σοφοῖς,
ἀγαστὸς θεοῖς· ζηλωτὸς ἀμοίροις, κτητὸς εὐμοίροις· τρυφῆς,
ἁβρότητος, χλιδῆς, χαρίτων, ἱμέρου, πόθου πατήρ· ἐπιμελὴς
ἀγαθῶν, ἀμελὴς κακῶν· ἐν πόνῳ, ἐν φόβῳ, ἐν πόθῳ, ἐν
e λόγῳ κυβερνήτης, ἐπιβάτης, παραστάτης τε καὶ σωτὴρ
ἄριστος, συμπάντων τε θεῶν καὶ ἀνθρώπων κόσμος, ἡγεμὼν
κάλλιστος καὶ ἄριστος, ᾧ χρὴ ἕπεσθαι πάντα ἄνδρα ἐφυμ-
νοῦντα καλῶς, ᾠδῆς μετέχοντα ἣν ᾄδει θέλγων πάντων θεῶν
5 τε καὶ ἀνθρώπων νόημα.

    Οὗτος, ἔφη, ὁ παρ' ἐμοῦ λόγος, ὦ Φαῖδρε, τῷ θεῷ
ἀνακείσθω, τὰ μὲν παιδιᾶς, τὰ δὲ σπουδῆς μετρίας, καθ'
ὅσον ἐγὼ δύναμαι, μετέχων.

ἁβρότης, -ητος, ἡ: splendor, elegance, luxury
ἀγαστός, -ή, -όν: to be admired, admirable
ἀγριότης, -ητος, ἡ: savageness, fierceness
ᾄδω: to sing*
ἄ-δωρος, -ον: taking no gifts, not giving
ἀλλοτριότης, ἡ: alienation, estrangement
ἀ-μελής, -ές: careless, negligent, heedless
ἄ-μοιρος, -ον: without a share in (+ gen.)*
Ἀνάγκη, ἡ: Necessity, Force, Constraint
ἀνά-κειμαι: to be dedicated, to be set up
ἄνεμος, ου, ὁ: wind*
βασιλεία, ας, ἡ: rule, dominion, kingdom*
γαλήνη, ἡ: calm, stillness
δυσ-μένεια, ἡ: ill-will, enmity, hatred
εἰρήνη, ἡ: peace*
ἔμ-μετρος, -ον: in meter; measured, moderate
ἐξ-ορίζω: to banish, remove
ἑορτή, ἡ: a feast, festival
ἐπ-έρχομαι: to come upon, approach; attack*
ἐπι-βάτης, -ου, ὁ: hoplite on a ship, marine
ἐπι-μελής, -ές: careful about, attentive
εὐ-μένεια, ἡ: goodwill, kindness, favor
εὔ-μοιρος, -ον: with a large share
ἐφ-υμνέω: to sing a hymn, chant
ζηλωτός -ή, -όν: to be coveted, enviable
ἡγεμών, -όνος, ὁ: leader, commander, guide*
θεατός, -ή, -όν: to be gazed upon; observable
θέλγω: to charm, enchant, bewitch
ἵλαος, -ον: propitious, gracious, kind
ἵμερος, ὁ: a longing, yearning, desire

κῆδος, -εος, τό: care, concern, trouble, sorrow
κοίτη, ἡ: repose, allaying, lying down; bed
κόσμος, ὁ: order, good order, world-order*
κτητός, -ή, -όν: to be acquired, desirable
κυβερνήτης, -ου, ὁ: helmsman, pilot
μέτριος, -α, -ον: moderate, measured, fair
νηνεμία, ἡ: ceasing of winds, stillness of air
νόημα, -ατος, τό: thought, purpose, design
οἰκειότης, ἡ: intimacy, affection, relationship
παιδιή, ἡ: childish play, sport, game, pastime
παρα-στάτης, ὁ: comrade-in-arms
πέλαγος, -εος, τό: the sea
πληρόω: to fill, make full of (+ gen.)
πόθος, ὁ: a longing, yearning, desire
πόνος, ὁ: work, toil, labor*
πορίζω: to provide, procure, furnish, supply*
πρᾳότης, -ητος, ὁ: mildness, gentleness
σύμ-πας, -ασα, -αν: all together, all at once*
συν-έρχομαι: to come or go together, go with*
σύν-οδος, ἡ: gathering, meeting, assembly
σωτήρ, ὁ: savior, deliverer, preserver
τοιόσδε, -άδε, -όνδε: such, the following*
τρυφή, ἡ: luxury, wantonness
ὕπνος, ὁ: sleep, slumber
φιλό-δωρος, -ον: fond of giving, generous
φόβος, ὁ: fear, terror, panic*
χάρις, χάριτος, ἡ: grace, favor, gratitude*
χλιδή, ἡ: delicacy, luxury, effeminacy
χορός, ὁ: a dance, chorus
ᾠδή, ἡ: a song, lay, ode

197b8 ἔφυ: *was born*; ἔφυε, impf. φύω
  γέγονεν: *have come to be*; neuter pl. subj.
c1 πρῶτος: *foremost, supreme*
c2 τοῖς ἄλλοις: *for others*; dat. of interest
c3 τι...εἰπεῖν: *(the desire) to say something in meter comes upon me*
  ὅτι: *(namely) that*
  ὁ ποιῶν: *the one bringing about...*; governs both of the verses below
c5 πελάγει: *to the sea*; dat. of interest
  γαλήνην νηνεμίαν: *windless calm* "a calm, a ceasing of winds,"
c6 κοίτην ὕπνον τ᾽: *the allaying...and the sleep...*; τε is the sole conjunction
  ἐν κήδει: *amidst troubles*; "in trouble"
d1 ἀλλοτριότητος...οἰκειότητος: *of estrangement...with affection*; partitive

d2 τιθείς: *causing*; pres. pple, τίθημι
  συνιέναι: inf. συνέρχομαι
d5 ἵλεως: *propitious*; ἵλαος, nom. sg.
  σοφοῖς...θεοῖς...ἀμοίροις...εὐμοίροις: *by...by...*; dat. of agent with verbal adjs.
e2 κόσμος: *ornament, adornment*
e3 ᾧ: *whom*; dat. obj. of ἕπεσθαι
  ἕπεσθαι: *to follow*; ἄνδρα is acc. subj.
e4 μετέχοντα: *participating in* (+ gen.); pple
e6 παρ᾽ ἐμοῦ: *from me*
e7 ἀνακείσθω: *let..be dedicated*; 3rd s. imp.
  τὰ μὲν παιδιᾶς...τὰ δὲ μετρίας: *in some respect...in other respect*; acc. respect, the genitives are obj. of μετέχων
e8 καθ᾽ ὅσον: *insofar as*

198   Εἰπόντος δὲ τοῦ Ἀγάθωνος πάντας ἔφη ὁ Ἀριστόδημος
ἀναθορυβῆσαι τοὺς παρόντας, ὡς πρεπόντως τοῦ νεανίσκου
εἰρηκότος καὶ αὑτῷ καὶ τῷ θεῷ. τὸν οὖν Σωκράτη εἰπεῖν
βλέψαντα εἰς τὸν Ἐρυξίμαχον, ἆρά σοι δοκῶ, φάναι, ὦ
5   παῖ Ἀκουμενοῦ, ἀδεὲς πάλαι δέος δεδιέναι, ἀλλ' οὐ μαντικῶς
ἃ νυνδὴ ἔλεγον εἰπεῖν, ὅτι Ἀγάθων θαυμαστῶς ἐροῖ, ἐγὼ δ'
ἀπορήσοιμι;

Τὸ μὲν ἕτερον, φάναι τὸν Ἐρυξίμαχον, μαντικῶς μοι
δοκεῖς εἰρηκέναι, ὅτι Ἀγάθων εὖ ἐρεῖ· τὸ δὲ σὲ ἀπορήσειν,
10   οὐκ οἶμαι.

b   Καὶ πῶς, ὦ μακάριε, εἰπεῖν τὸν Σωκράτη, οὐ μέλλω
ἀπορεῖν καὶ ἐγὼ καὶ ἄλλος ὁστισοῦν, μέλλων λέξειν μετὰ
καλὸν οὕτω καὶ παντοδαπὸν λόγον ῥηθέντα; καὶ τὰ μὲν ἄλλα
οὐχ ὁμοίως μὲν θαυμαστά· τὸ δὲ ἐπὶ τελευτῆς τοῦ κάλλους
5   τῶν ὀνομάτων καὶ ῥημάτων τίς οὐκ ἂν ἐξεπλάγη ἀκούων;
ἐπεὶ ἔγωγε ἐνθυμούμενος ὅτι αὐτὸς οὐχ οἷός τ' ἔσομαι οὐδ'
ἐγγὺς τούτων οὐδὲν καλὸν εἰπεῖν, ὑπ' αἰσχύνης ὀλίγου
c   ἀποδρὰς ᾠχόμην, εἴ πη εἶχον. καὶ γάρ με Γοργίου ὁ λόγος
ἀνεμίμνησκεν, ὥστε ἀτεχνῶς τὸ τοῦ Ὁμήρου ἐπεπόνθη·
ἐφοβούμην μή μοι τελευτῶν ὁ Ἀγάθων Γοργίου κεφαλὴν
δεινοῦ λέγειν ἐν τῷ λόγῳ ἐπὶ τὸν ἐμὸν λόγον πέμψας αὐτόν
5   με λίθον τῇ ἀφωνίᾳ ποιήσειεν. καὶ ἐνενόησα τότε ἄρα
καταγέλαστος ὤν, ἡνίκα ὑμῖν ὡμολόγουν ἐν τῷ μέρει μεθ'
d   ὑμῶν ἐγκωμιάσεσθαι τὸν ἔρωτα καὶ ἔφην εἶναι δεινὸς τὰ
ἐρωτικά, οὐδὲν εἰδὼς ἄρα τοῦ πράγματος, ὡς ἔδει ἐγκωμιάζειν
ὁτιοῦν. ἐγὼ μὲν γὰρ ὑπ' ἀβελτερίας ᾤμην δεῖν τἀληθῆ
λέγειν περὶ ἑκάστου τοῦ ἐγκωμιαζομένου, καὶ τοῦτο μὲν
5   ὑπάρχειν, ἐξ αὐτῶν δὲ τούτων τὰ κάλλιστα ἐκλεγομένους
ὡς εὐπρεπέστατα τιθέναι· καὶ πάνυ δὴ μέγα ἐφρόνουν ὡς εὖ
ἐρῶν, ὡς εἰδὼς τὴν ἀλήθειαν τοῦ ἐπαινεῖν ὁτιοῦν. τὸ δὲ ἄρα,

ἀ-βελτερία, ἡ: stupidity, silliness
ἀ-δεής, -ές: without fear, causing no fear
αἰσχύνη, ἡ: shame, disgrace, dishonor*
ἀλήθεια, ἡ: truth*
ἀνα-θορυβέω: to cry out loudly, to applaud
ἀνα-μιμνήσκω: to remind (acc.) of (gen.),
    remember*
ἀπο-διδράσκω: to run away, flee, escape
ἀ-τεχνῶς: simply, really, entirely*
ἀ-φωνια, ἡ: speechlessness
δείδω: to fear*
δέος, δέους, τό: fear, alarm, dread, awe
ἐγγύς: near, close to (+ gen.); adv. nearby*
ἐκ-λέγω: to pick out, select, choose
ἐκ-πλήττω: to strike with fear, amaze,
    astound, to drive out of one senses*
ἐν-θυμέομαι: to consider, reflect, ponder*
ἐν-νοέω: to have in mind, notice, consider*
εὐ-πρεπής, -ές: attractive; suitable, fitting

ἡνίκα: at which time, when, since*
κατα-γέλαστος, -ον: ridiculous
λίθος, ὁ: a stone*
μακάριος, -α, -ον: blessed, happy*
μέρος, -έος, τό: a part, share, portion*
νεανίσκος, ὁ: a youth
νοέω: to think, mean, indicate, suppose
νυν-δή: just now*
πάλαι: long ago, formerly, of old*
παντο-δαπός, -ή, -όν: of every sort, varied*
πέμπω: to send, conduct, convey, dispatch*
πῃ: in some way, in any way, somehow
πρεπόντως: fittingly, suitably
ῥῆμα, τό: a word, saying, phrase*
τελευτή, ἡ: an end, completion; death*
ὑπ-άρχω: to be ready, available; be possible*
φοβέομαι: to fear, be seized with fear, flee*
φρονέω: to think, to be wise, prudent*

198a2 ἀναθορυβῆσαι: applauded; aor. inf.
    τοὺς παρόντας: those present; pple,
    πάρ-ειμι, acc. subject
    ὡς πρεπόντως: so fittingly for (+ dat.)
a3 εἰρηκότος: the youth having spoken; pf.
    pple, ἐρέω in a gen. abs.
    αὐτῷ: ἑαυτῷ, reflexive pronoun
a5 ἀδεὲς...δέος δεδιέναι: to have feared a
    fear not to be feared; pf. inf., δείδω, a
    wordplay in response to the speech
a6 ὅτι: (namely) that
    ἔροι...ἀπορήσοιμι: would speak...I would
    be at a loss...; fut. opt. replacing fut.
    indicative in secondary sequence, ἐρέω
a8 τὸ ἕτερον...ὅτι: the former (point)
    ...namely that; object of εἰρηκέναι
a9 εἰρηκέναι: pf. inf., ἐρέω
    ἐρεῖ: 3ʳᵈ sg. ἐρέω, fut. of λέγω
    τὸ...ἀπορήσειν: that you will be at
    a loss; articular infinitive; acc. respect
b2 λέξειν: μέλλω governs a fut. inf., λέγω
b3 ῥηθέντα: spoken; acc. sg, aor. pple, ἐρέω
    τὰ μὲν ἄλλα...τὸ δὲ ἐπὶ τελευτῆς: the
    other (parts)...but that (part) at the end
b5 τοῦ κάλλους: because of the beauty; gen.
    of cause governed by the verb ἐξεπλάγη
    ἂν ἐξεπλάγη: who would not have been
    astounded; aor. pass. ἐκ-πλήττω

expressing past potential
b6 οὐχ...οὐδ...οὐδὲν: not...even...anything;
    last two negatives redundant
    οἷός τ᾽ ἔσομαι: I will be able; fut., εἰμί
b7 ὀλίγου: almost; "(it lacks) from a little"
c1 ἀποδρὰς: aor. pple, ἀπο-διδράσκω
    ᾠχόμην: impf. οἴχομαι
    εἶχον: I was able; impf. ἔχω
c2 τὸ τοῦ Ὁμήρου: that (described in)
    Homer's (epic); i.e. Medusa's head
    ἐπεπόνθη: 1ˢᵗ sg. plpf. act. πάσχω
c3 μὴ...ποιήσειεν: lest he make; aor. opt.,
    fearing clause with μή in secondary seq.
    τελευτῶν: finally; pple acts as an adv.
    Γοργίου...πέμψας: sending the head of
    Gorgias, clever at speaking in the
    speech, against my speech; δεινός often
    governs an explanatory inf., wordplay on
    Medusa, the Gorgon, and Gorgias
c5 τῇ ἀφωνίᾳ: by my speechlessness; means
d1 ἐγκωμιάσεσθαι: fut. inf., ἐγκωμιάζω
    ἐρωτικὰ: in erotic matters; acc. respect
d2 εἰδὼς: knowing; pple οἶδα, cf. d7
d3 ᾤμην: 1ˢᵗ sg. impf. οἴομαι
    τἀληθῆ: the truth; crasis τὰ ἀληθῆ
d4 τοῦτο...ὑπάρχειν: this was a given
d6 ὡς εὐπρεπέστατα: as attractive as
    possible

ὡς ἔοικεν, οὐ τοῦτο ἦν τὸ καλῶς ἐπαινεῖν ὁτιοῦν, ἀλλὰ τὸ ὡς

e μέγιστα ἀνατιθέναι τῷ πράγματι καὶ ὡς κάλλιστα, ἐάν τε ᾖ
οὕτως ἔχοντα ἐάν τε μή· εἰ δὲ ψευδῆ, οὐδὲν ἄρ' ἦν πρᾶγμα.
προυρρήθη γάρ, ὡς ἔοικεν, ὅπως ἕκαστος ἡμῶν τὸν Ἔρωτα
ἐγκωμιάζειν δόξει, οὐχ ὅπως ἐγκωμιάσεται. διὰ ταῦτα δὴ
5 οἶμαι πάντα λόγον κινοῦντες ἀνατίθετε τῷ Ἔρωτι, καί
φατε αὐτὸν τοιοῦτόν τε εἶναι καὶ τοσούτων αἴτιον, ὅπως ἂν
199 φαίνηται ὡς κάλλιστος καὶ ἄριστος, δῆλον ὅτι τοῖς μὴ γιγνώσκουσιν—οὐ γὰρ δήπου τοῖς γε εἰδόσιν—καὶ καλῶς γ' ἔχει
καὶ σεμνῶς ὁ ἔπαινος. ἀλλὰ γὰρ ἐγὼ οὐκ ᾔδη ἄρα τὸν
τρόπον τοῦ ἐπαίνου, οὐ δ' εἰδὼς ὑμῖν ὡμολόγησα καὶ αὐτὸς
5 ἐν τῷ μέρει ἐπαινέσεσθαι. ἡ γλῶσσα οὖν ὑπέσχετο, ἡ δὲ
φρὴν οὔ· χαιρέτω δή. οὐ γὰρ ἔτι ἐγκωμιάζω τοῦτον τὸν
τρόπον—οὐ γὰρ ἂν δυναίμην—οὐ μέντοι ἀλλὰ τά γε ἀληθῆ,

b εἰ βούλεσθε, ἐθέλω εἰπεῖν κατ' ἐμαυτόν, οὐ πρὸς τοὺς
ὑμετέρους λόγους, ἵνα μὴ γέλωτα ὄφλω. ὅρα οὖν, ὦ Φαῖδρε,
εἴ τι καὶ τοιούτου λόγου δέῃ, περὶ Ἔρωτος τἀληθῆ λεγόμενα
ἀκούειν, ὀνομάσει δὲ καὶ θέσει ῥημάτων τοιαύτῃ ὁποία δἂν
5 τις τύχῃ ἐπελθοῦσα.

Τὸν οὖν Φαῖδρον ἔφη καὶ τοὺς ἄλλους κελεύειν λέγειν,
ὅπῃ αὐτὸς οἴοιτο δεῖν εἰπεῖν, ταύτῃ.

Ἔτι τοίνυν, φάναι, ὦ Φαῖδρε, πάρες μοι Ἀγάθωνα σμίκρ'
ἄττα ἐρέσθαι, ἵνα ἀνομολογησάμενος παρ' αὐτοῦ οὕτως ἤδη
10 λέγω.

c Ἀλλὰ παρίημι, φάναι τὸν Φαῖδρον, ἀλλ' ἐρώτα. μετὰ
ταῦτα δὴ τὸν Σωκράτη ἔφη ἐνθένδε ποθὲν ἄρξασθαι.

Καὶ μήν, ὦ φίλε Ἀγάθων, καλῶς μοι ἔδοξας καθηγή-
σασθαι τοῦ λόγου, λέγων ὅτι πρῶτον μὲν δέοι αὐτὸν ἐπιδεῖξαι
5 ὁποῖός τίς ἐστιν ὁ Ἔρως, ὕστερον δὲ τὰ ἔργα αὐτοῦ. ταύτην

σάνα-τίθημι: to set up, dedicate; attribute
ἀν-ομολογέομαι: to agree, receive agreement
γέλως, -ωτος, ὁ: laughter
γλῶσσα, ἡ: tongue*
ἐνθένδε: from here, from this place
ἐπ-έρχομαι: to come upon, approach; attack*
ἐπι-δείκνυμι: to show forth, display, point out*
θέσις, -εως, ἡ: a placing, arranging; position
καθ-ηγέομαι: to lead the way, begin; explain
κινέω: to set in motion, move; arouse, irritate*
μέρος, -έος, τό: a part, share, portion*
ὀνόμασις, -εως, ἡ: wording, choice of words
ὅπῃ: by which way, in what way, how*

ὁποῖος, -α, -ον: what sort or kind*
ὀφλισκάνω: to incur, be liable to pay, owe
παρ-ίημι: to pass over, yield, allow, permit*
ποθεν: from somewhere, from some place
προ-ερέω: to say first, say beforehand*
ῥῆμα, τό: a word, saying, phrase*
σεμνῶς: solemnly, with reverence
ὑμέτερος, -α, -ον: your, yours*
ὑπ-ισχνέομαι: to promise, profess, swear
ὕστερον: later*
φρήν, φρενός, ἡ: the midriff; heart, mind, wits
ψευδής, -ές: false

198d7 τὸ δέ: but; here δέ is adversative

d8 ἄρα...ἦν: it turns out, as it seems, this is not,; ἄρα + impf. (in this case, εἰμί) expresses a truth just realized, translate in the present; see also e2
τὸ...ἀνατιθέναι: to attribute (+ dat.)
ὡς μέγιστα...καὶ ὡς κάλλιστα: the... things as possible; objects of ἀνατιθέναι

e1 ἐάν τε...ἐάν τε: whether...or
ᾖ: they are; 3rd sg. pres. subj., εἰμί; the implicit neuter pl. subj. takes a 3rd sg.

e2 οὕτως ἔχοντα: something being so; ἔχω + adv. modifies a missing neuter subject
ψευδῆ: (they are) lies; ψευδέα, neuter pl., supply ἐστίν
οὐδὲν...πρᾶγμα: no big deal

e3 προυρρήθη: it was said earlier; aor. pass. of προ-ερέω used impersonally
ὅπως: how; indirect statement

e4 ἐγκωμιάσεται: 3rd sg. fut. mid.

e5 πάντα λόγον: every word; object of both κινοῦντες and ἀνατίθετε

e6 αὐτὸν: acc. subj.
ὅπως ἄν: in order that; purpose clause

199a1 ὡς κάλλιστος: as...as possible
δῆλον ὅτι: clearly; "it is clear that"
τοῖς γιγνώσκουσιν: follows φαίνεται

a2 οὐ γὰρ δήπου: for surely...not
τοῖς...εἰδόσιν: dat. pl., pple, οἶδα

a3 καλῶς γ' ἔχει: is beautiful; ἔχω + adv.
ἀλλὰ γάρ: and yet
ἤδη, εἰδώς: 3rd sg. past and pple, οἶδα

a5 ὑπέσχετο: 3rd sg. aor., ὑπ-ισχνέομαι

a6 χαιρέτω δή: just let it go; "just let it say farewell," 3rd sg. imperative
τοῦτον τὸν τρόπον: in this manner

a7 οὐ μέντοι ἀλλὰ...γε: (I do) not (praise in this manner) however, but I...

b1 κατὰ ἐμαυτόν, οὐ πρὸς: in my own way ...not against; "according to me"

b2 ὄφλω: aor. subj., ὀφλισκάνω
ὅρα...εἰ: see whether...; sg. imperative

b3 τι...δέῃ: you at all want, you have any need; δέε(σ)αι, 2nd sg. pres. mid. of δέομαι, (+gen., inf.); τι is an inner acc.

b4 ὀνομάσει...ὁποία: with such wording and arrangement of phrases that; dat. of manner with λεγόμενα
δᾶν: δὴ ἄν

b5 τύχῃ: happens to (pple); 3rd sg. aor. subj.

b7 ὅπῃ...ταύτῃ: in this way in which...; "in which way...in this way," the antecedent follows the relative pronoun and clause
οἴοιτο: pres opt. in secondary sequence

b8 πάρες: allow; sg. imperative, παρ-ίημι
σμικρ' ἄττα: some minor things; σμίκρα τινα

b9 ἀνομολογησάμενος παρ' αὐτοῦ: once having received agreement from him

c1 ἐρώτα: sg. imperative, ἐρωτάω

c4 δέοι: opt. of δεῖ in secondary sequence
ἐπιδεῖξαι: aor. inf. ἐπιδείκνυμι

c5 ὁποῖός τίς: what sort at all...; τις is indefinite, the accent comes from ἐστιν

τὴν ἀρχὴν πάνυ ἄγαμαι. ἴθι οὖν μοι περὶ Ἔρωτος, ἐπειδὴ
καὶ τἆλλα καλῶς καὶ μεγαλοπρεπῶς διῆλθες οἷός ἐστι, καὶ
d τόδε εἰπέ· πότερόν ἐστι τοιοῦτος οἷος εἶναί τινος ὁ Ἔρως
ἔρως, ἢ οὐδενός; ἐρωτῶ δ᾽ οὐκ εἰ μητρός τινος ἢ πατρός
ἐστιν—γελοῖον γὰρ ἂν εἴη τὸ ἐρώτημα εἰ Ἔρως ἐστὶν ἔρως
μητρὸς ἢ πατρός—ἀλλ᾽ ὥσπερ ἂν εἰ αὐτὸ τοῦτο πατέρα
5 ἠρώτων, ἆρα ὁ πατήρ ἐστι πατήρ τινος ἢ οὔ; εἶπες ἂν
δήπου μοι, εἰ ἐβούλου καλῶς ἀποκρίνασθαι, ὅτι ἔστιν ὑέος
γε ἢ θυγατρὸς ὁ πατὴρ πατήρ· ἢ οὔ;

Πάνυ γε, φάναι τὸν Ἀγάθωνα.

Οὐκοῦν καὶ ἡ μήτηρ ὡσαύτως; Ὁμολογεῖσθαι καὶ τοῦτο.

e Ἔτι τοίνυν, εἰπεῖν τὸν Σωκράτη, ἀπόκριναι ὀλίγῳ πλείω,
ἵνα μᾶλλον καταμάθῃς ὃ βούλομαι. εἰ γὰρ ἐροίμην, "Τί
δέ; ἀδελφός, αὐτὸ τοῦθ᾽ ὅπερ ἔστιν, ἔστι τινὸς ἀδελφὸς ἢ
οὔ;" φάναι εἶναι.

5 Οὐκοῦν ἀδελφοῦ ἢ ἀδελφῆς; Ὁμολογεῖν.

Πειρῶ δή, φάναι, καὶ τὸν ἔρωτα εἰπεῖν. ὁ Ἔρως ἔρως
ἐστὶν οὐδενὸς ἢ τινός;

Πάνυ μὲν οὖν ἔστιν.

200 Τοῦτο μὲν τοίνυν, εἰπεῖν τὸν Σωκράτη, φύλαξον παρὰ
σαυτῷ μεμνημένος ὅτου· τοσόνδε δὲ εἰπέ, πότερον ὁ Ἔρως
ἐκείνου οὗ ἔστιν ἔρως, ἐπιθυμεῖ αὐτοῦ ἢ οὔ;

Πάνυ γε, φάναι.

5 Πότερον ἔχων αὐτὸ οὗ ἐπιθυμεῖ τε καὶ ἐρᾷ, εἶτα ἐπιθυμεῖ
τε καὶ ἐρᾷ, ἢ οὐκ ἔχων;

Οὐκ ἔχων, ὡς τὸ εἰκός γε, φάναι.

Σκόπει δή, εἰπεῖν τὸν Σωκράτη, ἀντὶ τοῦ εἰκότος εἰ
ἀνάγκη οὕτως, τὸ ἐπιθυμοῦν ἐπιθυμεῖν οὗ ἐνδεές ἐστιν, ἢ μὴ
b ἐπιθυμεῖν, ἐὰν μὴ ἐνδεὲς ᾖ; ἐμοὶ μὲν γὰρ θαυμαστῶς δοκεῖ,
ὦ Ἀγάθων, ὡς ἀνάγκη εἶναι· σοὶ δὲ πῶς;

Κἀμοί, φάναι, δοκεῖ.

ἄγαμαι: to wonder at, marvel at, admire*
ἀδελφός, ὁ: brother*
ἀδελφής, ἡ: sister*
ἀπο-κρίνομαι: to answer, reply*
διέρχομαι: to go through, pass; relate,explain*
εἰκός, -ότος, τό: likely, probably, reasonable
εἶτα: then, next, and so, therefore*
ἐρώτημα, τό: question, inquiry
θυγάτηρ, ἡ: daughter*
κατα-μανθάνω: to learn thoroughly,
    understand; discover, find

μεγαλοπρεπῶς: magnificently
μιμνήσκω: to recall, remember*
οὐκοῦν: therefore, then, accordingly*
πότερον: whether*
σκοπέω: to look at, examine, consider*
τοσόσδε, -ήδε, -όνδε: so great, so much, so
    many
υἱός, -οῦ, ὁ: a son*
φυλάττω: keep watch, guard, keep in mind*
ὡσαύτως: in the same manner, just so*

199c6 ἴθι: *come then*; imperative of ἔρχομαι,
    often precedes an imperative, here εἰπέ
c7 διῆλθες: 2nd sg. aor. διέρχομαι
    τἆλλα: *in other respects*; acc. respect
    καὶ τόδε: *the following also*; "this here"
d1 πότερόν...ἤ: in direct questions leave
    πότερόν untranslated; cf. 200a2, a5
    τοιοῦτος οἷος εἶναί: *the sort such to be*;
    τοιοῦτος is a pred. adj. modifying the
    subject ὁ Ἔρως
d2 τινος...ἔρως: *desire for something*;
    objective genitive, frequent in this pasage
d5 ἄν: belongs to a missing apodosis, leave
    untranslated
    αὐτὸ τοῦτο πατέρα: *this very thing,
    "father"*; αὐτο is an intensive pronoun
    ἠρώτων: 1st sg. imperf., ἐρωτάω
    εἶπες ἄν: *you would say;* past potential
d6 ἐβούλου: ἐβούλε(σ)ο, 2nd sg. impf.
    ὑέος: gen. sg. υἱος
d8 πάνυ γε: *quite so*; a common way to
    say "yes" in Plato's dialogues
d9 ὁμολογεῖσθαι καὶ τοῦτο: (Aristodemus
    said) *he agreed to this as well;* Agathon
    is the subject in this indirect discourse
e1 ἀπόκριναι: aor. mid. imperative
    ὀλίγῳ: *a little*; dat. degree of difference
    πλείω: *more*; πλειο(ν)α, acc. sg.
e2 καταμάθῃς: aor. subj. καταμανθάνω
    βούλομαι: supply λέγειν

ἐροίμην: *I should ask*; pres. opt. ἔρομαι
e2 Τί δέ: *What then?*
e3 αὐτὸ τοῦθ᾽ ὅπερ ἔστιν: *this very thing
    which it is*; in apposition to ἀδελφός
e4 φάναι εἶναι: *he said that it was*; again,
    understand "Aristodemus said", cf. d9
e5 Ὁμολογεῖν: Agathon is the subject, see
    d9 and e4 above
e9 Πειρῶ: πειρά(σ)ο, sg. mid. imperative
200a1 φύλαξον: aor. imperative, obj. is τοῦτο
    παρὰ σαυτῷ: *within yourself*
a2 ὅτου: *what (it is)*; ὅτινος, gen. object
    of μεμνημένος, perf. pple.; add ἐστίν
    τοσόνδε: *this much*
a3 ὁ Ἔρως...ἔρως: *Love for that for which
    there is love*; οὗ is a rel. pronoun
    αὐτοῦ: *it*; the antecedent is ἐκείνου
a7 ὡς τὸ εἰκός γε: *as is likely at any rate*
a8 Σκόπει: sg. imperative; Σκόπεε
    ἀντὶ τοῦ εἰκότος: *instead of what is
    likely, instead of the likelihood*
a9 ἐπιθυμοῦν: *thing desiring*; neuter sg. pple
    οὗ: *(that) which*; gen. obj. of ἐνδεές, the
    antecedent, obj. of ἐπιθυμεῖν, is missing
b1 ᾖ: 3rd sg. pres. subj. εἰμί
    θαυμαστῶς...ὡς: *how strongly it
    seems to me*; lit. "it seems marvelously
    to me how…"
d8 σοὶ δὲ πῶς: supply δοκεῖ
    Κἀμοί: καὶ ἐμοί

Καλῶς λέγεις. ἆρ᾽ οὖν βούλοιτ᾽ ἄν τις μέγας ὢν μέγας
5 εἶναι, ἢ ἰσχυρὸς ὢν ἰσχυρός;

Ἀδύνατον ἐκ τῶν ὡμολογημένων.

Οὐ γάρ που ἐνδεὴς ἂν εἴη τούτων ὅ γε ὤν.

Ἀληθῆ λέγεις.

Εἰ γὰρ καὶ ἰσχυρὸς ὢν βούλοιτο ἰσχυρὸς εἶναι, φάναι τὸν
10 Σωκράτη, καὶ ταχὺς ὢν ταχύς, καὶ ὑγιὴς ὢν ὑγιής—ἴσως
γὰρ ἄν τις ταῦτα οἰηθείη καὶ πάντα τὰ τοιαῦτα τοὺς ὄντας
c τε τοιούτους καὶ ἔχοντας ταῦτα τούτων ἅπερ ἔχουσι καὶ
ἐπιθυμεῖν, ἵν᾽ οὖν μὴ ἐξαπατηθῶμεν, τούτου ἕνεκα λέγω—
τούτοις γάρ, ὦ Ἀγάθων, εἰ ἐννοεῖς, ἔχειν μὲν ἕκαστα
τούτων ἐν τῷ παρόντι ἀνάγκη ἃ ἔχουσιν, ἐάντε βούλωνται
5 ἐάντε μή, καὶ τούτου γε δήπου τίς ἂν ἐπιθυμήσειεν; ἀλλ᾽
ὅταν τις λέγῃ ὅτι ἐγὼ ὑγιαίνων βούλομαι καὶ ὑγιαίνειν,
καὶ πλουτῶν βούλομαι καὶ πλουτεῖν, καὶ ἐπιθυμῶ αὐτῶν
τούτων ἃ ἔχω, εἴποιμεν ἂν αὐτῷ ὅτι σύ, ὦ ἄνθρωπε,
d πλοῦτον κεκτημένος καὶ ὑγίειαν καὶ ἰσχὺν βούλει καὶ εἰς
τὸν ἔπειτα χρόνον ταῦτα κεκτῆσθαι, ἐπεὶ ἐν τῷ γε νῦν
παρόντι, εἴτε βούλει εἴτε μή, ἔχεις· σκόπει οὖν, ὅταν
τοῦτο λέγῃς, ὅτι ἐπιθυμῶ τῶν παρόντων, εἰ ἄλλο τι λέγεις
5 ἢ τόδε, ὅτι βούλομαι τὰ νῦν παρόντα καὶ εἰς τὸν ἔπειτα
χρόνον παρεῖναι. ἄλλο τι ὁμολογοῖ ἄν; Συμφάναι ἔφη τὸν
Ἀγάθωνα.

Εἰπεῖν δὴ τὸν Σωκράτη, οὐκοῦν τοῦτό γ᾽ ἐστὶν ἐκείνου
ἐρᾶν, ὃ οὔπω ἕτοιμον αὐτῷ ἐστιν οὐδὲ ἔχει, τὸ εἰς τὸν
ἔπειτα χρόνον ταῦτα εἶναι αὐτῷ σῳζόμενα καὶ παρόντα;

10 Πάνυ γε, φάναι.

e Καὶ οὗτος ἄρα καὶ ἄλλος πᾶς ὁ ἐπιθυμῶν τοῦ μὴ ἑτοίμου
ἐπιθυμεῖ καὶ τοῦ μὴ παρόντος, καὶ ὃ μὴ ἔχει καὶ ὃ μὴ ἔστιν

ἐάν-τε: whether…or*
ἐν-νοέω: to have in mind, notice, consider*
ἕτοιμος, -η, -ον: ready, prepared, at hand*
ἰσχύς, ὁ: strength, power, force
οὔ-πω: not yet*
πλουτέω: to be wealthy, rich*
πλοῦτος, ὁ: wealth, riches*

που: anywhere, somewhere; I suppose
σκοπέω: to look at, examine, consider*
σύμ-φημι: to assent, approve*
σῴζω: to save, keep, preserve*
ὑγιαίνω: to be sound, healthy, wholesome
ὑγίεια, ἡ: soundness, health, wholesomeness
ὑγιής, -ές: sound, healthy, wholesome*

200b6 ἀδύνατον: impersonal, supply ἐστίν
  ὡμολογημένων: *what was agreed
  upon*; "things having been agreed," pf.
b7 ὅ γε ὤν: *since he is (large or strong)*;
  γε adds causal force; ὁ is the article ὁ
  with an accent from the enclitic γε
b9 βούλοιτο…ἄν οἰηθείη: *should…would*;
  future less vivid; aor. dep. οἴομαι
b11 ταῦτα…πάντα τὰ τοιαῦτα: *in respect
  to…*; acc. of respect
  οἰηθείη: 3rd sg. aor. pass. dep, governs
  ἐπιθυμεῖν, τοὺς ὄντας… ἔχοντας
  ταῦτα as its subject and τούτων…
  ἔχουσι as its gen. object
c2 ἐξαπατηθῶμεν: aor. pass. subj., purpose
  λέγω: supply the object τοῦτο
c3 τούτοις: *for these people*; dat. of
  interest with ἀνάγκη (ἐστίν) ἔχειν
c4 ἐν τῷ παρόντι: *at the present (time)*
  ἐάντε…ἐάντε: *whether…or*; ἐάν τε
c5 τούτου: gen. object of ἐπιθυμήσειεν,
  the antecedent is ἔχειν…ἃ ἔχουσιν
  ἐπιθυμήσειεν: 3rd pl. aor. potential opt.
d1 κεκτημένος, κεκτῆσθαι: pf. mid. pple

and inf., κτάομαι
βούλει: *you wish*; βούλε(σ)αι, 2nd sg.
καί εἰς τὸν ἔπειτα χρόνον: *in(to) the
  future as well*; "the thereafter time"
d2 ἐν τῷ…νῦν παρόντι: *now in the
  present (time)*
d3 εἴτε…εἴτε: *whether…or*
  σκόπει: sg. imperative; σκόπεε
d4 τοῦτο…ὅτι: *this…(namely) this*
  παρόντων, παρόντα: *things at hand*
  ἄλλο τι…ἤ: *anything other than…*
d5 καί εἰς τὸν ἔπειτα χρόνον: see d1
d6 παρεῖναι: pres. inf., πάρ-ειμι
  Συμφάναι ἔφη: *(Aristodemus) said*
  Aristodemus is the subject of ἔφη, and
d9 ἕτοιμον αὐτῷ: *at hand to him,
  available to him*; predicate adjective
  τὸ…εἶναι: *that these things are…*;
  articular inf., ταῦτα is the subject
e2 τοῦ μὴ ἑτοίμου…παρόντος: gen.
  objects of ἐπιθυμεῖ not ἐπιθυμῶν
e3 ὃ μὴ ἔχει…ὃ μὴ…οὖ ἐνδεής…: a series
  of 3 relative clauses looking forward to
  τοιαῦτα ἄττα in e4

Optatives in Subordinate Clauses

In secondary sequence an optative may replace a subjunctive with or without ἄν in a
subordinate clause. Translate an indefinite opt. in the past and an opt. of purpose/fearing with
may or *might*.

Indefinite	subjunctive		optative	
relative	ὅ τι ἄν ποιῇ	→	ὅ τι ποιοῖ	whatever she does/did
temporal	ἐπειδὰν ποιῇ	→	ἐπειδὴ ποιοῖ	whenever she does/did
conditional	ἐάν ποιῇ	→	εἰ ποιοῖ	if ever she does/did
Purpose/Fearing	ἵνα ποιῇ	→	ἵνα ποιοῖ	so that she may/might do

αὐτὸς καὶ οὗ ἐνδεής ἐστι, τοιαῦτ᾽ ἄττα ἐστὶν ὧν ἡ ἐπιθυμία
5 τε καὶ ὁ ἔρως ἐστίν;

Πάνυ γ᾽, εἰπεῖν.

Ἴθι δή, φάναι τὸν Σωκράτη, ἀνομολογησώμεθα τὰ εἰρημένα. ἄλλο τι ἔστιν ὁ Ἔρως πρῶτον μὲν τινῶν, ἔπειτα
τούτων ὧν ἂν ἔνδεια παρῇ αὐτῷ;

201 Ναί, φάναι.

Ἐπὶ δὴ τούτοις ἀναμνήσθητι τίνων ἔφησθα ἐν τῷ λόγῳ
εἶναι τὸν ἔρωτα· εἰ δὲ βούλει, ἐγώ σε ἀναμνήσω. οἶμαι
γάρ σε οὑτωσί πως εἰπεῖν, ὅτι τοῖς θεοῖς κατεσκευάσθη τὰ
5 πράγματα δι᾽ ἔρωτα καλῶν· αἰσχρῶν γὰρ οὐκ εἴη ἔρως. οὐχ
οὑτωσί πως ἔλεγες;

Εἶπον γάρ, φάναι τὸν Ἀγάθωνα.

Καὶ ἐπιεικῶς γε λέγεις, ὦ ἑταῖρε, φάναι τὸν Σωκράτη·
καὶ εἰ τοῦτο οὕτως ἔχει, ἄλλο τι ὁ Ἔρως κάλλους ἂν εἴη
5 ἔρως, αἴσχους δὲ οὔ; ὡμολόγει.

b Οὐκοῦν ὡμολόγηται, οὗ ἐνδεής ἐστι καὶ μὴ ἔχει, τούτου
ἐρᾶν;

Ναί, εἰπεῖν.

Ἐνδεὴς ἄρ᾽ ἐστὶ καὶ οὐκ ἔχει ὁ Ἔρως κάλλος.

5 Ἀνάγκη, φάναι.

Τί δέ; τὸ ἐνδεὲς κάλλους καὶ μηδαμῇ κεκτημένον κάλλος
ἆρα λέγεις σὺ καλὸν εἶναι;

Οὐ δῆτα.

Ἔτι οὖν ὁμολογεῖς ἔρωτα καλὸν εἶναι, εἰ ταῦτα οὕτως
10 ἔχει;

Καὶ τὸν Ἀγάθωνα εἰπεῖν κινδυνεύω, ὦ Σώκρατες, οὐδὲν
εἰδέναι ὧν τότε εἶπον.

c Καὶ μὴν καλῶς γε εἶπες, φάναι, ὦ Ἀγάθων. ἀλλὰ
σμικρὸν ἔτι εἰπέ· τἀγαθὰ οὐ καὶ καλὰ δοκεῖ σοι εἶναι;

Ἔμοιγε.

αἶσχος, -εος, τό: shame, disgrace; ugliness*
ἀνα-μιμνήσκω: to remind (acc.) of (gen.), remember*
ἀν-ομολογέομαι: to agree, receive agreement
δῆτα: certainly, to be sure, of course*

ἔν-δεια, ἡ: need, lack, deficiency*
ἐπιεικῶς: suitably, reasonably
κατα-σκευάζω: to prepare, construct, equip*
μηδαμῇ: in no way, not at all
ναί: yes, yeah

200e4 οὗ: *(that) for which*; gen. obj. of ἐνδεής
τοιαῦτ' ἄττα: *some such things*; subject
ὧν: *(that) for which*; the antecedent, which is the pred. of ἐστίν , is missing

e6 πάνυ γ': *quite so*; πάνυ γε

e7 ἴθι δὴ: *come, then*; imp., ἔρχομαι (ι-)
ἀνομολογησώμεθα: *let us...*; aor. hortatory subj., ἀν-ομολογέομαι
τὰ εἰρημένα: pf. pass. pple, ἐρέω

e8 ἄλλο τι: *is it anything other (than)*; introduces a question that expects a "yes" response, often left untranslated
πρῶτον μὲν τινῶν, ἔπειτα τούτων: *love first for something, next for these things...*; gen. objects of Ἔρως

e9 ὧν ἄν...παρῇ: *of which...is present*; 3rd sg. subj. πάρειμι, gen. after ἔνδεια

201a2 ἐπὶ...τούτοις: *in addition to these things*; in addition to the points in 200e8
ἀναμνήσθητι: aor. dep. imperative
ἔφησθα: *you said*; alternative impf. ἔφην

a3 τίνων: *for what*; interrogative pronoun introducing an indirect question, once again an objective genitive of ἔρως
βούλει: *you wish*; βούλε(σ)αι, 2nd sg.
ἀναμνήσω: 1st sg. fut. ἀνα-μιμνήσκω

a4 οὑτωσί: *in this here way*; deictic iota suffix strengthens οὕτως, cf. a6
κατεσκευάσθη: 3rd sg. aor. pass.

a5 εἴη: *there was*; opt. is simply replacing an indicative in indirect discourse
αἰσχρῶν: *of ugly things*; objective gen.
οὐχ...ἔλεγες: *Were you not saying...?*

a7 εἶπον γάρ: *(yes), for I did say (that)*

a9 οὕτως ἔχει: *this is so*; ἔχω + adv.
ἄλλο τι: leave untranslated, see 200e8
κάλλους, αἴσχους: gen., ε-stem nouns

a10 Ὡμολόγει: *he continued to agree*; impf. Agathon is subject; Apollodorus, speaker.

b1 ὡμολόγηται: *it has been agreed*; pf. pass ἐστι, ἔχει, ἐρᾶν: ὁ Ἔρως is the subj.

b6 Τί δέ: *What then?*

b7 κεκτημένον: pf. pple, κτάομαι

b11 κινδυνεύω...οὐδὲν εἰδέναι: *it looks as though I know nothing*; "I run the risk of knowing nothing", inf. of ὁράω

b12 ὧν: *(of those things) which*; ἐκείνων ἅ, acc. relative pronoun attracted into the gen. case of a missing antecedent

c2 σμικρὸν ἔτι: *a little further*; adv. acc.
τἀγαθὰ: crasis τὰ ἀγαθά
οὐ: used to anticipate a "yes" response

Optative in Indirect Statement and Indirect Question

In secondary sequence an optative may replace an indicative main verb in indirect statement or question. Although the optative will retain the tense of the direct statement or question, English requires that you shift the optative into the past when you translate.

Ind. Statement	ὅτι ἐστίν	→	ὅτι εἴη	that she is/was
	ὡς ἐποίησε	→	ὡς ποιήσειε	that she did/had done
Ind. Question	ὅποι ἔρχεται	→	ὅποι ἴοι	where she is/was going
	πόθεν ἦλθε	→	πόθεν ἔλθοι	whence she came/had come

Εἰ ἄρα ὁ Ἔρως τῶν καλῶν ἐνδεής ἐστι, τὰ δὲ ἀγαθὰ καλά,
5 κἂν τῶν ἀγαθῶν ἐνδεὴς εἴη.

Ἐγώ, φάναι, ὦ Σώκρατες, σοὶ οὐκ ἂν δυναίμην ἀντιλέγειν, ἀλλ᾽ οὕτως ἐχέτω ὡς σὺ λέγεις.

Οὐ μὲν οὖν τῇ ἀληθείᾳ, φάναι, ὦ φιλούμενε Ἀγάθων,
δύνασαι ἀντιλέγειν, ἐπεὶ Σωκράτει γε οὐδὲν χαλεπόν.

d   Καὶ σὲ μέν γε ἤδη ἐάσω· τὸν δὲ λόγον τὸν περὶ τοῦ
Ἔρωτος, ὅν ποτ᾽ ἤκουσα γυναικὸς Μαντινικῆς Διοτίμας, ἣ
ταῦτά τε σοφὴ ἦν καὶ ἄλλα πολλά—καὶ Ἀθηναίοις ποτὲ
θυσαμένοις πρὸ τοῦ λοιμοῦ δέκα ἔτη ἀναβολὴν ἐποίησε τῆς
5 νόσου, ἣ δὴ καὶ ἐμὲ τὰ ἐρωτικὰ ἐδίδαξεν—ὃν οὖν ἐκείνη
ἔλεγε λόγον, πειράσομαι ὑμῖν διελθεῖν ἐκ τῶν ὡμολογημένων ἐμοὶ καὶ Ἀγάθωνι, αὐτὸς ἐπ᾽ ἐμαυτοῦ, ὅπως ἂν
δύνωμαι. δεῖ δή, ὦ Ἀγάθων, ὥσπερ σὺ διηγήσω, διελθεῖν
e   αὐτὸν πρῶτον, τίς ἐστιν ὁ Ἔρως καὶ ποῖός τις, ἔπειτα τὰ
ἔργα αὐτοῦ. δοκεῖ οὖν μοι ῥᾷστον εἶναι οὕτω διελθεῖν, ὡς
ποτέ με ἡ ξένη ἀνακρίνουσα διῄει. σχεδὸν γάρ τι καὶ ἐγὼ
πρὸς αὐτὴν ἕτερα τοιαῦτα ἔλεγον οἷάπερ νῦν πρὸς ἐμὲ
5 Ἀγάθων, ὡς εἴη ὁ Ἔρως μέγας θεός, εἴη δὲ τῶν καλῶν·
ἤλεγχε δή με τούτοις τοῖς λόγοις οἷσπερ ἐγὼ τοῦτον, ὡς
οὔτε καλὸς εἴη κατὰ τὸν ἐμὸν λόγον οὔτε ἀγαθός.

Καὶ ἐγώ, πῶς λέγεις, ἔφην, ὦ Διοτίμα; αἰσχρὸς ἄρα ὁ
Ἔρως ἐστὶ καὶ κακός;

10   Καὶ ἥ, οὐκ εὐφημήσεις; ἔφη· ἢ οἴει, ὅτι ἂν μὴ καλὸν
ᾖ, ἀναγκαῖον αὐτὸ εἶναι αἰσχρόν;

202   Μάλιστά γε.

Ἦ καὶ ἂν μὴ σοφόν, ἀμαθές; ἢ οὐκ ᾔσθησαι ὅτι ἔστιν
τι μεταξὺ σοφίας καὶ ἀμαθίας;

Τί τοῦτο;

αἰσθάνομαι: to perceive, feel, learn, realize*
ἀλήθεια, ἡ: truth*
ἀ-μαθής, -ές: ignorant, foolish, stupid*
ἀ-μαθία, ἡ: ignorance, folly*
ἀνα-βολή, ἡ: postponement, delay; cloak
ἀνα-κρίνω: to examine closely, question
ἀντι-λέγω: to speak against, challenge*
δέκα: ten*
διδάσκω: to teach, instruct*
διέρχομαι: go through, pass; relate, explain*
ἐλέγχω: to cross-examine, test, refute*

ἔτος, -εως, τό: a year*
εὐ-φημέω: to keep quiet, keep religious silence
θύω: to sacrifice, make a sacrifice*
λοιμός, ὁ: a plague, pestilence
Μαντινικός, -ή, -όν:: from Mantinea
νόσος, ὁ: sickness, illness, disease*
ξένη, ἡ: a female guest, foreigner, stranger*
οἷοσ-περ, -απερ, -ουπερ: which sort, as
ποῖος, -α, -ον: what sort of? what kind of?*
σχεδόν: nearly, almost, just about, practically*

201c4 τὰ ἀγαθὰ: good things (are); add ἐστίν
  c5 κἂν: then (Eros) would...; καὶ ἄν, καὶ is
    inferential, "then"
  c6 ἂν δυναίμην: pres. (not aor.) potential
    opt., the stem is δυνα- and the common
    present thematic vowel ο is not used
  c7 ἐχέτω: let it be so...; "let it be disposed
    as," 3rd sg. imperative, ἔχω + adv.
  c8 οὐ μὲν οὖν: nay, rather...not; μὲν οὖν,
    often affirmative, indicates a correction
  c9 φιλούμενε: O beloved; vocative, pple
    τῇ ἀληθείᾳ: dat. obj. of ἀντιλέγειν
    ἐπεὶ Σωκράτει γε: (I say this) since to
    challenge Socrates is; supply τὸ
    ἀντιλέγειν from the previous clause as
    the subject; Σωκράτει is the dat. obj.
  d1 ἐάσω: I will let you go; fut. ἐάω
    τὸν...λόγον τὸν περὶ...: the speech
    concerning...; the article is repeated
  d2 ἤκουσα: I heard (acc.) from (gen.)
  d3 ταῦτά τε...καὶ ἄλλα πολλὰ: in both
    these and many other things, acc. respect
  d4 θυσαμένοις πρὸ τοῦ λοιμοῦ: to the
    Athenians making sacrifices for the
    plague; aor. mid. pple
    δέκα ἔτη: for 10 years; acc. duration
    ἀναβολὴν ἐποίησε: put off, delayed
  d5 ἣ δὴ: the very one who; common
    translation of δή before pronouns
  d6 πειράσομαι: fut. πειράζω
    τῶν ὡμολογημένων: what was agreed
    upon; "things having been agreed upon",
    pf. pass. pple + dat. of agent
  d7 ἐπ᾽ ἐμαυτοῦ: on my own
    ὅπως ἄν...: in whatever way, however

  d8 διηγήσω: explained; διηγήσα(σ)ο 2nd sg.
  e1 ποῖός τις: what sort of thing at all (it is);
    supply ἐστίν
  e2 ῥᾷστον: very easy; irreg. superlative adj.
    from ῥάδιος
    οὕτω...ὥς: in the way that, just as
  e3 διῄει: she related; "went through," 3rd sg.
    impf. διέρχομαι
    σχεδόν...τι: just about, almost
  e4 οἷάπερ...᾽Αγάθων: supply ἔλεγε
  e5 ὡς...: (namely) that
    τῶν καλῶν: (desire) for fine things;
    supply ἔρως
  e6 ἤλεγχε: she was cross-examining; impf.
    suggests ongoing action
    τούτοις τοῖς λόγοις: dat. of means
    τοῦτον: I was cross-examining this one;
    i.e. Agathon; supply ἤλεγχον
    ὡς...: (namely) that
  e7 κατὰ τὸν ἐμὸν λόγον: according to my
    argument
  e8 πῶς λέγεις: what do you mean?
  e10 ἦ: she (said); a demonstrative pronoun
    οἴει: you think; 2nd sg. pres. mid., οἴομαι
    ὅτι...ᾖ: whatever is; ὅ τι, antecedent is
    the following αὐτό; 3rd sg. subj. εἰμί
    ἀναγκαῖον: it is necessary; add ἐστίν
202a2 Μάλιστά γε: very much so
    ἄν: ἐάν, supply ᾖ from above
  b2 ἀμαθές: aor. μανθάνω, supply
    ἀναγκαῖον αὐτὸ εἶναι
    ᾔσθησαι: you perceived; 2nd sg. pf.
    αἰσθάνομαι
  a4 Τί τοῦτο: what is this?; supply ἐστίν

5   Τὸ ὀρθὰ δοξάζειν καὶ ἄνευ τοῦ ἔχειν λόγον δοῦναι οὐκ
οἶσθ᾽, ἔφη, ὅτι οὔτε ἐπίστασθαί ἐστιν—ἄλογον γὰρ πρᾶγμα
πῶς ἂν εἴη ἐπιστήμη; —οὔτε ἀμαθία—τὸ γὰρ τοῦ ὄντος
τυγχάνον πῶς ἂν εἴη ἀμαθία; —ἔστι δὲ δήπου τοιοῦτον ἡ
ὀρθὴ δόξα, μεταξὺ φρονήσεως καὶ ἀμαθίας.

10   Ἀληθῆ, ἦν δ᾽ ἐγώ, λέγεις.

b   Μὴ τοίνυν ἀνάγκαζε ὃ μὴ καλόν ἐστιν αἰσχρὸν εἶναι,
μηδὲ ὃ μὴ ἀγαθόν, κακόν. οὕτω δὲ καὶ τὸν ἔρωτα ἐπειδὴ
αὐτὸς ὁμολογεῖς μὴ εἶναι ἀγαθὸν μηδὲ καλόν, μηδέν τι
μᾶλλον οἴου δεῖν αὐτὸν αἰσχρὸν καὶ κακὸν εἶναι, ἀλλά τι
5   μεταξύ, ἔφη, τούτοιν.

Καὶ μήν, ἦν δ᾽ ἐγώ, ὁμολογεῖταί γε παρὰ πάντων μέγας
θεὸς εἶναι.

Τῶν μὴ εἰδότων, ἔφη, πάντων λέγεις, ἢ καὶ τῶν εἰδότων;
Συμπάντων μὲν οὖν.

10   Καὶ ἣ γελάσασα καὶ πῶς ἄν, ἔφη, ὦ Σώκρατες,
c   ὁμολογοῖτο μέγας θεὸς εἶναι παρὰ τούτων, οἵ φασιν αὐτὸν
οὐδὲ θεὸν εἶναι;

Τίνες οὗτοι; ἦν δ᾽ ἐγώ.

Εἶς μέν, ἔφη, σύ, μία δ᾽ ἐγώ.

5   Κἀγὼ εἶπον, πῶς τοῦτο, ἔφην, λέγεις;

Καὶ ἥ, Ῥᾳδίως, ἔφη. λέγε γάρ μοι, οὐ πάντας θεοὺς
φῂς εὐδαίμονας εἶναι καὶ καλούς; ἢ τολμήσαις ἄν τινα μὴ
φάναι καλόν τε καὶ εὐδαίμονα θεῶν εἶναι;

Μὰ Δί᾽ οὐκ ἔγωγ᾽, ἔφην.

10   Εὐδαίμονας δὲ δὴ λέγεις οὐ τοὺς τἀγαθὰ καὶ τὰ καλὰ
κεκτημένους;

Πάνυ γε.

d   Ἀλλὰ μὴν Ἔρωτά γε ὡμολόγηκας δι᾽ ἔνδειαν τῶν

84

ἄ-λογος, -ον: without account, without reason
ἀ-μαθία, ἡ: ignorance, folly*
γελάω: to laugh*
δόξα, ἡ: opinion, reputation, honor, glory*
δοξάζω: to opine, think, suppose, imagine*
ἔν-δεια, ἡ: need, lack, deficiency*

ἐπί-σταμαι: to know, know how, understand*
μά: by, in affirmation*
σύμ-πας, -ασα, -αν: all together, all at once*
φρόνησις, -εως, ἡ: wisdom, intelligence,
    prudence*

202a5 τὸ...δοξάζειν...δοῦναι: together, these
    two art. infinitives are the subject of
    ἐστιν within the ὅτι clause below
    τοῦ ἔχειν: without being able; ἔχω + inf.
    λόγον δοῦναι: to give an account; aor.
    inf., δίδωμι

a6 οἶσθ᾽: you know; οἶσθα, 2ⁿᵈ sg., οἶδα
    οὔτε ἐπίστασθαι...οὔτε ἀμαθία:
    neither...nor; these predicates lack
    parallelism: infinitive vs. nominative
    ἄλογον...πρᾶγμα: a matter without an
    account; cf. λόγον δοῦναι in a5

a7 τὸ...τυγχάνον: the attaining of what
    really is; i.e. the truth; τυγχάνω. + gen.,
    neuter pple of τυγχάνω and εἰμί

a8 ἂν εἴη: would be; 3ʳᵈ sg. potential opt.

a9 ὀρθὴ δόξα: right opinion, true opinion; a
    term commonly distinguished from
    ἐπιστήμη, knowledge, in Plato

a10 ἦν: I said; impf. ἠμί

b1 μὴ ἀνάκαζε: negative sg. imperative

b3 μηδέν τι μᾶλλον οἴου: think nothing at
    all more that; οἴε(σ)ο, mid. imperative

b5 τούτοιν: these two; dual genitive

b6 καὶ μήν: and yet
    ὁμολογεῖταί: (Eros) is agreed; pass.
    παρὰ πάντων: by all; gen. of agent

b8 τῶν...εἰδότων: gen. pl. pple οἶδα
    πάντων λέγεις: do you mean by "all";
    in response to the previous sentence,
    πάντων and the other genitives are
    governed by the παρὰ in b6

b9 μὲν οὖν: certainly

b10 ἥ: she; demonstrative pronoun

c1 ἂν ὁμολογοῖτο: (Eros) could be agreed;
    opt. pass., Eros is the implicit subject
    παρὰ τούτων: by these; gen. agent

c4 εἰς μέν...μία δ᾽: supply ἐστίν twice

c5 Κἀγὼ: καὶ ἐγὼ
    εἶπον...ἔφην: said; ἔφην is redundant
    Πῶς τοῦτο λέγεις: what do you mean
    by this; "How do you say this?"

c6 ἥ: she
    λέγε...μοι: sg. imperative; introducing
    a direct question
    οὐ φῇς: do you deny, do you claim
    that...not

c7 μὴ φάναι: to deny; pres. inf., φημί

c9 Μὰ Δί᾽: By Zeus!; Μὰ Δία
    ἔγωγ᾽: ἔγωγε

c11 κεκτημένους: those possessing; "having
    possessed" perf. mid. pple, κτάομαι

d1 ἀλλὰ μήν: but then; often introducing a
    point in contrast to the previous one

Verbal Adjectives ending in -τέος, -τέα, -τέον

Together with εἰμί and a dative of agent, the verbal adjective ending in -τεός expresses
necessity or obligation. Often the construction is impersonal, and the verb εἰμί or the dative is
omitted. In translation, we often make the dative of agent the subject of an active verb.

πειρατέον ἐστὶν ἡμῖν	it is to be attempted by us	→ we **ought to/must** attempt
λεκτέον ἐστίν	it is to be said (by me)	→ I **ought to/should/must** say

ἀγαθῶν καὶ καλῶν ἐπιθυμεῖν αὐτῶν τούτων ὧν ἐνδεής ἐστιν.

5 Ὡμολόγηκα γάρ.

Πῶς ἂν οὖν θεὸς εἴη ὅ γε τῶν καλῶν καὶ ἀγαθῶν ἄμοιρος;

Οὐδαμῶς, ὥς γ᾽ ἔοικεν.

Ὁρᾷς οὖν, ἔφη, ὅτι καὶ σὺ ἔρωτα οὐ θεὸν νομίζεις;

Τί οὖν ἄν, ἔφην, εἴη ὁ Ἔρως; θνητός;

10 Ἥκιστά γε.

Ἀλλὰ τί μήν;

Ὥσπερ τὰ πρότερα, ἔφη, μεταξὺ θνητοῦ καὶ ἀθανάτου.

Τί οὖν, ὦ Διοτίμα;

e Δαίμων μέγας, ὦ Σώκρατες· καὶ γὰρ πᾶν τὸ δαιμόνιον μεταξύ ἐστι θεοῦ τε καὶ θνητοῦ.

Τίνα, ἦν δ᾽ ἐγώ, δύναμιν ἔχον;

Ἑρμηνεῦον καὶ διαπορθμεῦον θεοῖς τὰ παρ᾽ ἀνθρώπων

5 καὶ ἀνθρώποις τὰ παρὰ θεῶν, τῶν μὲν τὰς δεήσεις καὶ θυσίας, τῶν δὲ τὰς ἐπιτάξεις τε καὶ ἀμοιβὰς τῶν θυσιῶν, ἐν μέσῳ δὲ ὂν ἀμφοτέρων συμπληροῖ, ὥστε τὸ πᾶν αὐτὸ αὑτῷ συνδεδέσθαι. διὰ τούτου καὶ ἡ μαντικὴ πᾶσα χωρεῖ

203 καὶ ἡ τῶν ἱερέων τέχνη τῶν τε περὶ τὰς θυσίας καὶ τελετὰς καὶ τὰς ἐπῳδὰς καὶ τὴν μαντείαν πᾶσαν καὶ γοητείαν. θεὸς δὲ ἀνθρώπῳ οὐ μείγνυται, ἀλλὰ διὰ τούτου πᾶσά ἐστιν ἡ ὁμιλία καὶ ἡ διάλεκτος θεοῖς πρὸς ἀνθρώπους, καὶ ἐγρη-

5 γορόσι καὶ καθεύδουσι· καὶ ὁ μὲν περὶ τὰ τοιαῦτα σοφὸς δαιμόνιος ἀνήρ, ὁ δὲ ἄλλο τι σοφὸς ὢν ἢ περὶ τέχνας ἢ χειρουργίας τινὰς βάναυσος. οὗτοι δὴ οἱ δαίμονες

ἀμοιβή, ἡ: compensation; answer, exchange
ἄ-μοιρος, -ον: without a share in (+ gen.)*
βάναυσος, -ον: mechanical, base, ignoble
γοητεία, ἡ: sorcery, magic; juggling, cheating
δαιμόνιον, τό: divine being, divinity*
δαιμόνιος, -α, -ον: divine, daimon-like*
δαίμων, -ονος, ὁ: a divine being, spirit*
δέησις, -εως, ἡ: a prayer, entreaty
διάλεκτος, ἡ: discourse: discussion, debate
δια-πορθμεύω: to carry over, communicate
ἐγείρω: to awaken, wake up, rouse*
ἐπίταξις, -εως, ἡ: an injunction, command
ἐπῳδή, ἡ: an enchantment, charm, spell
ἑρμηνεύω: to interpret, explain

ἥκιστος, -η, -ον: least; not at all*
ἱερεύς, -έως, ὁ: a priest, sacrificer*
καθ-εύδω: to lie down to sleep, sleep*
μαντεία, ἡ: oracle, prophetic power
μείγνυμι: mix, mingle, join, have intercourse
μέσος, -η, -ον: middle, in the middle of*
ὁμιλία, ἡ: association, company, society
οὐδαμῶς: in no way, not at all
συν-δέω: to bind together
συμ-πληρόω: to fill up, fill up completely
τελετή, ἡ: mystic rites, initiation
χειρου-ργία, ἡ: handicraft, practice of a skill
χωρέω: to come or go, pass; have room for

202d2 Ὡμολόγηκα: 1ˢᵗ sg. pf. ὁμολογέω

d2 γάρ: *yes, indeed*; as often in responses

d7 Ἔρωτα οὐ θεὸν: supply εἶναι

d8 Τί οὖν: *What then…?*

d9 Ἥκιστά γε: *not in the least*; a strong negative response, "least (of all)"

d10 Ἀλλὰ τί μήν: *well, what then?*

d11 τὰ πρότερα: *previously*; adverbial acc.

d13 πᾶν τὸ δαιμόνιον: *the entire class of* δαίμονες

e2 Τίνα…ἔχον: possessing what power?; a sentence fragment; ἔχον is a neuter pple.

e2 ἦν: *I said*; impf. ἠμί

e3 Ἑρμηνεῦον…διαπορθμεῦον: *interpreting and communicating…*; neuter pres. pples modifying τὸ δαιμόνιον, the implicit subject of συμπληροῖ below in e6

e3 τὰ παρ' ἀνθρώπων…τὰ παρὰ θεῶν: *messages from humans…messages from the gods*

e4 τῶν μὲν…τῶν δὲ: *from humans…from the gods*; "from these…from those"

e5 ἀμοιβὰς: acc. pl., ἡ ἀμοιβή

e6 ἐν μέσῳ…ὄν: *being..*; pres. pple εἰμί modifying τὸ δαιμόνιον, the subject

e6 συμπληροῖ: *fills up the middle ground*; not opt. but 3ʳᵈ sg. pres., o-contract

e6 τὸ πᾶν: *the All*; i.e. the universe

e7 αὐτῷ: *itself*; ἑαυτῷ, 3ʳᵈ sg. reflexive συνδεδέσθαι: pf. pass. inf., συν-δέω ἡ μαντικὴ: *art of prophecy*; add τέχνη

e8 τῶν ἱερέων…τῶν…περὶ: *of the priests concerned with* (+ acc.); "of the priests regarding…"

203a2 ἐστιν…θεοῖς: *the gods have*; dat. poss.

a3 ἐγρηγορόσι…καθεύδουσι: *while being awake and sleeping*; both are dat. pl. pples, ἐγρηγορόσι is a pf. act. pple from ἐγείρω with middle sense; the pples modifying πρὸς ἀνθρώπους, which construction is dative in sense

a5 δαιμόνιος ἀνήρ: predicate; add ἐστίν ἄλλο τι…ἤ..ἤ: *in anything else…than …or*; acc. of respect with σοφὸς

a6 βάναυσος: nom., supply ἐστίν and ἀνήρ, in parallelism to δαιμόνιος ἀνήρ above

πολλοὶ καὶ παντοδαποί εἰσιν, εἷς δὲ τούτων ἐστὶ καὶ ὁ
Ἔρως.

Πατρὸς δέ, ἦν δ᾽ ἐγώ, τίνος ἐστὶ καὶ μητρός;

b   Μακρότερον μέν, ἔφη, διηγήσασθαι· ὅμως δέ σοι ἐρῶ.
ὅτε γὰρ ἐγένετο ἡ Ἀφροδίτη, ἡστιῶντο οἱ θεοὶ οἵ τε ἄλλοι
καὶ ὁ τῆς Μήτιδος υὸς Πόρος. ἐπειδὴ δὲ ἐδείπνησαν,
προσαιτήσουσα οἷον δὴ εὐωχίας οὔσης ἀφίκετο ἡ Πενία, καὶ
5 ἦν περὶ τὰς θύρας. ὁ οὖν Πόρος μεθυσθεὶς τοῦ νέκταρος—
οἶνος γὰρ οὔπω ἦν—εἰς τὸν τοῦ Διὸς κῆπον εἰσελθὼν
βεβαρημένος ηὗδεν. ἡ οὖν Πενία ἐπιβουλεύουσα διὰ τὴν
αὑτῆς ἀπορίαν παιδίον ποιήσασθαι ἐκ τοῦ Πόρου, κατα-
c κλίνεταί τε παρ᾽ αὐτῷ καὶ ἐκύησε τὸν ἔρωτα. διὸ δὴ καὶ
τῆς Ἀφροδίτης ἀκόλουθος καὶ θεράπων γέγονεν ὁ Ἔρως,
γεννηθεὶς ἐν τοῖς ἐκείνης γενεθλίοις, καὶ ἅμα φύσει ἐραστὴς ὢν περὶ τὸ καλὸν καὶ τῆς Ἀφροδίτης καλῆς οὔσης.
5 ἅτε οὖν Πόρου καὶ Πενίας υὸς ὢν ὁ Ἔρως ἐν τοιαύτῃ τύχῃ
καθέστηκεν. πρῶτον μὲν πένης ἀεί ἐστι, καὶ πολλοῦ δεῖ
ἁπαλός τε καὶ καλός, οἷον οἱ πολλοὶ οἴονται, ἀλλὰ σκληρὸς
d καὶ αὐχμηρὸς καὶ ἀνυπόδητος καὶ ἄοικος, χαμαιπετὴς ἀεὶ
ὢν καὶ ἄστρωτος, ἐπὶ θύραις καὶ ἐν ὁδοῖς ὑπαίθριος κοιμώ-
μενος, τὴν τῆς μητρὸς φύσιν ἔχων, ἀεὶ ἐνδείᾳ σύνοικος.
κατὰ δὲ αὖ τὸν πατέρα ἐπίβουλός ἐστι τοῖς καλοῖς καὶ τοῖς
5 ἀγαθοῖς, ἀνδρεῖος ὢν καὶ ἴτης καὶ σύντονος, θηρευτὴς
δεινός, ἀεί τινας πλέκων μηχανάς, καὶ φρονήσεως ἐπι-
θυμητὴς καὶ πόριμος, φιλοσοφῶν διὰ παντὸς τοῦ βίου,
δεινὸς γόης καὶ φαρμακεὺς καὶ σοφιστής· καὶ οὔτε ὡς
e ἀθάνατος πέφυκεν οὔτε ὡς θνητός, ἀλλὰ τοτὲ μὲν τῆς αὐτῆς
ἡμέρας θάλλει τε καὶ ζῇ, ὅταν εὐπορήσῃ, τοτὲ δὲ ἀποθνή-

ἀκόλουθος, ὁ: follower*
ἀν-υπόδητος, -η, -ον: unshod, barefoot*
ἄ-οικος, -ον: homeless, houseless
ἀ-πορία, ἡ: poverty, difficulty, bewilderment*
ἄ-στρωτος, -ον: without bedding, uncovered
αὐχμηρός, -ά, -όν: dry, dusty, rough
ἀφ-ικνέομαι: to come, arrive*
βαρέω: to weigh down, depress
γενέθλιος, -ον: belonging to one's birth
γόης, -ητος ,ἡ: a enchanter, sorcerer; cheat
ἔν-δεια, ἡ: need, lack, deficiency*
ἐπι-βουλεύω: to plot against, contrive against*
ἐπί-βουλος, -ον: plotting against, treacherous
ἐπιθυμητής, -οῦ, ὁ: desirer, lover
ἑστιάω: to entertain, give a feast
εὕδω: to sleep, lie down to sleep
εὐ-πορέω: to prosper, thrive, be well off*
εὐωχία, ἡ: feast, banquet, good cheer
θάλλω: to bloom, abound, be luxuriant
θεράπων, -οντος, ὁ: an attendant, servant
θηρευτής, ὁ: a hunter, huntsman
ἴτης, ὁ: eager, reckless, headlong, hasty
καθ-ίστημι: to set down, establish, put into a
    state; become, fall into a state*
κῆπος, ὁ: a garden, orchard
κοιμάω: to put to sleep; mid. to fall asleep
μακρός, ά, όν: long, far, distant, large*
μεθύω: to become drunk, be drunk*

Μῆτις, ἡ: Metis
μηχανή, ἡ: means, device, contrivance*
νέκταρ, -αρος, τό: nectar
ὁδός, ἡ: road, way, path, journey*
οἶνος, ὁ: wine*
ὅτε: when, at some time*
οὔ-πω: not yet*
παιδίον, τό: a little or young child, child
παντο-δαπός, -ή, -όν: of every sort, varied*
πένης, -ητος, ὁ: a poor man, a day-laborer*
Πενία, ἡ: Poverty, Need*
πλέκω: to twist, weave
πόριμος, -ον: resourceful, inventive
Πόρος, ὁ: Plenty, Means, Way, Path*
προσ-αιτέω: to ask in addition, beg
σκληρός, -ά, -όν: hard, harsh, severe*
σοφιστής, ὁ: sophist, wise man*
σύν-οικος, -ον: co-inhabitant, associated with
σύν-τονος, -ον: intense, serious, severe
τοτέ: at one time*
τύχη, ἡ: chance, luck, fortune, success*
υἱός, -οῦ, ὁ: a son*
ὑπ-αίθριος, -α, -ον: under the open sky
φαρμακεύς, -έως, ὁ: a sorcerer of potions
φιλο-σοφέω: to pursue wisdom, investigate*
φρόνησις, -εως, ἡ: wisdom, intelligence,
    prudence*
χαμαιπετής, -ές: lying on the ground

203a9 Πατρὸς...τίνος...μητρός: From what
    father and mother...; gen. of origin
b1 μακρότερον: (it is) rather long; add ἐστίν
    ἐρῶ: I will say; ἐρέω
b2 ἐγένετο: was born; "came to be"
    ἡστιῶντο: 3rd pl. impf. ἑστιάω
    τῆς Μήτιδος ὑὸς: son of Metis
b4 προσαιτήσουσα: intending to beg; fut.
    οἷον δὴ εὐωχίας οὔσης: since it was a
    feast; οἷον + pple is causal; gen. abs.
    ἀφίκετο: 3rd sg, aor. ἀφ-ικνέομαι
b5 μεθυσθείς: becoming drunk; ingressive,
    aor. dep. pple. nom. sg.
    τοῦ νέκταρος: from...;partitive gen.
b6 εἰσελθὼν: nom. sg. aor. pple. εἰσέρχομαι
b7 βεβαρημένος: feeling heavy; pf. mid.
    ηὗδεν: fell asleep; inceptive impf. εὕδω
b8 αὑτῆς: of her own; ἑαυτῆς, reflexive
c2 γέγονεν: has become; pf. γίγνομαι

c3 γεννηθεὶς: born; aor. pass. pple, γεννάω
    τοῖς γενεθλίοις: birthday
    φύσει: by nature; dat. of respect
c4 τῆς Ἀφροδίτης...οὔσης: since
    Aphrodite is...; causal gen. abs.
c5 ἐν τοιαύτῃ τύχῃ καθέστηκεν: has come
    into such circumstances; "has come into
    such fortune," pf. καθίστημι
c6 πολλοῦ δεῖ: far from; "it lacks from
    much", treat this construction as an adv.
d2 ἐπὶ θύραις: in doorways; "near doors"
d4 ἐπιβουλός: governs a dative object
e1 οὔτε ὡς...πέφυκεν: is by nature neither
    like...; 3rd sg. pf. φύω
    τοτὲ μὲν...δὲ: at one time...at another
    τῆς αὐτῆς ἡμέρας: in the same day; gen.
    of time within
e2 ζῇ: ζάει, 3rd sg. pres. α-contract, ζάω
    εὐπορήσῃ: prospers; aor. subjunctive

σκει, πάλιν δὲ ἀναβιώσκεται διὰ τὴν τοῦ πατρὸς φύσιν, τὸ
δὲ ποριζόμενον ἀεὶ ὑπεκρεῖ, ὥστε οὔτε ἀπορεῖ Ἔρως ποτὲ
5   οὔτε πλουτεῖ, σοφίας τε αὖ καὶ ἀμαθίας ἐν μέσῳ ἐστίν.
204 ἔχει γὰρ ὧδε. θεῶν οὐδεὶς φιλοσοφεῖ οὐδ' ἐπιθυμεῖ σοφὸς
γενέσθαι—ἔστι γάρ—οὐδ' εἴ τις ἄλλος σοφός, οὐ φιλοσοφεῖ.
οὐδ' αὖ οἱ ἀμαθεῖς φιλοσοφοῦσιν οὐδ' ἐπιθυμοῦσι σοφοὶ
γενέσθαι· αὐτὸ γὰρ τοῦτό ἐστι χαλεπὸν ἀμαθία, τὸ μὴ
5   ὄντα καλὸν κἀγαθὸν μηδὲ φρόνιμον δοκεῖν αὑτῷ εἶναι
ἱκανόν. οὔκουν ἐπιθυμεῖ ὁ μὴ οἰόμενος ἐνδεὴς εἶναι οὗ ἂν
μὴ οἴηται ἐπιδεῖσθαι.

Τίνες οὖν, ἔφην ἐγώ, ὦ Διοτίμα, οἱ φιλοσοφοῦντες, εἰ
μήτε οἱ σοφοὶ μήτε οἱ ἀμαθεῖς;

b   Δῆλον δή, ἔφη, τοῦτό γε ἤδη καὶ παιδί, ὅτι οἱ μεταξὺ
τούτων ἀμφοτέρων, ὧν ἂν εἴη καὶ ὁ Ἔρως. ἔστιν γὰρ δὴ τῶν
καλλίστων ἡ σοφία, Ἔρως δ' ἐστὶν ἔρως περὶ τὸ καλόν,
ὥστε ἀναγκαῖον ἔρωτα φιλόσοφον εἶναι, φιλόσοφον δὲ
5   ὄντα μεταξὺ εἶναι σοφοῦ καὶ ἀμαθοῦς. αἰτία δὲ αὐτῷ καὶ
τούτων ἡ γένεσις· πατρὸς μὲν γὰρ σοφοῦ ἐστι καὶ εὐπόρου,
μητρὸς δὲ οὐ σοφῆς καὶ ἀπόρου. ἡ μὲν οὖν φύσις τοῦ
δαίμονος, ὦ φίλε Σώκρατες, αὕτη· ὃν δὲ σὺ ᾠήθης Ἔρωτα
c   εἶναι, θαυμαστὸν οὐδὲν ἔπαθες. ᾠήθης δέ, ὡς ἐμοὶ δοκεῖ
τεκμαιρομένη ἐξ ὧν σὺ λέγεις, τὸ ἐρώμενον ἔρωτα εἶναι,
οὐ τὸ ἐρῶν· διὰ ταῦτά σοι οἶμαι πάγκαλος ἐφαίνετο ὁ
Ἔρως. καὶ γὰρ ἔστι τὸ ἐραστὸν τὸ τῷ ὄντι καλὸν καὶ
5   ἁβρὸν καὶ τέλεον καὶ μακαριστόν· τὸ δέ γε ἐρῶν ἄλλην
ἰδέαν τοιαύτην ἔχον, οἵαν ἐγὼ διῆλθον.

Καὶ ἐγὼ εἶπον, εἶεν δή, ὦ ξένη, καλῶς γὰρ λέγεις·
τοιοῦτος ὢν ὁ Ἔρως τίνα χρείαν ἔχει τοῖς ἀνθρώποις;

Τοῦτο δὴ μετὰ ταῦτ', ἔφη, ὦ Σώκρατες, πειράσομαί σε
d   διδάξαι. ἔστι μὲν γὰρ δὴ τοιοῦτος καὶ οὕτω γεγονὼς ὁ

ἀβρός, -ά, -όν: delicate, graceful
αἰτία, ἡ: cause, reason; charge, blame*
ἀ-μαθής, -ές: ignorant, foolish, stupid*
ἀ-μαθία, ἡ: ignorance, folly*
ἀνα-βιώσκομαι: to come back to life
ἄ-πορος, -ον: without means, poor, difficult
δαίμων, -ονος, ὁ: a divine being, spirit*
διδάσκω: to teach, instruct*
διέρχομαι: to go through, pass; relate, explain*
εἶεν: well! well now!
ἐπι-δέομαι: to want, need; to ask, beg
εὔ-πορος, -ον: resourceful, easily done, easy*
ἰδέα, ἡ: look, appearance, form, kind*
μακαριστός, ή, όν: most blessed, most happy

μέσος, - η, -ον: middle, in the middle of*
ξένη, ἡ: a female guest, foreigner, stranger*
οὔκ-ουν: certainly not, and so not
πάγκαλος, -η, -ον: all-beautiful, good, noble*
πλουτέω: to be wealthy, rich*
πορίζω: to provide, procure, furnish, supply*
τεκμαίρομαι: to judge, calculate, conjecture
τέλεος, -α, -ον: perfect, complete; last*
ὑπ-εκρέω: to flow out from under, slip away
φιλο-σοφέω: to pursue wisdom, investigate*
φιλό-σοφος, ὁ: a pursuer or lover of wisdom*
φρόνιμος, -ον: sensible, intelligent, prudent
χρεία, ἡ: use, advantage, service; need, want`
ὧδε: in this way, so, thus*

203e3 τὸ ποριζόμενον: *what is being provided*
e4 ἀπορεῖ: *is poor*; in contrast to πλουτεῖ
204a1 ἔχει...ὧδε: *it is as follows*; ἔχω + adv.
a2 ἔστι γάρ: supply σοφός
   οὐδ...οὐ: the second οὐ is redundant
a3 σοφοὶ: predicate adj. after γενέσθαι
   αὐτὸ...ἀμαθία: *ignorance is harmful in respect to this very thing (namely)* ...; acc. of respect followed by τὸ...δοκεῖν
a4 μὴ ὄντα: *though not being*...; pple with concessive force, modifies the implicit acc. subj. of δοκεῖν
a5 καλὸν κἀγαθὸν: καλὸν καὶ ἀγαθὸν
   αὑτῷ: *to oneself*, ἑαυτῷ, reflexive
a6 ὁ μὴ...εἶναι: subj. of ἐπιθυμεῖ
   οὗ: *(that) which*; the gen. antecedent, obj. of ἐπιθυμεῖ, is missing; οὗ is the obj. of ἐπιδεῖσθαι within the relative clause
b1 Δῆλον...τοῦτο...ὅτι: *this is clear ...(namely) that*; add ἐστίν
   καὶ παιδὶ: *even to a child*
   ὅτι οἱ μεταξὺ: *that (those pursuing wisdom are) those between*...; add οἱ φιλοσοφοῦντες from above and εἰσίν
b2 ὧν: *among whom*; partitive genitive
   τῶν καλλίστων: *(one) of the most beautiful things, among the most*

beautiful things; partitive genitive
b4 ἀναγκαῖον: *to be necessary*; supply a second εἶναι
b5 αἰτία...καὶ τούτων: *reason these things as well*; objective gen.
   πατρός...μητρὸς: *he is from a father... from a mother..*; gen. of origin
b8 ὅν...εἶναι: *with regard to what you*...; acc. of respect
   ᾠήθης: *you thought*; aor. dep. οἴομαι
c1 ἔπαθες: *experienced*; 2nd sg. aor. πάσχω
c2 Ἔρωτα: acc. subject of εἶναι
c3 ἐφαίνετο: *appeared*; a linking verb
c4 τὸ ἐραστὸν: *what is desirable*; subject
   τῷ ὄντι: *really, actually*; dat. of respect
c6 ἰδέαν: *character*
   ἔχον: *is something having*...; neuter pple is a predicate, modifying the subject τὸ ἐρῶν; supply ἐστίν
   διῆλθον: *related*; 3rd pl. aor. διέρχομαι
c3 εἶεν δὴ: *well then*
d1 πειράσομαι: fut., πειράζω
   διδάξαι: aor. inf. διδάσκω
d2 οὕτω γεγονὼς: *has come to be in this way*; lit. "something having come to be in this way" perf. pple + verb εἰμί is a a perf. periphrastic form

Ἔρως, ἔστι δὲ τῶν καλῶν, ὡς σὺ φῄς. εἰ δέ τις ἡμᾶς
ἔροιτο· Τί τῶν καλῶν ἐστιν ὁ Ἔρως, ὦ Σώκρατές τε
5 καὶ Διοτίμα; ὧδε δὲ σαφέστερον· ἐρᾷ ὁ ἐρῶν τῶν καλῶν·
τί ἐρᾷ;

Καὶ ἐγὼ εἶπον ὅτι Γενέσθαι αὑτῷ.

Ἀλλ᾽ ἔτι ποθεῖ, ἔφη, ἡ ἀπόκρισις ἐρώτησιν τοιάνδε· Τί
ἔσται ἐκείνῳ ᾧ ἂν γένηται τὰ καλά;

5 Οὐ πάνυ ἔφην ἔτι ἔχειν ἐγὼ πρὸς ταύτην τὴν ἐρώτησιν
προχείρως ἀποκρίνασθαι.

e Ἀλλ᾽, ἔφη, ὥσπερ ἂν εἴ τις μεταβαλὼν ἀντὶ τοῦ καλοῦ
τῷ ἀγαθῷ χρώμενος πυνθάνοιτο· φέρε, ὦ Σώκρατες, ἐρᾷ ὁ
ἐρῶν τῶν ἀγαθῶν· τί ἐρᾷ;

Γενέσθαι, ἦν δ᾽ ἐγώ, αὑτῷ.

5 Καὶ τί ἔσται ἐκείνῳ ᾧ ἂν γένηται τἀγαθά;

Τοῦτ᾽ εὐπορώτερον, ἦν δ᾽ ἐγώ, ἔχω ἀποκρίνασθαι, ὅτι
εὐδαίμων ἔσται.

205 Κτήσει γάρ, ἔφη, ἀγαθῶν οἱ εὐδαίμονες εὐδαίμονες, καὶ
οὐκέτι προσδεῖ ἐρέσθαι Ἵνα τί δὲ βούλεται εὐδαίμων εἶναι
ὁ βουλόμενος; ἀλλὰ τέλος δοκεῖ ἔχειν ἡ ἀπόκρισις.

Ἀληθῆ λέγεις, εἶπον ἐγώ.

5 Ταύτην δὴ τὴν βούλησιν καὶ τὸν ἔρωτα τοῦτον πότερα
κοινὸν οἴει εἶναι πάντων ἀνθρώπων, καὶ πάντας τἀγαθὰ
βούλεσθαι αὑτοῖς εἶναι ἀεί, ἢ πῶς λέγεις;

Οὕτως, ἦν δ᾽ ἐγώ· κοινὸν εἶναι πάντων.

Τί δὴ οὖν, ἔφη, ὦ Σώκρατες, οὐ πάντας ἐρᾶν φαμεν,
b εἴπερ γε πάντες τῶν αὐτῶν ἐρῶσι καὶ ἀεί, ἀλλά τινάς φαμεν
ἐρᾶν, τοὺς δ᾽ οὔ;

Θαυμάζω, ἦν δ᾽ ἐγώ, καὶ αὐτός.

Ἀλλὰ μὴ θαύμαζ᾽, ἔφη· ἀφελόντες γὰρ ἄρα τοῦ ἔρωτός

ἀντί: instead of, in place of (+ gen.) *
ἀπο-κρίνομαι: to answer, reply*
ἀπόκρισις, -εως, ἡ: answer
ἀφ-αιρέω: to take away from, pick out*
βούλησις, -εως, ὁ: a wish, intention, purpose
ἐρώτησις, -εως, ἡ: question, inquiry
εὔ-πορος, -ον: resourceful, easily done, easy*
κτῆσις, -εως, ἡ: possession, acquisition
μετα-βάλλω: to change, alter; turn about*
οὐκ-έτι: no more, no longer, no further*
ποθέω: to long for, yearn after

πότερος, -α, -ον: which of the two?
   whether?*
προσ-δεῖ: to be necessary in addition
προ-χείρως: handily, readily
πυνθάνομαι: to learn by inquiry, learn by
   hearsay; inquire, ask about*
σαφής, -ές: clear, distinct, definite*
τέλος, -εος, τό: end, goal, result; sacred rites*
τοιόσδε, -άδε, -όνδε: such, the following*
ὧδε: in this way, so, thus*

204d3 τῶν καλῶν: is (love) for beautiful things; i.e. "Eros is eros of beautiful things," objective gen., governed by ἔρως the implicit predicate of ἐστίν

d4 ἔροιτο: should ask; pres. opt., ἔρομαι
Τί: why?; "in what respect," acc. respect

d5 ὧδε δὲ σαφέστερον: or (to put it) more clearly in the following way; comp. adv.
ἐρᾷ: ἐράει, 3rd sg. pres. α-contract,
τῶν καλῶν: object of ὁ ἐρῶν not ἐρᾷ

d6 τί ἐρᾷ;: What does he desire?; neuter singular, acc. direct object

d7 ὅτι Γενέσθαι αὑτῷ: that he possess them; "that (beautiful things) come to be for him," dat. of possession

d8 ἔσται ἐκείνῳ: that one will possess; dat. of possession and 3rd sg. fut. εἰμί

d9 ᾧ ἂν γένηται: who comes to possess; "to whom...comes to be" dat. possession

d10 ἔχειν...προχείρως: to be readily able; ἔχω + inf.

e1 ὥσπερ ἂν εἰ: just as if; future less vivid condition with missing apodosis, leave ἄν untranslated

e2 πυνθάνοιτο: one should inquire; 3rd sg. pres. opt., πυνθάνομαι

e3 φέρε: come now; usually introduces an imperative, here introducing a question

e4 Γενέσθαι...τἀγαθά: see d7-9 above

e6 εὐπορώτερον: more easily; comp. adv.
ἔχω: I am able; ἔχω + inf.

e7 ἔσται: 3rd sg. fut. εἰμί

205a1 Κτήσει: by possession of; dat. of cause

a2 ἐρέσθαι: to ask; inf. ἔρομαι
Ἵνα τί δὲ: but for what purpose; "but in order that what (may happen)...?"

a5 Ταύτην...ἔρωτα: acc. subject of the infinitive εἶναι, κοινόν is a predicate
πότερα...ἤ: a two-part question, do not translate πότερα

a6 οἴει: you think; 2nd sg. pres. οἴομαι
τἀγαθὰ: crasis, τὰ ἀγαθὰ

a7 αὑτοῖς εἶναι: that they have; ἑαυτοῖς, dat. of possession
πῶς λέγεις: What do you say?

a9 Τί δὴ οὖν: just why then...; "in respect to just what then", acc. respect

a7 οὐ...φαμεν: οὐ modifies φαμεν

b1 τῶν αὑτῶν: the same things
ἀλλά: but instead; in contrast to a9
τινάς...τοὺς δ: some...others

b4 μὴ θαύμαζ: don't be amazed; μὴ θαύμαζε, neg. pres. imperative
ἀφελόντες: picking out; nom. pl. aor. pple ἀφ-αιρέω, governing the neuter sg. accusative τι εἶδος in b5

5 τι εἶδος ὀνομάζομεν, τὸ τοῦ ὅλου ἐπιτιθέντες ὄνομα, ἔρωτα,
τὰ δὲ ἄλλα ἄλλοις καταχρώμεθα ὀνόμασιν.

Ὥσπερ τί; ἦν δ᾽ ἐγώ.

Ὥσπερ τόδε. οἶσθ᾽ ὅτι ποίησίς ἐστί τι πολύ· ἡ γάρ
τοι ἐκ τοῦ μὴ ὄντος εἰς τὸ ὂν ἰόντι ὁτῳοῦν αἰτία πᾶσά ἐστι

c ποίησις, ὥστε καὶ αἱ ὑπὸ πάσαις ταῖς τέχναις ἐργασίαι
ποιήσεις εἰσὶ καὶ οἱ τούτων δημιουργοὶ πάντες ποιηταί.

Ἀληθῆ λέγεις.

Ἀλλ᾽ ὅμως, ἦ δ᾽ ἥ, οἶσθ᾽ ὅτι οὐ καλοῦνται ποιηταὶ ἀλλὰ

5 ἄλλα ἔχουσιν ὀνόματα, ἀπὸ δὲ πάσης τῆς ποιήσεως ἓν
μόριον ἀφορισθὲν τὸ περὶ τὴν μουσικὴν καὶ τὰ μέτρα τῷ
τοῦ ὅλου ὀνόματι προσαγορεύεται. ποίησις γὰρ τοῦτο
μόνον καλεῖται, καὶ οἱ ἔχοντες τοῦτο τὸ μόριον τῆς ποιήσεως
ποιηταί.

5 Ἀληθῆ λέγεις, ἔφην.

d Οὕτω τοίνυν καὶ περὶ τὸν ἔρωτα. τὸ μὲν κεφάλαιόν ἐστι
πᾶσα ἡ τῶν ἀγαθῶν ἐπιθυμία καὶ τοῦ εὐδαιμονεῖν ὁ "μέ-
γιστός τε καὶ δολερὸς ἔρως" παντί· ἀλλ᾽ οἱ μὲν ἄλλῃ
τρεπόμενοι πολλαχῇ ἐπ᾽ αὐτόν, ἢ κατὰ χρηματισμὸν ἢ κατὰ

5 φιλογυμναστίαν ἢ κατὰ φιλοσοφίαν, οὔτε ἐρᾶν καλοῦνται
οὔτε ἐρασταί, οἱ δὲ κατὰ ἕν τι εἶδος ἰόντες τε καὶ ἐσπουδακότες τὸ τοῦ ὅλου ὄνομα ἴσχουσιν, ἔρωτά τε καὶ ἐρᾶν καὶ
ἐρασταί.

Κινδυνεύεις ἀληθῆ, ἔφην ἐγώ, λέγειν.

10 Καὶ λέγεται μέν γέ τις, ἔφη, λόγος, ὡς οἳ ἂν τὸ ἥμισυ

e ἑαυτῶν ζητῶσιν, οὗτοι ἐρῶσιν· ὁ δ᾽ ἐμὸς λόγος οὔτε ἡμίσεός
φησιν εἶναι τὸν ἔρωτα οὔτε ὅλου, ἐὰν μὴ τυγχάνῃ γέ που,
ὦ ἑταῖρε, ἀγαθὸν ὄν, ἐπεὶ αὐτῶν γε καὶ πόδας καὶ χεῖρας
ἐθέλουσιν ἀποτέμνεσθαι οἱ ἄνθρωποι, ἐὰν αὐτοῖς δοκῇ τὰ

αἰτία, ἡ: cause, reason; charge, blame*
ἀπο-τέμνω: to cut off, sever
ἀφ-ορίζω: to mark off by boundaries, distinguish, define
δολερός, -ά, -όν: treacherous, deceptive
ἐργασία, ἡ: work, labor, creation, practicing
εὐ-δαιμονέω: to be happy, fortunate
ἴσχω: to have, hold back, check, restrain*
κατα-χράομαι: to use, apply; misuse, abuse
κεφάλαιον, τό: main or chief point, gist, sum*
μέτρον, τό: meter, measure, verse; length*

μόριον, τό: a piece, portion, section
ὀνομάζω: to name, call by name*
πολλα-χῆ: many times, often
που: anywhere, somewhere; I suppose
πούς, ποδός, ὁ: a foot*
προσ-αγορεύω: to address, call by name*
σπουδάζω: to pursue earnestly, be serious, be eager for, make haste*
φιλο-γυμναστία, ἡ: fondness for gymnastics
χρηματισμός, ὁ: money-making, gain, profit

205b5 τι εἶδος: *a certain type, a particular kind*; in contrast with "whole," τοῦ ὅλου
ἐπιτιθέντες: *attributing, applying*; pres. pple, ἐπι-τίθημι
ἔρωτα: acc. object of ὀνομάζομεν
b6 τὰ ἄλλα: *in respect to other (types of love)*; acc. of respect, supply n. pl. εἴδη
b7 Ὥσπερ τί: *Like what?, just as what?*
b8 Ὥσπερ τόδε: *Like this, like the following*
οἶσθ᾽: οἶσθα, 2ⁿᵈ sg., οἶδα
τι πολύ: *something complex*; "multiple"
b9 τοι: *you know*; perhaps an ethical dative
ἰόντι ὁτῳοῦν: *for whatsoever coming, going*; dat. pple, ἔρχομαι (ι)
ἡ...αἰτία πᾶσά: *entire cause for*
c2 ποιηταί: *(are) poets*; add εἰσίν
c4 καλοῦνται: *they are called*; governs a predicate nominative
c5 ἓν μόριον...τὸ περὶ: *one part regarding...*
c6 ἀφορισθὲν: *having been defined*; neuter sg. aor. pass. pple. ἀφ-ορίζω
τὰ μέτρα: *verse*; "the measures"
c7 τῷ...ὀνόματι: dat. of means
ποίησις: predicate nom. of καλεῖται
c9 ποιηταί: *(are) poets*; add εἰσίν
d1 τὸ κεφάλαιόν: *in general, in sum*

d3 παντί: *for everyone*
d4 τρεπόμενοι...ἐπ᾽ αὐτόν: *turning (themselves) toward it*; i.e. pursuing it
ἄλλη...πολλαχῆ: *in many different ways*; "in many other ways"
κατὰ...κατὰ...κατὰ: *through* (+ acc.)
d5 οὔτε ἐρᾶν καλοῦνται οὔτε ἐρασταί: *they are neither said to love nor are called lovers*; two uses of καλοῦνται
d6 κατὰ ἕν τι εἶδος: *through one particular type (of love)*
ἰόντες: *going, coming*; pple, ἔρχομαι (ι)
ἐσπουδακότες: pf. pple, σπουδάζω
d9 Κινδυνεύεις: *you are probably*; "you run the risk (+ infinitive)"
d10 τις...λόγος, ὡς: *a certain story... (namely) that...*
οἳ ἄν...ζητῶσιν: *whoever...*; the antecedent is the following οὗτοι
e1 ἡμίσεός...ὅλου: *(a lover) of half...of the whole*; both are objective genitive
τυγχάνῃ...ὄν: *it happens to be*; 3ʳᵈ sg. pres. subj., τυγχάνω + pple
e3 ἐπεὶ...γε: *(I say this) since*
αὐτῶν: *their own*; ἑαυτῶν, reflexive

5 ἑαυτῶν πονηρὰ εἶναι. οὐ γὰρ τὸ ἑαυτῶν οἶμαι ἕκαστοι
ἀσπάζονται, εἰ μὴ εἴ τις τὸ μὲν ἀγαθὸν οἰκεῖον καλεῖ καὶ

206 ἑαυτοῦ, τὸ δὲ κακὸν ἀλλότριον· ὡς οὐδέν γε ἄλλο ἐστὶν οὗ
ἐρῶσιν ἄνθρωποι ἢ τοῦ ἀγαθοῦ. ἢ σοὶ δοκοῦσιν;

Μὰ Δί᾽ οὐκ ἔμοιγε, ἦν δ᾽ ἐγώ.

Ἆρ᾽ οὖν, ἦ δ᾽ ἥ, οὕτως ἁπλοῦν ἐστι λέγειν ὅτι οἱ
ἄνθρωποι τἀγαθοῦ ἐρῶσιν;

5 Ναί, ἔφην.

Τί δέ; οὐ προσθετέον, ἔφη, ὅτι καὶ εἶναι τὸ ἀγαθὸν
αὑτοῖς ἐρῶσιν;

Προσθετέον.

Ἆρ᾽ οὖν, ἔφη, καὶ οὐ μόνον εἶναι, ἀλλὰ καὶ ἀεὶ εἶναι;

10 Καὶ τοῦτο προσθετέον.

Ἔστιν ἄρα συλλήβδην, ἔφη, ὁ ἔρως τοῦ τὸ ἀγαθὸν αὑτῷ
εἶναι ἀεί.

Ἀληθέστατα, ἔφην ἐγώ, λέγεις.

b Ὅτε δὴ τοῦτο ὁ ἔρως ἐστὶν ἀεί, ἦ δ᾽ ἥ, τῶν τίνα τρόπον
διωκόντων αὐτὸ καὶ ἐν τίνι πράξει ἡ σπουδὴ καὶ ἡ σύντασις
ἔρως ἂν καλοῖτο; τί τοῦτο τυγχάνει ὂν τὸ ἔργον; ἔχεις
εἰπεῖν;

5 Οὐ μεντἂν σέ, ἔφην ἐγώ, ὦ Διοτίμα, ἐθαύμαζον ἐπὶ
σοφίᾳ καὶ ἐφοίτων παρὰ σὲ αὐτὰ ταῦτα μαθησόμενος.

Ἀλλὰ ἐγώ σοι, ἔφη, ἐρῶ. ἔστι γὰρ τοῦτο τόκος ἐν
καλῷ καὶ κατὰ τὸ σῶμα καὶ κατὰ τὴν ψυχήν.

Μαντείας, ἦν δ᾽ ἐγώ, δεῖται ὅτι ποτε λέγεις, καὶ οὐ
5 μανθάνω.

c Ἀλλ᾽ ἐγώ, ἦ δ᾽ ἥ, σαφέστερον ἐρῶ. κυοῦσιν γάρ, ἔφη,
ὦ Σώκρατες, πάντες ἄνθρωποι καὶ κατὰ τὸ σῶμα καὶ κατὰ

ἀλλότριος, -α, -ον: of another, alien, foreign*
ἁπλόος, -η, -ον: single, simple, absolute*
ἀσπάζομαι: to welcome, embrace*
μά: by, *in affirmation**
μανθάνω: to learn, understand*
μαντεία, ἡ: oracle, prophetic power
ναί: yes, yeah*
οἰκεῖος, -α, -ον: one's own; belonging to one,
    private, *subst.* relatives*
πονηρός, -ά, -όν: wicked, base; defective*

πρᾶξις, -εως, ἡ: action, deed, activity,
    business*
προσ-τίθημι: to add, attribute, impose, give*
σαφής, -ές: clear, distinct, definite*
συλλήβδην: collectively, in sum, altogether
σύν-τασις, -εως, ἡ: effort
τόκος, ὁ: giving birth; childbirth, offspring,
    child*
φοιτάω: to go to and fro, visit, come regularly

205e5 τὰ ἑαυτῶν: *their own (body parts)*;
    neuter plural governs the singular δοκῇ
    τὸ ἑαυτῶν: *their own (traits)*
e6 εἰ μὴ εἴ: *unless if, except if*
    τις...καλεῖ: *one calls (acc.) (acc.)*; καλεῖ
    takes a double accusative
    οἰκεῖον...καὶ ἑαυτοῦ: *"what belongs to
    oneself" and "one's own"*
206a1 τοῦ ἀγαθοῦ: parallel to οὐδέν ἄλλο,
    the acc. is attracted into the gen. by οὗ
a2 Μὰ Δί': *By Zeus*; Μὰ Δία
a3 ἦ δ' ἥ: *she said*; ἦ is 3ʳᵈ sg. ἠμί
    ἁπλοῦν: *simply true*; "simple", neuter
    acc. sg. of uncontracted ἁπλοον
a6 Τί δέ: *What then?*
    οὐ προσθετέον: *should we not add?*; οὐ is
    used in a question expecting a yes
    answer, προσθετέον is a verbal adj. from
    προσ-τίθημι, supply ἐστίν
    εἶναι...αὐτοῖς: *they possess*; ἑαυτοῖς,
    reflexive, dat. of possession
a9 οὐ μόνον...ἀλλὰ καί: *not only...but also*
a13 Ἀληθέστατα: superlative adverb
b1 ὅτε: *since*

τῶν...καλοῖτο: *in what manner do they
    pursue it and in what activity are
    enthusiasm and effort called love?*; two
    interrogatives govern ἔρως ἄν καλοῖτο
b3 τοῦτο...τὸ ἔργον: *this function
    ἔχεις: are you able?*; ἔχω + pple
b5 μεντἄν: *certainly*; μέντοι ἄν
    οὐ..ἄν..ἐθαύμαζον: *I would not be
    amazed at...*; ἄν + impf. indicates a
    past potential
    ἐπὶ σοφίᾳ: *at your wisdom*
b6 ἐφοίτων: ἐφοίταον, impf. + ἄν in b5
    μαθησόμενος: *intending to learn, in
    order to learn*; fut., expressing purpose
    ἐρῶ: fut. ἐρέω
b7 τόκος ἐν καλῷ: *giving birth in the
    presence of beauty* or *in beauty*
b8 κατὰ τὸ σῶμα καὶ κατὰ τὴν ψυχήν:
    in regard to body and in regard to soul
b9 μαντείας...δεῖται: *what in the world you
    mean is in need of prophetic power*,
    object of separation with δεῖται
c1 σαφέστερον: *more clearly*; comparative
    adverb

τὴν ψυχήν, καὶ ἐπειδὰν ἔν τινι ἡλικίᾳ γένωνται, τίκτειν
ἐπιθυμεῖ ἡμῶν ἡ φύσις.   τίκτειν δὲ ἐν μὲν αἰσχρῷ οὐ
5   δύναται, ἐν δὲ τῷ καλῷ.   ἡ γὰρ ἀνδρὸς καὶ γυναικὸς
συνουσία τόκος ἐστίν.   ἔστι δὲ τοῦτο θεῖον τὸ πρᾶγμα,
καὶ τοῦτο ἐν θνητῷ ὄντι τῷ ζῴῳ ἀθάνατον ἔνεστιν, ἡ κύησις
καὶ ἡ γέννησις. τὰ δὲ ἐν τῷ ἀναρμόστῳ ἀδύνατον γενέ-
d   σθαι.   ἀνάρμοστον δ᾽ ἐστὶ τὸ αἰσχρὸν παντὶ τῷ θείῳ, τὸ
δὲ καλὸν ἁρμόττον.   Μοῖρα οὖν καὶ Εἰλείθυια ἡ Καλλονή
ἐστι τῇ γενέσει.   διὰ ταῦτα ὅταν μὲν καλῷ προσπελάζῃ
τὸ κυοῦν, ἵλεών τε γίγνεται καὶ εὐφραινόμενον διαχεῖται
5   καὶ τίκτει τε καὶ γεννᾷ· ὅταν δὲ αἰσχρῷ, σκυθρωπόν τε
καὶ λυπούμενον συσπειρᾶται καὶ ἀποτρέπεται καὶ ἀνείλλεται
καὶ οὐ γεννᾷ, ἀλλὰ ἴσχον τὸ κύημα χαλεπῶς φέρει. ὅθεν δὴ
τῷ κυοῦντί τε καὶ ἤδη σπαργῶντι πολλὴ ἡ πτοίησις γέγονε
e   περὶ τὸ καλὸν διὰ τὸ μεγάλης ὠδῖνος ἀπολύειν τὸν ἔχοντα.
ἔστιν γάρ, ὦ Σώκρατες, ἔφη, οὐ τοῦ καλοῦ ὁ ἔρως, ὡς
σὺ οἴει.

Ἀλλὰ τί μήν;
5   Τῆς γεννήσεως καὶ τοῦ τόκου ἐν τῷ καλῷ.
Εἶεν, ἦν δ᾽ ἐγώ.

Πάνυ μὲν οὖν, ἔφη.   τί δὴ οὖν τῆς γεννήσεως; ὅτι
ἀειγενές ἐστι καὶ ἀθάνατον ὡς θνητῷ ἡ γέννησις. ἀθα-
207   νασίας δὲ ἀναγκαῖον ἐπιθυμεῖν μετὰ ἀγαθοῦ ἐκ τῶν ὡμολογημένων, εἴπερ τοῦ ἀγαθοῦ ἑαυτῷ εἶναι ἀεὶ ἔρως ἐστίν.
ἀναγκαῖον δὴ ἐκ τούτου τοῦ λόγου καὶ τῆς ἀθανασίας τὸν
ἔρωτα εἶναι.

5   Ταῦτά τε οὖν πάντα ἐδίδασκέ με, ὁπότε περὶ τῶν ἐρω-

ἀει-γενής, -ές: everlasting
ἀ-θανασία, ἡ: immortality*
ἀν-άρμοστος, -ον: not harmonious, unsuitable
    disproportionate (+ dat.); disharmony
ἀν-είλω: to roll up, shrink back
ἀπο-λύω: to loose from, release*
ἀπο-τρέπω: to turn away, avert, deter
ἀρμόττος, -ον: harmonious, suitable,
    proportionate; subst. harmony
γέννησις, -εως, ἡ: engendering, producing*
δια-χέω: to disperse, break up, mid. to relax
διδάσκω: to teach, instruct*
εἶεν: well! well now!*
Εἰλείθυια, ἡ: Eilithyia, goddess of childbirth
ἐν-είμί: to be in, exist in*
εὐ-φραίνω: to cheer, gladden, delight
ἡλικία, ἡ: age, time of life*
ἵλαος, -ον: propitious, gracious, kind

ἴσχω: to have, hold back, check, restrain*
Καλλονή, ἡ: Beauty
κύημα, -ατος, τό: what is conceived, fetus
κύησις, -εως, ἡ: conception, pregnancy
λυπέω: to cause pain, distress, grief*
Μοῖρα, ἡ: Moira, goddess of one's lot in life
ὅ-θεν: from where, from which*
ὁπότε: when, by what time*
προσ-πελάζω: to approach, bring near (+ dat.)
πτοίησις, -εως, ἡ: excitement
σκυθρ-ωπός, -όν: sullen-looking, frowning
σπαργάω: to swell up, ripen
συ-σπειράομαι: to coil up
τόκος, ὁ: giving birth; childbirth, offspring,
    child*
ὠδίς, -ῖνος, ἡ: the pangs of labor, labor-pains

206c3 ἔν τινι ἡλικίᾳ γένωνται: they come to
    be a certain age; "in a certain age"
c4 ἐν αἰσχρῷ: in the presence of ugliness,
    in ugliness; the meaning is ambiguous
c5 ἐν δὲ τῷ καλῷ: but in the presence of
    beauty, but in beauty
c6 τόκος: (a sort of) birth; pred. noun
    τοῦτο: this; subject of both verbs
c7 ἐν θνητῷ...ζῴῳ: in an animal though
    being mortal; the pple is concessive
    ἀθάνατον ἔνεστιν: is immortal
    ἡ κύησις...γέννησις: namely...; in
    apposition to the preceding τοῦτο
c8 τὰ δὲ: these things; i.e. ἡ κύησις
    ...γέννησις, acc. subj. of γενέσθαι
    ἐν τῷ ἀναρμόστῳ: out of harmony;
    "in disharmony"
    ἀδύνατον: it is impossible; add ἐστίν
d1 ἀνάρμοστον: out of harmony with + dat.
d2 Μοῖρα...Εἰλείθυια: as Moira and
    Eilithyia
    ἡ Καλλονή: Beauty
d3 τῇ γενέσει: in the presence of birth
    καλῷ: dat. object of προσ-πελάζῃ
c7 προσπελάζῃ: 3rd sg. pres. subj.
d4 τὸ κυοῦν: one being pregnant; neuter.
    pple from κυέω
    ἵλεών: ἵλαον, neuter predicate nom.

διαχεῖται: relaxes; or "speads out"
d5 αἰσχρῷ: supply προσ-πελάζῃ
d6 ἀνείλεται: ἀνείλεται; the image is
    similar to the physical response of a penis
d7 ἴσχον τὸ κύημα χαλεπῶς φέρει: by
    holding onto what is conceived it
    bears it with difficulty; pple, ἴσχω
    ὅ-θεν δὴ: for this very reason
e1 μεγάλης ὠδῖνος: from great pain; gen.
    of separation with τὸ ἀπολύειν
    τὸν ἔχοντα: the one having (the pain);
    acc. object of τὸ ἀπολύειν
e3 οἴει: you think; 2nd sg. οἴομαι
e4 ἀλλὰ τί μήν: Well, what then?
e7 τί...τῆς γεννήσεως: why (is love love)
    for reproduction?; objective genitive
    ὅτι: because
e8 ὡς θνητῷ: for a mortal at least
207a1 ἀναγκαῖον: (it is) necessary; add ἐστίν
    ὡμολογημένων: what has been agreed
a2 εἴπερ...ἐστίν: if desire for the good is
    to possess (it) always; ἑαυτῷ is dat.
    of possession, "to be for itself"
a3 ἀναγκαῖον: (it is) necessary; add ἐστίν
    ἐκ τούτου τοῦ λόγου: according to this
argument

τικῶν λόγους ποιοῖτο, καί ποτε ἤρετο τί οἴει, ὦ Σώκρατες,
αἴτιον εἶναι τούτου τοῦ ἔρωτος καὶ τῆς ἐπιθυμίας; ἢ οὐκ
αἰσθάνῃ ὡς δεινῶς διατίθεται πάντα τὰ θηρία ἐπειδὰν γεννᾶν ἐπιθυμήσῃ, καὶ τὰ πεζὰ καὶ τὰ πτηνά, νοσοῦντά τε
b πάντα καὶ ἐρωτικῶς διατιθέμενα, πρῶτον μὲν περὶ τὸ συμμιγῆναι ἀλλήλοις, ἔπειτα περὶ τὴν τροφὴν τοῦ γενομένου,
καὶ ἕτοιμά ἐστιν ὑπὲρ τούτων καὶ διαμάχεσθαι τὰ ἀσθενέστατα τοῖς ἰσχυροτάτοις καὶ ὑπεραποθνήσκειν, καὶ αὐτὰ τῷ
5 λιμῷ παρατεινόμενα ὥστ' ἐκεῖνα ἐκτρέφειν, καὶ ἄλλο πᾶν
ποιοῦντα. τοὺς μὲν γὰρ ἀνθρώπους, ἔφη, οἴοιτ' ἄν τις ἐκ
λογισμοῦ ταῦτα ποιεῖν· τὰ δὲ θηρία τίς αἰτία οὕτως ἐρω-
c τικῶς διατίθεσθαι; ἔχεις λέγειν;

Καὶ ἐγὼ αὖ ἔλεγον ὅτι οὐκ εἰδείην· ἡ δ' εἶπεν, Διανοῇ
οὖν δεινός ποτε γενήσεσθαι τὰ ἐρωτικά, ἐὰν ταῦτα μὴ
ἐννοῇς;

5 Ἀλλὰ διὰ ταῦτά τοι, ὦ Διοτίμα, ὅπερ νυνδὴ εἶπον, παρὰ
σὲ ἥκω, γνοὺς ὅτι διδασκάλων δέομαι. ἀλλά μοι λέγε
καὶ τούτων τὴν αἰτίαν καὶ τῶν ἄλλων τῶν περὶ τὰ ἐρωτικά.

Εἰ τοίνυν, ἔφη, πιστεύεις ἐκείνου εἶναι φύσει τὸν ἔρωτα,
οὗ πολλάκις ὡμολογήκαμεν, μὴ θαύμαζε. ἐνταῦθα γὰρ
d τὸν αὐτὸν ἐκείνῳ λόγον ἡ θνητὴ φύσις ζητεῖ κατὰ τὸ δυνατὸν
ἀεί τε εἶναι καὶ ἀθάνατος. δύναται δὲ ταύτῃ μόνον, τῇ
γενέσει, ὅτι ἀεὶ καταλείπει ἕτερον νέον ἀντὶ τοῦ παλαιοῦ,
ἐπεὶ καὶ ἐν ᾧ ἓν ἕκαστον τῶν ζῴων ζῆν καλεῖται καὶ εἶναι
5 τὸ αὐτό—οἷον ἐκ παιδαρίου ὁ αὐτὸς λέγεται ἕως ἂν πρεσβύτης γένηται· οὗτος μέντοι οὐδέποτε τὰ αὐτὰ ἔχων ἐν
αὑτῷ ὅμως ὁ αὐτὸς καλεῖται, ἀλλὰ νέος ἀεὶ γιγνόμενος, τὰ
δὲ ἀπολλύς, καὶ κατὰ τὰς τρίχας καὶ σάρκα καὶ ὀστᾶ καὶ
e αἷμα καὶ σύμπαν τὸ σῶμα. καὶ μὴ ὅτι κατὰ τὸ σῶμα,
ἀλλὰ καὶ κατὰ τὴν ψυχὴν οἱ τρόποι, τὰ ἤθη, δόξαι, ἐπιθυ-

αἷμα, -ατος τό: blood*
αἰσθάνομαι: to perceive, feel, learn, realize*
ἀντί: instead of, in place of (+ gen.)*
ἀπ-όλλυμι: to destroy, kill, ruin*
ἀ-σθενής, -ές: without strength, weak, feeble*
διδάσκαλος, ὁ: a teacher*
δια-μάχομαι: to fight, strive, struggle against,
δια-νοέομαι: to think, suppose, intend*
δια-τίθεμαι: to be disposed, arranged, treated*
δόξα, ἡ: opinion, reputation, honor, glory*
δυνατός, -ή, -όν: capable, strong, possible*
ἐκ-τρέφω: to bring up from childhood, rear
ἐν-νοέω: to have in mind, notice, consider*
ἕτοιμος, -η, -ον: ready, prepared, at hand*
ἦθος, -εος, τό: custom; disposition, character*
θηρίον, τό: a wild animal, beast*
θρίξ, τριχός, ὁ: the hair of the head, hair
κατα-λείπω: to leave behind, abandon*

λιμός. ὁ, ἡ: hunger, famine
λογισμός, ὁ: calculation; account, reasoning
νοσέω: to be sick, ill*
νυν-δή: just now*
ὀστέον, τό: bone
οὐδέ-ποτε: not ever, never*
παιδάριον, τό: a small child, child
παρα-τείνω: to stretch out along, to extend
πεζός, -ή, -όν: on foot
πιστεύω: to trust, believe in, rely on
πρεσβύτης, ὁ: old man
πτηνός, -ή, -όν: feathered, winged
σάρξ, σαρκός, ἡ: flesh
συμ-μίγνυμι: to mix together, have intercourse
σύμ-πας, -ασα, -αν: all together, all at once*
τροφή, ἡ: nourishment; rearing, upbringing*
ὑπερ-αποθνήσκω: to die on behalf of, die for*

207a6 λόγους ποιοῖτο: *made speeches*; opt. replacing ἄν + subj. in an indefinite clause in secondary sequence
ἤρετο: *she asked*; 3rd sg. aor., ἔρομαι
οἴει: 2nd sg. pres., οἴομαι

a8 αἰσθάνῃ: αἰσθάνε(σ)αι, 2nd sg. pres.
ὡς δεινῶς διατίθεται: *how strangely ...are disposed*; with a neuter pl. subject

a9 ἐπιθυμήσῃ: 3rd sg. aor. subj.; pl. subject

b1 ἐρωτικῶς διατιθέμενα: *being erotically disposed*
συμμιγῆναι: aor. pass. dep. inf.

b2 τοῦ γενομένου: *of what has been born*

b3 ἕτοιμά ἐστιν: *are ready to*; the subject is τὰ ἀσθενέστατα (θηρία) below

b4 ἰσχυροτάτοις: obj. of διαμάχομαι
αὐτά: *they*; i.e. τὰ ἀσθενέστατα
τῷ λιμῷ: dat. of means

b5 παρατεινόμενα: *laid low*; "stretched out", pres. pass. pple
ἐκεῖνα: *those*; i.e. the new-born θηρία

b6 οἴοιτ᾽ ἄν τις: *one might think*; οἴοιτο

b7 τίς αἰτία: *what (is) the reason (that)...*

c1 ἔχεις: *are you able*; ἔχω + inf.

c2 εἰδείην: 1st s. opt. οἶδα; indirect discourse
διανοῇ: *do you intend*; δια-νοέ(σ)αι, 2nd sg. pres.

c3 γενήσεσθαι: fut. inf., γίγνομαι ; the subject is the subject of διανοῇ
τὰ ἐρωτικά: *in (respect to) erotic matters*; acc. of respect with δεινός

c5 ὅπερ νυνδὴ εἶπον: *as I said just now*; "the very thing I said just now"

c6 γνοὺς: nom. aor. act. pple, γιγνώσκω

c9 οὗ: *which*; an acc. made gen. by ἐκείνου
φύσει: *by nature*; dat. of respect
ἐνταῦθα: *there*; i.e. in the animal world

d1 τὸν αὐτὸν ἐκείνῳ λόγον: *according to the same principle as that one*; adv. acc.
κατὰ τὸ δυνατόν: *insofar as it is possible*

d2 ταύτῃ: *in this way*

d3 τῇ γενέσει: dat. means, in apposition
ὅτι: *because*

d4 ἐπεὶ καὶ ἐν ᾧ: *since in fact while...*; the main clause missing
καλεῖται: *is said to*; governs 2 infinitives

d5 οἷον: *for example*
ὁ αὐτὸς: *the same*

d8 τὰ δὲ ἀπολλύς: *losing other (parts)*; nom. sg. pres. pple.
κατὰ...τρίχας: *with respect to hair...*

e1 μὴ ὅτι...ἀλλὰ καὶ: *not only...but also*

μίαι, ἡδοναί, λῦπαι, φόβοι, τούτων ἕκαστα οὐδέποτε τὰ
αὐτὰ πάρεστιν ἑκάστῳ, ἀλλὰ τὰ μὲν γίγνεται, τὰ δὲ ἀπόλ-
5 λυται. πολὺ δὲ τούτων ἀτοπώτερον ἔτι, ὅτι καὶ αἱ ἐπιστῆμαι
208 μὴ ὅτι αἱ μὲν γίγνονται, αἱ δὲ ἀπόλλυνται ἡμῖν, καὶ οὐδέ-
ποτε οἱ αὐτοί ἐσμεν οὐδὲ κατὰ τὰς ἐπιστήμας, ἀλλὰ καὶ
μία ἑκάστη τῶν ἐπιστημῶν ταὐτὸν πάσχει. ὃ γὰρ καλεῖται
μελετᾶν, ὡς ἐξιούσης ἐστὶ τῆς ἐπιστήμης· λήθη γὰρ
5 ἐπιστήμης ἔξοδος, μελέτη δὲ πάλιν καινὴν ἐμποιοῦσα ἀντὶ
τῆς ἀπιούσης μνήμην σῴζει τὴν ἐπιστήμην, ὥστε τὴν
αὐτὴν δοκεῖν εἶναι. τούτῳ γὰρ τῷ τρόπῳ πᾶν τὸ θνητὸν
σῴζεται, οὐ τῷ παντάπασιν τὸ αὐτὸ ἀεὶ εἶναι ὥσπερ τὸ
b θεῖον, ἀλλὰ τῷ τὸ ἀπιὸν καὶ παλαιούμενον ἕτερον νέον
ἐγκαταλείπειν οἷον αὐτὸ ἦν. ταύτῃ τῇ μηχανῇ, ὦ Σώκρατες, ἔφη, θνητὸν ἀθανασίας μετέχει, καὶ σῶμα καὶ τἆλλα
πάντα· ἀθάνατον δὲ ἄλλῃ. μὴ οὖν θαύμαζε εἰ τὸ αὑτοῦ
5 ἀποβλάστημα φύσει πᾶν τιμᾷ· ἀθανασίας γὰρ χάριν παντὶ
αὕτη ἡ σπουδὴ καὶ ὁ ἔρως ἕπεται.

Καὶ ἐγὼ ἀκούσας τὸν λόγον ἐθαύμασά τε καὶ εἶπον
εἶεν, ἦν δ' ἐγώ, ὦ σοφωτάτη Διοτίμα, ταῦτα ὡς ἀληθῶς
οὕτως ἔχει;

c Καὶ ἥ, ὥσπερ οἱ τέλεοι σοφισταί, εὖ ἴσθι, ἔφη, ὦ
Σώκρατες· ἐπεί γε καὶ τῶν ἀνθρώπων εἰ ἐθέλεις εἰς τὴν
φιλοτιμίαν βλέψαι, θαυμάζοις ἂν τῆς ἀλογίας περὶ ἃ ἐγὼ
εἴρηκα εἰ μὴ ἐννοεῖς, ἐνθυμηθεὶς ὡς δεινῶς διάκεινται ἔρωτι
5 τοῦ ὀνομαστοὶ γενέσθαι "καὶ κλέος ἐς τὸν ἀεὶ χρόνον
ἀθάνατον καταθέσθαι", καὶ ὑπὲρ τούτου κινδύνους τε
κινδυνεύειν ἕτοιμοί εἰσι πάντας ἔτι μᾶλλον ἢ ὑπὲρ τῶν
d παίδων, καὶ χρήματα ἀναλίσκειν καὶ πόνους πονεῖν οὑστινασοῦν καὶ ὑπεραποθνῄσκειν. ἐπεὶ οἴει σύ, ἔφη, Ἄλκηστιν

ἀ-θανασία, ἡ: immortality*
ἄλλη: in another place; in another way*
ἀ-λογία, ἡ: unreasonableness, absurdity
ἀν-αλίσκω: to use up, to spend, squander
ἀπο-βλάστημα, -ατος, τό: a shoot, offspring
ἀπ-όλλυμι: to destroy, kill, ruin*
ἄ-τοπος, -ον: strange, odd, extraordinary*
διά-κειμαι: to be disposed, be affected*
ἐγ-καταλείπω: to leave behind, leave out
εἶεν: well! well now!*
ἐν-θυμέομαι: to consider, reflect, ponder*
ἐν-νοέω: to have in mind, consider, reflect*
ἐξ-έρχομαι: to go out, come out*
ἔξ-οδος, ἡ: exit, way out, outlet
ἕτοιμος, -η, -ον: ready, prepared, at hand*
καινός, -ή, -όν: new, novel, strange*
κατα-τίθημι: to put down, lay up in store
κίνδυνος, ὁ: risk, danger, venture
κλέος, -εος, τό: glory, fame, rumor

λήθη, ἡ: forgetfulness
λύπη, ἡ: pain, distress, grief*
μελετάω: to care for, practice, study
μελέτη, ἡ: care, attention, study, practice
μηχανή, ἡ: means, device, contrivance*
μνήμη, ἡ: a remembrance, memory, record*
ὀνομαστός, -ή, -όν: named, notable, famous
οὐδέ-ποτε: not ever, never*
παλαιόω: to be old, become old, make old*
παντά-πασι: all in all, altogether, absolutely*
πονέω: to work hard, toil
πόνος, ὁ: work, toil, labor*
σοφιστής, ὁ: sophist, wise man*
σῴζω: to save, keep, preserve*
τέλεος, -α, -ον: perfect, complete; last*
ὑπερ-αποθνήσκω: to die on behalf of, die for*
φιλο-τιμία, ἡ: love of honor, ambition
φόβος, ὁ: fear, terror, panic*
χάρις, χάριτος, ἡ: grace, favor, gratitude*

207e3 τὰ αὐτὰ πάρεστιν: *is the same* (+ dat.)
  e4 τὰ μὲν...τὰ δέ: *some...others*
  e5 πολύ...τούτων ἀτοπώτερον ἔτι: *still much more extraordinary than these things (is)*; gen. of comparison, add ἐστίν
    αἱ ἐπιστῆμαι: *(items of) knowledge*
208a1 μὴ ὅτι...ἀλλὰ καί: *not only...but also*
    αἱ μὲν...αἱ δέ: *some...others*
    ἐσμεν: *we are*; οἱ αὐτοί is a pred. adj.
  a2 οὐδὲ κατὰ τὰς ἐπιστήμας: *not even in regards to our knowledge*
  a3 ταὐτόν: *the same thing*; τὸ αὐτόν ὅ...καλεῖται μελετᾶν...ἐστί: *what is called studying exists*; inf., α-contract
  a4 ὡς ἐξιούσης...ἐπιστήμης: *since knowledge goes out (of us)*; ὡς + pple
  a5 ἔξοδος: *(is) the exit*; predicate noun
    καινὴν...μνήμην: *new memory*
  a6 ἀντὶ τῆς ἀπιούσης: *in place of the (memory) slipping away*; supply μνήμης, pple ἀπέρχομαι
    ὥστε...δοκεῖν εἶναι: *so as to...*; result
  a7 τὴν αὐτήν: *the same*; pred. of εἶναι
    τούτῳ...τῷ τρόπῳ: *in this way*
  a8 τῷ...εἶναι: *because it is*; "by its being"; articular inf., dat. of means or cause
  b1 τῷ...ἐγκαταλείπειν: *because...leaves behind*" dat. of means or cause; cf. a8
    τὸ ἀπιὸν καὶ παλαιούμενον: *(the*

mortal part) growing old and departing; acc. subject; pple. ἀπέρχομαι
  b2 οἷον αὐτὸ ἦν: *(something) such as it was*
    ταύτῃ τῇ μηχανῇ: *in this way*
  b3 σῶμα...πάντα: *in respect to body and all other things*; τὰ ἄλλα, acc. respect
  b4 ἄλλη: *in a different way, another way*
  b5 πᾶν: *everything*; subject of 3rd sg. τιμᾷ
    ἀθανασίας...χάριν: *for the sake of immortality*; "thanks to immortality"
  b6 ἔπεται: *accompanies* (+ dat.)
  b8 ὡς ἀληθῶς: *truly*
  b9 οὕτως ἔχει: *are so*; "hold in this way," ἔχω + inf.
  c1 ἥ: *she*; demonstrative pronoun
    τέλεοι σοφισταί: *consummate sophists*
    εὖ ἴσθι: *know well*; sg. imperative, οἶδα
  c2 τῶν ἀνθρώπων: *with* φιλοτιμίαν
  c3 βλέψαι: *to look*; aor. inf. βλέπω
    τῆς ἀλογίας: *your folly*; obj. of verb
    περὶ ἃ ἐγὼ εἴρηκα: *regarding that which I have said*; 1st sg. pf. ἐρέω
  c4 ἐνθυμηθείς: *considering*; aor. dep. pple
    ὡς δεινῶς: *how strangely*
  c5 τοῦ γενέσθαι...καταθέσθαι: *for becoming ...storing up*; aor. κατατίθημι; articular infinitives, objective gen. with ἔρωτι
    ἐς...χρόνον: *everlasting*; "for all time"
  c3 οὑστινασοῦν: *whatsoever toils*

ὑπὲρ Ἀδμήτου ἀποθανεῖν ἄν, ἢ Ἀχιλλέα Πατρόκλῳ ἐπαποθανεῖν, ἢ προαποθανεῖν τὸν ὑμέτερον Κόδρον ὑπὲρ τῆς
5 βασιλείας τῶν παίδων, μὴ οἰομένους ἀθάνατον μνήμην
ἀρετῆς πέρι ἑαυτῶν ἔσεσθαι, ἣν νῦν ἡμεῖς ἔχομεν; πολλοῦ
γε δεῖ, ἔφη, ἀλλ' οἶμαι ὑπὲρ ἀρετῆς ἀθανάτου καὶ τοιαύτης
δόξης εὐκλεοῦς πάντες πάντα ποιοῦσιν, ὅσῳ ἂν ἀμείνους
e ὦσι, τοσούτῳ μᾶλλον· τοῦ γὰρ ἀθανάτου ἐρῶσιν. οἱ μὲν
οὖν ἐγκύμονες, ἔφη, κατὰ τὰ σώματα ὄντες πρὸς τὰς γυναῖκας
μᾶλλον τρέπονται καὶ ταύτῃ ἐρωτικοί εἰσιν, διὰ παιδογονίας
ἀθανασίαν καὶ μνήμην καὶ εὐδαιμονίαν, ὡς οἴονται, αὑτοῖς
5 εἰς τὸν ἔπειτα χρόνον πάντα ποριζόμενοι· οἱ δὲ κατὰ τὴν
209 ψυχήν—εἰσὶ γὰρ οὖν, ἔφη, οἳ ἐν ταῖς ψυχαῖς κυοῦσιν ἔτι
μᾶλλον ἢ ἐν τοῖς σώμασιν, ἃ ψυχῇ προσήκει καὶ κυῆσαι
καὶ τεκεῖν· τί οὖν προσήκει; φρόνησίν τε καὶ τὴν ἄλλην
ἀρετήν—ὧν δή εἰσι καὶ οἱ ποιηταὶ πάντες γεννήτορες καὶ
5 τῶν δημιουργῶν ὅσοι λέγονται εὑρετικοὶ εἶναι· πολὺ δὲ
μεγίστη, ἔφη, καὶ καλλίστη τῆς φρονήσεως ἡ περὶ τὰ τῶν
πόλεών τε καὶ οἰκήσεων διακόσμησις, ᾗ δὴ ὄνομά ἐστι
σωφροσύνη τε καὶ δικαιοσύνη—τούτων δ' αὖ ὅταν τις ἐκ
b νέου ἐγκύμων ᾖ τὴν ψυχήν, ἤθεος ὢν καὶ ἡκούσης τῆς
ἡλικίας, τίκτειν τε καὶ γεννᾶν ἤδη ἐπιθυμῇ, ζητεῖ δὴ
οἶμαι καὶ οὗτος περιὼν τὸ καλὸν ἐν ᾧ ἂν γεννήσειεν· ἐν
τῷ γὰρ αἰσχρῷ οὐδέποτε γεννήσει. τά τε οὖν σώματα τὰ
5 καλὰ μᾶλλον ἢ τὰ αἰσχρὰ ἀσπάζεται ἅτε κυῶν, καὶ ἂν
ἐντύχῃ ψυχῇ καλῇ καὶ γενναίᾳ καὶ εὐφυεῖ, πάνυ δὴ ἀσπάζεται τὸ συναμφότερον, καὶ πρὸς τοῦτον τὸν ἄνθρωπον
εὐθὺς εὐπορεῖ λόγων περὶ ἀρετῆς καὶ περὶ οἷον χρὴ εἶναι
c τὸν ἄνδρα τὸν ἀγαθὸν καὶ ἃ ἐπιτηδεύειν, καὶ ἐπιχειρεῖ

ἀ-θανασία, ἡ: immortality*
ἀσπάζομαι: to welcome, embrace*
βασιλεία, ας, ἡ: rule, dominion, kingdom*
γενναῖος, -α, -ον: noble, well-bred*
γεννήτωρ, -ορος, ὁ: begetter, father, ancestor
δημιουργός, ὁ: a skilled workman, craftsman*
δικαιοσύνη, ἡ: justice, righteousness*
δια-κόσμησις, -εως, ἡ: a setting in order,
    regulating, management
δόξα, ἡ: opinion, reputation, honor, glory*
ἐγ-κύμων, -ον: pregnant
ἐπ-αποθνῄσκω: to die after, die afterwards
ἐπιτηδεύω: to pursue. follow, practice
εὐ-δαιμονία, ἡ: happiness, good fortune*
εὐθύς: right away, straight, directly, at once*
εὐ-κλεής, -ές: glorious, famous
εὐ-πορέω: to prosper, thrive, be well off*

εὑρετικός, -όν: inventive, ingenious
εὐ-φυής, -ές: naturally gifted, naturally suited
ἤθεος, ὁ: a young man, unmarried man
ἡλικία, ἡ: age, time of life*
Κόδρος, ὁ: Codros
μνήμη, ἡ: a remembrance, memory, record*
οἴκησις, ἡ: dwelling, house, household
οὐδέ-ποτε: not ever, never*
παιδο-γονία, ἡ: begetting of children
περι-έρχομαι: to go around, come round
πορίζω: to provide, procure, furnish, supply*
προ-αποθνῄσκω: to die before or first
προσ-ήκει: it is fitting, is suitable (dat.) (inf.)*
συν-αμφότεροι: both together
ὑμέτερος, -α, -ον: your, yours*
φρόνησις, -εως, ἡ: wisdom, intelligence,
    prudence*

208d3 ἀποθανεῖν ἄν: *would have died*; ἄν +
aor. inf., past potential. subject Ἄλκηστιν

d6 ἀρετῆς πέρι: *concerning the exellence*
ἔσεσθαι: fut. inf., εἰμί; subj. is μνήμην
πολλοῦ δεῖ: *far from it*; "it lacks from
much" cf. 203c6

d8 εὐκλεοῦς: εὐ-κλεεός, gen. sg.
ὅσῳ...τοσούτῳ μᾶλλον: *the better
they are, the more (they do it)*; "by as
much as they are better, by that much
more (they do it)", ὅσῳ and τοσούτῳ
are dat. of the decree of difference with
a comparative adj. and adv. ἀμείνους
(ἀμεινο(ν)ες) and μᾶλλον respectively

e1 ὦσι: 3ʳᵈ pl. pres. subj., εἰμί

e2 ἐγκύμονες: predicate adj. of οἱ...ὄντες
κατὰ τὰ σώματα: *in bodies*

e3 ταύτῃ: *in this way*

e5 εἰς τὸν ἔπειτα χρόνον πάντα: *for all
time hereafter, for the entire future*
οἱ...ψυχήν: *those (pregnant) in their soul*

209a1 εἰσί...οἱ: *for there are those who*...

a2 ἅ...τεκεῖν: *(pregnant with) things
which*...; direct object of κυοῦσιν
κυῆσαι: aor. act. inf., κυέω

a4 ὧν: *of which*; governed by γεννήτορες

a5 τῶν δημιουργῶν ὅσοι: *as many of the
craftsmen as*...; δημιουργῶν is a

partitive gen. within the relative clause
πολὺ μεγίστη: *by far the greatest*

a7 ἣ...ἐστι: *which has*; dat. of possession

a8 τούτων: *with these things*; neuter gen.
obj. governed by ἐγκύμων below
ἐκ νέου: *from youth*

b1 ᾗ: *is*; 3ʳᵈ sg. pres. subj., εἰμί
τὴν ψυχήν: *in the soul*; acc. of respect
ἡκούσης τῆς ἡλικίας: gen. abs.

b2 ἐπιθυμῇ: *(and) desires*; 3ʳᵈ sg. pres. subj;

b3 περιιών: pres. pple, περι-έρχομαι (-ι)
τὸν καλόν: *beauty*; obj. of ζητεῖ
γεννήσειεν: *might beget*; 3ʳᵈ sg. aor.
potential subj.
ἐν τῷ...αἰσχρῷ: *in ugliness, in the
presence of ugliness*

b5 μᾶλλον ἤ: *rather than*
ἅτε κυῶν: *since*...; ἅτε + pple κυέω
ἄν: *ἐάν*

b6 ἐντύχῃ: 3ʳᵈ sg. aor. subj., ἐν-τυγχάνω

b8 πρὸς...ἄνθρωπον: *toward this person*
εὐπορεῖ λόγων: *he possesses a wealth
of words*
περὶ οἷον: *regarding what sort (of
man)*

c1 ἅ ἐπιτηδεύειν: *(regarding) what
things (a good man ought) to practice*

παιδεύειν. ἁπτόμενος γὰρ οἶμαι τοῦ καλοῦ καὶ ὁμιλῶν
αὐτῷ, ἃ πάλαι ἐκύει τίκτει καὶ γεννᾷ, καὶ παρὼν καὶ ἀπὼν
μεμνημένος, καὶ τὸ γεννηθὲν συνεκτρέφει κοινῇ μετ᾽ ἐκείνου,
5 ὥστε πολὺ μείζω κοινωνίαν τῆς τῶν παίδων πρὸς ἀλλήλους
οἱ τοιοῦτοι ἴσχουσι καὶ φιλίαν βεβαιοτέραν, ἅτε καλλιόνων
καὶ ἀθανατωτέρων παίδων κεκοινωνηκότες. καὶ πᾶς ἂν
δέξαιτο ἑαυτῷ τοιούτους παῖδας μᾶλλον γεγονέναι ἢ τοὺς
d ἀνθρωπίνους, καὶ εἰς Ὅμηρον ἀποβλέψας καὶ Ἡσίοδον καὶ
τοὺς ἄλλους ποιητὰς τοὺς ἀγαθοὺς ζηλῶν, οἷα ἔκγονα ἑαυτῶν
καταλείπουσιν, ἃ ἐκείνοις ἀθάνατον κλέος καὶ μνήμην παρέχεται αὐτὰ τοιαῦτα ὄντα· εἰ δὲ βούλει, ἔφη, οἵους Λυκοῦργος
5 παῖδας κατελίπετο ἐν Λακεδαίμονι σωτῆρας τῆς Λακεδαί-
μονος καὶ ὡς ἔπος εἰπεῖν τῆς Ἑλλάδος. τίμιος δὲ παρ᾽
ὑμῖν καὶ Σόλων διὰ τὴν τῶν νόμων γέννησιν, καὶ ἄλλοι
e ἄλλοθι πολλαχοῦ ἄνδρες, καὶ ἐν Ἕλλησι καὶ ἐν βαρβάροις,
πολλὰ καὶ καλὰ ἀποφηνάμενοι ἔργα, γεννήσαντες παντοίαν
ἀρετήν· ὧν καὶ ἱερὰ πολλὰ ἤδη γέγονε διὰ τοὺς τοιούτους
παῖδας, διὰ δὲ τοὺς ἀνθρωπίνους οὐδενός πω.
5 Ταῦτα μὲν οὖν τὰ ἐρωτικὰ ἴσως, ὦ Σώκρατες, κἂν σὺ
210 μυηθείης· τὰ δὲ τέλεα καὶ ἐποπτικά, ὧν ἕνεκα καὶ ταῦτα
ἔστιν, ἐάν τις ὀρθῶς μετίῃ, οὐκ οἶδ᾽ εἰ οἷός τ᾽ ἂν εἴης.
ἐρῶ μὲν οὖν, ἔφη, ἐγὼ καὶ προθυμίας οὐδὲν ἀπολείψω·
πειρῶ δὲ ἕπεσθαι, ἂν οἷός τε ᾖς. δεῖ γάρ, ἔφη, τὸν ὀρθῶς
5 ἰόντα ἐπὶ τοῦτο τὸ πρᾶγμα ἄρχεσθαι μὲν νέον ὄντα ἰέναι
ἐπὶ τὰ καλὰ σώματα, καὶ πρῶτον μέν, ἐὰν ὀρθῶς ἡγῆται
ὁ ἡγούμενος, ἑνὸς αὐτὸν σώματος ἐρᾶν καὶ ἐνταῦθα γεννᾶν
λόγους καλούς, ἔπειτα δὲ αὐτὸν κατανοῆσαι ὅτι τὸ κάλλος
b τὸ ἐπὶ ὁτῳοῦν σώματι τῷ ἐπὶ ἑτέρῳ σώματι ἀδελφόν ἐστι,
καὶ εἰ δεῖ διώκειν τὸ ἐπ᾽ εἴδει καλόν, πολλὴ ἄνοια μὴ οὐχ

ἀδελφός, -ή, -όν: akin to, just like (+ dat.)
ἄλλο-θι: in another place, elsewhere*
ἀνθρώπινος, -η, -ον: human, of a human*
ἄ-νοια, ἡ: folly, foolishness
ἀπο-βλέπω: look away from, look at, gaze*
ἀπο-λείπω: to leave behind, abandon*
ἀπο-φαίνω: to show, make clear; perform*
βάρβαρος, ὁ: foreigner, a non-Greek*
βέβαιος, -ον: firm, steadfast, sure, certain*
γέννησις, -εως, ἡ: engendering, producing*
δέχομαι: to receive, accept, take*
ἔκ-γονος, -ον: offspring, a child
Ἑλλάς, Ἑλλάδος, ἡ: Hellas, Greece
Ἕλλην, Ἕλληνος, ὁ: Greek
ἐποπτικός, -όν: subst. highest mysteries
ἔπος, -εος, τό: a word
ζηλόω: to be jealous of, rival, emulate
ἱερόν, τό: temple, shrine, holy place
ἴσχω: to have, hold back, check, restrain*
κατα-λείπω: to leave behind, abandon*
κατα-νοέω: to observe, understand, consider
κλέος, -εος, τό: glory, fame, rumor

κοινῇ: in common, together, by consent*
κοινωνέω: to have a share of, partake in
κοινωνία, ἡ: association, partnership*
Λακεδαίμων, -ονος, ἡ: Lacedaemon*
Λυκοῦργος, ὁ: Lycurgus
μείζων, μεῖζον: larger, greater*
μέτ-ειμι: to go after, pursue
μιμνήσκω: to recall, remember*
μνήμη, ἡ: a remembrance, memory, record*
μυέω: to initiate into the mysteries
ὁμιλέω: to associate, consort, converse with
παιδεύω: to educate, to teach*
πάλαι: long ago, formerly, of old*
παντοῖος, -α, -ον: every sort, various
πολλα-χοῦ: in many places
προ-θυμία, ἡ: eagerness, zeal, readiness
πω: yet, up to this time*
Σόλων, -ονος, ὁ: Solon
συν-εκτρέφω: to rear up together or along with
σωτήρ, ὁ: savior, deliverer, preserver
τέλος, -εος, τό: end, goal, result; sacred rites*
τίμιος, -α, -ον: honored, valued, worthy*

209c3 ἁπτόμενος: *touching*; + partitive gen.
παρὼν...ἀπὼν μεμνημένος: *recalling (him) both (being) present and (being) absent*; πάρειμι, ἄπειμι, μιμνήσκω

c4 τὸ γεννηθέν: *the thing (having been) born*; neuter aor. pass. pple

c5 μείζω: μείζονα, modifying κοινωνίαν τῆς τῶν παίδων: *than the partnership for children*; gen. of comparison supply κοινωνίας

c6 ἅτε...κεκοινωνηκότες: *since they have in common* (+ gen.); ἅτε + pf. pple καλλιόνων: gen., irregular comparative

c7 ἂν δέξαιτο...μᾶλλον.ἤ: *would prefer than...than...*; "*would rather accept that*"

c8 τοὺς ἀνθρωπίνους: *human (children)*

d2 ζηλῶν, οἷα: *envying what sort of...*

d3 παρέχεται: *provides*; subj. is neuter pl. αὐτά...ὄντα: *(since) they are such*; i.e. immortal, "*themselves being such*"

d4 εἰ δὲ βούλει: *If you wish*; parenthetical οἵους...παῖδας: *what sort of children*; i.e. his laws, same as οἷα ἔγκονα above

d5 σωτῆρας: *as deliverers*

d6 ὡς ἔπος εἰπεῖν: *so to speak, as it were*

d7 παρ' ὑμῖν: *among you*; supply ἐστίν

e1 ἄλλοθι πολλαχοῦ: *in many other places*; "*in many places elsewhere*"

e2 ἀποφηνάμενοι: *performing*; aor. pple

e3 ὧν...ἱερὰ πολλὰ ἤδη γέγονε: *for whom many shrines have come to be*

e4 οὐδενός πω: *for no one yet (a shrine has come to be)*; parallel to e3

e5 Ταῦτα...ἐρωτικά: *in...*; acc. respect κἂν σὺ μυηθείης: *even you might be initiated*; aor. pass. potential opt. μυέω

210a1 τέλεα...ἐποπτικά: *rites and mysteries*

a2 μετίῃ: *one pursues*, 3rd sg. subj., μέτ-ειμι οἷος τε...εἴης: *you would be able*; opt.

a3 ἐρῶ μὲν...πειρῶ δὲ: *I, on the one hand, will speak...you, on the other hand, try*; fut. ἐρέω, sg. imperative πειρα(σ)ο

a4 ἂν οἷός τε ᾖς: *if you are able*; ἐάν

e5 τὸν.ἰόντα: *the one proceeding*; ἔρχομαι ἰέναι: *to proceed*; inf. ἔρχομαι

e7 ἑνός...σώματος: obj. of inf. ἐρᾶν κατανοῆσαι:8; aor. inf.

b1 ἐπὶ...σώματι: *in whatsoever body* τῷ...σώματι ἀδελφόν: *akin to (beauty) in another body*; add dat. κάλλει

b2 ἐπὶ εἴδει: *in (the case of) physical form* μὴ οὐχ...ἡγεῖσθαι: *not to consider...*

ἕν τε καὶ ταὐτὸν ἡγεῖσθαι τὸ ἐπὶ πᾶσιν τοῖς σώμασι κάλλος·
τοῦτο δ' ἐννοήσαντα καταστῆναι πάντων τῶν καλῶν σωμάτων
5 ἐραστήν, ἑνὸς δὲ τὸ σφόδρα τοῦτο χαλάσαι καταφρονή-
σαντα καὶ σμικρὸν ἡγησάμενον· μετὰ δὲ ταῦτα τὸ ἐν ταῖς
ψυχαῖς κάλλος τιμιώτερον ἡγήσασθαι τοῦ ἐν τῷ σώματι,
ὥστε καὶ ἐὰν ἐπιεικὴς ὢν τὴν ψυχήν τις κἂν σμικρὸν ἄνθος
c ἔχῃ, ἐξαρκεῖν αὐτῷ καὶ ἐρᾶν καὶ κήδεσθαι καὶ τίκτειν λόγους
τοιούτους καὶ ζητεῖν, οἵτινες ποιήσουσι βελτίους τοὺς
νέους, ἵνα ἀναγκασθῇ αὖ θεάσασθαι τὸ ἐν τοῖς ἐπιτηδεύμασι
καὶ τοῖς νόμοις καλὸν καὶ τοῦτ' ἰδεῖν ὅτι πᾶν αὐτὸ αὑτῷ
5 συγγενές ἐστιν, ἵνα τὸ περὶ τὸ σῶμα καλὸν σμικρόν τι
ἡγήσηται εἶναι· μετὰ δὲ τὰ ἐπιτηδεύματα ἐπὶ τὰς ἐπιστήμας
ἀγαγεῖν, ἵνα ἴδῃ αὖ ἐπιστημῶν κάλλος, καὶ βλέπων πρὸς
d πολὺ ἤδη τὸ καλὸν μηκέτι τὸ παρ' ἑνί, ὥσπερ οἰκέτης,
ἀγαπῶν παιδαρίου κάλλος ἢ ἀνθρώπου τινὸς ἢ ἐπιτηδεύ-
ματος ἑνός, δουλεύων φαῦλος ἢ καὶ σμικρολόγος, ἀλλ' ἐπὶ
τὸ πολὺ πέλαγος τετραμμένος τοῦ καλοῦ καὶ θεωρῶν πολ-
5 λοὺς καὶ καλοὺς λόγους καὶ μεγαλοπρεπεῖς τίκτῃ καὶ διανοή-
ματα ἐν φιλοσοφίᾳ ἀφθόνῳ, ἕως ἂν ἐνταῦθα ῥωσθεὶς καὶ
αὐξηθεὶς κατίδῃ τινὰ ἐπιστήμην μίαν τοιαύτην, ἥ ἐστι καλοῦ
e τοιοῦδε. πειρῶ δέ μοι, ἔφη, τὸν νοῦν προσέχειν ὡς οἷόν
τε μάλιστα. ὃς γὰρ ἂν μέχρι ἐνταῦθα πρὸς τὰ ἐρωτικὰ
παιδαγωγηθῇ, θεώμενος ἐφεξῆς τε καὶ ὀρθῶς τὰ καλά, πρὸς
τέλος ἤδη ἰὼν τῶν ἐρωτικῶν ἐξαίφνης κατόψεταί τι θαυ-
5 μαστὸν τὴν φύσιν καλόν, τοῦτο ἐκεῖνο, ὦ Σώκρατες, οὗ δὴ
ἕνεκεν καὶ οἱ ἔμπροσθεν πάντες πόνοι ἦσαν, πρῶτον μὲν
211 ἀεὶ ὂν καὶ οὔτε γιγνόμενον οὔτε ἀπολλύμενον, οὔτε αὐξανό-
μενον οὔτε φθίνον, ἔπειτα οὐ τῇ μὲν καλόν, τῇ δ' αἰσχρόν,
οὐδὲ τοτὲ μέν, τοτὲ δὲ οὔ, οὐδὲ πρὸς μὲν τὸ καλόν, πρὸς

ἀγαπάω: to love, show affection, be fond of*
ἄνθος, -εος, τό: a blossom, flower, bloom*
ἀπ-όλλυμι: to destroy, kill, ruin*
αὐξάνω: to increase, augment, develop
ἄ-φθονος, ον: ungrudging, unenvied
βελτίων, -ον: better
δια-νόημα, -ατος, τό: a thought, notion
δουλεύω: to be a slave, serve, be subject to*
ἔμ-προσθεν: before, former; earlier*
ἐν-νοέω: to have in mind, notice, consider*
ἐξαίφνης: suddenly, immediately*
ἐξ-αρκέω: to be enough, suffice, be sufficient*
ἐπιτήδευμα, τό: a pursuit, activity, practice*
ἐπιεικής, -ές: fitting, suitable, decent, good
ἐφεξῆς: in succession, in a row, in order
θεωρέω: to see, watch, look at*
καθ-ίστημι: to establish, put into a state, make
   become; fall into a state, become*
κατα-φρονέω: to think down upon, despise*

κήδομαι: to care for, be troubled for (+ gen.)
μεγαλο-πρεπής, -ές: magnificent
μέχρι: up to; until, as long as (+ gen.)*
μηκέτι: no longer, no more
οἰκέτης, -ου, ὁ: a house-slave, slave
παιδ-αγωγέω: to educate
παιδάριον, τό: a small child, child
πέλαγος, -εος, τό: sea
πόνος, ὁ: work, toil, labor*
ῥώννυμι: to strengthen, make strong; be fit*
σμικρο-λόγος, -α, -ον: petty, counting trifles
συγ-γενής, -ές: own kind, kin; natural, inborn
τέλος, -εος, τό: end, goal, result; sacred rites*
τίμιος, -α, -ον: honored, valued, worthy*
τοιόσδε, -άδε, -όνδε: such, the following*
τοτέ: at one time*
φθίνω: to wane, waste away, decay, perish
χαλάω: to slacken, loosen, release

210b3 ἕν..ταὐτόν: one and the same; τὸ αὐτὸ
   ἐπί...σώμασι: in (the case of) all bodies
b4 καταστῆναι: must become; aor. one of
   many infinitives governed by δεῖ in a4
b5 ἑνός...τοῦτο: this exceeding (love) for
   one (body); add τὸ ἐρᾶν, object of inf.
   χαλάσαι: must let go; aor. inf. with δεῖ
b6 σμικρὸν ἡγησάμενον: thinking (it) trivial
b7 τοῦ ἐν...σώματι: than that (beauty) in
   the body; gen. comparison;
b8 καὶ ἐάν...κἄν:: even if...even if; redundant
   τὴν ψυχήν: in soul; acc. of respect
   σμικρὸν ἄνθος: small bloom
c1 ἐξαρκεῖν...ζητεῖν: so as to..; with ὥστε
   τοιούτους...οἵτινες: the sorts...that
c2 βελτίους: better; βελτίο(ν)ες
c3 ἀναγκασθῇ: one be compelled; 3rd sg.
   aor. pass. dep. subj. in a purpose clause
   τό...καλόν: i.e. κάλλος, "beauty,"
c4 τοῦτο ἰδεῖν...ἐστιν: to see that all this
   (beauty) is akin itself to itself; aor. inf.
   ὁράω, αὑτῷ is the reflexive ἑαυτῷ
c5 σμικρόν τι: something trivial
c6 ἡγήσηται: 3rd sg. aor. subj. of purpose
   ἐπί...ἀγάγειν: (the guide) must lead
   (the youth) to fields of knowledge; add
   δεῖ from a4, note the change of subject

c7 ἴδῃ...τίκτῃ: one may see...may give
   birth; aor. subj. ὁράω and τίκτω,
   βλέπων...τὸ παρ' ἑνί: looking now to
   manifold beauty (and) no longer (to)
   (beauty) in one thing; supply κάλλος
   ᾖ: may be; 3rd sg. subj. εἰμί
d4 τὸ πολὺ πέλαγος: the manifold sea
   τετραμμένος: turned; pf. mid. τρέπομαι
   θεωρῶν: seeing (it); i.e. τὸ πέλαγος
d6 ἀφθόνῳ: unlimited, unstinting
   ῥωσθείς...αὐξηθείς: strengthened and
   developed; aor. pass. ῥώννυμι, αὐξάνω
d7 κατίδῃ: 3rd sg. aor. subj., καθ-οράω
e1 πειρῶ: try!; πειρά(σο)ο, sg. imperative
   ὡς...μάλιστα: as much as it is possible
e2 πρὸς τὰ ἐρωτικά: in regard to...
e3 παιδαγωγηθῇ: 3rd sg. aor. pass.
e4 ἰών: proceeding; pres. pple ἔρχομαι (ι)
   κατόψεταί: fut. dep., καθ-οράω (ὀπ-)
e5 τοῦτο ἐκεῖνο: this is that...; add ἐστίν
   ἦσαν: were; 3rd pl. impf. εἰμί
211a2 τῇ μὲν...τῇ δέ: in one way..in another..
a3 τοτὲ μέν...δέ: at one time...at another...
   πρὸς μὲν τὸ...πρὸς δὲ τὸ: in relation to
   this...in relation to that

δὲ τὸ αἰσχρόν, οὐδ᾽ ἔνθα μὲν καλόν, ἔνθα δὲ αἰσχρόν, ὡς
τισὶ μὲν ὂν καλόν, τισὶ δὲ αἰσχρόν· οὐδ᾽ αὖ φαντασθήσεται
αὐτῷ τὸ καλὸν οἷον πρόσωπόν τι οὐδὲ χεῖρες οὐδὲ ἄλλο
οὐδὲν ὧν σῶμα μετέχει, οὐδέ τις λόγος οὐδέ τις ἐπιστήμη,
οὐδέ που ὂν ἐν ἑτέρῳ τινι, οἷον ἐν ζῴῳ ἢ ἐν γῇ ἢ ἐν οὐρανῷ

b   ἢ ἔν τῳ ἄλλῳ, ἀλλ᾽ αὐτὸ καθ᾽ αὑτὸ μεθ᾽ αὑτοῦ μονοειδὲς ἀεὶ
ὄν, τὰ δὲ ἄλλα πάντα καλὰ ἐκείνου μετέχοντα τρόπον τινὰ
τοιοῦτον, οἷον γιγνομένων τε τῶν ἄλλων καὶ ἀπολλυμένων
μηδὲν ἐκεῖνο μήτε τι πλέον μήτε ἔλαττον γίγνεσθαι μηδὲ

5   πάσχειν μηδέν. ὅταν δή τις ἀπὸ τῶνδε διὰ τὸ ὀρθῶς παι-
δεραστεῖν ἐπανιὼν ἐκεῖνο τὸ καλὸν ἄρχηται καθορᾶν, σχεδὸν
ἄν τι ἅπτοιτο τοῦ τέλους. τοῦτο γὰρ δή ἐστι τὸ ὀρθῶς ἐπὶ

c   τὰ ἐρωτικὰ ἰέναι ἢ ὑπ᾽ ἄλλου ἄγεσθαι, ἀρχόμενον ἀπὸ
τῶνδε τῶν καλῶν ἐκείνου ἕνεκα τοῦ καλοῦ ἀεὶ ἐπανιέναι,
ὥσπερ ἐπαναβασμοῖς χρώμενον, ἀπὸ ἑνὸς ἐπὶ δύο καὶ ἀπὸ
δυοῖν ἐπὶ πάντα τὰ καλὰ σώματα, καὶ ἀπὸ τῶν καλῶν

5   σωμάτων ἐπὶ τὰ καλὰ ἐπιτηδεύματα, καὶ ἀπὸ τῶν ἐπιτηδευμάτων ἐπὶ τὰ καλὰ μαθήματα, καὶ ἀπὸ τῶν μαθημάτων ἐπ᾽
ἐκεῖνο τὸ μάθημα τελευτῆσαι, ὅ ἐστιν οὐκ ἄλλου ἢ αὐτοῦ
ἐκείνου τοῦ καλοῦ μάθημα, καὶ γνῷ αὐτὸ τελευτῶν ὃ ἔστι

d   καλόν. ἐνταῦθα τοῦ βίου, ὦ φίλε Σώκρατες, ἔφη ἡ Μαν-
τινικὴ ξένη, εἴπερ που ἄλλοθι, βιωτὸν ἀνθρώπῳ, θεωμένῳ
αὐτὸ τὸ καλόν. ὃ ἐάν ποτε ἴδῃς, οὐ κατὰ χρυσίον τε καὶ
ἐσθῆτα καὶ τοὺς καλοὺς παῖδάς τε καὶ νεανίσκους δόξει σοι

5   εἶναι, οὓς νῦν ὁρῶν ἐκπέπληξαι καὶ ἕτοιμος εἶ καὶ σὺ καὶ
ἄλλοι πολλοί, ὁρῶντες τὰ παιδικὰ καὶ συνόντες ἀεὶ αὐτοῖς,
εἴ πως οἷόν τ᾽ ἦν, μήτ᾽ ἐσθίειν μήτε πίνειν, ἀλλὰ θεᾶσθαι
μόνον καὶ συνεῖναι. τί δῆτα, ἔφη, οἰόμεθα, εἴ τῳ γένοιτο

e   αὐτὸ τὸ καλὸν ἰδεῖν εἰλικρινές, καθαρόν, ἄμεικτον, ἀλλὰ

ἄλλο-θι: in another place, elsewhere*
ἄ-μεικτος, -ον: unmixed, uniform
ἀπ-όλλυμι: to destroy, kill, ruin*
βιωτός, -όν: to be lived, worth living
γῆ, ἡ: earth*
δῆτα: certainly, to be sure, of course*
εἰλικρινής, -ές: unmixed, pure, absolute
ἐκ-πλήγνυμι: to strike with fear, amaze, astound, to drive out of one senses*
ἐλάττων, -ον: smaller, fewer*
ἔνθα: here, there*
ἐπ-αναβασμός, -οῦ, ὁ: ladder, steps of a stair
ἐπαν-έρχομαι: to go up; go back, return
ἐπιτήδευμα, τό: a pursuit, activity, practice*
ἐσθής, -ητος, ἡ: clothing, clothes
ἐσθίω: to eat

ἕτοιμος, -η, -ον: ready, prepared, at hand*
καθαρός, -ά, -όν: clean, pure, spotless*
μάθημα, -ατος, τό: instruction, teaching, lesson*
Μαντινικός, -ή, -όν: Mantinian
μονο-ειδής, -ές: uniform, of one kind or type
νεανίσκος, ὁ: a youth
ξένη, ἡ: a female guest, foreigner, stranger*
οὐρανός, ὁ: sky, heaven
παιδ-εραστέω: to be a lover of young men
που: anywhere, somewhere; I suppose
πρόσ-ωπον, τό: face, countenance*
σχεδόν: nearly, almost, just about, practically*
τέλος, -εος, τό: end, goal, result; sacred rites*
φαντάζομαι: to appear, seem, become visible
χρυσίον, τό: gold coin, money; jewelry

211a4 ἔνθα μὲν...ἔνθα δὲ: here...there
  ὡς...ὄν: as if it is, since it is; ὡς + pple
  τισὶ μὲν...τισὶ δὲ: for some...for others
a5 φαντασθήσεται: will appear; fut. dep.
a6 οἷον πρόσωπόν τι: like a face; as, for example, a face
a8 που...ἐν ἑτέρῳ τινι: being somewhere in something other (than itself)
  οἷον: for example
b1 τῳ ἄλλῳ: something else; τινι
  αὐτὸ καθ᾽ αὑτὸ μεθ᾽ αὑτοῦ: itself by itself with itself; intensive followed by two reflexive pronouns, ἑαυτὸ
b2 τρόπον τινὰ τοιοῦτον οἷον: in some such way that; adverbial acc.
b3 γιγνομένων...ἀπολλυμένων: although...; concessive, gen. abs.
b4 μηδὲν: not at all; adverbial
  ἐκεῖνο: that thing (i.e. absolute beauty); acc. subject of γίγνεσθαι
b6 ἐπανιὼν: pres. pple, ἐπαν-έρχομαι (ι-)
  καθορᾶν: pres. inf., καθ-οράω
  σχεδόν...τι: almost, just about
b7 ἂν ἅπτοιτο: would reach, grasp (+gen.)
c1 ἰέναι: to go, proceed; inf. ἔρχομαι
c2 ἐπανιέναι: pres. inf., ἐπαν-έρχομαι
c4 ἀπὸ δυοῖν: from two; dual gen. form
c7 τελευτῆσαι: one ends up at; aor. inf.

c8 γνῷ: (so that) one may learn; 3rd sg. aor. subj., γιγνώσκω; supply ἵνα
  τελευτῶν: finally; pple often adverbial
  αὐτό...ὅ ἐστι καλόν: the very thing that beauty is
d1 ἐνταῦθα τοῦ βίου: at that point of life; partitive genitive
d2 εἴπερ που ἄλλοθι: if anywhere; "if anywhere else(where)"
  βιωτὸν ἀνθρώπῳ: (life is) worth living for a human being; "it is worthy living"
d3 ὃ ἐάν ποτε ἴδῃς: which if you ever see; aor. subj., ὁράω
  κατά...: comparable with...
d4 δόξει: it will seem; 3rd s. fut.
d5 ἐκπέπληξαι: you are astounded; ἐκπέπληγσαι; 2nd sg. pf. pass.
  ἕτοιμος εἶ: you are ready; 2nd sg. εἰμί governing the infinitives below
d6 συνόντες...αὐτοῖς: being with them
d7 οἷόν τ᾽ ἦν: it was possible; impersonal use of οἷος τε + εἰμί; impf. of εἰμί
d8 συνεῖναι: pres. inf., σύν-ειμι
  εἴ τῳ γένοιτο...ἰδεῖν: if it should happen for anyone to see...; τῳ is an alternative form of the dat. τινι
e1 ἰδεῖν: inf. ὁράω

a   μὴ ἀνάπλεων σαρκῶν τε ἀνθρωπίνων καὶ χρωμάτων καὶ
ἄλλης πολλῆς φλυαρίας θνητῆς, ἀλλ᾽ αὐτὸ τὸ θεῖον καλὸν
δύναιτο μονοειδὲς κατιδεῖν; ἆρ᾽ οἴει, ἔφη, φαῦλον βίον
212 γίγνεσθαι ἐκεῖσε βλέποντος ἀνθρώπου καὶ ἐκεῖνο ᾧ δεῖ
θεωμένου καὶ συνόντος αὐτῷ; ἢ οὐκ ἐνθυμῇ, ἔφη, ὅτι ἐνταῦθα
αὐτῷ μοναχοῦ γενήσεται, ὁρῶντι ᾧ ὁρατὸν τὸ καλόν, τίκτειν
οὐκ εἴδωλα ἀρετῆς, ἅτε οὐκ εἰδώλου ἐφαπτομένῳ, ἀλλὰ
5   ἀληθῆ, ἅτε τοῦ ἀληθοῦς ἐφαπτομένῳ· τεκόντι δὲ ἀρετὴν
ἀληθῆ καὶ θρεψαμένῳ ὑπάρχει θεοφιλεῖ γενέσθαι, καὶ εἴπέρ
τῳ ἄλλῳ ἀνθρώπων ἀθανάτῳ καὶ ἐκείνῳ;

b   Ταῦτα δή, ὦ Φαῖδρέ τε καὶ οἱ ἄλλοι, ἔφη μὲν Διοτίμα,
πέπεισμαι δ᾽ ἐγώ· πεπεισμένος δὲ πειρῶμαι καὶ τοὺς ἄλλους
πείθειν ὅτι τούτου τοῦ κτήματος τῇ ἀνθρωπείᾳ φύσει συνεργὸν ἀμείνω Ἔρωτος οὐκ ἄν τις ῥᾳδίως λάβοι.   διὸ δὴ
5   ἔγωγέ φημι χρῆναι πάντα ἄνδρα τὸν ἔρωτα τιμᾶν, καὶ
αὐτὸς τιμῶ τὰ ἐρωτικὰ καὶ διαφερόντως ἀσκῶ, καὶ τοῖς
ἄλλοις παρακελεύομαι, καὶ νῦν τε καὶ ἀεὶ ἐγκωμιάζω τὴν
δύναμιν καὶ ἀνδρείαν τοῦ Ἔρωτος καθ᾽ ὅσον οἷός τ᾽ εἰμί. τοῦ-
c   τον οὖν τὸν λόγον, ὦ Φαῖδρε, εἰ μὲν βούλει, ὡς ἐγκώμιον εἰς
ἔρωτα νόμισον εἰρῆσθαι, εἰ δέ, ὅτι καὶ ὅπῃ χαίρεις ὀνομάζων,
τοῦτο ὀνόμαζε.

Εἰπόντος δὲ ταῦτα τοῦ Σωκράτους τοὺς μὲν ἐπαινεῖν, τὸν
5   δὲ Ἀριστοφάνη λέγειν τι ἐπιχειρεῖν, ὅτι ἐμνήσθη αὐτοῦ
λέγων ὁ Σωκράτης περὶ τοῦ λόγου· καὶ ἐξαίφνης τὴν αὔλειον
θύραν κρουομένην πολὺν ψόφον παρασχεῖν ὡς κωμαστῶν, καὶ
αὐλητρίδος φωνὴν ἀκούειν. τὸν οὖν Ἀγάθωνα, Παῖδες, φάναι,
d   οὐ σκέψεσθε; καὶ ἐὰν μέν τις τῶν ἐπιτηδείων ᾖ, καλεῖτε·
εἰ δὲ μή, λέγετε ὅτι οὐ πίνομεν ἀλλ᾽ ἀναπαυόμεθα ἤδη.

ἀνα-παύομαι: to rest*
ἀνά-πλεος, -α, -ον: full of (+ gen.)
ἀνδρεία, ἡ: manliness, bravery, courage*
ἀνθρώπειος, -α, -ον: human, of a human*
ἀνθρώπινος, -η, -ον: human, of a human*
ἀσκέω: to exercise, practice; fashion, adorn
αὔλειος, -α, -ον: of the court-yard
αὐλητρίς, -ίδος, ἡ: a flute-girl*
δια-φερόντως: differently from; especially*
ἐγ-κώμιον, τὸ: eulogy, speech of praise*
εἴδωλον, τό: an image, likeness, phantom
ἐκεῖ-σε: thither, to that place, to there*
ἐν-θυμέομαι: to consider, reflect, ponder*
ἐξαίφνης: suddenly, immediately*
ἐπιτήδειος, -α, -ον: suitable, useful. friendly;
    subst. close friend*
ἐφ-άπτω: to grab hold of, grasp, bind to*
θεο-φιλής, -ές: dear to the gods
κρούω: to strike, smite, knock, tap, clap

κτῆμα, -ατος, τό: possession, property
κωμαστής, -οῦ, ὁ: a reveler
μιμνήσκω: to recall, remember*
μοναχοῦ: alone, only
μονο-ειδής, -ές: uniform, of one kind or type
ὀνομάζω: to name, call by name*
ὅπη: by which way, in what way, how*
ὁρατός, -ή, -όν: able to be seen, visible
παρα-κελεύομαι: to order, urge, encourage*
σάρξ, σαρκός, ἡ: flesh
σκέπτομαι: to look at, examine, consider*
συν-εργός, -όν: collaborator; accomplice,
    fellow-worker, partner
ὑπ-άρχω: to be ready, available; be possible*
φλυαρία, ἡ: nonsense, silly talk, foolery
φωνή, ἡ: speech, voice*
χρῶμα, -ατος, τό: color, complexion; skin
ψόφος, ὁ: noise, sound

211e2 μὴ ἀνάπλεων: μὴ ἀνάπλεον, neut. sg.
  e4 δύναιτο: if he should be able; pres. opt.
    (stem δυνα-), governed by εἰ in d8
    κατιδεῖν: inf. καθοράω
    οἴει: you think; οἴε(σ)αι 2nd sg. mid.
212a1 γίγνεσθαι: belongs to + gen.
    ἐκεῖνο ᾧ δεῖ θεωμένου: beholding that
    thing (i.e. beauty itself) (with that) with
    which it is necessary (to behold it)
  a2 ἐνθυμῇ: ἐνθυμέε(σ)αι, 2nd sg. pres. mid.
  a3 αὐτῷ μοναχοῦ γενήσεται ὁρῶντι ᾧ
    ὁρατὸν τὸ καλόν: it will happen to
    him alone, looking (with that) with
    which beauty is able to be seen; cf. a1
  a4 ἅτε...ἐφαπτομένῳ: inasmuch...since...;
    ἅτε + pple is causal, same in a5
  a6 τεκόντι: for one...; aor. pple, τίκτω
    ἀρετὴν ἀληθῆ: true excellence; ἀληθέα
    is ε(σ) stem, 3rd decl. acc. sg.
    θρεψαμένῳ: nuturing; aor., τρέφω
    ὑπάρχει: it is possible; impersonal verb
    θεοφιλεῖ: dat., pred. adj. γενέσθαι
    εἴπέρ τῳ...ἐκείνῳ: if (it is possible) for
    any one else, (it is possible) for that one,
    too, (to become) immortal
  b2 πέπεισμαι: I am convinced of; "I have
    been persuaded" pf. pass., πείθω

  b3 ἀνθρωπείᾳ φύσει: for human nature; dat.
    of interest
    συνεργὸν ἀμείνω: a better partner for
    (gen.) than (gen.); ἀμείνο(ν)α, acc. sg.
    comparative adj.;first gen. κτήματος is
    the obj. Ἔρωτος is gen. of comparison
  b4 ἂν λάβοι: would find; aor. potential opt
  b5 χρῆναι: it is necessary; inf. χρή
    τιμᾶν: inf. α-contract τιμάω
  b8 καθ᾽ ὅσον: insofar as, in the extent that
    οἷός τ᾽ εἰμί: I am able
  c1 βούλει: βούλε(σ)αι, 2nd sg. pres. mid.
    ὡς ἐγκώμιον: as a speech of praise
  c2 νόμισον: consider; aor. imper. νομίζω
    εἰρῆσθαι: to have been said; pf. pass.
    εἰ δέ: or if (you wish); cf. εἰ μὲν in c1
    ὅτι καὶ ὅπῃ χαίρεις ὀνομάζων: what
    and how you are pleased to call it
  c5 ὅτι ἐμνήσθη αὐτοῦ: because (Socrates)
    had mentioned him; aor. dep. μιμνήσκω
  c7 ὡς κωμαστῶν: as if of revelers
  c8 Παῖδες: i.e. slaves, voc. direct address
  d1 οὐ σκέψεσθε: will you not look into it;
    fut. σκέπτομαι in a mild command
    ᾖ: he is; 3rd sg. pres. subj. εἰμί

Καὶ οὐ πολὺ ὕστερον Ἀλκιβιάδου τὴν φωνὴν ἀκούειν ἐν
τῇ αὐλῇ σφόδρα μεθύοντος καὶ μέγα βοῶντος, ἐρωτῶντος
5 ὅπου Ἀγάθων καὶ κελεύοντος ἄγειν παρ' Ἀγάθωνα. ἄγειν
οὖν αὐτὸν παρὰ σφᾶς τήν τε αὐλητρίδα ὑπολαβοῦσαν καὶ
ἄλλους τινὰς τῶν ἀκολούθων, καὶ ἐπιστῆναι ἐπὶ τὰς θύρας
e ἐστεφανωμένον αὐτὸν κιττοῦ τέ τινι στεφάνῳ δασεῖ καὶ
ἴων, καὶ ταινίας ἔχοντα ἐπὶ τῆς κεφαλῆς πάνυ πολλάς, καὶ
εἰπεῖν· ἄνδρες, χαίρετε· μεθύοντα ἄνδρα πάνυ σφόδρα
δέξεσθε συμπότην, ἢ ἀπίωμεν ἀναδήσαντες μόνον Ἀγάθωνα,
5 ἐφ' ᾧπερ ἤλθομεν; ἐγὼ γάρ τοι, φάναι, χθὲς μὲν οὐχ
οἷός τ' ἐγενόμην ἀφικέσθαι, νῦν δὲ ἥκω ἐπὶ τῇ κεφαλῇ
ἔχων τὰς ταινίας, ἵνα ἀπὸ τῆς ἐμῆς κεφαλῆς τὴν τοῦ σοφω-
τάτου καὶ καλλίστου κεφαλὴν ἐὰν εἴπω οὑτωσὶ ἀναδήσω.
ἆρα καταγελάσεσθέ μου ὡς μεθύοντος; ἐγὼ δέ, κἂν ὑμεῖς
213 γελᾶτε, ὅμως εὖ οἶδ' ὅτι ἀληθῆ λέγω. ἀλλά μοι λέγετε
αὐτόθεν, ἐπὶ ῥητοῖς εἰσίω ἢ μή; συμπίεσθε ἢ οὔ;

Πάντας οὖν ἀναθορυβῆσαι καὶ κελεύειν εἰσιέναι καὶ
κατακλίνεσθαι, καὶ τὸν Ἀγάθωνα καλεῖν αὐτόν. καὶ τὸν
5 ἰέναι ἀγόμενον ὑπὸ τῶν ἀνθρώπων, καὶ περιαιρούμενον ἅμα
τὰς ταινίας ὡς ἀναδήσοντα, ἐπίπροσθε τῶν ὀφθαλμῶν ἔχοντα
οὐ κατιδεῖν τὸν Σωκράτη, ἀλλὰ καθίζεσθαι παρὰ τὸν Ἀγά-
b θωνα ἐν μέσῳ Σωκράτους τε καὶ ἐκείνου· παραχωρῆσαι
γὰρ τὸν Σωκράτη ὡς ἐκεῖνον κατιδεῖν. παρακαθεζόμενον
δὲ αὐτὸν ἀσπάζεσθαί τε τὸν Ἀγάθωνα καὶ ἀναδεῖν.

Εἰπεῖν οὖν τὸν Ἀγάθωνα Ὑπολύετε, παῖδες, Ἀλκιβιάδην,
ἵνα ἐκ τρίτων κατακέηται.

5 Πάνυ γε, εἰπεῖν τὸν Ἀλκιβιάδην· ἀλλὰ τίς ἡμῖν ὅδε
τρίτος συμπότης; καὶ ἅμα μεταστρεφόμενον αὐτὸν ὁρᾶν

ἀκόλουθος, ὁ: follower*
ἀνα-θορυβέω: to cry out loudly, to applaud
ἀσπάζομαι: to welcome, embrace*
αὐλή, ἡ: the court-yard*
αὐλητρίς, -ίδος, ἡ: a flute-girl*
αὐτό-θεν: from the very spot or moment
ἀφ-ικνέομαι: to come, arrive*
βοάω: to shout, cry aloud
γελάω: to laugh*
δασύς, -εῖα, -ύ: thick, bushy, shaggy, rough
δέχομαι: to receive, accept, take*
ἐπί-προσθε: before, in front of
ἴον, τό: violet flower
καθ-ίζω: to make sit down, seat
κατα-γελάω: to laugh at, mock*
κιττός, ὁ: ivy
μεθύω: to be drunk with wine*
μέσος, -η, -ον: middle, in the middle of*6
μετα-στρέφω: to turn about, turn round*

ὅπου: where*
ὀφθαλμός, ὁ: the eye*
παρά-καθέζομαι: to sit down beside
παρα-χωρέω: to move over, make way, yield
περι-αιρέω: take off (from around), strip off
ῥητός, -ή, -όν: stated, specified, fixed*
στέφανος, ὁ: crown, wreath, garland
στεφανόω: to crown, wreathe, honor
συμ-πίνω: to drink together, join in drinking
συμ-πότης, ὁ: a fellow-drinker, symposiast*
ταινία, ἡ: a band, ribbon, fillet, head-band*
τοι: ya know, let me tell you, surely*
τρίτος, -η, -ον: a third*
ὑπο-λαμβάνω: to take up, reply; suppose*
ὑπο-λύω: to loosen from under, untie
ὕστερον: later*
φωνή, ἡ: speech, voice*
χθές: yesterday*

212d4 μέγα: *loudly*; adverbial acc.
  ἐρωτῶντος: pres. pple, ἐρωτάω
  d5 ὅπου Ἀγάθων: *where Agathon (is)*;
    indirect question, supply ἐστίν
    ἄγειν: *(a slave) to lead (him)*
  d6 σφᾶς: acc. of 3ʳᵈ pl. pronoun σφεῖς
    ὑπολαβοῦσαν: *supporting him*; "taking
    (him) up from underneath"
  d7 ἐπιστῆναι: *stood*; aor. inf., ἐφ-ίστημι
  e1 ἐστεφανωμένον: *crowned*; pf. pple
    στεφανόω
    τινι στεφάνῳ δασεῖ: dat. of means
  e2 ἐπὶ τῆς κεφαλῆς: *upon his head*
    χαίρετε: *hello!*; common greeting
  e4 δέξεσθε: *will you accept*; fut., δέχομαι
    συμπότην: *as a fellow drinker*
    ἀπίωμεν: *are we to depart*; deliberative
    subjunctive, ἀπ-έρχομαι (ι-)
    ἀναδήσαντες: *after crowning*; "tying
    (him) up (with ribbons or garlands)"
  e5 ἐφ' ᾧπερ: *for which very (reason)*
  e6 οὐχ οἷός τ' ἐγενόμην: *I happened to
    be unable, it turned out that I was
    unable*; a variation of οἷος τε + εἰμί
  e8 ἐὰν εἴπω οὑτωσί: *if I speak (of him) thus*

  ἀναδήσω: aor. subj., ἀνα-δέω cf. e4
  e9 καταγελάσεσθέ: fut., κατα-γελάω
    ὡς μεθύοντος: *since...*; ὡς + pple
    κἂν: *even if*; καὶ ἐάν
213a2 ἐπὶ ῥητοῖς: *on these stated terms*
    εἰσίω: *am I to enter*; deliberative subj. of
    εἰσ-έρχομαι (ι-)
    συμπίεσθε: fut. dep. συμ-πίνω
  a3 ἀναθορυβῆσαι: aor. inf.
    εἰσιέναι inf. εἰσέρχομαι
  a4 καὶ τὸν: *and he*; i.e. Alcibiades, acc. subj.
  a6 ὡς ἀναδήσοντα: *in order to...*; ὡς + fut.
    pple expresses purpose, ἀνα-δέω
    ἐπίπροσθε...ἔχοντα: *holding (the
    ribbons) over his own eyes...*
  a7 κατιδεῖν: inf. καθ-οράω
  b1 παραχωρῆσαι: aor. inf.
  b2 ὡς...κατιδεῖν: *when he saw...*
  b4 Ὑπολύετε...Ἀλκιβιάδην: *undo
    Alcibiades' (shoes)*; "undo Alcibiades"
  b5 ἐκ τρίτων: *in the third place (on the
    couch)*; along with Agathon and Socrates
    κατακέηται: pres. subj., κατα-κείμαι
  b7 ὁρᾶν: *to see*; inf.

τὸν Σωκράτη, ἰδόντα δὲ ἀναπηδῆσαι καὶ εἰπεῖν ὦ Ἡράκλεις,
τουτὶ τί ἦν; Σωκράτης οὗτος; ἐλλοχῶν αὖ με ἐνταῦθα κατέ-
c κεισο, ὥσπερ εἰώθεις ἐξαίφνης ἀναφαίνεσθαι ὅπου ἐγὼ ᾤμην
ἥκιστά σε ἔσεσθαι. καὶ νῦν τί ἥκεις; καὶ τί αὖ ἐνταῦθα
κατεκλίνης; ὡς οὐ παρὰ Ἀριστοφάνει οὐδὲ εἴ τις ἄλλος
γελοῖος ἔστι τε καὶ βούλεται, ἀλλὰ διεμηχανήσω ὅπως παρὰ
5 τῷ καλλίστῳ τῶν ἔνδον κατακείσῃ.

Καὶ τὸν Σωκράτη, Ἀγάθων, φάναι, ὅρα εἴ μοι ἐπαμύνεις·
ὡς ἐμοὶ ὁ τούτου ἔρως τοῦ ἀνθρώπου οὐ φαῦλον πρᾶγμα
γέγονεν. ἀπ᾽ ἐκείνου γὰρ τοῦ χρόνου, ἀφ᾽ οὗ τούτου
d ἠράσθην, οὐκέτι ἔξεστίν μοι οὔτε προσβλέψαι οὔτε διαλεχθῆναι καλῷ οὐδ᾽ ἑνί, ἢ οὑτοσὶ ζηλοτυπῶν με καὶ φθονῶν
θαυμαστὰ ἐργάζεται καὶ λοιδορεῖταί τε καὶ τὼ χεῖρε μόγις
ἀπέχεται. ὅρα οὖν μή τι καὶ νῦν ἐργάσηται, ἀλλὰ διάλ-
5 λαξον ἡμᾶς, ἢ ἐὰν ἐπιχειρῇ βιάζεσθαι, ἐπάμυνε, ὡς ἐγὼ
τὴν τούτου μανίαν τε καὶ φιλεραστίαν πάνυ ὀρρωδῶ.

Ἀλλ᾽ οὐκ ἔστι, φάναι τὸν Ἀλκιβιάδην, ἐμοὶ καὶ σοὶ διαλ-
λαγή. ἀλλὰ τούτων μὲν εἰς αὖθίς σε τιμωρήσομαι· νῦν
e δέ μοι, Ἀγάθων, φάναι, μετάδος τῶν ταινιῶν, ἵνα ἀναδήσω
καὶ τὴν τούτου ταυτηνὶ τὴν θαυμαστὴν κεφαλήν, καὶ μή μοι
μέμφηται ὅτι σὲ μὲν ἀνέδησα, αὐτὸν δὲ νικῶντα ἐν λόγοις
πάντας ἀνθρώπους, οὐ μόνον πρῴην ὥσπερ σύ, ἀλλ᾽ ἀεί,
5 ἔπειτα οὐκ ἀνέδησα. καὶ ἅμ᾽ αὐτὸν λαβόντα τῶν ταινιῶν
ἀναδεῖν τὸν Σωκράτη καὶ κατακλίνεσθαι.

Ἐπειδὴ δὲ κατεκλίνη, εἰπεῖν· εἶεν δή, ἄνδρες· δοκεῖτε
γάρ μοι νήφειν. οὐκ ἐπιτρεπτέον οὖν ὑμῖν, ἀλλὰ ποτέον·
ὡμολόγηται γὰρ ταῦθ᾽ ἡμῖν. ἄρχοντα οὖν αἱροῦμαι τῆς
5 πόσεως, ἕως ἂν ὑμεῖς ἱκανῶς πίητε, ἐμαυτόν. ἀλλὰ φερέτω,

αἱρέω: to seize, take; *mid.* choose*
ἀνα-πηδάω: to leap up, leap back, start up`
ἀνα-φαίνω: to show forth, display*
ἀπ-έχω: to be distant, keep away from
αὖθις: back again, later*
βιάζω: to constrain, use force, overpower*
δι-αλλαγή, ἡ: reconciliation, truce, exchange
δι-αλλάττω: to reconcile, give in an exchange
δια-μηχανάομαι: to bring about, contrive
εἶεν: well! well now! *
ἐλλοχάω: to lie in ambush for
ἐπ-αμύνω: to assist, help, defend, fend off
ἐπιτρεπτέος, -α, -ον: to be permitted, allowed
ἔνδον: within, at home*
ἐξαίφνης: suddenly, immediately*
ἔξ-εστι: it is allowed, permitted, possible*
ζηλοτυπέω: to be jealous of, rival, emulate
ἥκιστος, -η, -ον: least; not at all*

λοιδορέω: to abuse, rail against
μανία, ἡ: madness, frenzy; enthusiasm
μέμφομαι: to blame, censure, find fault with*
μετα-δίδωμι: to give a part of, give a share of
μόγις: with difficulty, reluctantly, hardly
νικάω: to conquer, defeat, win*
νήφω: to be sober*
ὅπου: where*
ὀρρωδέω: to fear, dread, shrink from
οὐκ-έτι: no more, no longer, no further*
πόσις, -εως, ὁ: drinking*
ποτέος, -α, -ον: to be drunk, drinkable,
προσ-βλέπω: to look at or upon
πρῴην: day before yesterday, other day
ταινία, ἡ: a band, ribbon, fillet, head-band*
τιμωρέω: to avenge, exact vengeance*
φθονέω: to begrudge, bear a grudge, envy
φιλ-εραστία, ἡ: devotion to a lover

213b8 ἰδόντα: acc. sg. pple ὁράω
  ἀναπηδῆσαι: aor. inf., ἀνα-πηδάω
  ῏Ω Ἡράκλεις: *Heracles!*; exclamation
b9 τουτὶ τί ἦν: *what is this here?*; τοῦτο
    with a deictic iota; the impf. of εἰμί
    expresses surprise
  κατέκεισο: 2nd sg. impf., κατάκειμαι
c1 ὥσπερ εἰώθεις: *just as you were
    accustomed*; plpf. εἴωθα with impf. sense
  ᾤμην: *I was thinking*; impf. οἴομαι
c2 ἔσεσθαι: fut. dep. inf., εἰμί
  τί: *why?*; same for both instances
c3 κατεκλίνης: *did you recline*; 2nd sg. aor.
    pass. dep., κατακλίνω
  ὡς: *since*; answering τί question in c2
  οὐδὲ εἴ τις ἄλλος: *nor (beside anyone)
    if anyone else*; supply παρά τινι in
    order to maintain the parallelism
c4 βούλεται: *wishes (to be funny)*
  διεμηχανήσω: διεμηχανήσα(σ)ο, 2nd
    sg. aor. mid.
c5 κατακείσῃ: *you will lie*; κατακείσε(σ)αι
c6 ὅρα εἰ: *see whether...*; sg. imperative
  ἐπαμύνεις: perhaps fut. form: ἐπαμυνεῖς
c7 ὡς...γέγονεν: *since...*; pf., γίγνομαι
c8 ἀφ᾽ οὗ: *from which (time)*; add χρόνου
d1 ἠράσθην: *I began to love, fell in love*;
    ingressive aor. pass. dep., ἐράω

προσβλέψαι: προσβλέπσαι, aor. inf.
διαλεχθῆναι: *to converse*; aor. pass. dep.
  infinitive from διαλέγομαι
d2 οὐδ᾽ ἑνί: *not even one*
  οὑτοσί: *this one here*; deictic iota
d3 τὼ χεῖρε μόγις ἀπέχεται: *he hardly
    keeps his two hands away*; dual form
d4 ὅρα...μή: *see to it that...not*
  διάλλαξον: *exchange (our positions on
    the couch)*; aor. imper., δι-αλλάττω
d5 ἐπιχειρῇ: *he attempts*; 3rd sg. pres. subj.
  ὡς...ὀρρωδῶ: *since I fear*
d8 εἰς αὖθις: *later, til later*
  τούτων: *for these things*; gen. charge
e1 μετάδος τῶν ταινιῶν: *give back (some)
    ribbons*; aor. imperative, partitive gen.
  ἀναδήσω: 1st sg. aor. subj. ἀναδέω
e3 μή...μέμφηται: *he may not..*; with ἵνα, e1
e5 τῶν ταινιῶν: *(some) ribbons*; partitive
  λαβόντα..ταινιῶν: *grabbing the ribbons*;
    partitive gen. aor. pple. λαμβάνω
e7 κατεκλίνη: 3rd sg. aor. pass. dep., cf. c3
e8 ἐπιτρεπτέον: *you must not be allowed*;
    verbal adj. + (εἰμί); same for ποτέον
e9 ὡμολόγηται: pf. pass. with dat. of agent
  ἄρχοντα...ἐμαυτόν: *myself as leader*
e10 φερέτω: *let (a slave) bring*; 3rd sg. imp.

Ἀγάθων, εἴ τι ἔστιν ἔκπωμα μέγα. μᾶλλον δὲ οὐδὲν δεῖ,
ἀλλὰ φέρε, παῖ, φάναι, τὸν ψυκτῆρα ἐκεῖνον, ἰδόντα αὐτὸν
214 πλέον ἢ ὀκτὼ κοτύλας χωροῦντα. τοῦτον ἐμπλησάμενον
πρῶτον μὲν αὐτὸν ἐκπιεῖν, ἔπειτα τῷ Σωκράτει κελεύειν
ἐγχεῖν καὶ ἅμα εἰπεῖν· πρὸς μὲν Σωκράτη, ὦ ἄνδρες, τὸ
σόφισμά μοι οὐδέν· ὁπόσον γὰρ ἂν κελεύῃ τις, τοσοῦτον
5 ἐκπιὼν οὐδὲν μᾶλλον μή ποτε μεθυσθῇ.

Τὸν μὲν οὖν Σωκράτη ἐγχέαντος τοῦ παιδὸς πίνειν· τὸν
δ᾽ Ἐρυξίμαχον πῶς οὖν, φάναι, ὦ Ἀλκιβιάδη, ποιοῦμεν;
b οὕτως οὔτε τι λέγομεν ἐπὶ τῇ κύλικι οὔτε τι ᾄδομεν, ἀλλ᾽
ἀτεχνῶς ὥσπερ οἱ διψῶντες πιόμεθα;

Τὸν οὖν Ἀλκιβιάδην εἰπεῖν ὦ Ἐρυξίμαχε, βέλτιστε
βελτίστου πατρὸς καὶ σωφρονεστάτου, χαῖρε.

5 Καὶ γὰρ σύ, φάναι τὸν Ἐρυξίμαχον· ἀλλὰ τί ποιῶμεν;

Ὅτι ἂν σὺ κελεύῃς. δεῖ γάρ σοι πείθεσθαι·

ἰητρὸς γὰρ ἀνὴρ πολλῶν ἀντάξιος ἄλλων·

ἐπίταττε οὖν ὅτι βούλει.

Ἄκουσον δή, εἰπεῖν τὸν Ἐρυξίμαχον. ἡμῖν πρὶν σὲ
10 εἰσελθεῖν ἔδοξε χρῆναι ἐπὶ δεξιὰ ἕκαστον ἐν μέρει λόγον
c περὶ Ἔρωτος εἰπεῖν ὡς δύναιτο κάλλιστον, καὶ ἐγκωμιάσαι.
οἱ μὲν οὖν ἄλλοι πάντες ἡμεῖς εἰρήκαμεν· σὺ δ᾽ ἐπειδὴ οὐκ
εἴρηκας καὶ ἐκπέπωκας, δίκαιος εἶ εἰπεῖν, εἰπὼν δὲ ἐπιτάξαι
Σωκράτει ὅτι ἂν βούλῃ, καὶ τοῦτον τῷ ἐπὶ δεξιὰ καὶ οὕτω
5 τοὺς ἄλλους.

Ἀλλά, φάναι, ὦ Ἐρυξίμαχε, τὸν Ἀλκιβιάδην, καλῶς μὲν
λέγεις, μεθύοντα δὲ ἄνδρα παρὰ νηφόντων λόγους παραβάλλειν μὴ οὐκ ἐξ ἴσου ᾖ. καὶ ἅμα, ὦ μακάριε, πείθει τί
d σε Σωκράτης ὧν ἄρτι εἶπεν; ἢ οἶσθα ὅτι τοὐναντίον ἐστὶ
πᾶν ἢ ὃ ἔλεγεν; οὗτος γάρ, ἐάν τινα ἐγὼ ἐπαινέσω τούτου

ᾄδω: to sing*
ἀντ-άξιος, -α, -ον: worth as much as (+ gen.)
ἄρτι: just, exactly*
ἀ-τεχνῶς: simply, really, entirely*
βέλτιστος, -η, -ον: best*
δεξιός, -ά, -όν: right, right side*
διψάω: to be thirsty, parched
ἐγ-χέω: to pour in, pour
ἐκ-πίνω: to drink up, drain dry*
ἔκ-πωμα, -ατος, τό: a drinking-cup
ἐμ-πίπλημι: to fill in
ἐπι-τάττω: to order, enjoin, command
ἰατρός, ὁ: physician, doctor*
κοτύλη, ἡ: a cup

κύλιξ, -ικος, ἡ: a cup, drinking-cup, kylix
μακάριος, -α, -ον: blessed, happy*
μεθύω: to be drunk with wine*
μέρος, -έος, τό: a part, share, portion*
νήφω: to be sober*
ὀκτώ: eight
ὁπόσος, -α, -ον: as much as, as many as, as great as*
παρα-βάλλω: to cast aside, compare
πρίν: until, before (+ inf.)*
σόφισμα, -ατος, τό: device, sly trick, fallacy
σώφρων, -ον: prudent, moderate, temperate*
χωρέω: to go, come; have room for
ψυκτήρ, -ῆρος, ὁ: a wine-cooler

213e11 μᾶλλον δὲ οὐδὲν δεῖ: *but rather, there is no need*; οὐδὲν is an internal acc.

e12 φέρε: *bring*; sg. imperative
ἰδόντα αὐτὸν...χωροῦντα: *seeing one (i.e. a wine-cooler) having room for...*; modifies Alcibiades, subject of φάναι

214a1 τοῦτον ἐμπλησάμενον: *having this (i.e. wine-cooler) filled up (for him)*; aor. mid. pple, ἐμ-πίπλημι

a2 ἐκπιεῖν: aor. inf., ἐκ-πίνω (stem πι-)
τῷ Σωκράτει κελεύειν ἐγχεῖν: *he bid (the slave) to pour one for Socrates*; dat. of advantage, not dat. object of κελεύειν

a3 Πρὸς...οὐδέν: *against Socrates my trick is worthless*; "against Socrates my trick is nothing for me"

a4 ὁπόσον...κελεύῃ τις: *however much one bids him (to drink)*; add ἐκπιεῖν
ἐκπιών: aor. pple ἐκ-πίνω (stem πι-)

a5 οὐδὲν μᾶλλον μή...μεθυσθῇ: *he not at all gets more drunk*; οὐδὲν is adverbial, 3rd sg. aor. pass. dep. subj.

a6 ἐγχέαντος τοῦ παιδός: gen. abs.

a7 Πῶς...ποιοῦμεν: *What's this we're doing?*; "how are we doing?"

b1 οὕτως: *in just this way?*; i.e. as before
ἐπὶ τῇ κύλικι: *over the cup*; i.e. while passing a cup of wine around

b2 ἀτεχνῶς...πιόμεθα: *will we simply drink?*; fut. deponent, πίνω (stem πι-)

b5 καὶ γὰρ σύ: *yes, and you too*
τί ποιῶμεν: *what are we to do?*; pres.

deliberative subjunctive

b6 Ὅτι ἄν: *whatever...*; in response to b5

b7 ἰητρὸς: Ionic for ἰατρὸς; supply ἐστίν

b8 βούλει: *you wish*; βούλε(σ)αι

b9 Ἄκουσον: aor. imperative
πρὶν...εἰσελθεῖν: *before you arrived*

b10 χρῆναι: inf. χρή
ἐπὶ δεξιὰ: *(from left) to right*

b10 ἐν μέρει: *in turn*; lit. "in part"

c1 ὡς...κάλλιστον: *as well as one could*
ἐγκωμιάσαι: aor. inf.

c2 εἰρήκαμεν: pf. ἐρέω, see also c3

c3 ἐκπέπωκας: 2nd sg. pf., ἐκ-πίνω
δίκαιος εἶ εἰπεῖν: *it is right that you speak*; "you are right to speak"
δὲ ἐπιτάξαι: *(it is right) that you order*; aor. inf.; add δίκαιος εἶ

c4 τοῦτον τῷ ἐπὶ δεξιά: *this one (must order) the one to the right*; add δεῖ ἐπιτάξαι

c7 παραβάλλειν μὴ οὐκ ἐξ ἴσου ᾖ: *perhaps it is not fair to compare (acc.) to (παρὰ) (acc.)*; μὴ + independent subj. expressing a doubtful assertion

c8 πείθει τί σε: *is Socrates persuading you of anything*; τι is an internal acc. and receives its accent from the enclitic σε

d1 τοὐναντίον: *the opposite*; τὸ ἐναντίον

d2 ἐπαινέσω: *I praise*; aor. subj., ἐπαινέω
τούτου: part of a gen. abs.

παρόντος ἢ θεὸν ἢ ἄνθρωπον ἄλλον ἢ τοῦτον, οὐκ ἀφέξεταί μου τὼ χεῖρε.

5 Οὐκ εὐφημήσεις; φάναι τὸν Σωκράτη.

Μὰ τὸν Ποσειδῶ, εἰπεῖν τὸν Ἀλκιβιάδην, μηδὲν λέγε πρὸς ταῦτα, ὡς ἐγὼ οὐδ᾽ ἂν ἕνα ἄλλον ἐπαινέσαιμι σοῦ παρόντος.

Ἀλλ᾽ οὕτω ποίει, φάναι τὸν Ἐρυξίμαχον, εἰ βούλει·
10 Σωκράτη ἐπαίνεσον.

e Πῶς λέγεις; εἰπεῖν τὸν Ἀλκιβιάδην· δοκεῖ χρῆναι, ὦ Ἐρυξίμαχε; ἐπιθῶμαι τῷ ἀνδρὶ καὶ τιμωρήσωμαι ὑμῶν ἐναντίον;

Οὗτος, φάναι τὸν Σωκράτη, τί ἐν νῷ ἔχεις; ἐπὶ τὰ
5 γελοιότερά με ἐπαινέσαι; ἢ τί ποιήσεις;

Τἀληθῆ ἐρῶ. ἀλλ᾽ ὅρα εἰ παρίῃς.

Ἀλλὰ μέντοι, φάναι, τά γε ἀληθῆ παρίημι καὶ κελεύω λέγειν.

Οὐκ ἂν φθάνοιμι, εἰπεῖν τὸν Ἀλκιβιάδην. καὶ μέντοι
10 οὑτωσὶ ποίησον. ἐάν τι μὴ ἀληθὲς λέγω, μεταξὺ ἐπιλαβοῦ, ἂν βούλῃ, καὶ εἰπὲ ὅτι τοῦτο ψεύδομαι· ἑκὼν γὰρ εἶναι οὐδὲν
215 ψεύσομαι. ἐὰν μέντοι ἀναμιμνῃσκόμενος ἄλλο ἄλλοθεν λέγω, μηδὲν θαυμάσῃς· οὐ γάρ τι ῥᾴδιον τὴν σὴν ἀτοπίαν ὧδ᾽ ἔχοντι εὐπόρως καὶ ἐφεξῆς καταριθμῆσαι.

Σωκράτη δ᾽ ἐγὼ ἐπαινεῖν, ὦ ἄνδρες, οὕτως ἐπιχειρήσω,
5 δι᾽ εἰκόνων. οὗτος μὲν οὖν ἴσως οἰήσεται ἐπὶ τὰ γελοιότερα, ἔσται δ᾽ ἡ εἰκὼν τοῦ ἀληθοῦς ἕνεκα, οὐ τοῦ γελοίου. φημὶ γὰρ δὴ ὁμοιότατον αὐτὸν εἶναι τοῖς σιληνοῖς τούτοις τοῖς
b ἐν τοῖς ἑρμογλυφείοις καθημένοις, οὕστινας ἐργάζονται οἱ δημιουργοὶ σύριγγας ἢ αὐλοὺς ἔχοντας, οἳ διχάδε διοιχθέντες φαίνονται ἔνδοθεν ἀγάλματα ἔχοντες θεῶν. καὶ φημὶ αὖ ἐοικέναι αὐτὸν τῷ σατύρῳ τῷ Μαρσύᾳ. ὅτι μὲν οὖν τό γε

ἄγαλμα, -ατος τό: statue, image*
ἄλλο-θεν: from another place, from elsewhere
ἀνα-μιμνήσκω: to remind (acc.) of (gen.),
    remember*
ἀπ-έχω: to be distant, keep away from*
ἀ-τοπία, ἡ: strangeness, oddness, bizarreness
αὐλός, ὁ: a flute
δι-οίγνυμι: to open*
διχάδε: apart, asunder; apart from (+ gen.)
εἰκών, -όνος, ἡ: a likeness, image; statue*
ἔνδο-θεν: from within*
ἐπι-λαμβάνω: to lay hold of, take over, seize
ἑρμογλυφεῖον, τό: a statuary's shop
εὔ-πορος, -ον: resourceful, easily done, easy*
εὐ-φημέω: to keep quiet, keep religious silence

ἐφεξῆς: in succession, in a row, in order
κάθ-ημαι: to sit*
κατ-αριθμέω: to count, reckon; recount
μά: by, in affirmation*
Μαρσύης, ὁ: Marsyas
παρ-ίημι: to pass over, yield, allow, permit*
Ποσειδῶν, -ῶνος, ὁ: Poseidon
σάτυρος, ὁ: satyr*
σιληνός, ὁ: silenus
σῦριγξ, σύριγγος, ἡ: a pipe
τιμωρέω: to avenge, exact vengeance*
φθάνω: to anticipate, do beforehand (+ pple)*
ψεύδομαι: to lie, cheat, beguile*
ὧδε: in this way, so, thus*

214d3 τούτου παρόντος: gen. abs.; πάρ-ειμι
ἢ θεὸν ἤ...: in apposition to τινα in d2
ἀφέξεταί: he will not keep away; fut.
mid. ἀπ-έχω ; ἔχω receives hard
breathing in the future: ἕξω

d4 τὼ χεῖρε: acc. d.o., dual form

d5 Οὐκ εὐφημήσεις: will you not be quiet;
fut. in a mild command, οὐ anticipates a
positive response

d6 Μὰ τὸν Ποσειδῶ: by Poseidon

d7 πρὸς ταῦτα: with regard to these things
ὡς: since, because

d9 ποίει: do!; ποίεε, pres. imperative

d10 ἐπαίνεσον: aor. imperative, ἐπαινέω

e1 Πῶς λέγεις: what do you mean?
χρῆναι: inf. from χρή

e2 ἐπιθῶμαι: am I to assail; deliberative
aor. subj., ἐπι-τίθημι (-θε)
τιμωρήσωμαι: aor. deliberative subj.
ὑμῶν ἐναντίον: in front of you

e4 ἐν νῷ: in mind; dat. sg. νοῦς
ἐπὶ τὰ γελοιότερα: for ridicule

e5 ἐπαινέσαι: aor. inf.; add ἐν νῷ ἔχεις

e6 ὅρα εἰ: see whether; sg. imp., ὁράω
παρίης: you allow (it); pres., παρ-ίημι

e9 οὐκ ἂν φθάνοιμι: I could not speak

sooner; supply λέγων, cf. 185e4

e10 οὑτωσί: in this here way; deictic iota
ποίησον: aor. imperative
ἐπιλαβοῦ: interrupt, take over; aor. mid.
imperative, ἐπι-λαβε(σ)ο

e11 ἂν βούλῃ: if you wish; 2nd sg. mid.
ἑκὼν εἶναι: willingly

215a1 ψεύσομαι: fut. ψεύδομαι

a1 ἄλλο ἄλλοθεν: something in a different
order; "a different thing from a
different place"

a2 μηδὲν θαυμάσῃς: do not at all become
amazed; prohibitive aor. subjunctive
ῥάδιον: (it is) easy; supply ἐστίν

a3 ὧδ᾽ ἔχοντι: for one being (disposed) in
this way; i.e. drunk, ἔχω + adv.
εὐπόρως: fluently; "resourcefully"

a5 οἰήσεται: will think (that I praise him);
add με ἐπαινέσαι, fut. of οἴομαι
ἐπὶ τὰ γελοιότερα: for ridicule
ἔσται: 3rd sg. fut., εἰμί

a7 ὁμοιότατον: most similar to; governs dat.

b1 οὕστινας: whom; acc. pl.

b2 διοιχθέντες: having been opened;. aor.
pass. pple, δι-οίγνυμι

b4 ἐοικέναι: to resemble + dat.; inf., ἔοικα

5 εἶδος ὅμοιος εἶ τούτοις, ὦ Σώκρατες, οὐδ᾽ αὐτὸς ἄν που
ἀμφισβητήσαις· ὡς δὲ καὶ τἆλλα ἔοικας, μετὰ τοῦτο ἄκουε.
ὑβριστὴς εἶ· ἢ οὔ; ἐὰν γὰρ μὴ ὁμολογῇς, μάρτυρας παρέξομαι. ἀλλ᾽ οὐκ αὐλητής; πολύ γε θαυμασιώτερος ἐκείνου.

c ὁ μέν γε δι᾽ ὀργάνων ἐκήλει τοὺς ἀνθρώπους τῇ ἀπὸ τοῦ
στόματος δυνάμει, καὶ ἔτι νυνὶ ὃς ἂν τὰ ἐκείνου αὐλῇ—ἃ γὰρ
Ὄλυμπος ηὔλει, Μαρσύου λέγω, τούτου διδάξαντος—τὰ οὖν
ἐκείνου ἐάντε ἀγαθὸς αὐλητὴς αὐλῇ ἐάντε φαύλη αὐλητρίς,

5 μόνα κατέχεσθαι ποιεῖ καὶ δηλοῖ τοὺς τῶν θεῶν τε καὶ
τελετῶν δεομένους διὰ τὸ θεῖα εἶναι. σὺ δ᾽ ἐκείνου τοσοῦτον
μόνον διαφέρεις, ὅτι ἄνευ ὀργάνων ψιλοῖς λόγοις ταὐτὸν

d τοῦτο ποιεῖς. ἡμεῖς γοῦν ὅταν μέν του ἄλλου ἀκούωμεν
λέγοντος καὶ πάνυ ἀγαθοῦ ῥήτορος ἄλλους λόγους, οὐδὲν
μέλει ὡς ἔπος εἰπεῖν οὐδενί· ἐπειδὰν δὲ σοῦ τις ἀκούῃ ἢ τῶν
σῶν λόγων ἄλλου λέγοντος, κἂν πάνυ φαῦλος ᾖ ὁ λέγων,

5 ἐάντε γυνὴ ἀκούῃ ἐάντε ἀνὴρ ἐάντε μειράκιον, ἐκπεπλη-
γμένοι ἐσμὲν καὶ κατεχόμεθα. ἐγὼ γοῦν, ὦ ἄνδρες, εἰ μὴ
ἔμελλον κομιδῇ δόξειν μεθύειν, εἶπον ὀμόσας ἂν ὑμῖν οἷα δὴ
πέπονθα αὐτὸς ὑπὸ τῶν τούτου λόγων καὶ πάσχω ἔτι καὶ

e νυνί. ὅταν γὰρ ἀκούω, πολύ μοι μᾶλλον ἢ τῶν κορυβαν-
τιώντων ἥ τε καρδία πηδᾷ καὶ δάκρυα ἐκχεῖται ὑπὸ τῶν
λόγων τῶν τούτου, ὁρῶ δὲ καὶ ἄλλους παμπόλλους τὰ
αὐτὰ πάσχοντας· Περικλέους δὲ ἀκούων καὶ ἄλλων ἀγαθῶν

5 ῥητόρων εὖ μὲν ἡγούμην λέγειν, τοιοῦτον δ᾽ οὐδὲν ἔπασχον,
οὐδ᾽ ἐτεθορύβητό μου ἡ ψυχὴ οὐδ᾽ ἠγανάκτει ὡς ἀνδραποδω-
δῶς διακειμένου, ἀλλ᾽ ὑπὸ τουτουῒ τοῦ Μαρσύου πολλάκις δὴ

216 οὕτω διετέθην ὥστε μοι δόξαι μὴ βιωτὸν εἶναι ἔχοντι ὡς
ἔχω. καὶ ταῦτα, ὦ Σώκρατες, οὐκ ἐρεῖς ὡς οὐκ ἀληθῆ. καὶ
ἔτι γε νῦν σύνοιδ᾽ ἐμαυτῷ ὅτι εἰ ἐθέλοιμι παρέχειν τὰ ὦτα,
οὐκ ἂν καρτερήσαιμι ἀλλὰ ταὐτὰ ἂν πάσχοιμι. ἀναγκάζει

ἀγανακτέω: to feel irritated, annoyed, angry
ἀμφισ-βητέω: to dispute, disagree with (dat.)
ἀνδραποδώδης, -ες: slavish, servile
αὐλέω: to play on the flute*
αὐλητής, -οῦ, ὁ: a flute-player
αὐλητρίς, -ίδος, ἡ: a flute-girl*
βιωτός, -όν: to be lived, worth living
γοῦν: γε οὖν, at least, at any rate, any way*
δάκρυον, τό: a tear
δηλόω: to make clear, show, reveal, exhibit*
διά-κειμαι: to be disposed, be affected*
δια-τίθεμαι: to be disposed, arranged, treated*
διδάσκω: to teach, instruct*
ἐκ-πλήγνυμι: to strike with fear, amaze,
     astound, to drive out of one senses*
ἐκ-χέω: to pour out
ἔπος, -εος, τό: a word*
θορυβέω: to throw into confusion, make an
     uproar; raise a shout; applaud*
καρδία, ἡ: heart
καρτερέω: to endure, be steadfast, staunch*
κατ-έχω: to hold fast, hold back; possess*

κηλέω: to charm, bewitch, enchant, beguile
κομιδῇ: exactly, just, absolutely, quite
κορυβαντιάω: to be in a Corybantic frenzy
μάρτυς, -υρος, ὁ, ἡ: a witness*
μεθύω: to be drunk with wine*
μειράκιον, τό: adolescent, boy, young man*
μέλω: there is a care for (dat.) for (gen.)
Ὄλυμπος, ὁ: Olympus (a pupil of Marsyas)
ὄμνυμι: to swear, take an oath*
ὄργανον, τό: instrument, tool, organ*
οὖς, ωτός, τό: ear*
παμ-πολύς, -πολλά, -πολύ: very much*
Περικλῆς, ὁ: Pericles
πηδάω: to leap, spring, bound
που: anywhere, somewhere; I suppose
ῥήτωρ, ὁ: a public speaker, orator*
στόμα, -ατος, τό: mouth*
σύν-οιδα: be conscious, cognizant of, know*
τελετή, ἡ: mystic rites, initiation
ὑβριστής, -οῦ, ἡ: an outrageous person*
ψιλός, -όν: naked, bare, stripped, simple

215b5 τό...εἶδος: *in form*; acc. of respect
    που: *I suppose*
b6 ὡς...ἔοικας: *how you are alike in other*
    respect; crasis τὰ ἄλλα, acc. of respect
b5 παρέξομαι: *I will provide*; fut. mid. in a
    future more vivid condition
b8 οὐκ αὐλητής;: *are you not a flute-player*;
    supply εἶ
    ἐκείνου: *than that one*; gen. comparison
c1 τῇ...δυνάμει: *by the power*; dat. means
c2 τὰ ἐκείνου: *the songs of that one*; cf. c3
    αὐλῇ: *plays*; 3ʳᵈ sg. pres. subj., αὐλέω
c3 ηὔλει: *used to play*; 3ʳᵈ sg. impf., αὐλέω
    Μαρσύου...διδάξαντος: *I say Marsyas'*
    (songs), since he taught (Olympus);
    causal gen. abs.
c4 ἐάντε...ἐάντε: *whether...or*
c5 μόνα κατέχεσθαι ποιεῖ: *alone cause*
    (one) to be possessed; neut. pl. subject
    τοὺς...δεομένους: *those in need of*
c6 διὰ τὸ θεῖα εἶναι: *on account of (their)*
    being divine; i.e. the songs
    τοσοῦτον...διαφέρεις...ὅτι: *you differ*
    this much from...namely that; inner acc.
c7 ψιλοῖς λόγοις: dat. of means
    ταὐτόν: *the same thing*; τὸ αὐτό

d1 του ἄλλου: *someone else*; τινός
d2 καὶ..ῥήτορος: *even a quite good rhetor*
    οὐδὲν μέλει: *it is no concern*; inner acc.
d3 ὡς ἔπος εἰπεῖν: *so to speak, as it were*
d4 κἂν: *even if*; καὶ ἐάν
d5 ἐάντε...ἐάντε: *whether...or*
    ἐκπεπληγμένοι ἐσμέν: *we are amazed*;
    pf. pple + εἰμί is a pf. periphrastic
d7 εἰ...ἔμελλον...εἶπον ὀμόσας ἄν: *if I*
    were going to...I would, swearing, say;
    past counterfactual; impf., ἄν aor.; aor.
    pple ὄμνυμι
d8 πέπονθα: 1ˢᵗ sg. pf. πάσχω
e6 ἐτεθορύβητό: *had been thrown into*
    confusion; plpf. pass., θορυβέω
    ὡς διακειμένου: *since I was disposed*
    slavishly; ὡς + pple, agrees with μου
216a1 διετέθην: *I was disposed*; aor. pass.
    ὥστε...δόξαι: *that it seemed*; "so as to
    seem" aor. inf. in a result clause
    ἔχοντι...ἔχω: *having (the life) as I have*
a2 ἐθέλοιμι, καρτερήσαιμι...πάσχοιμι:
    should...would...would; a future less
    vivid condition
    ταὐτὰ: *the same things*; crasis τὰ αὐτά

5 γάρ με ὁμολογεῖν ὅτι πολλοῦ ἐνδεὴς ὢν αὐτὸς ἔτι ἐμαυτοῦ
μὲν ἀμελῶ, τὰ δ᾽ Ἀθηναίων πράττω. βίᾳ οὖν ὥσπερ ἀπὸ
τῶν Σειρήνων ἐπισχόμενος τὰ ὦτα οἴχομαι φεύγων, ἵνα μὴ
αὐτοῦ καθήμενος παρὰ τούτῳ καταγηράσω. πέπονθα δὲ
b πρὸς τοῦτον μόνον ἀνθρώπων, ὃ οὐκ ἄν τις οἴοιτο ἐν ἐμοὶ
ἐνεῖναι, τὸ αἰσχύνεσθαι ὁντινοῦν· ἐγὼ δὲ τοῦτον μόνον
αἰσχύνομαι. σύνοιδα γὰρ ἐμαυτῷ ἀντιλέγειν μὲν οὐ δυναμένῳ ὡς οὐ δεῖ ποιεῖν ἃ οὗτος κελεύει, ἐπειδὰν δὲ ἀπέλθω,
5 ἡττημένῳ τῆς τιμῆς τῆς ὑπὸ τῶν πολλῶν. δραπετεύω οὖν
αὐτὸν καὶ φεύγω, καὶ ὅταν ἴδω, αἰσχύνομαι τὰ ὡμολογημένα.
c καὶ πολλάκις μὲν ἡδέως ἂν ἴδοιμι αὐτὸν μὴ ὄντα ἐν ἀνθρώποις·
εἰ δ᾽ αὖ τοῦτο γένοιτο, εὖ οἶδα ὅτι πολὺ μεῖζον ἂν ἀχθοίμην,
ὥστε οὐκ ἔχω ὅτι χρήσωμαι τούτῳ τῷ ἀνθρώπῳ.

Καὶ ὑπὸ μὲν δὴ τῶν αὐλημάτων καὶ ἐγὼ καὶ ἄλλοι πολλοὶ
5 τοιαῦτα πεπόνθασιν ὑπὸ τοῦδε τοῦ σατύρου· ἄλλα δὲ ἐμοῦ
ἀκούσατε ὡς ὅμοιός τ᾽ ἐστὶν οἷς ἐγὼ ᾔκασα αὐτὸν καὶ τὴν
δύναμιν ὡς θαυμασίαν ἔχει. εὖ γὰρ ἴστε ὅτι οὐδεὶς ὑμῶν
d τοῦτον γιγνώσκει· ἀλλὰ ἐγὼ δηλώσω, ἐπείπερ ἠρξάμην.
ὁρᾶτε γὰρ ὅτι Σωκράτης ἐρωτικῶς διάκειται τῶν καλῶν καὶ
ἀεὶ περὶ τούτους ἐστὶ καὶ ἐκπέπληκται, καὶ αὖ ἀγνοεῖ πάντα
καὶ οὐδὲν οἶδεν. ὡς τὸ σχῆμα αὐτοῦ τοῦτο οὐ σιληνῶδες;
5 σφόδρα γε. τοῦτο γὰρ οὗτος ἔξωθεν περιβέβληται, ὥσπερ
ὁ γεγλυμμένος σιληνός· ἔνδοθεν δὲ ἀνοιχθεὶς πόσης οἴεσθε
γέμει, ὦ ἄνδρες συμπόται, σωφροσύνης; ἴστε ὅτι οὔτε εἴ τις
καλός ἐστι μέλει αὐτῷ οὐδέν, ἀλλὰ καταφρονεῖ τοσοῦτον
e ὅσον οὐδ᾽ ἂν εἷς οἰηθείη, οὔτ᾽ εἴ τις πλούσιος, οὔτ᾽ εἰ ἄλλην
τινὰ τιμὴν ἔχων τῶν ὑπὸ πλήθους μακαριζομένων· ἡγεῖται
δὲ πάντα ταῦτα τὰ κτήματα οὐδενὸς ἄξια καὶ ἡμᾶς οὐδὲν
εἶναι—λέγω ὑμῖν—εἰρωνευόμενος δὲ καὶ παίζων πάντα τὸν
5 βίον πρὸς τοὺς ἀνθρώπους διατελεῖ. σπουδάσαντος δὲ αὐτοῦ

ἀ-γνοέω: to be ignorant of, not know*
Ἀθηναῖος, -α, -ον: Athenian, of Athens
ἀμελέω: to have no care for, neglect (+ gen.)*
ἀν-οίγνυμι: to open, open up*
ἀντι-λέγω: to speak against, challenge*
αὔλημα, -ατος, τό: music for the flute
ἄχθομαι: to be annoyed, vexed
βία, βιας, ἡ: violence; strength, force, might*
γέμω: to be full, teem (+ gen.)
γλύφω: to carve, engrave
δηλόω: to make clear, show, reveal, exhibit*
διά-κειμαι: to be disposed, be affected*
δια-τελέω: to live, continue, persevere
δραπετεύω: to run away
εἰκάζω: to portray, imagine, represent
εἰρωνεύομαι: to feign ignorance, fake modesty
ἐκ-πλήγνυμι: to strike with fear, amaze,
     astound, to drive out of one senses*
ἔνδο-θεν: from within, on the inside*
ἐν-ειμί: to be in, exist in*
ἔξω-θεν: from without, on the outside*
ἐπ-ίσχω: to withhold, check, restrain
ἡδέως: sweetly, pleasantly, gladly*
ἡττάομαι: to be less, weaker than, inferior to*

κάθ-ημαι: to sit*
κατα-γηράσκω: to grow old
κατα-φρονέω: to think down upon, despise*
κτῆμα, -ατος, τό: possession, property
μακαρίζω: to deem blessed or happy
μείζων, μείζον: larger, greater*
μέλω: imper. there is a care for (dat) for (gen.)
οὖς, ωτός, τό: ear*
παίζω: to play, sport, jest
περι-βάλλω: to throw round, enclose; clothe*
πλῆθος, τό: crowd, multitude; size*
πλούσιος, -α, -ον: rich, wealthy, opulent*
πόσος, -η, -ον: how much? how great? *
σάτυρος, ὁ: satyr*
Σειρήν, -ῆνος, ἡ: a Siren
σιληνός, ὁ: silenus*
σιληνώδης, -ες: Silenus-like
σπουδάζω: to pursue earnestly, be serious, be
     eager for, make haste*
σχῆμα, -ατος, τό: form, figure, appearance*
συμ-πότης, ὁ: a fellow-drinker, symposiast*
σύν-οιδα: be conscious, cognizant of, know*
φεύγω: to flee, escape; defend in court*

216a5 πολλοῦ...ὢν: *being deficient*; "being in need of much"

a6 τὰ...Ἀθηναίων: *the Athenians' affairs*

a7 ἐπισχόμενος τὰ ὦτα: *blocking my ears*

a8 αὐτοῦ: *there*; "in that very place"
πέπονθα: 1st sg. pf. πάσχω, see c5

b1 ὅ: *(that) which*...; missing antecedent

b2 τὸ αἰσχύνεσθαι ὁντιοῦν: *(namely) to feel shame before someone*; "whomsoever"

b3 σύνοιδα...ἐμαυτῷ...οὐ δυναμένῳ... ἡττημένῳ: *I am aware that I am not able...and am an inferior to/weaker than*; indirect discourse with participles

b4 ὡς οὐ δεῖ...: *that I ought not to* ἀπέλθω: 1st sg. aor. subj., ἀπ-έρχομαι

b5 τῆς τιμῆς τῆς ὑπὸ τῶν πολλῶν: *honor from the masses*; gen. obj. of ἡττημένῳ

b6 ἴδω...ἴδοιμι: aor. subj. and opt., ὁράω

c1 τὰ ὡμολογημένα: *things agreed upon* αὐτὸν μὴ ὄντα: *that he not exist*

c1 εἰ...γένοιτο..ἂν ἀχθοίμην: *should happen ... I would be pained*; future less vivid

c3 οὐκ ἔχω ὅτι χρήσωμαι: *I do not know what I am to do with this man*; "ὅ τι"

deliberative subj. aor. subj. χράομαι

c5 ὑπὸ...σατύρου: *because of...*

c6 ὡς ὅμοιός τ᾽ ἐστὶν: *how similar he is* οἷς ἐγὼ ἤκασα αὐτὸν: *(to those) to whom I likened him*; 1st sg. aor. εἰκάζω

c7 ὡς θαυμασίαν: *how amazing* ἴστε: pl. imperative, οἶδα

d1 ἐπείπερ ἠρξάμην: *since...*; aor. ἄρχω

d2 ἐρωτικῶς διάκειται: *is disposed erotically toward* (+ gen.)

d3 περὶ τούτους: *around them* ἐκπέπληκται: pf. pass., ἐκ-πλήττω

d4 ὡς τὸ σχῆμα...σιληνῶδες: *As for his appearance, (is) this not Silenus-like?*; acc. of respect

d5 τοῦτο...περιβέβληται: *This one has thrown this around (himself) on the outside*; pf. mid., περι-βάλλω

d6 γεγλυμμένος: pf. pass., γλύφω ἀνοιχθεὶς: aor. pass. pple, ἀν-οίγνυμι

d8 μέλει...οὐδέν: *it is no concern to him* τοσοῦτον ὅσον: *so much that...* οἰηθείη: *would think*; 3rd sg. aor. dep. opt.

a   καὶ ἀνοιχθέντος οὐκ οἶδα εἴ τις ἑώρακεν τὰ ἐντὸς ἀγάλματα·
ἀλλ' ἐγὼ ἤδη ποτ' εἶδον, καί μοι ἔδοξεν οὕτω θεῖα καὶ
217 χρυσᾶ εἶναι καὶ πάγκαλα καὶ θαυμαστά, ὥστε ποιητέον εἶναι
ἔμβραχυ ὅτι κελεύοι Σωκράτης. ἡγούμενος δὲ αὐτὸν ἐσπουδακέναι ἐπὶ τῇ ἐμῇ ὥρᾳ ἕρμαιον ἡγησάμην εἶναι καὶ εὐτύχημα
ἐμὸν θαυμαστόν, ὡς ὑπάρχον μοι χαρισαμένῳ Σωκράτει πάντ'
5   ἀκοῦσαι ὅσαπερ οὗτος ᾔδει· ἐφρόνουν γὰρ δὴ ἐπὶ τῇ ὥρᾳ
θαυμάσιον ὅσον. ταῦτα οὖν διανοηθείς, πρὸ τοῦ οὐκ εἰωθὼς
ἄνευ ἀκολούθου μόνος μετ' αὐτοῦ γίγνεσθαι, τότε ἀποπέμπων
b   τὸν ἀκόλουθον μόνος συνεγιγνόμην—δεῖ γὰρ πρὸς ὑμᾶς πάντα
τἀληθῆ εἰπεῖν· ἀλλὰ προσέχετε τὸν νοῦν, καὶ εἰ ψεύδομαι,
Σώκρατες, ἐξέλεγχε—συνεγιγνόμην γάρ, ὦ ἄνδρες, μόνος
μόνῳ, καὶ ᾤμην αὐτίκα διαλέξεσθαι αὐτόν μοι ἅπερ ἂν
5   ἐραστὴς παιδικοῖς ἐν ἐρημίᾳ διαλεχθείη, καὶ ἔχαιρον. τούτων
δ' οὐ μάλα ἐγίγνετο οὐδέν, ἀλλ' ὥσπερ εἰώθει διαλεχθεὶς ἄν
μοι καὶ συνημερεύσας ᾤχετο ἀπιών. μετὰ ταῦτα συγγυμνά-
c   ζεσθαι προυκαλούμην αὐτὸν καὶ συνεγυμναζόμην, ὥς τι
ἐνταῦθα περανῶν. συνεγυμνάζετο οὖν μοι καὶ προσεπάλαιεν
πολλάκις οὐδενὸς παρόντος· καὶ τί δεῖ λέγειν; οὐδὲν γάρ
μοι πλέον ἦν. ἐπειδὴ δὲ οὐδαμῇ ταύτῃ ἤνυτον, ἔδοξέ μοι
5   ἐπιθετέον εἶναι τῷ ἀνδρὶ κατὰ τὸ καρτερὸν καὶ οὐκ ἀνετέον,
ἐπειδήπερ ἐνεκεχειρήκη, ἀλλὰ ἰστέον ἤδη τί ἐστι τὸ πρᾶγμα.
προκαλοῦμαι δὴ αὐτὸν πρὸς τὸ συνδειπνεῖν, ἀτεχνῶς ὥσπερ
ἐραστὴς παιδικοῖς ἐπιβουλεύων. καί μοι οὐδὲ τοῦτο ταχὺ
d   ὑπήκουσεν, ὅμως δ' οὖν χρόνῳ ἐπείσθη. ἐπειδὴ δὲ ἀφίκετο
τὸ πρῶτον, δειπνήσας ἀπιέναι ἐβούλετο. καὶ τότε μὲν
αἰσχυνόμενος ἀφῆκα αὐτόν· αὖθις δ' ἐπιβουλεύσας, ἐπειδὴ
ἐδεδειπνήκεμεν διελεγόμην ἀεὶ πόρρω τῶν νυκτῶν, καὶ ἐπειδὴ

ἄγαλμα, -ατος τό: statue, image*
ἀκόλουθος, ὁ: follower*
ἀνετέος, -α, -ον: to be dismissed, given up
ἀν-οίγνυμι: to open, open up*
ἀνύτω: to achieve, accomplish, complete
ἀπο-πέμπω: to send away, to dismiss*
ἀ-τεχνῶς: simply, really, entirely*
αὖθις: back again, later*
αὐτίκα: straightway, at once; presently*
ἀφ-ικνέομαι: to come, arrive*
δια-νοέομαι: to think, suppose, intend*
ἐγ-χειρέω: to take in hand, attempt, begin
ἔμ-βραχυ: in brief, shortly
ἐντός: within, inside*
ἐξ-ελέγχω: to convict, refute, test
ἐπι-βουλεύω: to plot against, contrive against*
ἐπι-θετέος, -α, -ον: to be imposed, attacked
ἐρημία, ἡ: desert, wilderness; solitude
ἕρμαιον, τό: god-send, stroke of luck
εὐ-τύχημα, -ατος, τό: good luck, success
καρτερός, -ά, -όν: strong, steadfast, staunch

νύξ, νυκτός, ἡ: a night*
οὐδαμῇ: in no way, not at all
πάγκαλος, -η, -ον: all-beautiful, good, noble*
περαίνω: to bring about, finish, accomplish
ποιητέος, -α, -ον: to be done, to be made
πόρρω: far; advanced
προ-καλέω: to call forth, summon
προσ-παλαίω: to wrestle or struggle with
σπουδάζω: to pursue earnestly, be serious, be
　　eager for, make haste*
συγ-γίγνομαι: to be with, converse with,
　　associate with (+ dat.)
συγ-γυμνάζω: to exercise together*
συν-δειπνέω: to dine together with
συν-ημερεύω: to pass the day together
ὑπ-ακούω: to listen, heed, give ear, pay heed
ὑπ-άρχω: to be ready, available; be possible*
φρονέω: to think, to be wise, prudent*
χρύσεος, -η, -ον: golden, of gold*
ψεύδομαι: to lie, cheat, beguile*
ὥρα, ἡ: season, time, period of time; youth*

216e6 ἀνοιχθέντος: *opened*; aor. pass. pple,
　　gen. abs. ἀνοίγνυμι
　　ἑωράκεν: 3rd sg. pf. ὁράω
e7 εἶδον: 1st sg. aor. ὁράω
217a1 ποιητέον εἶναι: *I must do*; result clause,
　　"it is to be done (by me)," supply μοι
a2 ὅτι κελεύοι: *whatever...bids*; pres. opt.
　　replacing ἄν + subj. in secondary seq.
　　ἐσπουδακέναι...ὥρᾳ: *is eager for my*
　　youthful beauty; pf. inf., σπουδάζω
a4 ὡς ὑπάρχον...ἀκοῦσαι: *since it was*
　　available to me, after gratifying Socrates,
　　to hear...; "it being available," acc. abs.
a5 ᾔδει: *he knew*; past οἶδα
a6 ἐφρόνουν...ὅσον: *I had such amazing*
　　thoughts on my youthful beauty;
　　a difficult passage, perhaps internal acc.
　　διανοηθείς: *planning*; aor. pass. pple
　　πρὸ τοῦ οὐκ εἰωθώς: *before which*
　　(time) not being accustomed; pf. pple
b3 συνεγιγνόμην: *I began associating*; impf.
b4 ᾤμην: 1st sg. impf. οἴομαι
　　διαλέξεσθαι: fut. inf., διαλέγομαι
b5 ἅπερ ἄν...διαλεχθείη: *just as...would*
　　converse; "which very things," aor. opt.
　　replacing ἄν + past for repeated activity
　　ἔχαιρον: impf. χαίρω

b6 εἰώθει: *I was accustomed*; plpf.
　　διαλεχθείς: *conversing*; aor. dep. pple
　　ἄν...ᾤχετο: *he would go off*; ἄν + past
　　for repeated activity, not past potential
b7 ἀπιών: pres. pple, ἀπέρχομαι (stem ι)
c1 προυκαλούμην: προεκαλεόμην, impf.
　　ὡς...περανῶν: *so that..;* ὡς + fut.
c3 οὐδὲν γάρ μοι πλέον ἦν: *for I got no*
　　further; "for there was nothing more for
　　me,"
c4 ἤνυτον: *I accomplished*; impf.
c5 ἐπιθετέον εἶναι...οὐκ ἀνετέον: *that I must*
　　attack...and not give up; verbal adjectives
　　from ἐπι-τίθημι and ἀν-ίημι
　　κατὰ τὸ καρτερόν: *by force, strength*
c6 ἐνεκεχειρήκη: 1st s. plpf. ἐγ-χειρέω
　　ἰστέον...πράγμα: *I had to know what*
　　was the matter; verbal adj. from οἶδα
c8 οὐδὲ...ταχύ: *and not quickly;* adverb
　　ὑπήκουσεν: *accept (the dinner invitation);*
　　"heeded me"
d1 χρόνῳ ἐπείσθη: *in time was persuaded;*
　　3rd sg. aor. pass., dat. of time when
　　ἀφίκετο: 3rd sg. aor. mid., ἀφ-ικνέομαι
d3 ἀφῆκα: *I let go*; 1st sg. aor. ἀφ-ίημι
d4 ἐδεδειπνήκεμεν: plpf. δειπνέω

5 ἐβούλετο ἀπιέναι, σκηπτόμενος ὅτι ὀψὲ εἴη, προσηνάγκασα
αὐτὸν μένειν. ἀνεπαύετο οὖν ἐν τῇ ἐχομένῃ ἐμοῦ κλίνῃ, ἐν
ᾗπερ ἐδείπνει, καὶ οὐδεὶς ἐν τῷ οἰκήματι ἄλλος καθηῦδεν ἢ
e ἡμεῖς. μέχρι μὲν οὖν δὴ δεῦρο τοῦ λόγου καλῶς ἂν ἔχοι
καὶ πρὸς ὁντινοῦν λέγειν· τὸ δ' ἐντεῦθεν οὐκ ἄν μου ἠκούσατε
λέγοντος, εἰ μὴ πρῶτον μέν, τὸ λεγόμενον, οἶνος ἄνευ τε
παίδων καὶ μετὰ παίδων ἦν ἀληθής, ἔπειτα ἀφανίσαι Σω-
5 κράτους ἔργον ὑπερήφανον εἰς ἔπαινον ἐλθόντα ἄδικόν μοι
φαίνεται. ἔτι δὲ τὸ τοῦ δηχθέντος ὑπὸ τοῦ ἔχεως πάθος
κἄμ' ἔχει. φασὶ γάρ πού τινα τοῦτο παθόντα οὐκ ἐθέλειν
λέγειν οἶον ἦν πλὴν τοῖς δεδηγμένοις, ὡς μόνοις γνωσομένοις
218 τε καὶ συγγνωσομένοις εἰ πᾶν ἐτόλμα δρᾶν τε καὶ λέγειν
ὑπὸ τῆς ὀδύνης. ἐγὼ οὖν δεδηγμένος τε ὑπὸ ἀλγεινοτέρου
καὶ τὸ ἀλγεινότατον ὧν ἄν τις δηχθείη—τὴν καρδίαν γὰρ
ἢ ψυχὴν ἢ ὅτι δεῖ αὐτὸ ὀνομάσαι πληγείς τε καὶ δηχθεὶς
5 ὑπὸ τῶν ἐν φιλοσοφίᾳ λόγων, οἳ ἔχονται ἐχίδνης ἀγριώτερον,
νέου ψυχῆς μὴ ἀφυοῦς ὅταν λάβωνται, καὶ ποιοῦσι δρᾶν
τε καὶ λέγειν ὁτιοῦν—καὶ ὁρῶν αὖ Φαίδρους, Ἀγάθωνας,
b Ἐρυξιμάχους, Παυσανίας, Ἀριστοδήμους τε καὶ Ἀριστο-
φάνας· Σωκράτη δὲ αὐτὸν τί δεῖ λέγειν, καὶ ὅσοι ἄλλοι;
πάντες γὰρ κεκοινωνήκατε τῆς φιλοσόφου μανίας τε καὶ
βακχείας—διὸ πάντες ἀκούσεσθε· συγγνώσεσθε γὰρ τοῖς τε
5 τότε πραχθεῖσι καὶ τοῖς νῦν λεγομένοις. οἱ δὲ οἰκέται, καὶ
εἴ τις ἄλλος ἐστὶν βέβηλός τε καὶ ἄγροικος, πύλας πάνυ
μεγάλας τοῖς ὠσὶν ἐπίθεσθε.

Ἐπειδὴ γὰρ οὖν, ὦ ἄνδρες, ὅ τε λύχνος ἀπεσβήκει καὶ
c οἱ παῖδες ἔξω ἦσαν, ἔδοξέ μοι χρῆναι μηδὲν ποικίλλειν πρὸς
αὐτόν, ἀλλ' ἐλευθέρως εἰπεῖν ἅ μοι ἐδόκει· καὶ εἶπον κινήσας
αὐτόν, Σώκρατες, καθεύδεις;

Οὐ δῆτα, ἦ δ' ὅς.

ἄγριος, -α, -ον: wild, fierce
ἄγρ-οικος, -ον: rustic, unsophisticated, crude
ἄ-δικος, -ον: unjust, unrighteous*
ἀλγεινός, -ή, -όν: painful, grievous
ἀνα-παύομαι: to rest*
ἀπο-σβέννυμι: to put out, quench; be put out
ἀ-φανίζω: make invisible, conceal, destroy*
ἀ-φυής, -ές: without natural talent, witless
Βακχεία, ἡ: Bacchic frenzy
βέβηλος, -ον: impure, unhallowed
δάκνω: to bite; sting, prick*
δεῦρο: here, to this point, hither*
δῆτα: certainly, to be sure, of course*
δράω: to do*
ἐλεύθερος, -α, -ον: free*
ἐντεῦθεν: from here, from there*
ἔξω: out of (+ gen.); adv. outside*
ἔχις, -εως, ἡ: a snake, adder, viper
ἔχιδνα, ἡ: a snake, adder, viper
καθ-εύδω: to lie down to sleep, sleep*
καρδία, ἡ: heart
κινέω: to set in motion, move; arouse, irritate*
κλίνη, ἡ: a couch, bed

κοινωνέω: to have a share of, partake in (gen.)
λύχνος, ὁ: lamp, a portable light
μανία, ἡ: madness, frenzy; enthusiasm
μένω: to stay, remain*
μέχρι: up to; until, as long as (+ gen.)*
ὀδύνη, ἡ: pain of body, pain of mind
οἰκέτης, -ου, ὁ: a house-slave, slave
οἴκημα, -ατος, τό: room; workshop
οἶνος, ὁ: wine*
ὀνομάζω: to name, call by name*
οὖς, ωτός, τό: ear*
ὀψέ: late
πάθος, τό: suffering, experience, misfortune
πλήν: except, but*
πλήττω: to strike, beat
ποικίλλω: embroider; complicate, embellish
που: anywhere, somewhere; I suppose
προσ-αναγκάζω: to press, compel, force*
πύλη, ἡ: one wing of a pair of double gates*
σκήπτω: to allege, pretend, propose as support
συγ-γιγνώσκω: to sympathize, forgive (dat.)
ὑπερ-ήφανος, -ον: overweening, arrogant
φιλό-σοφος, ὁ: a pursuer or lover of wisdom

217d5 εἴη: *it was*; opt. εἰμί, secondary seq.
  d6 ἐχομένη ἐμοῦ: *next to me*; "clinging to me", partitive gen.
  e1 μέχρι..λόγου: *up to here of the speech*
  e2 καλῶς ἂν..λέγεν: *I could well say to anyone*; "it would be well…" ἔχω + adv.
  τὸ δ᾽ ἐντεῦθεν: *what (is said) from here*
  e3 ἂν ἠκούσατε…εἰ…ἦν: *you would not hear if wine were…*; contrafactual condition
  τὸ λεγόμενον: *as the saying goes*
  e4 ἔπειτα: *second*; second reason cf. e3
  ἀφανίσαι…ἄδικόν μοι φαίνεται: *it seems to me unjust that I…conceal*
  e5 εἰς ἔπαινον ἐλθόντα: *launching into a speech of praise*; modifies missing acc.
  e6 τοῦ δηχθέντος: *of one bitten*; aor. pass. pple δάκνω; following τὸ πάθος
  e7 κἄμ᾽ ἔχει: *is in fact same*; καὶ ἅμα
  e8 οἷον ἦν: *what it (i.e. the bite) was like*
  δεδηγμένοις: perf. pass. pple, δάκνω
218a1 ὡς..γνωσομένοις…συγγνωσομένοις: *so that…*; ὡς + fut. pple., purpose
  a3 τὸ ἀλγεινότατον…δηχθείη: *in respect to the most painful part of those (in which) one could be bitten*; acc. respect

καρδίαν, ψυχὴν: *in…in…in…*; respect
ὀνομάσαι: aor. inf. ὀνομάζω
  a4 πληγείς…δηχθείς: *struck and bitten*; aor. pass. pple. in apposition to a2
  a5 ἔχονται ἀγριώτερον: *cling more fiercely* comparative adv. and gen. comparison
  a6 μὴ ἀφυοῦς: *not untalented*; with ψυχῆς
  λάβωνται: *(the words) grab hold of*; aor. subj. governing a partitive genitive
  a7 Φαίδρους, Ἀγάθωνας…: *the Phaedruses (of the world), the Agathons (of the world)…*; i.e. people like Phaedrus…
  b2 Σωκράτη…λέγειν: *need I mention Socrates?*; "why must I mention…"
  b3 κεκοινωνήκατε: 2nd pl. pf.
  b4 ἀκούσεσθε: 2nd pl. fut. dep. ἀκούω
  συγγνώσεσθε: *forgive*; 2nd pl. fut. dep.
  b5 τοῖς πραχθεῖσι: *things done*; aor. pass.
  b6 πύλας…ἐπίθεσθε: *shut very large gates over your ears*; dat. pl. οὖς, aor. imperative of ἐπι-τίθημι
  b8 ἀπεσβήκει: *had been quenched*; plpf. ἀπο-σβέννυμι
  c1 χρῆναι: *that I ought*; inf. χρή
  c2 κινήσας αὐτόν: *shaking him*; aor. pple.

5   Οἶσθα οὖν ἅ μοι δέδοκται;

    Τί μάλιστα, ἔφη.

Σὺ ἐμοὶ δοκεῖς, ἦν δ' ἐγώ, ἐμοῦ ἐραστὴς ἄξιος γεγονέναι μόνος, καί μοι φαίνῃ ὀκνεῖν μνησθῆναι πρός με. ἐγὼ δὲ οὑτωσὶ ἔχω· πάνυ ἀνόητον ἡγοῦμαι εἶναι σοὶ μὴ οὐ καὶ
5 τοῦτο χαρίζεσθαι καὶ εἴ τι ἄλλο ἢ τῆς οὐσίας τῆς ἐμῆς
d δέοιο ἢ τῶν φίλων τῶν ἐμῶν. ἐμοὶ μὲν γὰρ οὐδέν ἐστι πρεσβύτερον τοῦ ὡς ὅτι βέλτιστον ἐμὲ γενέσθαι, τούτου δὲ οἶμαί μοι συλλήπτορα οὐδένα κυριώτερον εἶναι σοῦ. ἐγὼ δὴ τοιούτῳ ἀνδρὶ πολὺ μᾶλλον ἂν μὴ χαριζόμενος αἰσχυνοίμην
5 τοὺς φρονίμους, ἢ χαριζόμενος τούς τε πολλοὺς καὶ ἄφρονας.

Καὶ οὗτος ἀκούσας μάλα εἰρωνικῶς καὶ σφόδρα ἑαυτοῦ τε καὶ εἰωθότως ἔλεξεν ὦ φίλε Ἀλκιβιάδη, κινδυνεύεις τῷ ὄντι οὐ φαῦλος εἶναι, εἴπερ ἀληθῆ τυγχάνει ὄντα ἃ λέγεις
e περὶ ἐμοῦ, καί τις ἔστ' ἐν ἐμοὶ δύναμις δι' ἧς ἂν σὺ γένοιο ἀμείνων· ἀμήχανόν τοι κάλλος ὁρῴης ἂν ἐν ἐμοὶ καὶ τῆς παρὰ σοὶ εὐμορφίας πάμπολυ διαφέρον. εἰ δὴ καθορῶν αὐτὸ κοινώσασθαί τέ μοι ἐπιχειρεῖς καὶ ἀλλάξασθαι κάλλος
5 ἀντὶ κάλλους, οὐκ ὀλίγῳ μου πλεονεκτεῖν διανοῇ, ἀλλ' ἀντὶ δόξης ἀλήθειαν καλῶν κτᾶσθαι ἐπιχειρεῖς καὶ τῷ
219 ὄντι χρύσεα χαλκείων διαμείβεσθαι νοεῖς. ἀλλ', ὦ μακάριε, ἄμεινον σκόπει, μή σε λανθάνω οὐδὲν ὤν. ἤ τοι τῆς διανοίας ὄψις ἄρχεται ὀξὺ βλέπειν ὅταν ἡ τῶν ὀμμάτων τῆς ἀκμῆς λήγειν ἐπιχειρῇ· σὺ δὲ τούτων ἔτι πόρρω.

5 Κἀγὼ ἀκούσας, τὰ μὲν παρ' ἐμοῦ, ἔφην, ταῦτά ἐστιν, ὧν οὐδὲν ἄλλως εἴρηται ἢ ὡς διανοοῦμαι· σὺ δὲ αὐτὸς οὕτω βουλεύου ὅτι σοί τε ἄριστον καὶ ἐμοὶ ἡγῇ.

Ἀλλ', ἔφη, τοῦτό γ' εὖ λέγεις· ἐν γὰρ τῷ ἐπιόντι χρόνῳ
b βουλευόμενοι πράξομεν ὃ ἂν φαίνηται νῷν περί τε τούτων καὶ περὶ τῶν ἄλλων ἄριστον.

ἀκμή, ἡ: highest point, prime, bloom, flower
ἀλήθεια, ἡ: truth*
ἀλλάττω: to change, alter; exchange
ἀ-μήχανος, -ον: impossible, inconceivable
ἀ-νόητος, -ον: foolish, unintelligent*
ἄ-φρων, -ον: senseless, foolish, silly
βέλτιστος, -η, -ον: best*
βουλεύω: to deliberate, plan, take counsel*
δι-αμείβω: to exchange
διάνοια, ἡ: thought, intention; intellect*
δια-νοέομαι: to think, consider, intend*
δόξα, ἡ: opinion, reputation, honor, glory*
εἰωθότως: customarily, according to custom
εἰρωνικῶς: with feigned innocence
ἐπ-έρχομαι: to come upon, approach; attack*
εὐ-μορφία, ἡ: shapeliness, good looks
κοινωνέω: to have a share of, partake of
κύριος, -α, -ον: legitimate, authoritative*
λανθάνω: to escape notice of, act unnoticed*

λήγω: to stop, cease, leave off*
μάλα: very, very much, exceedingly*
μακάριος, -α, -ον: blessed, happy*
μιμνήσκω: to recall, remember*
νοέω: to think, mean, indicate, suppose
ὀκνέω: to shirk from, hesitate, hang back
ὄμμα, -ατος, τό: the eye
ὀξύς, -εῖα, -ύ: sharp, keen*
οὐσία, ἡ: property, substance; being, essence
ὄψις, -εως, ἡ: vision, appearance, form; face*
πάμ-πολυ: very much, greatly
πλεονεκτέω: to have or gain advantage over
πόρρω: far; advanced, far from (+ gen.)
σκοπέω: to look at, examine, consider*
συλλήπτωρ, -ορος, ὁ: a partner, assistant
τοι: ya know, let me tell you, surely*
φρόνιμος, -ον: sensible, intelligent, prudent
χάλκειος, -η, -ον: of copper or bronze; bronze
χρύσεος, -η, -ον: golden, of gold; gold*

218c5 μοι δέδοκται: *I have decided*; lit. "has seemed good to me", neuter pl. subject

c7 ἐμοῦ: *for me*; obj. of ἐραστὴς

c8 φαίνῃ: *you seem*; 2ⁿᵈ sg. pres. mid.
μνησθῆναι: *from mentioning (it)*; aor dep.

c9 μὴ οὐ...χαρίζεσθαι: *not to gratify*

c10 τοῦτο: *in this*; i.e. sex, acc. of respect
εἴ...δέοιο: *if you should request anything else from*; δέοι(σ)ο, 2ⁿᵈ sg. opt.

d2 πρεσβύτερον: *more important*
τοῦ...γενέσθαι: *than becoming*; articular inf. as a gen. of comparison
ὡς ὅτι βέλτιστον: *as good as possible*; ὡς ὅτι is redundant with a superlative
τούτου...συλλήπτορα οὐδένα κυριώτερον: *no one is more capable a helper for this (task)*; objective genitive σοῦ: *than...*; gen. comparision

d4 ἂν αἰσχυνοίμην: *I would be ashamed before sensible men*; apodosis of a fut. less vivid, the protasis is the μή + pple

d6 σφόδρα ἑαυτοῦ: *very much in character*; "very much of himself"

d7 ἔλεξεν: 3ʳᵈ sg. aor., λέγω, usually εἶπον
κινδυνεύεις...εἶναι: *it looks as though you are*; "you run the risk of being"
τῷ ὄντι: *really, actually*; dat. respect

d8 τυγχάνει ὄντα: *happened to be*

e1 ἂν γένοιο: *you might become*; γένοι(σ)ο,

e2 ὁρῴης ἄν: *you must see*; opt. ὁράω
τῆς παρὰ σοὶ πάμπολυ διαφέρον: *differing very much from the good looks in you*; gen. separation

e4 κοινώσασθαι: *bargain with* (+ dat.); governed by ἐπιχειρεῖς
ἀλλάξασθαι: *exchange*; aor. ἀλλάττω
ἀντὶ κάλλους: *in place of..* gen. κάλλεος

e5 οὐκ ὀλίγῳ...διανοῇ: *you plan to have not a small advantage over me*; dat. of degree of difference, gen. of comparison; 2ⁿᵈ sg. pres. mid.

219a1 χαλκείων: *for bronze*; gen. of price

a2 ἄμεινον σκόπει: *consider better*; imper.
μή σε λανθάνω...ὤν: *lest it escapes your notice that I am (worth) nothing*; "lest I escape your notice, being not worthy"

a4 ἡ τῶν ὀμμάτων: *the (vision) of the eyes*
τῆς ἀκμῆς..ἐπιχειρῇ: *begins to decline*
σὺ δὲ: *but you (are)...*; supply εἶ

a5 τὰ..ἐστιν...διανοοῦμαι: *the things (said) by me are these, none of which has been said otherwise than as I intend*; pf. ἐρέω

a7 βουλεύου: *deliberate!*; βουλεύε(σ)ο, imp.
ὅτι...ἡγῇ: *what you think best*; 2ⁿᵈ s. pres.

a8 ἐπιόντι χρόνῳ: *future*; "coming time"

b1 πράξομεν: 1ˢᵗ pl. fut., πράττω
νῷν: *to us two*; 1ˢᵗ pl. dual form, dat.

Ἐγὼ μὲν δὴ ταῦτα ἀκούσας τε καὶ εἰπών, καὶ ἀφεὶς
ὥσπερ βέλη, τετρῶσθαι αὐτὸν ᾤμην· καὶ ἀναστάς γε, οὐδ᾽
5 ἐπιτρέψας τούτῳ εἰπεῖν οὐδὲν ἔτι, ἀμφιέσας τὸ ἱμάτιον
τὸ ἐμαυτοῦ τοῦτον—καὶ γὰρ ἦν χειμών—ὑπὸ τὸν τρίβωνα
κατακλινεὶς τὸν τουτουί, περιβαλὼν τὼ χεῖρε τούτῳ τῷ
c δαιμονίῳ ὡς ἀληθῶς καὶ θαυμαστῷ, κατεκείμην τὴν νύκτα
ὅλην. καὶ οὐδὲ ταῦτα αὖ, ὦ Σώκρατες, ἐρεῖς ὅτι ψεύδομαι.
ποιήσαντος δὲ δὴ ταῦτα ἐμοῦ οὗτος τοσοῦτον περιεγένετό
τε καὶ κατεφρόνησεν καὶ κατεγέλασεν τῆς ἐμῆς ὥρας καὶ
5 ὕβρισεν—καὶ περὶ ἐκεῖνό γε ᾤμην τὶ εἶναι, ὦ ἄνδρες δικασταί·
δικασταὶ γάρ ἐστε τῆς Σωκράτους ὑπερηφανίας—εὖ γὰρ
ἴστε μὰ θεούς, μὰ θεάς, οὐδὲν περιττότερον καταδεδαρθηκὼς
d ἀνέστην μετὰ Σωκράτους, ἢ εἰ μετὰ πατρὸς καθηῦδον ἢ
ἀδελφοῦ πρεσβυτέρου.

Τὸ δὴ μετὰ τοῦτο τίνα οἴεσθέ με διάνοιαν ἔχειν, ἡγού-
μενον μὲν ἠτιμάσθαι, ἀγάμενον δὲ τὴν τούτου φύσιν τε καὶ
5 σωφροσύνην καὶ ἀνδρείαν, ἐντετυχηκότα ἀνθρώπῳ τοιούτῳ
οἵῳ ἐγὼ οὐκ ἂν ᾤμην ποτ᾽ ἐντυχεῖν εἰς φρόνησιν καὶ εἰς
καρτερίαν; ὥστε οὔθ᾽ ὅπως οὖν ὀργιζοίμην εἶχον καὶ ἀπο-
στερηθείην τῆς τούτου συνουσίας, οὔτε ὅπῃ προσαγαγοίμην
e αὐτὸν ηὐπόρουν. εὖ γὰρ ᾔδη ὅτι χρήμασί γε πολὺ μᾶλλον
ἄτρωτος ἦν πανταχῇ ἢ σιδήρῳ ὁ Αἴας, ᾧ τε ᾤμην αὐτὸν
μόνῳ ἁλώσεσθαι, διεπεφεύγει με. ἠπόρουν δή, καταδε-
δουλωμένος τε ὑπὸ τοῦ ἀνθρώπου ὡς οὐδεὶς ὑπ᾽ οὐδενὸς
5 ἄλλου περιῇα. ταῦτά τε γάρ μοι ἅπαντα προυγεγόνει, καὶ
μετὰ ταῦτα στρατεία ἡμῖν εἰς Ποτείδαιαν ἐγένετο κοινὴ
καὶ συνεσιτοῦμεν ἐκεῖ. πρῶτον μὲν οὖν τοῖς πόνοις οὐ
μόνον ἐμοῦ περιῆν, ἀλλὰ καὶ τῶν ἄλλων ἁπάντων—ὁπότ᾽
ἀναγκασθεῖμεν ἀποληφθέντες που, οἷα δὴ ἐπὶ στρατείας,

ἄγαμαι: to wonder at, marvel at, admire*
ἀδελφός, ὁ: a brother*
Αἴας, -αντος, ὁ: Ajax
ἁλίσκομαι: to be caught, be taken*
ἀμφι-έννυμι: to put (acc) around (acc), clothe
ἀνδρεία, ἡ: manliness, bravery, courage*
ἀν-ίστημι: to make stand up, raise up, get up*
ἀπο-λαμβάνω: to take from; intercept, cut off
ἀπο-στερέω: to deprive from, rob, defraud
ἀ-τιμάζω: to dishonor, esteem lightly, slight
ἄ-τρωτος, -ον: unwoundable, invulnerable
βέλος, -εος, τό: an arrow, missile, dart*
δαιμόνιος, -α, -ον: divine, daimon-like*
διάνοια, ἡ: thought, intention; intellect*
δια-φεύγω: to flee, get away from, escape*
δικαστής, οῦ, ὁ: a juror, dicast*
ἐκεῖ: there, in that place*
ἐπιτρέπω: to commit, entrust; permit, allow*
εὐ-πορέω: to have means, prosper, thrive*
ἱμάτιον, τό: a cloak, mantle*
καθ-εύδω: to lie down to sleep, sleep*
καρτερία, ἡ: strength, steadfastness
κατα-γελάω: to laugh at, mock*
κατα-δαρθάνω: to fall asleep, be asleep*
κατα-δουλόω: to enslave, reduce to slavery
κατα-φρονέω: to think down upon, despise*
μά: by, *in affirmation*

νύξ, νυκτός, ἡ: a night*
ὅπῃ: by which way, in what way, how*
ὁπότε: when, by what time*
ὀργίζω: to make angry, provoke, irritate
παντα-χῆ: everywhere; in every way
περι-βάλλω: to throw round, enclose; clothe*
περι-γίγνομαι: to prevail over (gen.); survive
περί-ειμι: to surpass, excel, (+ gen.)*
περι-έρχομαι: to go around, run round
περιττός, -ή, -όν: extraordinary, remarkable*
πόνος, ὁ: work, toil, labor*
Ποτείδαια, ἡ: Potidaea
που: anywhere, somewhere; I suppose
προ-γίγνομαι: to happen, occur before
προσ-άγω: to bring near, apply; win over*
σίδηρος, ὁ: iron; sword, knife
στρατεία, ἡ: an expedition, campaign
συσ-σιτέω: to share a mess with, eat with
τιτρώσκω: to wound, inflict, damage
τρίβων, -ωνος, ὁ: worn or threadbare cloak
ὑβρίζω: to commit outrage, assault, insult*
ὑπερηφανία, ἡ: arrogance, disdain, contempt
φρόνησις, -εως, ἡ: intelligence, wisdom*
χειμών, -ῶνος τό: storm, winter*
ψεύδομαι: to lie, cheat, beguile*
ὥρα, ἡ: season, time, period of time; youth*

219b3 ἀφείς: *having shot*; aor. pple, ἀφ-ίημι
  b4 τετρῶσθαι: perf. pass. inf., τιτρώσκω
    ἀναστάς: *standing up*; pple, ἀν-ίστημι
  b5 ἐπιτρέψας: *allowing* (+ dat.); aor. pple
    ἀμφιέσας: aor. pple, ἀμφι-έννυμι
  b7 τὸν τουτουί: *of this her man*; deictic -ι
    τὼ χεῖρε: *both of my hands*; dual acc.
  c1 τὴν νύκτα ὅλην: *for...*; acc. of duration
  c3 τοσοῦτον: *so far, so much*; adverbial
  c4 τῆς ἐμῆς ὥρας: *my youthful beauty*
  c5 περὶ ἐκεῖνο: *regarding that* (i.e. beauty)
    τὶ εἶναι: *that it was something* (special)
  c6 ἐστε: *you are*; 2nd pl. pres. εἰμί
  c7 εὖ ἴστε: *know well*; pl. imperative, οἶδα
    μὰ θεούς: *by the gods! by*
    οὐδὲν περιττότερον...ἤ: *no more
    remarkably...than*; comparative adverb
  d1 καταδεδαρθηκώς: nom. sb. pf. pple
    ἀνέστην: *I got up*; aor., ἀν-ίστημι
  d3 τὸ δὴ μετὰ τοῦτο: *as for after this*; acc.
    of respect

τίνα...διάνοιαν: *what frame of mind...?*
  d5 ἐντετυχηκότα: pf. pple ἐν-τυγχάνω
  d6 ἂν ἐντυχεῖν: *would meet*; past potential
    εἰς φρόνησιν: *with regard to intelligence*
  d7 οὔθ' ὅπως...εἶχον: *I did not know how
    I was to be angry*; deliberative optatives
  d8 οὔτε ὅπῃ...ηὐπόρουν: *nor did I have the
    means how I might attract him*; aor.
    deliberative aor.opt. προσάγω
  e1 ἤδη: *I knew*; 1st sg. past, οἶδα
    χρήμασί...σιδήρῳ: *by money, by iron*;
    both governed by ἄτρωτος
  e2 ᾧ τε ᾤμην: *and (as for that) by which I
    thought*; lost antecedent is acc. respect,
  e3 ἁλώσεσθαι: fut. mid. inf., ἁλίσκομαι
  e5 περιῇα: 1st sg. impf. περι-έρχομαι
    προυγεγόνει: *had occurred beforehand*
  e7 τοῖς πόνοις: *in hardships*; dat. respect
  e8 περιῆν: *he prevailed over*; + gen. impf.
    ἀποληφθέντες: *being cut off*; aor. pass.
    οἷα δή...: *as (happens) on campaign*

220 ἀσιτεῖν, οὐδὲν ἦσαν οἱ ἄλλοι πρὸς τὸ καρτερεῖν—ἔν τ' αὖ
ταῖς εὐωχίαις μόνος ἀπολαύειν οἷός τ' ἦν τά τ' ἄλλα καὶ
πίνειν οὐκ ἐθέλων, ὁπότε ἀναγκασθείη, πάντας ἐκράτει, καὶ
ὃ πάντων θαυμαστότατον, Σωκράτη μεθύοντα οὐδεὶς πώποτε
5 ἑώρακεν ἀνθρώπων. τούτου μὲν οὖν μοι δοκεῖ καὶ αὐτίκα ὁ
ἔλεγχος ἔσεσθαι. πρὸς δὲ αὖ τὰς τοῦ χειμῶνος καρτερήσεις
—δεινοὶ γὰρ αὐτόθι χειμῶνες—θαυμάσια ἠργάζετο τά τε
b ἄλλα, καί ποτε ὄντος πάγου οἵου δεινοτάτου, καὶ πάντων ἢ
οὐκ ἐξιόντων ἔνδοθεν, ἢ εἴ τις ἐξίοι, ἠμφιεσμένων τε
θαυμαστὰ δὴ ὅσα καὶ ὑποδεδεμένων καὶ ἐνειλιγμένων τοὺς
πόδας εἰς πίλους καὶ ἀρνακίδας, οὗτος δ' ἐν τούτοις ἐξῄει
5 ἔχων ἱμάτιον μὲν τοιοῦτον οἷόνπερ καὶ πρότερον εἰώθει
φορεῖν, ἀνυπόδητος δὲ διὰ τοῦ κρυστάλλου ῥᾷον ἐπορεύετο
ἢ οἱ ἄλλοι ὑποδεδεμένοι, οἱ δὲ στρατιῶται ὑπέβλεπον
c αὐτὸν ὡς καταφρονοῦντα σφῶν. καὶ ταῦτα μὲν δὴ ταῦτα·

οἷον δ' αὖ τόδ' ἔρεξε καὶ ἔτλη καρτερὸς ἀνὴρ

ἐκεῖ ποτε ἐπὶ στρατιᾶς, ἄξιον ἀκοῦσαι. συννοήσας γὰρ
αὐτόθι ἕωθέν τι εἱστήκει σκοπῶν, καὶ ἐπειδὴ οὐ προυχώρει
5 αὐτῷ, οὐκ ἀνίει ἀλλὰ εἱστήκει ζητῶν. καὶ ἤδη ἦν μεσημβρία, καὶ ἄνθρωποι ᾐσθάνοντο, καὶ θαυμάζοντες ἄλλος ἄλλῳ
ἔλεγεν ὅτι Σωκράτης ἐξ ἑωθινοῦ φροντίζων τι ἕστηκε.
τελευτῶντες δέ τινες τῶν Ἰώνων, ἐπειδὴ ἑσπέρα ἦν, δειπνή-
d σαντες—καὶ γὰρ θέρος τότε γ' ἦν—χαμεύνια ἐξενεγκάμενοι
ἅμα μὲν ἐν τῷ ψύχει καθηῦδον, ἅμα δ' ἐφύλαττον αὐτὸν εἰ
καὶ τὴν νύκτα ἑστήξοι. ὁ δὲ εἱστήκει μέχρι ἕως ἐγένετο
καὶ ἥλιος ἀνέσχεν· ἔπειτα ᾤχετ' ἀπιὼν προσευξάμενος τῷ
5 ἡλίῳ. εἰ δὲ βούλεσθε ἐν ταῖς μάχαις—τοῦτο γὰρ δὴ
δίκαιόν γε αὐτῷ ἀποδοῦναι—ὅτε γὰρ ἡ μάχη ἦν ἐξ ἧς ἐμοὶ

αἰσθάνομαι: to perceive, feel, learn, realize*
ἀμφι-έννυμι: to put round one, clothe
ἀν-έχω: to uphold, endure; rise up, emerge*
ἀν-ίημι: to send up, let go, give up*
ἀν-υπόδητος, -η, -ον: unshod, barefoot*
ἀπο-δίδωμι: to give back, return, render*
ἀπο-λαύω: to enjoy, have enjoyment (gen.)*
ἀρνακίς, -ίδος, ἡ: a sheep's skin, fleece
ἀ-σιτέω: to be without food; fast
αὐτίκα: straightway, at once; presently*
αὐτό-θι: on the very spot, here, there*
ἐκεῖ: there, in that place*
ἐκ-φέρω: to carry out, bring forth, produce*
ἔλεγχος, ὁ: proof; examination, refutation
ἔνδο-θεν: from within*
ἐν-ελίττω: to roll up in, wrap
ἐξ-έρχομαι: to go out, come out*
ἑσπέρα, ἡ: evening, eve
εὐωχία, ἡ: feast, banquet
ἕωθεν: from dawn, at earliest dawn
ἑωθινός, -ή, -όν: in the morning, early
ἥλιος, ὁ: the sun*
θέρος, τό: summer, summertime
ἱμάτιον, τό: a cloak or mantle*
Ἴωνες, -ων, οἱ: Ionians
καθ-εύδω: to lie down to sleep, sleep*
κατα-φρονέω: to think down upon, despise*
καρτερέω: to endure, be steadfast, staunch*

καρτέρησις, -εως, ὁ: feat of endurance
καρτερός, -ά, -όν: steadfast, staunch, strong
κρατέω: overcome (+ gen.); rule; be strong*
κρύσταλλος, ὁ: ice
μάχη, ἡ: battle, fight, combat*
μεθύω: to be drunk with wine*
μεσημβρία, ἡ: mid-day, noon
νύξ, νυκτός, ἡ: a night
ὁπότε: when, by what time*
πάγος, ὁ: frost
πῖλος, ὁ: wool, felt
πούς, ποδός, ὁ: a foot*
προσ-εύχομαι: to pray to, worship
προ-χωρέω: go on, advance, make progress
πώ-ποτε: ever yet, ever
ῥέζω: to do, accomplish, make, perform
στρατία, ἡ: an army
στρατιώτης, -ου, ὁ: soldier
συν-νοέω: to reflect, comprehend, understand
τλάω: to bear, suffer, undergo
ὑπο-βλέπω: to look askance at, eye
ὑπο-δέω: to bind from under, put on shoes*
φορέω: to carry regularly, wear
φροντίζω: to think, worry, give heed to
φυλάττω: keep watch, guard, keep in mind*
χαμεύνιον, τό: bedding, small bed
χειμών, -ῶνος τό: storm, winter*
ψῦχος, -εος, ὁ: cold; frost

220a1 οὐδὲν...πρὸς τὸ καρτερεῖν: *not at all near to enduring (this)*; strong negative

a2 οἷός τ᾽ ἦν: *he was able*; impf. εἰμί
τά τ᾽ ἄλλα καὶ: *and in particular*; "both in other respects and...", also a7

a3 ἐθέλων: *although...*; concessive pple
ἀναγκασθείη: *whenever he was forced*; aor. pass. opt., general temporal clause
ἐκράτει: *used to beat*; iterative impf.

a4 ὃ: *and what (is)...*; supply ἐστίν

a5 ἑώρακεν: 3rd sg. pf. ὁράω

a6 ἔσεσθαι: fut. dep. inf. εἰμί
πρὸς: *regarding, in respect to*

a7 χειμῶνες: *the storms (were)*; add ἦσαν

b1 ὄντος...δεινοτάτου: gen. abs.
πάντων...ἐνειλιγμένων: *while all (the soldiers)...*; gen. abs. with pf. pass. pples.

b2 ἐξίοι: *went out*; opt. ἐξέρχομαι

b3 θαυμαστὰ...ὅσα: *it's amazing how much*

b4 ἐξῆει: *used to go out*; iterative impf.

b6 εἰώθει: *was accustomed*; plpf., εἴωθα
ῥᾷον ἤ: *more easily than*; comp. adv.

c1 ὡς: *on the grounds that*; alleged cause
ταῦτα...ταῦτα: *and that is that*

c2 οἷον: *what sort of thing the steadfast man accomplished and endured*; ῥέζω, τλάω

c3 ἄξιον ἀκοῦσαι: *(is) worthy to hear*; add ἐστίν, predicate of οἷον, explanatory inf.

c4 εἰστήκει: *stood*; plpf. ἵστημι, cf. c5

c5 οὐκ ἀνίει: *did not give up*; impf., ἀν-ίημι

c6 ᾐσθάνοντο: *perceived*; impf. αἰσθάνομαι

c8 τελευτῶντες: *in the end*; pple is an adv.

d1 ἐξενεγκάμενοι: aor. mid. pple, ἐκ-φέρω

d2 ἅμα μὲν...ἅμα δ᾽: *both...and*

d3 τὴν νύκτα: *for the night*; acc. duration
ἑστήξοι: *would stand*; fut. pf. opt.

d4 ἀνέσχεν: *rose up*; aor. ἀνέχω
ᾤχετ᾽ ἀπιών: *walked (going) away*

d6 δίκαιόν: *it is right to*; supply ἐστίν
ἀποδοῦναι: *to render*; aor. ἀποδίδωμι

καὶ τἀριστεῖα ἔδοσαν οἱ στρατηγοί, οὐδεὶς ἄλλος ἐμὲ ἔσωσεν
e ἀνθρώπων ἢ οὗτος, τετρωμένον οὐκ ἐθέλων ἀπολιπεῖν, ἀλλὰ
συνδιέσωσε καὶ τὰ ὅπλα καὶ αὐτὸν ἐμέ. καὶ ἐγὼ μέν, ὦ Σώκρατες, καὶ τότε ἐκέλευον σοὶ διδόναι τἀριστεῖα τοὺς στρατηγούς, καὶ τοῦτό γέ μοι οὔτε μέμψῃ οὔτε ἐρεῖς ὅτι ψεύδομαι·
5 ἀλλὰ γὰρ τῶν στρατηγῶν πρὸς τὸ ἐμὸν ἀξίωμα ἀποβλεπόντων
καὶ βουλομένων ἐμοὶ διδόναι τἀριστεῖα, αὐτὸς προθυμότερος
ἐγένου τῶν στρατηγῶν ἐμὲ λαβεῖν ἢ σαυτόν. ἔτι τοίνυν,
ὦ ἄνδρες, ἄξιον ἦν θεάσασθαι Σωκράτη, ὅτε ἀπὸ Δηλίου
221 φυγῇ ἀνεχώρει τὸ στρατόπεδον· ἔτυχον γὰρ παραγενόμενος
ἵππον ἔχων, οὗτος δὲ ὅπλα. ἀνεχώρει οὖν ἐσκεδασμένων
ἤδη τῶν ἀνθρώπων οὗτός τε ἅμα καὶ Λάχης· καὶ ἐγὼ περι-
τυγχάνω, καὶ ἰδὼν εὐθὺς παρακελεύομαί τε αὐτοῖν θαρρεῖν,
5 καὶ ἔλεγον ὅτι οὐκ ἀπολείψω αὐτώ. ἐνταῦθα δὴ καὶ κάλλιον ἐθεασάμην Σωκράτη ἢ ἐν Ποτειδαίᾳ—αὐτὸς γὰρ ἧττον
ἐν φόβῳ ἦ διὰ τὸ ἐφ᾽ ἵππου εἶναι—πρῶτον μὲν ὅσον περιῆν
b Λάχητος τῷ ἔμφρων εἶναι· ἔπειτα ἔμοιγ᾽ ἐδόκει, ὦ Ἀριστόφανες, τὸ σὸν δὴ τοῦτο, καὶ ἐκεῖ διαπορεύεσθαι ὥσπερ
καὶ ἐνθάδε, "βρενθυόμενος καὶ τὠφθαλμὼ παραβάλ-
λων, ἠρέμα παρασκοπῶν καὶ τοὺς φιλίους καὶ τοὺς πολεμίους,
5 δῆλος ὢν παντὶ καὶ πάνυ πόρρωθεν ὅτι εἴ τις ἅψεται τούτου
τοῦ ἀνδρός, μάλα ἐρρωμένως ἀμυνεῖται. διὸ καὶ ἀσφαλῶς
ἀπῄει καὶ οὗτος καὶ ὁ ἑταῖρος· σχεδὸν γάρ τι τῶν οὕτω
διακειμένων ἐν τῷ πολέμῳ οὐδὲ ἅπτονται, ἀλλὰ τοὺς προ-
c τροπάδην φεύγοντας διώκουσιν.

Πολλὰ μὲν οὖν ἄν τις καὶ ἄλλα ἔχοι Σωκράτη ἐπαινέσαι
καὶ θαυμάσια· ἀλλὰ τῶν μὲν ἄλλων ἐπιτηδευμάτων τάχ᾽ ἄν
τις καὶ περὶ ἄλλου τοιαῦτα εἴποι, τὸ δὲ μηδενὶ ἀνθρώπων
5 ὅμοιον εἶναι, μήτε τῶν παλαιῶν μήτε τῶν νῦν ὄντων, τοῦτο

ἀμύνω: to fend off, ward off, defend*
ἀνα-χωρέω: to go back, withdraw, retreat*
ἀξίωμα, -ατος, τό: status, rank, standing
ἀπο-βλέπω: to look (away) to, look at, gaze*
ἀπο-λείπω: to leave behind, abandon*
ἀριστεῖα, τά: prize for valor*
ἀ-σφαλής, -ές: safe, secure, not liable to fall
βρενθύομαι: to swagger, move haughtily
Δήλιος, ὁ: Delium
διά-κειμαι: to be disposed, be affected*
δια-πορεύω: to journey along, proceed
ἔμ-φρων, -ον: sensible, shrewd, intelligent
ἐπιτήδευμα, τό: a pursuit, activity, practice*
ἐρρωμένος, -η, -ον: vigorous, stout, strong
εὐθύς: right away, straight, directly, at once*
ἠρέμα: calmly, quietly, gently, softly
θαρρέω: to be confident, bold; take courage*
ἵππος, ὁ: a horse*
Λάχης, ὁ: Laches
μέμφομαι: to blame, censure, find fault with*
ὅπλον, τό: arms; tool, implement*
ὀφθαλμός, ὁ: the eye*
παρα-βάλλω: to cast aside, compare

παρα-γίγνομαι: to be present; to arrive*
παρα-κελεύομαι: to order, urge, encourage*
παρα-σκοπέω: to give a sidelong glance at
περί-ειμι: to surpass, excel, (+ gen.)*
περι-τυγχάνω: to happen upon, meet with
πολέμιος, -α, -ον: hostile, of the enemy*
πόλεμος, ὁ: battle, fight, war*
πόρρω-θεν: from afar, at a distance
Ποτειδαία, ἡ: Potidaea
πρό-θυμος, -ον: eager, zealous, ready, willing
προ-τροπάδην: headlong, headforemost
σκεδάννυμι: to scatter, disperse
στρατηγός, ὁ: a general, leader*
στρατόπεδον, τό: camp, encampment; army*
συν-διασῴζω: to save together; help save
σχεδόν: nearly, almost, just about, practically*
σῴζω: to save, keep, preserve*
τάχα: perhaps, possibly
τιτρώσκω: to wound, inflict, damage
φεύγω: to flee, escape; defend in court*
φόβος, ὁ: fear, terror, panic*
φυγή, ἡ: flight, escape, exile*
ψεύδομαι: to lie, cheat, beguile*

220d7 ἔδοσαν: 3rd pl. aor., δίδωμι
  ἔσωσεν: 3rd sg. aor., σῴζω
  e1 τετρωμένον: wounded; pf. pass. pple.
    ἀπολιπεῖν: aor. inf., ἀπο-λείπω
  e2 συνδιέσωσε: 3rd sg. aor., συν-διασῴζω
    ὅπλα...αυτὸν ἐμέ: my armor and myself
  e3 διδόναι: inf. δίδωμι, subj. στρατηγούς
    μέμψῃ: μέμψε(σ)αι, 2nd sg. fut.
  e6 αὐτὸς ἐγένου: you yourself became; aor.
    τῶν στρατηγῶν: gen. of comparison
221a1 φυγῇ: in flight from Delium
    ἀνεχώρει: he was retreating; impf.
    ἔτυχον: I happened; 1st sg. aor. τυγχάνω
  a2 ἵππον ἔχων: to be serving in the cavalry;
    "having a horse," governed by ἔτυχον
    οὗτος δὲ ὅπλα: this one...(serving) as a
    hoplite soldier; "this one (having) arms"
  a3 ἀνεχώρει: see a1, but the subject is plural
    ἐσκεδασμένων: having scattered; pf.
    mid. pple in a gen. abs.
  a4 ἰδών: aor. pple, ὁράω
    αὐτοῖν: them; dual dative
  a5 αὐτώ: them; dual accusative
    κάλλιον: more nobly; comp. adverb
  a6 ἧττον ἐν φόβῳ ἦ: I was less in fear;

ἧττον is a comp. adv.; impf. εἰμί
  a7 ὅσον περιήν: how much he surpassed +
    gen.; impf. περί-ειμι
  b1 τῷ...εἶναι: in being; dat. respect
  b2 τὸ σὸν...: as this (verse) of yours (says);
    Alcibiades is addressing Aristophanes as
    "you" here: Aristophanes' Clouds 362
    ἐκεῖ...ὥσπερ...ἐνθάδε: there just as
    here; i.e. in battle just as in your play
  b3 Βρενθυόμενος...τὠφθαλμὼ
    παραβάλλων: swaggering and casting
    his two eyes from side to side; crasis τὼ
    ὀφθαλμὼ, dual acc.
  b5 δῆλος...παντὶ: being obvious to everyone
    πάνυ πόρρωθεν: from quite afar
    ἄψεται: touches; 3rd sg. fut., ἅπτομαι
  b6 ἀμυνεῖται: 3rd sg. fut. mid., ἀμύνω
  b7 ἀπῄει: departed; impf. ἀπ-έρχομαι
    σχεδόν...τι: pretty much, practically
  b8 οὐδὲ ἅπτονται: (the enemy soldiers)
    don't even touch; i.e. attack Socrates
  c1 διώκουσιν: (the enemy) chase the
    (Athenian soldiers)...
  c2 ἂν ἔχοι: one would be able, one could
  c3 τῶν...ἐπιτηδευμάτων: about...; add περί

ἄξιον παντὸς θαύματος. οἷος γὰρ Ἀχιλλεὺς ἐγένετο, ἀπει-
κάσειεν ἄν τις καὶ Βρασίδαν καὶ ἄλλους, καὶ οἷος αὖ
Περικλῆς, καὶ Νέστορα καὶ Ἀντήνορα—εἰσὶ δὲ καὶ ἕτεροι—

d καὶ τοὺς ἄλλους κατὰ ταῦτ᾽ ἄν τις ἀπεικάζοι· οἷος δὲ οὑτοσὶ
γέγονε τὴν ἀτοπίαν ἄνθρωπος, καὶ αὐτὸς καὶ οἱ λόγοι αὐτοῦ,
οὐδ᾽ ἐγγὺς ἂν εὕροι τις ζητῶν, οὔτε τῶν νῦν οὔτε τῶν
παλαιῶν, εἰ μὴ ἄρα εἰ οἷς ἐγὼ λέγω ἀπεικάζοι τις αὐτόν,

5 ἀνθρώπων μὲν μηδενί, τοῖς δὲ σιληνοῖς καὶ σατύροις, αὐτὸν
καὶ τοὺς λόγους.

Καὶ γὰρ οὖν καὶ τοῦτο ἐν τοῖς πρώτοις παρέλιπον, ὅτι
καὶ οἱ λόγοι αὐτοῦ ὁμοιότατοί εἰσι τοῖς σιληνοῖς τοῖς διοιγο-

e μένοις. εἰ γὰρ ἐθέλοι τις τῶν Σωκράτους ἀκούειν λόγων,
φανεῖεν ἂν πάνυ γελοῖοι τὸ πρῶτον· τοιαῦτα καὶ ὀνόματα
καὶ ῥήματα ἔξωθεν περιαμπέχονται, σατύρου δή τινα ὑβρι-
στοῦ δοράν. ὄνους γὰρ κανθηλίους λέγει καὶ χαλκέας τινὰς

5 καὶ σκυτοτόμους καὶ βυρσοδέψας, καὶ ἀεὶ διὰ τῶν αὐτῶν τὰ
αὐτὰ φαίνεται λέγειν, ὥστε ἄπειρος καὶ ἀνόητος ἄνθρωπος

222 πᾶς ἂν τῶν λόγων καταγελάσειεν. διοιγομένους δὲ ἰδὼν ἄν
τις καὶ ἐντὸς αὐτῶν γιγνόμενος πρῶτον μὲν νοῦν ἔχοντας
ἔνδον μόνους εὑρήσει τῶν λόγων, ἔπειτα θειοτάτους καὶ
πλεῖστα ἀγάλματ᾽ ἀρετῆς ἐν αὑτοῖς ἔχοντας καὶ ἐπὶ πλεῖ-

5 στον τείνοντας, μᾶλλον δὲ ἐπὶ πᾶν ὅσον προσήκει σκοπεῖν
τῷ μέλλοντι καλῷ κἀγαθῷ ἔσεσθαι.

Ταῦτ᾽ ἐστίν, ὦ ἄνδρες, ἃ ἐγὼ Σωκράτη ἐπαινῶ· καὶ αὖ
ἃ μέμφομαι συμμείξας ὑμῖν εἶπον ἅ με ὕβρισεν. καὶ μέν-

b τοι οὐκ ἐμὲ μόνον ταῦτα πεποίηκεν, ἀλλὰ καὶ Χαρμίδην
τὸν Γλαύκωνος καὶ Εὐθύδημον τὸν Διοκλέους καὶ ἄλλους
πάνυ πολλούς, οὓς οὗτος ἐξαπατῶν ὡς ἐραστὴς παιδικὰ
μᾶλλον αὐτὸς καθίσταται ἀντ᾽ ἐραστοῦ. ἃ δὴ καὶ σοὶ

ἄγαλμα, -ατος τό: statue, image*
ἀ-νόητος, -ον: foolish, unintelligent*
Ἀντήνωρ, ὁ: Antenor
ἀπ-εικάζω: to represent, liken to, compare to
ἄ-πειρος, -ον: inexperienced, unacquainted
ἀ-τοπία, ἡ: strangeness, oddness, bizarreness
Βρασίδης, ὁ: Brasidas
βυρσο-δέψης, ὁ: a tanner
Γλαύκων, ὁ: Glaucon
δι-οίγω: διοίγνυμι, to open, open up*
Διοκλῆς, ὁ: Diocles
δορά, ἡ: an animal skin, hide
ἐγγύς: near, close to (+ gen.); adv. nearby*
ἔνδον: within, at home*
ἐντός: within, inside*
ἔξω-θεν: from without, on the outside*
Εὐθύδημος, ὁ: Euthydemus
εὑρίσκω: to find, discover, devise, invent*
θαῦμα, -ατος, τό: wonder, astonishment*
καθ-ίστημι: to establish, put into a state, make
    become; fall into a state, become*
κανθήλιος, ὁ: a pack-mule

κατα-γελάω: to laugh at, mock*
μέμφομαι: to blame, censure, find fault with*
Νέστωρ, ὁ: Nestor
ὄνος, ὁ, ἡ: a mule
παρα-λείπω: to pass over, pass by
περι-αμπέχω: to wrap in, clothe in (acc.)
Περικλῆς, ὁ: Pericles
πλεῖστος, -η, -ον: most, very many, greatest*
προσ-ήκει: it is fitting, is suitable (dat.) (inf.)*
ῥῆμα, τό: a word, saying, phrase*
σάτυρος, ὁ: satyr*
σιληνός, ὁ: silenus*
σκοπέω: to look at, examine, consider*
σκυτο-τόμος, ὁ: a leather-cutter, shoemaker
συμ-μίγνυμι: to mix together, have intercourse
τείνω: to tend, extend, direct; stretch, spread
ὑβρίζω: to commit outrage, assault, insult*
ὑβριστός, -η, -ον: outrageous, insolent
χαλκεύς, -έως, ὁ: blacksmith
Χαρμίδης, ὁ: Charmides

221c6 οἷος: (to) the sort of man who; missing
    antecedent is dat. object of ἀπεικάσειεν
    ἀπεικάσειεν ἄν: one might liken (acc.) to
    (dat.); aor. potential opt., ἀπ-εικάζω

c7 οἷος αὖ Περικλῆς: (to) the sort of man
    who Perikles (became); supply ἐγένετο

d1 κατὰ ταῦτ': in the same way; τὰ αὐτα
    ἀπεικάζοι: one might liken; pres. opt.

d1 οἷος δὲ...ἄνθρωπος: but the sort of man
    this one here has become; adversative δὲ,
    pf. γίγνομαι, acc. of respect

d3 οὐδ' ἐγγύς: not anyone close; add τινα
    ἄν εὕχοι: aor. potential opt., εὑρίσκω
    τῶν νῦν...τῶν παλαιῶν: among those
    now...those long ago; partitive genitive

d4 εἰ μὴ ἄρα εἰ: except, it seems, if...
    οἷς..λέγω: to those (whom) I am
    speaking; relative attracted into the dat.
    of the missing antecedent

d7 τοῦτο...ὅτι: this, namely that
    ἐν τοῖς πρώτοις: in the beginning

d8 τοῖς διοιγομένοις: being opened; pres.
    pass. pple, διοίγω

e1 ἐθέλοι...φανεῖν ἄν: should be willing,
    would appear; future less vivid condition

e2 τὸ πρῶτον: at first; adverbial acc.

e3 τινα δοράν: a sort of hide; appositive

e5 διὰ τῶν αὐτῶν: with the same (words)
    τὰ αὐτὰ: the same things; obj. λέγειν

222a1 καταγελάσειεν: aor. opt. with gen. obj.
    διοιγομένους ἰδών: seeing them being
    opened; i.e. words, aor. pple. ὁράω

a2 μόνους τῶν λόγων: these arguments
    alone; "alone of arguments", direct obj.
    of εὑρήσει; ἔχοντας, θειοτάτους,
    ἔχοντας and τείνοντας are modifiers
    νοῦν ἔχοντες: having sense

a3 εὑρήσει: fut. εὑρίσκω, ignore the ἄν

a4 ἐν αὐτοῖς: in themselves; ἐν ἑαυτοῖς
    ἐπὶ πλεῖστον τείνοντας, μᾶλλον δὲ
    ἐπὶ πᾶν ὅσον: extending to very much,
    or rather to everything that...

a5 τῷ μέλλοντι...ἔσεσθαι: for one intended
    to be; fut. dep. inf. εἰμί

a6 καλῷ κἀγαθῷ: noble and good; pred. adj

a8 ἃ μέμφομαι συμμείξας: having mixed
    what I blame him for together (with
    praise); aor. pple, συμ-μίγνυμι

b1 οὐκ..μόνον...ἀλλὰ καί: not only...but also
    πεποίηκεν: 3rd sg. pf. ποιέω

b3 ἐξαπατῶν ὡς : deceiving as if an erastes

b4 καθίσταται: becomes; παιδικὰ is pred.

5 λέγω, ὦ Ἀγάθων, μὴ ἐξαπατᾶσθαι ὑπὸ τούτου, ἀλλ᾽ ἀπὸ τῶν
ἡμετέρων παθημάτων γνόντα εὐλαβηθῆναι, καὶ μὴ κατὰ
τὴν παροιμίαν ὥσπερ νήπιον παθόντα γνῶναι.

c   Εἰπόντος δὴ ταῦτα τοῦ Ἀλκιβιάδου γέλωτα γενέσθαι
ἐπὶ τῇ παρρησίᾳ αὐτοῦ, ὅτι ἐδόκει ἔτι ἐρωτικῶς ἔχειν τοῦ
Σωκράτους. τὸν οὖν Σωκράτη, Νήφειν μοι δοκεῖς, φάναι,
ὦ Ἀλκιβιάδη. οὐ γὰρ ἄν ποτε οὕτω κομψῶς κύκλῳ περι-
5 βαλλόμενος ἀφανίσαι ἐνεχείρεις οὗ ἕνεκα ταῦτα πάντα
εἴρηκας, καὶ ὡς ἐν παρέργῳ δὴ λέγων ἐπὶ τελευτῆς αὐτὸ
ἔθηκας, ὡς οὐ πάντα τούτου ἕνεκα εἰρηκώς, τοῦ ἐμὲ καὶ
d Ἀγάθωνα διαβάλλειν, οἰόμενος δεῖν ἐμὲ μὲν σοῦ ἐρᾶν καὶ
μηδενὸς ἄλλου, Ἀγάθωνα δὲ ὑπὸ σοῦ ἐρᾶσθαι καὶ μηδ᾽ ὑφ᾽
ἑνὸς ἄλλου. ἀλλ᾽ οὐκ ἔλαθες, ἀλλὰ τὸ σατυρικόν σου
δρᾶμα τοῦτο καὶ σιληνικὸν κατάδηλον ἐγένετο. ἀλλ᾽, ὦ
5 φίλε Ἀγάθων, μηδὲν πλέον αὐτῷ γένηται, ἀλλὰ παρασκευάζου ὅπως ἐμὲ καὶ σὲ μηδεὶς διαβαλεῖ.

Τὸν οὖν Ἀγάθωνα εἰπεῖν, καὶ μήν, ὦ Σώκρατες, κινδυ-
e νεύεις ἀληθῆ λέγειν. τεκμαίρομαι δὲ καὶ ὡς κατεκλίνη ἐν
μέσῳ ἐμοῦ τε καὶ σοῦ, ἵνα χωρὶς ἡμᾶς διαλάβῃ. οὐδὲν οὖν
πλέον αὐτῷ ἔσται, ἀλλ᾽ ἐγὼ παρὰ σὲ ἐλθὼν κατακλινήσομαι.

Πάνυ γε, φάναι τὸν Σωκράτη, δεῦρο ὑποκάτω ἐμοῦ
5 κατακλίνου.

Ὦ Ζεῦ, εἰπεῖν τὸν Ἀλκιβιάδην, οἷα αὖ πάσχω ὑπὸ τοῦ
ἀνθρώπου. οἴεταί μου δεῖν πανταχῇ περιεῖναι. ἀλλ᾽ εἰ
μή τι ἄλλο, ὦ θαυμάσιε, ἐν μέσῳ ἡμῶν ἔα Ἀγάθωνα
κατακεῖσθαι.

10 Ἀλλ᾽ ἀδύνατον, φάναι τὸν Σωκράτη. σὺ μὲν γὰρ ἐμὲ
ἐπῄνεσας, δεῖ δὲ ἐμὲ αὖ τὸν ἐπὶ δεξί᾽ ἐπαινεῖν. ἐὰν οὖν
ὑπὸ σοὶ κατακλινῇ Ἀγάθων, οὐ δήπου ἐμὲ πάλιν ἐπαι-

ἀ-φανίζω: to make invisible, conceal, destroy*
γέλως, -ωτος, ὁ: laughter
δεξιός, -ά, -όν: right, right side*
δεῦρο: here, to this point, hither*
δια-βάλλω: to pass over; slander, set (acc.) at variance, make (acc.) quarrel
δια-λαμβάνω: to take separately; divide
δρᾶμα, -ατος, ὁ: a play; deed, act
ἐγ-χειρέω: to take in hand, attempt, begin
εὐλαβέομαι: to be cautious, be careful, beware
κατά-δηλος, -η, -ον: quite clear, evident*
κομψός, -ή, -όν: fine, exquisite, clever
κύκλος, ὁ: a circle, round, ring*
λανθάνω: to escape notice, act unnoticed*
μέσος, - η, -ον: middle, in the middle of*
νήπιος, -α, -ον: foolish, childish, silly

νήφω: to be sober*
πάθημα, -ατος, τό: suffering, misfortune
παντα-χῆ : everywhere, in every way
παρα-σκευάζω: to prepare, get ready*
πάρ-εργον, τό: subordinate or incidental business, secondary matter
παρ-οιμία, ἡ: common saying, proverb*
παρρησία,ἡ: frankness, frank speech
περι-βάλλω: to throw round, enclose; clothe*
περί-ειμι: to surpass, excel, (+ gen.)*
σατυρικός, -ή, -όν: satyr, satyr-like
σίληνικός, -ή, -όν: silenus, silenus-like
τεκμαίρομαι: to judge, calculate, conjecture
τελευτή, ἡ: end, completion; death*
ὑπο-κάτω: under, below (+ gen.)
χωρίς: separately, apart; apart from (+ gen.)*

222b5 ἃ δη...λέγω: *that's why I am telling you...*; "with respect to these very things"
  b6 γνόντα: *having learned*; aor. pple γιγνώσκω modifying the acc. subject
  b7 εὐλαβηθῆναι: *to beware*; aor. pass. dep.
  κατά: *according to...*
  νήπιον: *fool*; "foolish man"
  παθόντα γνῶναι: *to learn by suffering*; aor. pple of πάσχω, aor. inf., γιγνώσκω
  c2 ἐρωτικῶς ἔχειν: *still be amorous toward*; + objective gen, "be disposed amorously"
  c4 οὐ...ἄν....ἐνεχείρεις: *you would not have attempted to conceal*; ἄν + impf. ἐγ-χειρέω expresses past potential
  c5 κύκλῳ περιβαλλόμενος: *enclosing yourself all around*; dat. of respect
  οὗ ἕνεκα: *(that) for the sake of which*
  c6 εἴρηκας: 2nd sg. pf. ἐρέω
  ὡς...λέγων: *as if speaking in an afterthought*; "on secondary matters," ὡς + pple for alleged cause, see b5 above
  ἐπὶ τελευτῆς: *at the end (of the speech)*
  c7 ἔθηκας: *placed*; 2nd sg. aor. τίθημι
  ὡς...εἰρηκώς: *as if having spoken...*
  τοῦ...διαβάλλειν: *namely, making (acc.)quarrel*; in apposition to τούτου
  d3 ἔλαθες: *you did not escape notice*; 2nd sg. aor. λανθάνω
  τὸ σατυρικόν...σιληνικὸν: *this satyr-play and silenus-play of yours*

d5 μηδὲν...γένηται: *let him get no further*; "let nothing more come to be for him," prohibitive subj., dat. of possession
  παρασκευάζου ὅπως: *take care that*; "prepare yourself" mid. imperative, ὅπως + fut. in a clause of effort
  d6 διαβαλεῖ: διαβαλέει, fut., δια-βάλλω
  d7 κινδυνεύεις...λέγειν: *it looks as though you are speaking*; lit. "you run the risk of speaking"
  e1 ὡς κατεκλίνη: *that he lay down*; 3rd sg. aor. pass. deponent
  e2 ἵνα...διαλάβῃ: *so that....*; 3rd sg. aor. subj. in a purpose clause
  οὐδὲν...ἔσται: *he will get no further*; 3rd sg. fut. εἰμί, see d5 above
  e4 ὑποκάτω ἐμοῦ: *(the place) below me*; i.e. the seat on the right
  e5 κατακλίνου: *lie down*; καταλίνε(σ)ο mid. imperative
  e6 οἷα: *what things...!*; in exclamation
  e7 μου περιεῖναι: *prevail over me*; περί-ειμι
  e8 τι ἄλλο: *(it is) something else*; add ἐστίν
  ἔα: *allow*; sg. imperative, ἐάω
  e10 ἀδύνατον: *it is impossible*; add ἐστίν
  e11 ἐπῄνεσας: *you praised*; aor., ἐπαινέω
  τὸν ἐπὶ δεξί : *the one to the right*
  ὑπὸ σοὶ: *beneath me*; cf. e4
  e12 κατακλινῇ: *lies down*; 3rd sg. pres. subj.

νέσεται, πρὶν ὑπ᾽ ἐμοῦ μᾶλλον ἐπαινεθῆναι; ἀλλ᾽ ἔασον,
223 ὦ δαιμόνιε, καὶ μὴ φθονήσῃς τῷ μειρακίῳ ὑπ᾽ ἐμοῦ
ἐπαινεθῆναι· καὶ γὰρ πάνυ ἐπιθυμῶ αὐτὸν ἐγκωμιάσαι.

ἰοῦ ἰοῦ, φάναι τὸν Ἀγάθωνα, Ἀλκιβιάδη, οὐκ ἔσθ᾽ ὅπως
ἂν ἐνθάδε μείναιμι, ἀλλὰ παντὸς μᾶλλον μεταναστήσομαι,
5 ἵνα ὑπὸ Σωκράτους ἐπαινεθῶ.

Ταῦτα ἐκεῖνα, φάναι τὸν Ἀλκιβιάδην, τὰ εἰωθότα·
Σωκράτους παρόντος τῶν καλῶν μεταλαβεῖν ἀδύνατον ἄλλῳ.
καὶ νῦν ὡς εὐπόρως καὶ πιθανὸν λόγον ηὗρεν, ὥστε παρ᾽
ἑαυτῷ τουτονὶ κατακεῖσθαι.

b Τὸν μὲν οὖν Ἀγάθωνα ὡς κατακεισόμενον παρὰ τῷ
Σωκράτει ἀνίστασθαι· ἐξαίφνης δὲ κωμαστὰς ἥκειν παμπόλλους ἐπὶ τὰς θύρας, καὶ ἐπιτυχόντας ἀνεῳγμέναις ἐξιόντος
τινὸς εἰς τὸ ἄντικρυς πορεύεσθαι παρὰ σφᾶς καὶ κατακλί-
5 νεσθαι, καὶ θορύβου μεστὰ πάντα εἶναι, καὶ οὐκέτι ἐν
κόσμῳ οὐδενὶ ἀναγκάζεσθαι πίνειν πάμπολυν οἶνον. τὸν
μὲν οὖν Ἐρυξίμαχον καὶ τὸν Φαῖδρον καὶ ἄλλους τινὰς ἔφη
ὁ Ἀριστόδημος οἴχεσθαι ἀπιόντας, ἓ δὲ ὕπνον λαβεῖν,
c καὶ καταδαρθεῖν πάνυ πολύ, ἅτε μακρῶν τῶν νυκτῶν οὐσῶν,
ἐξεγρέσθαι δὲ πρὸς ἡμέραν ἤδη ἀλεκτρυόνων ᾀδόντων, ἐξεγρόμενος δὲ ἰδεῖν τοὺς μὲν ἄλλους καθεύδοντας καὶ οἰχο-
μένους, Ἀγάθωνα δὲ καὶ Ἀριστοφάνη καὶ Σωκράτη ἔτι
5 μόνους ἐγρηγορέναι καὶ πίνειν ἐκ φιάλης μεγάλης ἐπὶ δεξιά.
τὸν οὖν Σωκράτη αὐτοῖς διαλέγεσθαι· καὶ τὰ μὲν ἄλλα ὁ
d Ἀριστόδημος οὐκ ἔφη μεμνῆσθαι τῶν λόγων—οὔτε γὰρ ἐξ
ἀρχῆς παραγενέσθαι ὑπονυστάζειν τε—τὸ μέντοι κεφάλαιον,
ἔφη, προσαναγκάζειν τὸν Σωκράτη ὁμολογεῖν αὐτοὺς τοῦ
αὐτοῦ ἀνδρὸς εἶναι κωμῳδίαν καὶ τραγῳδίαν ἐπίστασθαι
5 ποιεῖν, καὶ τὸν τέχνῃ τραγῳδοποιὸν ὄντα ⟨καὶ⟩ κωμῳδοποιὸν
εἶναι. ταῦτα δὴ ἀναγκαζομένους αὐτοὺς καὶ οὐ σφόδρα
ἑπομένους νυστάζειν, καὶ πρότερον μὲν καταδαρθεῖν τὸν

ᾄδω: to sing*
ἀλεκτρυών, -όνος, ὁ: a rooster
ἀν-ίστημι: to make stand up, raise up, get up*
ἀν-οίγνυμι: to open, open up*
ἄντικρυς: straight on, right on; outright
δαιμόνιος, -α, -ον: divine, daimon-like*
δεξιός, -ά, -όν: right, right side*
ἐγείρω: to awaken, wake up, rouse*
ἐξαίφνης: suddenly, immediately*
ἐξ-εγείρω: to wake up, awaken, rouse
ἐξ-έρχομαι: to go out, come out*
ἐπί-σταμαι: to know, know how, understand*
ἐπι-τυγχάνω: to hit upon, find, meet (+ dat.)
εὔ-πορος, -ον: resourceful, easily done, easy*
εὑρίσκω: to find, discover, devise, invent*
θόρυβος, ὁ: uproar, commotion, disturbance
ἰού: ho!, hurrah!
καθ-εύδω: to lie down to sleep, sleep*
κατα-δαρθάνω: to fall asleep, be asleep*
κεφάλαιον, τό: main or chief point, gist, sum*
κόσμος, ὁ: order, good order, world-order*
κωμαστής, -οῦ, ὁ: a reveler
κωμῳδία, ἡ: comedy

κωμῳδοποιός, ὁ: comic poet
μακρός, ά, όν: long, far, distant, large*
μειράκιον, τό: adolescent, boy, young man*
μένω: to stay, remain*
μεστός, -ή, -όν: full, filled, filled full*
μετα-λαμβάνω: to take a share of, partake of
μετ-ανίστημι: to get up and move, remove
μιμνήσκω: to recall, remember*
νύξ, νυκτός, ἡ: night*
νυστάζω: to nod off, doze off, fall asleep
οἶνος, ὁ: wine*
οὐκ-έτι: no more, no longer, no further*
παμ-πολύς, -πολλά, -πολύ: very much*
παρα-γίγνομαι: to be present; to arrive*
πιθανός, -ή, -όν: persuasive, plausible
πρίν: until, before
προσ-αναγκάζω: to press, compel, force*
τραγῳδία, ἡ: tragedy
τραγῳδοποιός, ὁ: a tragic poet, tragedian
ὕπνος, ὁ: sleep, slumber
ὑπο-νυστάζω: to nod off a little, get drowsy
φθονέω: to begrudge, bear a grudge, envy
φιάλη, ἡ: a broad, flat vessel; bowl

222e13 ἐπαινεθῆναι: aor. pass. inf.
  ἔασον: *allow it*; aor. imperative, ἐάω
223a1 μὴ φθονήσῃς: *don't...*; prohibitive subj.
a2 ἐγκωμιάσαι: aor. inf., ἐγκωμιάζω
a3 οὐκ ἔσθ᾽ ὅπως...μείναιμι: *I can't possibly stay here*; "there is not a way that I could stay here," aor. opt., μένω
a4 παντός: *than anything*; gen. comparison
  μετανστήσομαι: fut. μετ-ανίστημι
a5 ἐπαινεθῶ: 1st s. aor. pass. subj., purpose
a6 ταῦτα ἐκεῖνα...τὰ εἰωθότα: *here are those habits of his!*; "these are those accustomed things," pf. pple.
a7 Σωκράτους παρόντος: abs. πάρειμι
  τῶν καλῶν: partitive gen. with aor. inf.
  ἀδύνατον: *(it is) impossible*; add ἐστί
a8 ὡς...πιθανόν: *how fluently and persuasive*; conjoining an adv. and adj.
  ηὗρεν: 3rd sg. aor., εὑρίσκω
  τουτονὶ: *this here one*; i.e. Agathon, acc. subject of κατακεῖσθαι
b1 ὡς κατακεισόμενον: *in order to lie down*; ὡς + fut. pple expressing purpose
b3 ἀνεῳγμέναις: *(doors) opened*; pf. pass. pple, ἀν-οίγνυμι, supply θύραις

ἐξιόντος τινός: *while someone was leaving*; gen. abs., pple, ἐξ-έρχομαι
b4 εἰς τὸ ἄντικρυς: *straight on in*
b6 ἀναγκάζεσθαι: *(everyone) was compelled*; supply the acc. subj. πάντα
b8 οἴχεσθαι ἀπιόντας: *proceed to go out*. pres. pple, ἀπ-έρχομαι (1-)
  ἕ: *he*; i.e. Aristodemus, 3rd sg. reflexive
  λαβεῖν: *took*; aor. inf. λαμβάνω
c1 καταδαρθεῖν: aor. inf. κατα-δαρθάνω
  πάνυ πολύ: *for quite a long (time)*
  ἅτε...οὐσῶν: *since...*; ἅτε + pple
c2 ἐξεγρέσθαι: *to awake*; aor. mid. inf.
  πρὸς ἡμέραν: *near day(break)*
  ἐξεγρόμενος: *having awaken*; aor. pple
c3 ἰδεῖν: aor. inf. ὁράω
c5 ἐγρηγορέναι: *to be awake*, pf. inf.,
  ἐπὶ δεξιά: *(passing it from left) to right*
c6 τὰ ἄλλα...τὸ κεφάλαιον: *in respect to other things...but (as for) the main point*
d2 τε: *and*; joins the preceding infinitives
d3 τοῦ αὐτοῦ ἀνδρός: *(characteristic) of the same man*; predicate of εἶναι
d4 ἐπίστασθαι: *knows how*; governs inf.
d6 ταῦτα δή: *in respect to these very things*

Ἀριστοφάνη, ἤδη δὲ ἡμέρας γιγνομένης τὸν Ἀγάθωνα. τὸν
οὖν Σωκράτη, κατακοιμίσαντ᾽ ἐκείνους, ἀναστάντα ἀπιέναι,
10　καὶ ⟨ἓ⟩ ὥσπερ εἰώθει ἕπεσθαι, καὶ ἐλθόντα εἰς Λύκειον,
ἀπονιψάμενον, ὥσπερ ἄλλοτε τὴν ἄλλην ἡμέραν διατρίβειν,
καὶ οὕτω διατρίψαντα εἰς ἑσπέραν οἴκοι ἀναπαύεσθαι.

ἄλλ-οτε: at another time, at other times
ἀνα-παύομαι: to rest*
ἀν-ίστημι: to make stand up, raise up, get up*
ἀπο-νίζω: to wash, wash clean
δια-τρίβω: to pass time, consume, spend*

ἑσπέρα, ἡ: evening, eve
κατα-δαρθάνω: to fall asleep, be asleep*
κατα-κοιμίζω: to lull to sleep, put to sleep
Λύκειον, τό: the Lyceum
οἴκοι: at home, in the house

223d8 πρότερον μὲν ...ἤδη δὲ: *first...and now*

d8 τὸν Ἀγάθωνα: acc. subject, supply the inf. καταδαρθεῖν from d7 above

d9 κατακοιμίσαντ᾽ ἐκείνους: *after lulling them to sleep*; ingressive aor. pple. ἀναστάντα: aor. pple, ἀν-ίστημι

ἀπιέναι: went out; inf., ἀπ-έρχομαι (ι-)

d10 εἰώθει: *was accustomed*; plpf. with impf. sense εἴωθα

d12 εἰς ἑσπέραν: *at evening, near evening*

Particles in Plato

ἀλλά: *but* (strong adversative); *well, well then*
   ἀλλὰ γάρ: *but indeed, but in reality* (γαρ as adverb)
   ἀλλὰ δή: *but actually, but in fact*; *well then* (strengthens ἀλλὰ)
   ἀλλ᾽ ἤ: *except, other than*
ἄρα: *so, then, it seems, it turns out*
ἆρα (ἦ ἄρα): (untranslated, introduces a yes/no question)
αὖ: *again, in turn; moreover*
γάρ: *for, since* (conjunction)
   in fact, indeed (adverb)
  καὶ γάρ: *and in fact, and indeed* (γάρ as adverb)
      for even, for also (καὶ as adverb)
   γὰρ δή: *and in fact, and indeed*
γε: *at least, at any rate* (restrictive and intensive, as if italicizing the previous word)
   indeed, yes
   γοῦν (γέ...οὖν): *at least, at any rate*
δέ: *but, and* (conjunction)
   on the other hand (adverb with μέν)
δή: *just, really, very, certainly, indeed* (emphatic, expresses exactness)
δήπου: *perhaps, I suppose, not doubt*
ἦ: *truly, in truth* (introduces a question)`
καί: *and* (conjunction),
    also, even, too, in fact (adverb)
  καὶ δὴ καί: *and in particular, and especially, and indeed also*
  καί εἰ: *even if* (εἰ καί: *although*)
  καὶ δέ: *and also* (καί adverbial)
  καὶ μέντοι καί: *yes indeed and* (1st καί adverbial)
μέν: *on the one hand* (often untranslated); *certainly* (affirmative)
  μὲν οὖν: *certainly in fact* (affirmative)
      no, rather; on the contrary (marks a correction)
μέντοι: *certainly, of course, moreover; however, yet*
μήν: *surely, truly* (strong emphatic)
  τί μήν: *naturally, of course, what indeed?*
οὐ-δέ: *and not, but not, nor* (conjunction); *not even* (adverb)
οὖν: *and so, then, therefore* (inferential)
  δ᾽ οὖν (δέ...οὖν): *and so, then, therefore* (inferential)
  οὐκοῦν: *and so....not? not then?* (interrogative)
      and so, then, therefore (inferential)
  οὔκουν: *and so....not, not then*
που: *I suppose, somehow*
τοί: *you know, to be sure* (ethical dat. of σύ)
  τοί-νυν: *well then; therefore, accordingly*

For more details see Denniston's *The Greek Particles* or Smyth's *Greek Grammar* pp. 631-671.

ἵημι, ἥσω, ἧκα, εἷκα, εἷμαι, εἵθην: to send, release, let go

	Present		Imperfect		Aorist	
Active	ἵημι	ἵεμεν	ἵην	ἵεμεν	ἧκα	εἷμεν
	ἵης	ἵετε	ἵεις	ἵετε	ἧκας	εἷτε
	ἵησιν	ἱᾶσι	ἵει	ἵεσαν	ἧκεν	εἷσαν
Imp	ἵει	ἵετε			ἕς	ἕτε
Pple	ἱείς, ἱεῖσα, ἱέν				εἵς, εἷσα, ἕν	
	ἱέντος, ἱείσης, ἱέντος				ἕντος, εἵσης, ἕντος	
Inf.	ἱέναι				εἷναι	
Middle	ἵεμαι	ἱέμεθα	ἱέμην	ἱέμεθα	εἵμην	εἵμεθα
	ἵεσαι	ἵεσθε	ἵεσο	ἵεσθε	εἷσο	εἷσθε
	ἵεται	ἵενται	ἵετο	ἵεντο	εἷτο	εἷντο
Imp	ἵεσο	ἵεσθε			οὗ	ἕσθε
Pple	ἱέμενος, η, ον				ἕμενος, η, ον	
Inf.	ἵεσθαι				ἕσθαι	

εἰμί (to be)

	present		imperfect		imp.	pple	inf.
1st	εἰμί	ἐσμέν	ἦ, ἦν	ἦμεν	ἴσθι	ὤν	εἷναι
2nd	εἶ	ἐστέ	ἦσθα	ἦτε	ἔστε	οὖσα	
3rd	ἐστίν	εἰσίν	ἦν	ἦσαν		ὄν	

	subjunctive		optative	
1st	ὦ	ὦμεν	εἴην	εἷμεν
2nd	ᾖς	ἦτε	εἴης	εἷτε
3rd	ᾖ	ὦσιν	εἴη	εἷεν

εἷμι (to go, present translates as the future of ἔρχομαι)

	present		imperfect		imp.	pple	inf.
1st	εἷμι	ἴμεν	ᾖα	ᾖμεν	ἴθι	ἰών	ἰέναι
2nd	εἶ	ἴτε	ᾖεισθα	ᾖτε	ἴτε	ἰοῦσα	
3rd	εἷσι	ἴασιν	ᾖειν	ᾖσαν		ἰόν	

	subjunctive		optative	
1st	ἴω	ἴωμεν	ἴοιμι	ἴοιμεν
2nd	ἴῃς	ἴητε	ἴοις	ἴοιτε
3rd	ἴῃ	ἴωσιν	ἴοι	ἴοιεν

λύω, λύσω, ἔλυσα, λέλυκα, λέλυμαι, ἐλύθην: loosen, ransom

	PRESENT		FUTURE		
	Active	Middle/Pass.	Active	Middle	Passive
Primary Indiative	λύω λύεις λύει λύομεν λύετε λύουσι(ν)	λύομαι λύε(σ)αι λύεται λυόμεθα λύεσθε λύονται	λύσω λύσεις λύσει λύσομεν λύσετε λύσουσι(ν)	λύσομαι λύσε(σ)αι λύσεται λυσόμεθα λύσεσθε λύσονται	λυθήσομαι λυθήσε(σ)αι λυθήσεται λυθησόμεθα λυθήσεσθε λυθήσονται
Secondary Indicative	ἔλυον ἔλυες ἔλυε(ν) ἐλύομεν ἐλύετε ἔλυον	ἐλυόμην ἐλύε(σ)ο ἐλύετο ἐλυόμεθα ἐλύεσθε ἐλύοντο			
Subjunctive	λύω λύῃς λύῃ λύωμεν λύητε λύωσι(ν)	λύωμαι λύῃ λύηται λυώμεθα λύησθε λύωνται			
Optative	λύοιμι λύοις λύοι λύοιμεν λύοιτε λύοιεν	λυοίμην λύοιο λύοιτο λυοίμεθα λύοισθε λύοιντο	λύσοιμι λύσοις λύσοι λύσοιμεν λύσοιτε λύσοιεν	λυσοίμην λύσοιο λύσοιτο λυσοίμεθα λύσοισθε λύσοιντο	λυθησοίμην λυθήσοιο λυθήσοιτο λυθησοίμεθα λυθήσοισθε λυθήσοιντο
Imp	λῦε λύετε	λύε(σ)ο λύεσθε			
Pple	λύων, λύουσα, λύον	λυόμενος, λυομένη, λυόμενον	λύσων, λύσουσα, λύσον	λυσόμενος, λυσομένη, λυσόμενον	λυθησόμενος, λυθησομένη, λυθησόμενον
Inf.	λύειν	λύεσθαι	λύσειν	λύσεσθαι	λυθήσεσθαι

2nd sg. mid/pass -σ is often dropped except in pf. and plpf. tenses: ε(σ)αι → ῃ,ει   ε(σ)ο → ου

| AORIST | | | PERFECT | | |
Active	Middle	Passive	Middle	Passive	
			λέλυκα λέλυκας λέλυκε λελύκαμεν λελύκατε λελύκασι(ν)	λέλυμαι λέλυσαι λέλυται λελύμεθα λέλυσθε λέλυνται	Primary Indiative
ἔλυσα ἔλυσας ἔλυε(ν) ἐλύσαμεν ἐλύσατε ἔλυσαν	ἐλυσάμην ἐλύσα(σ)ο ἐλύσατο ἐλυσάμεθα ἐλύσασθε ἐλύσαντο	ἐλύθην ἐλύθης ἐλύθη ἐλύθημεν ἐλύθητε ἐλύθησαν	ἐλελύκη ἐλελύκης ἐλελύκει ἐλελύκεμεν ἐλελύκετε ἐλελύκεσαν	ἐλελύμην ἐλέλυσο ἐλέλυτο ἐλελύμεθα ἐλέλυσθε ἐλέλυντο	Secondary Indiative
λύσω λύσῃς λύῃ λύσῃ λύσωμεν λύσωσι(ν)	λυσώμαι λύσῃ λύσηται λυσώμεθα λύσησθε λύσωνται	λυθῶ λυθῇς λυθῇ λυθῶμεν λυθῆτε λυθῶσι(ν)	λελύκω λελύκῃς λελύκῃ λελύκωμεν λελύκητε λελύκωσι(ν)	λελυμένος ὦ -- ᾖς -- ᾖ -- ὦμεν -- ἦτε -- ὦσιν	Subjunctive
λύσαιμι λύσαις λύσαι λύσαιμεν λύσαιτε λύσαιεν	λυσαίμην λύσαιο λύσαιτο λυσαίμεθα λύσαισθε λύσαιντο	λυθείην λυθείης λυθείη λυθεῖμεν λυθεῖτε λυθεῖεν	λελύκοιμι λελύκοις λελύκοι λελύκοιμεν λελύκοιτε λελύκοιεν	λελυμένος εἴην -- εἴης -- εἴη -- εἴημεν -- εἴητε -- εἴησαν	Optative
λῦσον λύσατε	λῦσαι λύσασθε	λύθητι λύθητε		λέλυσο λέλυσθε	Imp
λύσᾶς, λύσᾶσα, λῦσαν	λυσάμενος, λυσαμένη, λυσάμενον	λύθείς, λυθεῖσα, λυθέν	λελυκώς, λελυκυῖα λελυκός	λελυμένος, λελυμένη λελυμένον	Pple
λῦσαι	λύσασθαι	λυθῆναι	λελυκέναι	λελύσθαι	Inf.

Adapted from a handout by Dr. Helma Dik (http://classics.uchicago.edu/faculty/dik/niftygreek)

Core Vocabulary List
(Words 7 or More Times)

Readers should memorize this core list as soon as possible and then begin to master the high frequency words (6-3 times or fewer) as they encounter them in the reading. A complete list of words occurring 6-3 times may be found at the end of this book. If you encounter a word that is not found in the facing vocabulary or commentary, it is most likely in this list.

The number of occurrences of each word in the *Symposium* was tabulated with the help of vocabulary tools in the Perseus Digital Library (perseus.tufts.edu).

ἀγαθός, -ή, -όν: good, brave, noble
Ἀγάθων, -ονος, ὁ: Agathon
ἄγω, ἄξω, ἤγαγον, ἦχα, ἦγμαι, ἤχθην: to lead, bring, carry, convey; keep, maintain
ἀ-δύνατος, -ον: unable, incapable, impossible
ἀεί: always, forever, in every case
ἀ-θάνατος, -ον: undying, immortal
αἴρω, ἀρῶ, ἦρα, ἦρκα, ἦρμαι, ἤρθην: to lift, take up, raise up; exalt, extol
αἰσχρός, -ά, -όν: shameful, disgraceful, base; ugly
αἰσχρῶς: shamefully, disgracefully
αἰσχύνω, αἰσχυνῶ, ᾔσχυνα, –, ᾔσχυμμαι, ᾐσχύνθην: to shame, dishonor; *mid.* feel shame
αἴτιος, -α, -ον: culpable, responsible, blameworthy
ἀκούω, ἀκούσομαι, ἤκουσα, ἀκήκοα, –, ἠκούσθην: to hear, listen to (acc. thing; gen. person)
ἀληθής, -ές: true
ἀληθῶς: truly
Ἀλκιβιάδης, ὁ: Alcibiades
ἀλλά: but
ἀλλήλων, -λοις, -λους: one another (no nom. forms)
ἄλλος, -η, -ο: other, one...another
ἄλλου (ἄλλο-σε): to another place, to elsewhere
ἄλλως: otherwise, in another way``
ἅμα: at once, at the same time; together with (+ dat.)
ἀμείνων, -ον: better (comparative of ἀγαθός)
ἀμφότερος, -α, -ον: each of two, both
ἄν: *modal adv.*
ἀνά: up, upon (+ dat.); up to, on to (+ acc.)
ἀναγκάζω, ἀναγκάσω, ἠνάγκασα, ἠνάγκακα, –, ἠναγκάσθην: to force, compel, require
ἀναγκαῖος, -α, -ον: necessary, inevitable
ἀνάγκη, ἡ: necessity, force, constraint
ἀνα-δέω, -δήσω, -έδησα, -δέδεκα, -δέδεμαι, -εδέθην: to tie up, bind up, crown, wreathe
ἀνδρεῖος, -α, -ον: brave, courageous, manly
ἄνευ: without (+ gen.)
ἀνήρ, ἀνδρός, ὁ: man, male human being
ἄνθρωπος, ὁ: human being, person
ἄνω: up, above, aloft
ἄξιος, -α, -ον: worthy of, deserving of (+ gen.)
ἀξίως: worthily, deservingly
ἁπαλός, -ή, -όν: delicate, tender, soft, gentle
ἄπ-ειμι -έσομαι: to be away, be absent

ἀπ-έρχομαι, -ελεύσομαι, -ῆλθον, -ελήλυθα, –, –: to go away, depart
ἀπό: from, away from. (+ gen.)
ἀπο-θνῄσκω, -θανοῦμαι, -έθανον, -τέθνηκα, –, –: to die, die off, perish
ἀ-πορέω, ἀπορήσω: to be at a loss, puzzled, bewildered; be poor
ἅπτω, ἅψω, ἧψα, –, ἧμμαι, ἥφθην: to fasten, join; *mid.* touch, grasp (+ gen.)
ἄρα: then, therefore, it seems, it turns out
ἆρα: *untranslated particle introducing a yes/no question*
ἀρετή, ἡ: excellence, virtue, goodness
Ἀριστόδημος, ὁ: Aristodemus
ἄριστος, -η, -ον: best, most excellent (superl. ἀγαθός)
Ἀριστοφάνης, ὁ: Aristophanes
ἁρμονία, ἡ: attunement, harmony; fastening, joint
ἄρρην, -ενος, ὁ, ἡ, τό: male, masculine
ἀρχή, ἡ: the beginning; rule, office
ἄρχω, ἄρξω, ἦρξα, ἦρχα, ἦργμαι, ἤρχθην: to begin; rule, be leader of
ἅτε: inasmuch as, since, seeing that (+ pple.)
αὖ: again, in turn; further, moreover
αὐτός, -ή, -ό: he, she, it; the same; -self
αὐτοῦ: at the very place, here, there
ἀφ-ίημι, -ήσω, -ῆκα, -εῖκα, -εῖμαι, -είθην: to let go, release, give up, send forth, launch
Ἀφροδίτη, ἡ: Aphrodite

βίος, ὁ: life
βιόω, βιώσομαι, ἐβίωσα, βεβίωκα, βεβίωμαι, –: to live
βλέπω, βλέψω, ἔβλεψα, –, –, –: to see, look, look to, look at, gaze upon
βούλομαι, βουλήσομαι, –, –, βεβούλημαι, ἐβουλήθην: to wish, be willing, desire, choose

Γαῖα, ἡ: Gaia, Earth
γάρ: for, since
γε: at least, at any rate; indeed
γελοῖος, -α, -ον: laughable, ridiculous
γένεσις, -εως, ἡ: origin, beginning, birth, generation
γεννάω, γεννήσω: to beget, engender, bring forth, produce
γένος, -εος, τό: race, clan; offspring, child; type, kind
γίγνομαι, γενήσομαι, ἐγενόμην, γέγονα, γεγένημαι, –: to become, come into being, be
    born, happen, occur
γιγνώσκω, γνώσομαι, ἔγνων, ἔγνωκα, ἔγνωσμαι, ἐγνώσθην: to learn, realize; know
γυνή, γυναικός, ἡ: woman, wife

δέ: but, and, on the other hand
δεῖ: it is necessary, must, ought (+acc. + inf.)
δεινός, -ή, -όν: terrible; strange, marvelous; clever
δειπνέω, δειπνήσω, ἐδείπνησα, δεδείπνηκα, –, –: to make dinner, eat dinner
δέω (δέομαι), δεήσω, ἐδέησα, δεδέηκα, δεδέημαι, ἐδεήθην: to lack, want, need; *mid.* ask, beg
δέω, δήσω, ἔδησα, δέδεκα, δέδεμαι, ἐδέθην: to bind
δή: indeed, surely, really, certainly, just
δῆλος, -η, -ον: clear, evident, conspicuous, obvious
δημιουργός, ὁ: craftsman, skilled workman*
δή-που: perhaps, I suppose, I presume, of course
διά: through (+ gen.); on account of, because of (+ acc.)

δια-λέγομαι, -λέξομαι, -ελεξάμην, –, -είλεγμαι, -ελέχθην: to converse with, discuss, talk to
δια-φέρω, -οἴσω, -ἤνεγκον, -ενήνοχα, -ενήνεγμαι, -ηνέχθην: to disagree, differ; be superior
δίδωμι, δώσω, ἔδωκα, δέδωκα, δέδομαι, ἐδόθην: to give, offer, grant, provide
δι-ηγέομαι, -ηγήσομαι, -ηγησάμην, –, -ήγημαι, –: to set out in detail, relate, narrate, explain
δίκαιος, -α, -ον: just, right, lawful, fair
δικαίως: justly, rightly, lawfully, fairly
διό: δι᾽ ὅ, on account of which, on which account
Διοτίμα, ἡ: Diotima
διώκω, διώξω, ἐδίωξα, δεδίωχα, –, ἐδιώχθην: to pursue, follow; prosecute
δοκέω, δόξω, ἔδοξα, δεδόκηκα, δέδογμαι, ἐδοκήθην: to seem, seem good; think, suppose
δύναμαι, δυνήσομαι, –, –, δεδύνημαι, ἐδυνήθην: to be able, can, be capable
δύναμις, -εως, ἡ: power, force, ability, influence
δύο: two

ἕ: *3rd person sg., acc. reflexive pronoun (οὗ, gen., οἷ, dat.)*
ἐάν: εἰ ἄν, if ever (+ subj.)
ἑαυτοῦ, -ῆς, -οῦ: himself, herself, itself, themselves
ἐάω, ἐάσω, εἴασα, εἴακα, εἴαμαι, εἰάθην: to allow, permit, let be, suffer
ἐγκωμιάζω, ἐγκωμιάσω, –, ἐγκεκωμίακα, –, –: to praise, laud, extol
ἐγώ: I
ἐθέλω, ἐθελήσω, ἠθέλησα, ἠθέληκα, –, –:: to be willing, wish, desire
εἰ: if, whether
εἶδον: saw, beheld, (aor. of ὁράω)
εἶδος, -εος, τό: form, shape, appearance; kind, sort
εἷλον: seized, took; *mid.* chose (aor. of αἱρέω)
εἰμί, ἔσομαι: to be, exist
εἶμι: will go, will come, (fut. of ἔρχομαι,)
εἶπον: said, spoke (aor. λέγω, φημί)
εἰς: into, to, for, in regard to (+ acc.)
εἷς, μία, ἕν: one, single, alone
εἰσ-έρχομαι, -ελεύσομαι, -ἦλθον, -ελήλυθα, –, –: to go in, enter
εἴωθα: to be accustomed (pf. with pres. sense)
ἐκ: out of, from (+ gen.)
ἕκαστος, -η, -ον: each, each one, every every one
ἐκεῖνος, -η, -ον: that, those
ἑκών, ἑκοῦσα, ἑκόν: willing, intentional
ἐμ-αυτοῦ, -ῆς, -οῦ: myself
ἐμός, -ή, -όν: my, mine
ἐμ-ποιέω, ποιήσω, ἐποίησα, πεποίηκα, πεποίημαι, ἐποιήθην: to engender, implant, cause
ἐν: in, on, among. (+ dat.)
ἐν-αντίος, -α, -ον: opposite, contrary, facing
ἐν-δεής, -ές: in need of, lacking, deficient (+ gen.)
ἐν-δίδωμι, -δώσω, -έδωκα, -δέδωκα, -δέδομαι, -εδόθην: to give in, surrender; give, lend
ἕνεκα: for the sake of, because of, for (+ preceding gen.)
ἐνθάδε: here, hither, there, thither; now, in this case
ἐνταῦθα: here, hither, there, thither; then, at that time
ἐν-τυγχάνω, τεύξομαι, ἔτυχον, τετύχηκα, –, –: to chance upon, meet with, encounter (dat)
ἐξ-απατάω, -απατήσω: to deceive, beguile, trick
ἔοικα: to be like, seem like, resemble, be likely (pf. with pres. sense)
ἐπ-αινέω, -αινέσω, -ἤνεσα, -ἤνεκα, –, -ἠνέθην, : to praise, praise for, approve, commend

ἔπαινος, ὁ: praise, approval, commendation
ἐπεί: since, because; when, after
ἐπειδάν: whenever
ἐπειδή: since, because; when, after
ἔπ-ειτα: then, next, secondly
ἐπί: near, at (+ gen. + dat.), to, (+ acc), upon, after (+ dat)
ἐπι-θυμέω, ἐπιθυμήσω: to desire, long for
ἐπι-θυμία, ἡ: desire, longing, yearning
ἐπιστήμη, ἡ: knowledge
ἐπι-τίθημι, θήσω, ἔθηκα, τέθηκα, τέθειμαι, ἐτέθην: to put on, impose, attribute; set on, attack
ἐπι-χειρέω: to attempt, try, endeavor; attack, set upon
ἕπομαι, ἕψομαι, ἑσπόμην, –, –, –: to follow, accompany, escort
ἐραστής, -οῦ, ὁ: lover
ἐραστός, -ή, -όν: beloved, lovely
ἐράω, –, ἠράσθην: to love, to be in love with, desire (+ gen.) (aor. deponent)
ἐργάζομαι, ἐργάσομαι, ἠργασάμην, –, εἴργασμαι, ἠργάσθην: to work, accomplish, perform
ἔργον, τό: work, labor, deed, act
ἐρέω: will say, will speak, will mention (fut. of λέγω, pf. εἴρημαι)
ἔρομαι, ἐρήσομαι, ἠρόμην: to ask, question, inquire
Ἐρυξίμαχος, ὁ: Eryximachus
ἔρχομαι, ἐλεύσομαι, ἦλθον, ἐλήλυθα, –, –: to come, go
ἐρώμενος, ὁ, ἡ: beloved, the one loved
Ἔρως, -ωτος, ὁ: Eros, Love, Desire
ἔρως, -ωτος, ὁ: love, desire
ἐρωτάω, ἐρωτήσω, ἠρόμην, ἠρώτηκα, ἠρώτημαι, ἠρωτήθην: to ask, inquire, question
ἐρωτικός, -ή, -όν: erotic, amorous, of desire
ἑταῖρος, ὁ: companion, comrade, mate
ἕτερος, -α, -ον: one (of two), other; different
ἔτι: still, besides, further, yet, any longer, moreover
εὖ: well
εὐ-δαίμων, -ον: happy, fortunate, blessed
ἐφ-ίστημι, -στήσω, -έστησα, -έστηκα, -έσταμαι, -εστάθην: to set, stop, or stand near or over
ἔχω, ἕξω, ἔσχον, ἔσχηκα, ἔσχημαι, –: to have, hold, possess; be able; be disposed
ἕως: until, as long as

ζάω, ζήσω, ἔζησα, : to live
Ζεύς, Διός, ὁ: Zeus
ζητέω, ζητήσω, ἐζήτησα, ἐζήτηκα, –, –: to seek, look for, search, investigate
ζῷον, τό: animal, living creature

ἤ: or, either...or; than
ἦ: in truth, truly (introduces a question)`
ἡγέομαι, ἡγήσομαι, ἡγησάμην, –, ἥγημαι, –: to lead, guide; consider, think, believe
ἤδη: already, now, at this time
ἡδονή, ἡ: pleasure, enjoyment, delight
ἧδος, -εος, τό: pleasure, enjoyment, delight
ἥκω, ἥξω: to have come, be present (impf. ἧκον as plpf.)
ἡμεῖς: we
ἡμέρα, ἡ: day
ἡμέτερος, -α, -ον: our
ἠμί: I say

ἥμισυ, τό: a half
ἥμισυς, -εια, -υ: half
ἡμός, -ή, -όν: our
ἥττων, -ον: less, weaker, inferior (comp. of κακός)

θαυμάζω, θαυβάσομαι, ἐθαύμασα, τεθαύμακα, –, ἐθαυμάσθην: to wonder, be amazed
θαυμάσιος, -α, -ον: wonderful, marvelous, amazing
θαυμαστής, ὁ: an admirer
θαυμαστός, -ή, -όν: wonderful, marvelous, amazing
θεά, ἡ: a goddess
θεάομαι, θεάσομαι, ἐθεασάμην, –, τεθέαμαι, –: to see, watch, look at; contemplate, consider
θεῖος, -α, -ον: divine, god-like, sent by the gods
θεός, ὁ: god, divinity
θνήσκω, ἀποθάνομαι, ἀπέθανον, τέθνηκα, –, –: to die, die off, perish
θνητός, -ή, -όν: mortal, able to die
θύρα, ἡ: door
θυσία, ἡ: sacrifice, offering

ἰατρικός, -ή, -όν: medical, of a physician; medicine
ἱκανός, -ή, -όν: enough, sufficient, adequate, competent
ἱκανῶς: enough, sufficiently, adequately
ἵνα: in order that (+ subj.); where (+ ind.)
ἴσος, -η, -ον: equal to, same as, like
ἵστημι, στήσω, ἔστησα, ἔστηκα, ἔσταμαι, ἐστάθην:: to make stand, set up, stop, establish
ἰσχυρός, -ά, -όν: strong, powerful; severe`
ἴσως: perhaps, probably; equally, likely

καθά: καθ᾽ ἅ, according as, just as
καθ-οράω, -όψομαι, -εῖδον, -εωρακα, -ωμμαι, -ώφθην: to look down upon, perceive, observe
καί: and, also, even, too, in fact
κακός, -ή, -όν: bad, base, cowardly, evil
καλέω, καλέω, ἐκάλεσα, κέκληκα, κέκλημαι, ἐκλήθην: to call, summon, invite
κάλλος, -εος, ὁ: beauty
καλός, -ή, -όν: beautiful, fair, noble, fine
καλῶς: well, nobly
κἄν: καὶ ἐαν, and if, even if, although
κατά: down; in accordance with, according to (+ acc.)
κατα-κεῖμαι, κείσομαι: to lie (down), recline (often equivalent to pass. of τίθημι)
κατα-κλίνομαι, -κλινέομαι, –, –, –, κατεκλίθην: to lie down, recline; act. make recline
κελεύω, κελεύσω, ἐκέλευσα, κεκέλευκα, κεκελεύσομαι, ἐκελεύσθην: to bid, order, exhort
κενόω, κενώσω, ἐκένωσα, –, κεκένωμαι, ἐκενώθην: to empty out, drain of (+ gen.)
κεφαλή, ἡ: head
κινδυνεύω, κινδυνεύσω: to run the risk, risk, be likely do, be in danger
κοινός, -ή, -όν: common, ordinary; public
κόσμιος, -α, -ον: well-ordered, regular, moderate
κτάομαι, κτήσομαι, ἐκτησάμην, –, κέκτημαι, ἐκτήθην: to acquire, get, gain, procure, possess
κυέω, κυήσω, ἐκύησα: to conceive, be pregnant with

λαμβάνω, λήψομαι, ἔλαβον, εἴληφα, εἴλημμαι, ἐλήφθην: to take, receive, catch, grasp
λέγω, λέξω, ἔλεξα, εἴλοχα, λέλεγμαι, ἐλέχθην: to say, speak, (fut. is often ἐρέω)

λείπω, λείψω, ἔλιπον, λέλοιπα, λέλειμμαι, ἐλείφθην: to leave, forsake, abandon
λόγος, ὁ: word, speech, account, argument, reason

μάλιστα: especially, in particular, most of all, certainly
μᾶλλον: more, rather (comparative of μαλά)
μαντικός, -ή, -όν: prophetic, oracular; *subst.* prophecy
μέγας, μεγάλη, μέγα: big, great, important; haughty
μεγίστος, -η, -ον: very big, greatest, most important
μέλλω, μελλήσω, ἐμέλλησα: to be about to, be going to; intend to
μέν: on the one hand
μέντοι: however, nevertheless; certainly
μετά: with, along with (+ gen.); after (+ acc.)
μεταξύ: betwixt, between
μετ-έχω, -έξω, -έσχον, -έσχηκα, -έσχημαι, –: to partake, take a part in, have a share in (gen.)
μή: not, lest
μη-δέ: and not, but not, not even, nor
μηδ-είς, μηδ-εμία, μηδ-έν: no one, nothing
μήν: truly, surely, then; yet
μή-τε: and not, neither...nor
μήτηρ, ἡ: mother
μικρός, ή, όν: small, little; trifle, insignificant
μόνος, -η, -ον: alone, only, solitary, single
μουσική, ἡ: music, the art of music, the arts
μουσικός, -ή, -όν: musical, educated, cultured

νέος, -α, -ον: new, novel, strange, young; *sub.* a youth
νομίζω, νομιῶ, ἐνόμισα, νενόμικα, νενόμισμαι, ἐνομίσθην: to believe, consider, deem, hold
νόμος, ὁ: custom, law
νοῦς, ὁ: mind, thought, reason, attention, sense
νῦν: now; as it is

ὁ, ἡ, τό: the
ὅδε, ἥδε, τόδε: this, this here, the following
οἶδα: to know (pf. with pres. sense)
οἴομαι, οἰήσομαι, –, –, –, ᾠήθην: to suppose, think, imagine
οἷος, -α, -ον: what sort, which sort, such as, as
οἴχομαι, οἰχήσομαι: to go, go off, depart
ὀλίγος -η, -ον: few, small, little
ὅλος, -η, -ον: whole, entire, complete
Ὅμηρος, ὁ: Homer
ὅμοιος, -α, -ον: like, resembling, similar to (+ dat.)
ὁμοίως: similarly, in the same way, in the same manner
ὁμο-λογέω, ὁμολογήσω, ὡμολόγησα, ὡμολόγηκα, –, ὡμολογήθην: to agree, acknowledge
ὅμως: nevertheless, however, yet
ὄνομα, -ατος, τό: name, word
ὅπως: how, in what way; in order that, that
ὁράω, ὄψομαι, εἶδον, ἑώρακα, ὦμμαι, ὤφθην: to see, look, behold
ὀρθός, -ή, -όν: straight, upright, right
ὀρθῶς: rightly, correctly
ὅς, ἥ, ὅ: who, which, that

ὅσος, -η, -ον: as much as, as many as; all who, all that
ὅσ-περ, ἥ-περ, ὅ-περ: whoever, whatever, the very one
　　who, the very thing which
ὅσ-τις, ἥ-τις, ὅ τι: who, which; whoever, whichever,
　　anyone who, anything which, anything that
ὁστισ-οῦν, ἡτισ-οῦν, ὁτι-οῦν: whosoever, whatsoever
ὅταν: ὅτε ἄν, whenever
ὅτι: that; because
οὐ, οὐκ, οὐχ: not, no
οὗ: where
οὐ-δέ: and not, but not, not even, nor
οὐδ-είς, οὐδε-μία, οὐδ-έν: no one, nothing
οὖν: and so, then; at all events
οὐράνιος, -α, -ον: heavenly, dwelling in heaven
οὔ-τε: and not, neither...nor
οὗτος, αὕτη, τοῦτο: this, these
οὕτως: in this way, thus, so

παιδικά, τά: darling, favorite, boyfriend
παιδικός, -ή, -όν: boyish, playful, sportive
παῖς, παιδός, ὁ, ἡ: child, boy, girl; slave
παλαιός, -ά, -όν: old, aged, ancient
πάλιν: again, once more; back, backwards
πάν-δημος, -ον: common, popular, vulgar
πάνυ: quite, very, entirely, completely
παρά: from, at, to the side of (+ gen., dat., acc.); in respect to, contrary to
πάρ-ειμι, -έσομαι: to be near, be present, be at hand
παρ-έχω, -έξω, -έσχον, -έσχηκα, -έσχημαι, –: to provide, furnish, supply, produce
πᾶς, πᾶσα, πᾶν: every, all, the whole, entire
πάσχω, πείσομαι, ἔπαθον, πέπονθα: to suffer, experience; allow
πατήρ, ὁ: father
Παυσανίης, ὁ: Pausanias
παύω, παύσομαι, ἔπαυσα, πέπαυκα, πέπαυμαι, ἐπαύθην: to stop, make cease; *mid.* cease
πείθω, πείσω, ἔπεισα, πέποιθα, πέπεισμαι, ἐπείσθην: to persuade, win over, trust; *mid.* obey
πειράζω: to make an attempt, endeavor
πειράομαι, -ήσομαι, ἐπειρησάμην, –, πεπείρημαι, ἐπειρήθην: to attempt, make trial of (gen)
περί: concerning, about, around (+ gen., dat., acc.)
πηρός, -ή, -όν: maimed, disabled
πίνω, πίομαι, ἔπιον, πέπωκα, –, ἐπόθην: to drink
πλέων, -ον: more, greater (comparative of πολύς)
πλέως, πλέα, πλέων: full, full of (+ gen.)
ποιέω, -ήσω, ἐποίησα, πεποίηκα, πεποίημαι, ἐποιήθην: to do, make, create; *mid.* consider
ποίησις, -εως, ἡ: creation, production; poetry
ποιητής, οῦ, ὁ: maker, creator, poet
πόλις, ἡ: a city
πολλά-κις: many times, often, frequently
πολύ: *adv.* much, quite, by far, far
πολύς, πολλά, πολύ: much, many, great, large, long
πορεύομαι, πορεύσομαι, ἐπορευσάμην, –, πεπορεύμαι, ἐπορεύθην: to travel, proceed
ποτέ: ever, at some time, once

που: somewhere, anywhere; I suppose
ποῦ: where?
πρᾶγμα, τό: deed, act; matter, affair, trouble
πράττω, πράξω, ἔπραξα, πέπραχα, πέπραγμαι, ἐπράχθην: to do, accomplish, make, act
πρέσβυς, -εως, ὁ: old man, elder, ambassador
πρέσβύτατος, -η, -ον: oldest, most important
πρέσβύτερος, -α -ον: older, more important
πρό: before, in front; in place of (+ gen.)
πρός: to, towards (+ acc.), near, in addition to (+ dat.)
προσ-έχω, -έξω, -έσχον, -έσχηκα, -έσχημαι, –: to offer, provide; direct
πρότερος, -α, -ον: before, in front; earlier
πρῶτον: adv. first
πρῶτος, -η, -ον: first, earliest
πως: somehow, in some way
πῶς: how? in what way?

ῥᾴδιος, -α, -ον: easy, ready

σε-αυτοῦ, -ῆ, -οῦ: yourself
σεύω: to put in quick motion; drive, chase away
σμικρός, -ά, -όν: small, little, insignificant
σός, -ή, -όν: your, yours
σοφία, ἡ: wisdom, skill, judgment, intelligence
σοφός, -ή, -όν: wise, skilled
σπουδή, ἡ: effort, earnestness, zeal, enthusiasm; haste
σύ: you
σύν-ειμι, -έσομαι: to be with, associate with
συν-ουσία, ἡ: gathering, association, union
σφεῖς: they
σφόδρα: very, very much, exceedingly, earnestly
σφός, -ή, -όν: their, their own
Σωκράτης, -ους, ὁ: Socrates
σῶμα, -ατος, τό: body
σωφροσύνη, ἡ: moderation, temperance, prudence

ταύτῃ: in this way, in this respect, so, thus
ταχύς, εῖα, ύ: fast, quick, swift, rapid
ταχύ: quickly, swiftly, hastily
τε: and, both
τελευτάω, τελευτήσω, ἐτέλευσα, τετελεύτηκα, –, –: to end, complete, finish; die
τέχνη, ἡ: art, skill, craft
τῇ: here, there
τίθημι, θήσω, ἔθηκα, τέθηκα, τέθειμαι, ἐτέθην: to set, put, place, arrange, make, cause
τίκτω, τέξομαι, ἔτεκον, τέτοκα, –, –: to give birth, beget, bring forth, bear, produce
τιμάω, τιμήσω, ἐτίμησα, τετίμηκα, τετιμήσομαι, ἐτιμήθην: to honor, value, esteem
τιμή, ἡ: honor; office
τις, τι: anyone, anything, someone, something
τίς, τί: who? which?
τοί-νυν: well then; therefore, accordingly
τοι-οῦτος, -αύτη, -οῦτο: such, this sort

τολμάω, τολμήσω, ἐτόλμησα, τετόλμηκα, –, –: to dare, undertake, venture
τοσ-οῦτος, -αύτη, -οῦτο: so great, so much, so many
τότε: at that time, then
τρέπω: to turn, direct; alter, change
τρόπος, ὁ: way, manner; turn, direction; custom
τυγχάνω, τεύξομαι, ἔτυχον, τετύχηκα, –, –: to chance, happen to (+ pple); get (+ gen.)

ὑμεῖς: you
ὑμός, -ή, -όν: your, yours
ὑπέρ: above, on behalf of (+ gen.); over, beyond (+ acc.)
ὑπό: by, because of, from (+ gen.), under (+ dat., + acc.)

Φαῖδρος, ὁ: Phaedrus
φαίνω, φανῶ, ἔφηνα, πέφηνα, πέφασμαι, ἐφάνθην: to show; *mid.* appear, seem
φαῦλος, -η, -ον: worthless, insignificant, mediocre
φέρω, οἴσω, ἤνεγκον, ἐνήνοχα, ἐνήνεγμαι, ἠνέχθην: to bear, carry, bring, convey
φημί, ἐρέω, εἶπον, εἴρηκα, εἴρημαι, ἐρρήθην: to say, claim, assert
φιλία, ἡ: friendship, affection, love, devotion
φίλος, -η, -ον: dear, friendly, beloved; *subst.* friend, kin
φιλο-σοφία, ἡ: pursuit of wisdom, philosophy
φύσις, -εως, ἡ: nature, natural qualities, character
φύω, φύσω, ἔφυσα, πέφυκα, –, –: to bring forth, beget, engender; to be by nature

χαίρω, χαιρήσω, –, κεχάρηκα, κεχάρημαι, ἐχάρην: to rejoice, be glad; be pleased; fare well
χαλεπός, -ά, -όν: difficult, hard, harmful
χαρίζομαι, χαρίσομαι, ἐχαρισάμην, –, κεχάρισμαι: to (do a) favor, gratify, indulge (+ dat.)
χείρ, χειρός, ἡ: hand
χέω, χέω, ἔχεα, κέχυκα, κέχυμαι, ἐχύθην: to pour
χράομαι, χρήσομαι, ἐχρησάμην, –, κέχρημαι, ἐχρήσθην: to use, employ, engage in (+ dat.)
χρή: it is necessary, it is fitting; must, ought (+ inf.)
χρῆμα, -ατος, τό: thing; *pl.* money, goods
χρόνος, ὁ: time

ψυχή, ἡ: breath, life, spirit, soul

ὦ: O! oh!
ὡς: as, thus, so, that; when, since
ὥσπερ: just as, as, as if
ὥστε: so that, that, so as to